SRA Reading Mastery

Signature Edition

Presentation Book B
Grade 1

Siegfried Engelmann
Elaine C. Bruner

McGraw Hill — SRA

Columbus, OH

W9-CDD-096

SRAonline.com

Printed in the United States of America.

Send all inquiries to this address:
SRA/McGraw-Hill
4400 Easton Commons
Columbus, OH 43219

ISBN: 978-0-07-612451-0
MHID: 0-07-612451-7

7 8 9 RMN 13 12 11

Table of Contents

Individual Checkout Lessons

Curriculum Map *at the back of the book*

EXERCISE 1

Sound combination review

a. Here are some letters that go together. Get ready to tell me the sound they usually make.

b. (Point to **ou.**) What sound do these letters usually make? (Signal.) *ou.* Yes, **ou.**

c. (Repeat *b* with **ar.**)

d. (Repeat both sound combinations until firm.)

ou

ar

LETTER NAMES
EXERCISE 2

Say vowel names

a. Everybody, say the names of these letters.

b. (Point to each letter. Pause.) Get ready. (Touch each letter.) (The children respond.)

c. Again. (Repeat *b* until firm.)

Individual test

(Call on individual children. Each child is to identify two letters.)

a   u   i

o   e

READING VOCABULARY

Do not touch small letters.

Get ready to read all the words on this page without making a mistake.

EXERCISE 3

Sound out first

a. (Touch the ball for **fin.**) Sound it out. Get ready. (Quickly touch **f, i, n** as the children say:) *fffiiinnn.*

b. What word? (Signal.) *Fin.* Yes, **fin.**

c. (Repeat exercise until firm.)

EXERCISE 4

Sound out first

a. (Touch the ball for **fīne.**) Sound it out. Get ready. (Quickly touch **f, ī, n** as the children say:) *fffīīīnnn.*

b. What word? (Signal.) *Fine.* Yes, **fine.**

c. (Repeat exercise until firm.)

EXERCISE 5

Teach final-e rule

a. (Touch the ball for **fin.**) Everybody, read this word the fast way. Get ready. (Signal.) *Fin.* Yes, **fin.**

b. (Point to **i** in **fin.**) Here's a rule. If there is an **e** on the end of this word, you say the **name** of this letter. Remember that rule.

c. (Point to **i** in **fine.**) There's an **ē** on the end of this word. So tell me the **name** of this letter. Get ready. (Signal.) *ī.* Yes, **ī.**

d. (Touch the ball for **fine.**) Read this word the fast way and say the name **ī.** (Pause two seconds.) Get ready. (Signal.) *Fine.*

e. What word? (Signal.) *Fine.* Yes, **fine.**

f. (Touch the ball for **fin.**) Read the fast way. (Pause two seconds.) Get ready. (Signal.) *Fin.* Yes, **fin.**

• (Repeat until firm.)

g. (Touch the ball for **fine.**) Read the fast way. (Pause two seconds.) Get ready. (Signal.) *Fine.* Yes, **fine.**

• (Repeat until firm.)

h. (Repeat *f* and *g* until firm.)

EXERCISE 6

Listen, sound out with me

a. (Point to **children.**) I'll tell you this word. (Pause.) **Children.** What word? (Signal.) *Children.* Yes, **children.**

b. (Touch the ball for **children.**) Sound it out with me. Get ready. (Quickly touch each sound as you and the children say:) *chiiillldrrreeennn.*

c. What word? (Signal.) *Children.* Yes, **children.**

d. (Repeat *b* and *c* until firm.)

(Repeat any troublesome words.)

Individual test

(Call on individual children. Each child reads a different word.)

Do not touch small letters.

Get ready to read all the words on this page without making a mistake.

petted

EXERCISE 7

Read the fast way first

a. (Touch the ball for **petted.**) Read this word the fast way. (Pause two seconds.) Get ready. (Signal.) *Petted.* Yes, **petted.**

b. (Return to the ball.) Sound it out. Get ready. (Quickly touch **p, e,** between the **t**'s, **e, d** as the children say:) *peeeteeed.*

c. What word? (Signal.) *Petted.* Yes, **petted.**

d. (Repeat *b* and *c* until firm.)

e. (Repeat the exercise for **helped, sāved,** and **grass.**)

helped

sāved

grass

EXERCISE 8

Read the fast way

a. Read these words the fast way.

b. (Touch the ball for **would.** Pause two seconds.) Get ready. (Signal.) *Would.* Yes, **would.**

c. (Repeat *b* for **carmen, mooing, could, glad, called, thank, what,** and **who.**)

would

carmen

mooing

could

glad

called

thank

what

who

(Repeat any troublesome words.)

Individual test

(Call on individual children. Each child reads a different word.)

Do not touch small letters.

Get ready to read all the words on this page without making a mistake.

mouse

EXERCISE 9

ou word

a. (Point to **ou** in **mouse**.) What do these letters say? (Signal.) *ou.* Yes, **ou.**
b. (Touch the ball for **mouse**.) Read this word the fast way. Get ready. (Signal.) *Mouse.* Yes, **mouse.**

loud

EXERCISE 10

ou word

a. (Point to **ou** in **loud**.) What do these letters say? (Signal.) *ou.* Yes, **ou.**
b. (Touch the ball for **loud**.) Read this word the fast way. Get ready. (Signal.) *Loud.* Yes, **loud.**

EXERCISE 11

ou word

a. (Point to **ou** in **house**.) What do these letters say? (Signal.) *ou.* Yes, **ou.**
b. (Touch the ball for **house**.) Read this word the fast way. Get ready. (Signal.) *House.* Yes, **house.**

EXERCISE 12

ou word

a. (Touch the ball for **shouted**.) Read this word the fast way. (Pause two seconds.) Get ready. (Signal.) *Shouted.* Yes, **shouted.**
b. (Point to **ou** in **shout**.) Everybody, what do these letters say? (Signal.) *ou.* Yes, **ou.**
c. (Touch the ball for **shouted**.) Sound it out. Get ready. (Quickly touch **sh, ou, t, e, d** as the children say:) *shshshouteeed.*
d. What word? (Signal.) *Shouted.* Yes, **shouted.**
e. (Repeat *c* and *d* until firm.)

EXERCISE 13

ou word

a. (Touch the ball for **sounds**.) Read this word the fast way. (Pause two seconds.) Get ready. (Signal.) *Sounds.* Yes, **sounds.**
b. (Point to **ou** in **sounds**.) Everybody, what do these letters say? (Signal.) *ou.* Yes, **ou.**
c. (Touch the ball for **sounds**.) Sound it out. Get ready. (Quickly touch **s, ou, n, d, s** as the children say:) *sssounnndsss.*
d. What word? (Signal.) *Sounds.* Yes, **sounds.**
e. (Repeat *c* and *d* until firm.)

house

shouted

sounds

Individual test

(Call on individual children to read a column of words from this lesson. If the column contains only one or two words, direct the child to read additional words from an another column. Praise children who read all words with no errors.)

STORY 49

EXERCISE 14

First reading—title and three sentences

a. (Pass out Storybook 1.)

b. Everybody, open your reader to page 123.

c. Everybody, touch the title of the story and get ready to read the words in the title.

d. First word. ✔

• Get ready. (Tap.) *Carmen.*

e. (Tap for each remaining word in the title.)

f. Everybody, say the title. (Signal.)
Carmen calls for help.

g. Everybody, get ready to read this story.

h. First word. ✔

• Get ready. (Tap.) *Who.*

i. Next word. ✔

• Get ready. (Tap.) *Came.*

j. (Repeat *i* for the remaining words in the first three sentences. Have the children reread the first three sentences until firm.)

---

carmen calls for help[1]

who cāme to the farm to pet cows?[2]

whȳ didn't the children pet carmen?[3]

who fell into a dēēp, dēēp hōle?[4]

how did the other cows trȳ to help the girl?[5]

whȳ didn't the tēacher hēar the cows mooing?[6]

EXERCISE 15

Remaining sentences and questions

a. I'm going to call on individual children to read a sentence. Everybody, follow along and point to the words. If you hear a mistake, raise your hand.

b. (Call on a child.) Read the next sentence.

To Correct

word-identification errors
(**from,** for example)

1. That word is **from.** What word? *From.*
2. Go back to the beginning of the sentence and read the sentence again.

c. (Call on another child.) Read the next sentence.

d. (Repeat *c* for most of the remaining sentences in the story.)

e. (Occasionally have the group read a sentence. When the group is to read, say:) Everybody, read the next sentence. (Tap for each word in the sentence.)

---

f. (After each underlined sentence has been read, present each comprehension question specified below to the entire group.)

[1] What will Carmen do in this story? (Signal.) *Call for help.*

[2] Everybody, listen to that question. (Pause.) Who came to the farm to pet cows?

• Everybody, **say** that question. (Signal.) *Who came to the farm to pet cows?*

• What's the answer? (Signal.) *The children and their teacher.*

[3] Everybody, say that question. (Signal.) *Why didn't the children pet Carmen?*

• What's the answer? (Signal.) *Because she had such a loud moo.*

[4] Everybody, say that question. (Signal.) *Who fell into a deep, deep hole?*

• What's the answer? (Signal.) *A girl.*

[5] Everybody, say that question. (Signal.) *How did the other cows try to help the girl?*

• What's the answer? (Signal.) *They mooed.*

[6] Everybody, say that question. (Signal.) *Why didn't the teacher hear the cows mooing?*

• What's the answer? (Signal.) *They did not have loud moos.*

then carmen saw the girl. carmen called "moo" very loud. <u>she called "moo" so loud that the teacher could hear her.</u>[7] the teacher said, "that sounds like a call for help." the teacher ran to the little girl.

the teacher helped the little girl get out of the hole.[8] the teacher went over to carmen and said, "we are so glad that you have a loud moo. you said 'moo' so loud that you saved the little girl."

and what do you think the little girl did? the little girl kissed carmen and said, "thank you for mooing so loud."[9]

now carmen has lots of children pet her. carmen is happy that she has a big, loud moo.[10]

this is the end.

EXERCISE 16

Second reading—sentences and questions

a. You're going to read the story again. And I'm going to ask more questions.
b. Starting with the first word of the title. ✔ Get ready. (Tap as the children read the title.)
c. (Call on a child.) Read the first sentence.

To Correct

word-identification errors (**from,** for example)
1. That word is **from.** What word? *From.*
2. Go back to the beginning of the sentence and read the sentence again.

d. (Call on another child.) Read the next sentence.
e. (Repeat *d* for most of the remaining sentences in the story.)
f. (Occasionally have the group read a sentence.)
g. (After each underlined sentence has been read, present each comprehension question specified below to the entire group.)
  [7] How come the teacher heard Carmen's moo? (Signal.) *Because it was so loud.*
  [8] How did the girl get out of the hole? (Signal.) *The teacher helped her.*
  [9] What did the girl say? (Signal.) *Thank you for mooing so loud.*
  [10] Why is she happy with that big, loud moo? (The children respond.)
  • Yes, I think she knows that she helped save the little girl.

EXERCISE 17

Picture comprehension

a. Look at the picture.
b. (Ask these questions:)
  1. Where is the girl in this picture? (Signal.) *In a deep hole.*
  2. What is Carmen doing? (Signal.) *Mooing.*
  • Who is that coming up the hill? (Signal.) *The teacher.*
  3. What will the teacher do? (The children respond.)
  4. What will the little girl do? (The children respond.)

SUMMARY OF INDEPENDENT ACTIVITY
EXERCISE 18

Introduction to independent activity

a. (Pass out Worksheet 49 to each child.)
b. (Hold up side 1 of your worksheet.) Everybody, you're going to do this worksheet on your own. (Tell the children when they will work the items.)
• Let's go over the things you're going to do.

Story items

(Point to the story-items exercise.) Everybody, remember to write your answers in the blanks.

Following instructions

a. (Touch the sentence in the box.)
b. Everybody, first you're going to read the sentence in the box. Then you're going to read the instructions below the box and do what the instructions tell you to do.

Reading comprehension

(Point to the story on side 2.) You're going to read this story and then do the items. Remember to write the answers in the blanks.

Following instructions

(Point to the following-instructions exercise.) Everybody, you're going to read the instructions. Then you're going to do what the instructions tell you to do.

END OF LESSON 49

LETTER NAMES
EXERCISE 1

Say vowel names

a. Everybody, say the names of these letters.

b. (Point to each letter. Pause.) Get ready.
(Touch each letter.) (The children respond.)

c. Again. (Repeat *b* until firm.)

Individual test

(Call on several children. Each child is to
identify two letters.)

i   e   a

o   u

READING VOCABULARY

Do not touch small letters.

Get ready to read all the words on this page without making a mistake.

rod

EXERCISE 2

Sound out first

a. (Touch the ball for **rod.**) Sound it out. Get ready. (Quickly touch **r, o, d** as the children say:) *rrroood.*
b. What word? (Signal.) *Rod.* Yes, **rod.**
c. (Repeat exercise until firm.)

rōde

EXERCISE 3

Sound out first

a. (Touch the ball for **rōde.**) Sound it out. Get ready. (Quickly touch **r, ō, d** as the children say:) *rrrōōōd.*
b. What word? (Signal.) *Rode.* Yes, **rode.**
c. (Repeat exercise until firm.)

rod

rode

EXERCISE 4

Teach final-e rule

a. (Touch the ball for **rod.**) Everybody, read this word the fast way. Get ready. (Signal.) *Rod.* Yes, **rod.**
b. (Point to **o** in **rod.**) Here's a rule. If there is an **e** on the end of this word, you say the **name** of this letter. Remember that rule.
c. (Point to **ō** in **rōde.**) There's an e on the end of this word. So tell me the **name** of this letter. Get ready. (Signal.) *o.* Yes, **o.**
d. (Touch the ball for **rōde.**) Read this word the fast way and say the name **o.** (Pause two seconds.) Get ready. (Signal.) *Rode.*
e. What word? (Signal.) *Rode.* Yes, **rode.**
f. (Touch the ball for **rod.**) Read the fast way. (Pause two seconds.) Get ready. (Signal.) *Rod.* Yes, **rod.**
• (Repeat until firm.)
g. (Touch the ball for **rōde.**) Read the fast way. (Pause two seconds.) Get ready. (Signal.) *rode.* Yes, **rode.**
• (Repeat until firm.)
h. (Repeat *f* and *g* until firm.)

afrāid

EXERCISE 5

Listen, sound out with me

a. (Point to **afraid.**) I'll tell you this word. (Pause.) **Afraid.** What word? (Signal.) *Afraid.* Yes, **afraid.**
b. (Touch the ball for **afraid.**) Sound it out with me. Get ready. (Quickly touch each sound as you and the children say:) *aaafffrrrāāād.*
c. What word? (Signal.) *Afraid.* Yes, **afraid.**
d. (Repeat *b* and *c* until firm.)

EXERCISE 6

Read the fast way

a. Read this word the fast way.
b. (Touch the ball for **who.** Pause two seconds.) Get ready. (Signal.) *Who.* Yes, **who.**

(Repeat any troublesome words.)

Individual test

(Call on individual children. Each child reads a different word.)

Boo Leaves the House[1]

Boo was a ghost, but he was not mean like the other ghosts that lived with him. Those five ghosts were very mean and they liked to do mean things. But Boo was not mean. While the other ghosts went out to do mean things, he would read.[2]

Then one night, the other five ghosts made Boo leave the old house. They came back from playing mean tricks. Boo was sitting in his seat reading a book. The other ghosts said, "You are not a good ghost, so you must leave this house."[3]

"Where will I go?" Boo asked.

"We don't care where you go," the biggest ghost said. "Just get out of this house."

So Boo picked up his heap of books and left the old house. As he walked from the house, he could hear the other ghosts talking and laughing. They were planning to do mean things.⑤

Boo walked down the road. When he was near the town, he stopped. "I hear somebody crying."[4]

Boo looked around in the dark. At last he came to a stream and saw who was crying. It was a big green frog.[5] The frog looked at Boo and stopped crying. The frog said, "Are you really a ghost?"[6]

"Yes," Boo said. "And are you really a talking frog?"

"No," the frog said. "I am a king, but a monster cast a spell over me and turned me into a frog.[7] I am very sad."

"Can I help you?" Boo asked.[8]

"No," the frog said. "Nobody can help me now."[9]

More to come

[1] What's going to happen in this story? (Signal.) *Boo will leave the house.*

[2] What did the five ghosts like to do? (Signal.) *Mean things.*

• What did Boo do when the other ghosts were out? (Signal.) *Read.*

[3] What did they say? (Signal.) *You are not a good ghost, so you must leave this house.*

[4] What did he say? (Signal.) *I hear somebody crying.*

• I wonder who it was. Let's read and find out.

[5] Who was crying? (Signal.) *A big green frog.*

• Where was the frog? (Signal.) *In a stream.*

[6] What question did the frog ask? (Signal.) *Are you really a ghost?*

• What's the answer? (Signal.) *Yes.*

[7] Who was that frog? (Signal.) *A king.*

• How did he get to be a frog? (The children respond.) Yes, a monster cast a spell over him and turned him into a frog.

• What's a spell? (The children respond.) Yes, a spell is magic.

[8] What did Boo want to do? (Signal.) *Help the frog.*

[9] What did the frog say? (Signal.) *Nobody can help me now.*

• Do you think Boo will try to help? (The children respond.)

• We'll read more next time and see what happens.

EXERCISE 7

Picture comprehension

a. Look at the picture.

b. (Ask these questions:)
1. Who is sitting on a rock in the stream? (The children respond.) Yes, a big frog.
2. What is the frog doing? (Signal.) *Crying.*
3. How do you know he's crying? (The children respond.)
4. What do you think Boo is saying to him? (The children respond.)
5. Why does Boo have a book? (Signal.) *He likes to read.*

WORKSHEET 104

EXERCISE 8

Summary of independent activities

a. (Pass out Worksheet 104 to each child.)

b. Everybody, now you'll do your worksheet. Remember to do all parts of the worksheet and to read all the parts carefully.

END OF LESSON 104

Do not touch small letters.

Get ready to read all the words on this page without making a mistake.

also

EXERCISE 7

Two-part word

a. (Cover **so.** Point to **al.**) Everybody, tell me what this part of the word says. Get ready. (Signal.) *All.* Yes, **all.**

b. (Uncover **so.** Touch the ball for **also.**) Now tell me what the whole word says. Get ready. (Signal.) *Also.* Yes, **also.**

c. (Repeat exercise until firm.)

alwāys

EXERCISE 8

Two-part word

a. (Cover **wāys.** Point to **al.**) Everybody, tell me what this part of the word says. Get ready. (Signal.) *All.* Yes, **all.**

b. (Uncover **wāys.** Touch the ball for **alwāys.**) Now tell me what the whole word says. Get ready. (Signal.) *Always.* Yes, **always.**

c. (Repeat exercise until firm.)

almōst

EXERCISE 9

Two-part word

a. (Cover **mōst.** Point to **al.**) Everybody, tell me what this part of the word says. Get ready. (Signal.) *All.* Yes, **all.**

b. (Uncover **mōst.** Touch the ball for **almōst.**) Now tell me what the whole word says. Get ready. (Signal.) *Almost.* Yes, **almost.**

c. (Repeat exercise until firm.)

thēse

EXERCISE 10

Read the fast way first

a. (Touch the ball for **thēse.**) Read this word the fast way. (Pause two seconds.) Get ready. (Signal.) *These.* Yes, **these.**

b. (Return to the ball.) Sound it out. Get ready. (Quickly touch **th, ē, s** as the children say:) *thththēēēsss.*

c. What word? (Signal.) *These.* Yes, **these.**

d. (Repeat *b* and *c* until firm.)

e. (Repeat the exercise for **pink, thōse, they, pīled, scrēamed,** and **how.**)

pink

thōse

they

pīled

scrēamed

how

(Repeat any troublesome words.)

Individual test

(Call on individual children. Each child reads a different word.)

EXERCISE 5

Children spell, then read

a. First you're going to spell each word. Then you're going to read that word the fast way.

b. (Touch the ball for **hop.**) Spell it. Get ready. (Tap under each letter as the children say:) *H-O-P.* (Return to the ball.) Read it. Get ready. (Slash.) *Hop.*

c. (Repeat step *b* for each remaining word in the column.)

d. (Repeat steps *b* and *c* until firm.)

hop

hope

hoping

hopping

shopping

mopping

moping

Individual test

a. (Call on individual children to read one column of words from the lesson.)

b. (Praise children who read all words with no errors.)

EXERCISE 6

Reading—decoding

a. (Pass out Storybook 2.)

b. Everybody, open your reader to page 57.

c. Remember, if the group reads all the way to the red 5 without making more than five errors, we can go on.

d. Everybody, touch the title of the story. ✔

e. If you hear a mistake, raise your hand. Remember, children who do not have their place lose their turn. (Call on individual children to read two or three sentences. Do not ask comprehension questions. Tally all errors.)

To Correct

word-identification errors (**from,** for example)
1. That word is **from.** What word? *From.*
2. Go back to the beginning of the sentence and read the sentence again.

f. (If the children make more than five errors before they reach the red 5: when they reach the 5 return to the beginning of the story and have the children reread to the 5. Do not ask comprehension questions. Repeat step *f* until firm, and then go on to step *g*.)

g. (When the children read to the red 5 without making more than five errors: read the story to the children from the beginning to the 5. Ask the specified comprehension questions. When you reach the 5, call on individual children to continue reading the story. Have each child read two or three sentences.
Ask the specified comprehension questions.)

Do not touch small letters.

Get ready to read all the words on this page without making a mistake.

once

EXERCISE 11

Listen, sound out

a. (Point to **once**.) I'll tell you this word. (Pause.) **Once**. What word? (Signal.) *Once.* Yes, **once**.
b. (Touch the ball for **once**.) Sound it out. Get ready. (Quickly touch **o, n, c, e** as the children say:) *ooonnnceee.*
c. What word? (Signal.) *Once.* Yes, **once**.
d. (Repeat *b* and *c* until firm.)

mountain

EXERCISE 12

Listen, sound out with me

a. (Point to **mountain**.) I'll tell you this word. (Pause.) **Mountain**. What word? (Signal.) *Mountain.* Yes, **mountain**.
b. (Touch the ball for **mountain**.) Sound it out with me. Get ready. (Quickly touch **m, ou, n, t, a, i, n** as you and the children say:) *mmmounnntaaaiiinnn.*
c. What word? (Signal.) *Mountain.* Yes, **mountain**.
d. (Repeat *b* and *c* until firm.)

hound

EXERCISE 13

ou word

a. (Touch the ball for **hound**.) Read this word the fast way. (Pause two seconds.) Get ready. (Signal.) *Hound.* Yes, **hound**.
b. (Point to **ou** in **hound**.) Everybody, what do these letters say? (Signal.) *ou.* Yes, **ou**.
c. (Touch the ball for **hound**.) Sound it out. Get ready. (Quickly touch **h, ou, n, d** as the children say:) *hounnnd.*
d. What word? (Signal.) *Hound.* Yes, **hound**.
e. (Repeat *c* and *d* until firm.)

pouch

EXERCISE 14

ou word

a. (Touch the ball for **pouch**.) Read this word the fast way. (Pause two seconds.) Get ready. (Signal.) *Pouch.* Yes, **pouch**.
b. (Point to **ou** in **pouch**.) Everybody, what do these letters say? (Signal.) *ou.* Yes, **ou**.
c. (Touch the ball for **pouch**.) Sound it out. Get ready. (Quickly touch **p, ou, ch**. as the children say:) *pouch.*
d. What word? (Signal.) *Pouch.* Yes, **pouch**.
e. (Repeat *c* and *d* until firm.)

EXERCISE 15

Read the fast way

a. Read these words the fast way.
b. (Touch the ball for **around**. Pause two seconds.) Get ready. (Signal.) *Around.* Yes, **around**.
c. (Repeat *b* for **clouds** and **mouse**.)

around

clouds

mouse

Individual test

(Call on individual children to read a column of words from this lesson. If the column contains only one or two words, direct the child to read additional words from an another column. Praise children who read all words with no errors.)

EXERCISE 3

Words with underlined parts

a. First you're going to read the underlined part of each word in this column. Then you're going to read the whole word.

b. (Touch the ball for **Where.**) Read the underlined part. Get ready. (Tap the ball.) *wh.*

• Read the whole word. (Pause.) Get ready. (Slash.) *Where.*

c. (Repeat step *b* until firm.)

d. (Repeat steps *b* and *c* for each remaining word in the column.)

e. (Repeat the column until children read all the words in order without making a mistake.)

Where

there

Leaves

around

what

reading

stream

EXERCISE 4

Read the fast way

a. You're going to read all the words in this column the fast way.

b. (Touch the ball for **help.** Pause.) Get ready. (Slash.) *Help.*

c. (Repeat step *b* until firm.)

d. (Repeat steps *b* and *c* for each remaining word in the column.)

e. (Repeat the column until the children read all the words in order without making mistakes.)

help

new

spell

heap

hear

care

magic

STORYBOOK

STORY 50
EXERCISE 16

First reading—title and three sentences

a. (Pass out Storybook 1.)

b. Everybody, open your reader to page 125.

c. Everybody, touch the title of the story and get ready to read the words in the title.

d. First word. ✔

• Get ready. (Tap.) *Jill's.*

e. (Tap for the remaining word in the title.)

f. Everybody, say the title. (Signal.) *Jill's mouse.*

g. Everybody, get ready to read this story.

h. First word. ✔

• Get ready. (Tap.) *Jill.*

i. Next word. ✔

• Get ready. (Tap.) *Had.*

j. (Repeat *i* for the remaining words in the first three sentences. Have the children reread the first three sentences until firm.)

EXERCISE 17

Remaining sentences

a. I'm going to call on individual children to read a sentence. Everybody, follow along and point to the words. If you hear a mistake, raise your hand.

b. (Call on a child.) Read the next sentence.

To Correct

word-identification errors
(**from,** for example)

1. That word is **from.** What word? *From.*
2. Go back to the beginning of the sentence and read the sentence again.

c. (Call on another child.) Read the next sentence.

d. (Repeat *c* for most of the remaining sentences in the story.)

e. (Occasionally have the group read a sentence. When the group is to read, say:) Everybody, read the next sentence. (Tap for each word in the sentence.)

---

jill's mouse[1]

jill had a pet mouse. <u>her mouse</u>
<u>was little and pink.</u>[2] jill got a
little box for her little mouse. then
she went to her mother and said,
<u>"look what I have. I have a pet</u>
<u>mouse in this box."</u>[3]

<u>her mother jumped up. her</u>
<u>mother said, "get that mouse out of</u>
<u>this house."</u>[4]

jill said, "but I want to keep
this mouse."

her mother said, "you can't keep
that mouse in this house. I don't
like that mouse."

EXERCISE 18

Second reading—sentences and questions

a. You're going to read the story again. This time I'm going to ask questions.

b. Starting with the first word of the title. ✔

• Get ready. (Tap as the children read the title.)

c. (Call on a child.) Read the first sentence.

To Correct

word-identification errors
(**from,** for example)

1. That word is **from.** What word? *From.*
2. Go back to the beginning of the sentence and read the sentence again.

d. (Call on another child.) Read the next sentence.

e. (Repeat *d* for most of the remaining sentences in the story.)

f. (Occasionally have the group read a sentence.)

g. (After each underlined sentence has been read, present each comprehension question specified below to the entire group.)

[1] What will you read about in this story? (Signal.) *Jill's mouse.*

[2] What did her mouse look like? (Signal.) *Little and pink.*

[3] Who is Jill talking to? (Signal.) *Her mother.*

• What is she showing her? (Signal.) *The pet mouse.*

[4] What did her mother say? (Signal.) *Get that mouse out of this house.*

• Why did her mother say that? (The children respond.)

• It looks like her mother doesn't like mice.

READING VOCABULARY
EXERCISE 1

Teacher reads the words in red

a. I'll read each word in red. Then you'll spell each word.

b. (Touch the ball for **cast**.) My turn. (Slash as you say:) Cast. What word? (Signal.) *Cast.*

c. (Return to the ball.) Spell it. Get ready. (Tap under each letter as the children say:) *C-A-S-T.*
 • What word did you spell? (Signal.) *Cast.*

d. (Repeat steps *b* and *c* for each word in red.)

e. Your turn to read all the words in this column.

f. (Touch the ball for **cast**. Pause.) Get ready. (Slash.) *Cast.*

g. (Repeat step *f* for each remaining word in the column.)

h. (Repeat steps *f* and *g* until firm.)

cast

turned

watched

castle

monster

green

frog

EXERCISE 2

Read the fast way

a. You're going to read all the words in this column the fast way.

b. (Touch the ball for **sitting**. Pause.) Get ready. (Slash.) *Sitting.*

c. (Repeat step *b* until firm.)

d. (Repeat steps *b* and *c* for each remaining word in the column.)

e. (Repeat the column until the children read all the words in order without making mistakes.)

sitting

biggest

Nobody

picked

laughing

planning

somebody

jill asked, "would you let me
kēēp this mouse in the yard?⁵then
the mouse would not be around you."

"yes," her mother said, "but kēēp
that mouse out of this house."

so jill took the box and went to
the yard. she said, "I will māke a
house for this mouse." so she pīled
some grass around the box.

now jill is happy and her mother
is happy. and the mouse is happy.

whȳ was jill happy?⁶

whȳ was her mother happy?⁷

whȳ was the mouse happy?⁸

the end

---

⁵ What did Jill ask? (Signal.) *Would you let me keep this mouse in the yard?*
- (Repeat the question until the children give a firm response.)
⁶ Everybody, say that question. (Signal.) *Why was Jill happy?*
- What's the answer? (The children respond.)
- Yes, she got to keep her mouse.
⁷ Everybody, say that question. (Signal.) *Why was her mother happy?*
- What's the answer? (The children respond.)
- Yes, because the mouse is out of the house.
⁸ Everybody, say that question. (Signal.) *Why was the mouse happy?*
- What's the answer? (The children respond.)

EXERCISE 19

Picture comprehension

a. Look at the picture.

b. (Ask these questions:)

1. What is Jill's mother doing? (Let the children comment for ten seconds. Then comment briefly.)
2. Why is she doing that? (Signal.) *Because she doesn't like mice.*
3. What is Jill holding? (Signal.) *A box.*
- What is in the box? (Signal.) *Her pet mouse.*
4. Did you ever have a pet mouse? (The children respond.)
- Lots of people have pet dogs or cats, but not too many have a pet mouse.

SUMMARY OF INDEPENDENT ACTIVITY
EXERCISE 20

Summary of independent activities

a. (Pass out Worksheet 50 to each child.)

b. Everybody, now you'll do your worksheet. Remember to do all parts of the worksheet and to read all the parts carefully.

INDIVIDUAL CHECKOUT
EXERCISE 21

2-minute individual fluency checkout: rate/accuracy

a. As you are doing your worksheet, I'll call on children one at a time to read the **first page of the story.** Remember, you get two stars if you read the first page of the story in less than two minutes and make no more than three errors.

b. (Call on each child. Tell the child:) Start with the title and read the first page of the story very carefully. Go. (Time the child. Tell the child any words the child misses. Stop the child as soon as the child makes the fourth error or exceeds the time limit.)

c. (If the child meets the rate-accuracy criterion, record two stars on your chart for lesson 50. Congratulate the child. Give children who do not earn two stars a chance to read the first page of the story again before the next lesson is presented.) 101 words/**2 min** = 51 wpm **[3 errors]**

END OF LESSON 50

EXERCISE 6

Picture comprehension

a. What do you think you'll see in the picture?
(The children respond.)

b. Turn the page and look at the picture.

1. Show me the ghosts.
(The children respond.)
- Do they look mean? (Signal.) *Yes.*
2. What are they doing? (Signal.)
Scaring the horses.
- And what are the horses doing? (Signal.)
Running away.
3. Is Boo in this picture? (Signal.) *No.*
- How do you know? (The children respond.)
4. Would you be scared of those ghosts?
(The children respond.)
5. Are there really such things as ghosts?
(The children respond.)

EXERCISE 7

Summary of independent activities

a. (Pass out Worksheet 103 to each child.)

b. Everybody, now you'll do your worksheet.
Remember to do all parts of the worksheet
and to read all the parts carefully.

END OF LESSON 103

LETTER NAMES
EXERCISE 1

Say vowel names

a. Everybody, say the names of these letters.

b. (Point to each letter. Pause.) Get ready.
(Touch each letter.) (The children respond.)

c. Again. (Repeat *b* until firm.)

Individual test

(Call on individual children. Each child is to identify two letters.)

i   u   o

a   e

STORY 103

EXERCISE 5

Reading—decoding

a. (Pass out Storybook 2.)

b. Everybody, open your reader to page 54.

c. Remember, if the group reads all the way to the red 5 without making more than five errors, we can go on.

d. Everybody, touch the title of the story. ✔

e. If you hear a mistake, raise your hand. Remember, children who do not have their place lose their turn. (Call on individual children to read two or three sentences. Do not ask comprehension questions. Tally all errors.)

To Correct

word-identification errors (**from,** for example)
1. That word is **from.** What word? *From.*
2. Go back to the beginning of the sentence and read the sentence again.

f. (If the children make more than five errors before they reach the red 5: when they reach the 5 return to the beginning of the story and have the children reread to the 5. Do not ask comprehension questions. Repeat step *f* until firm, and then go on to step *g*.)

g. (When the children read to the red 5 without making more than five errors: read the story to the children from the beginning to the 5. Ask the specified comprehension questions. When you reach the 5, call on individual children to continue reading the story. Have each child read two or three sentences. Ask the specified comprehension questions.)

Boo the Ghost[1]

There was a big old house near the town. Six ghosts lived in that old house. And five of those ghosts were very mean. They liked to play tricks on boys and girls. They liked to scare people.[2]

Every night after the sun went down, those five ghosts would say, "What can we do that is mean?" The five ghosts would name some mean things.

Then the five ghosts would go out to do mean things. Sometimes they would hide on a dark street. When a child walked by, they would jump out and say, "Oooooow."[3] The child would run and they would say, "Ho, ho."

Sometimes they would go to a farm and make the horses so scared that the horses would run from the barn.[4] The farmer would come out to see what had happened. The ghosts would hide. ⑤ When he was near the barn, they would all jump at him and say, "Oooooow."[5] And the farmer would run back into his house.

Five ghosts were mean. But the other ghost who lived in the old house was not mean. His name was Boo.[6] He didn't like to scare horses. Boo liked to ride on horses. He didn't like to scare small boys and girls. He liked to play games with them.[7] He didn't like to do mean things. He liked to do things that made everybody happy.

But the people in town were afraid of him. Farmers were also afraid of him. Boys and girls were also afraid.[8] But the ghosts that he lived with were not afraid of him. They didn't like him. They said, "You are not a good ghost because you are not mean."[9]

More to come

---

[1] Who is this story about? (Signal.) *Boo the ghost.*

[2] Tell me some things the mean ghosts did. (The children respond.) Yes, they played tricks and scared people.

[3] What did they do? (Signal.) *Jumped out and said "Oooooow."*

[4] What did the ghosts do? (Signal.) *Scared the horses.*

[5] What would they do? (Signal.) *Jump at him and say, "Oooooow."*

[6] Did Boo live with the other ghosts? (Signal.) *Yes.*

• Was he mean? (Signal.) *No.*

[7] Did he like to scare small boys and girls? (Signal.) *No.*

• What did Boo like to do with them? (Signal.) *Play games.*

[8] Why were people afraid of Boo? (The children respond.)

[9] Were the other ghosts afraid of Boo? (Signal.) *No.*

• Why did they say he wasn't a good ghost? (Signal.) *He was not mean.*

READING VOCABULARY

Do not touch small letters.

Get ready to read all the words on this page without making a mistake.

rat

EXERCISE 2

Sound out first

a. (Touch the ball for **rat**.) Sound it out. Get ready. (Quickly touch **r, a, t** as the children say:) *rrraaat.*

b. What word? (Signal.) *Rat.* Yes, **rat.**

c. (Repeat exercise until firm.)

rāte

EXERCISE 3

Sound out first

a. (Touch the ball for **rāte**.) Sound it out. Get ready. (Quickly touch **r, ā, t** as the children say:) *rrrāāāt.*

b. What word? (Signal.) *Rate.* Yes, **rate.**

c. (Repeat exercise until firm.)

EXERCISE 4

Practice final-e rule

a. (Touch the ball for **rate**.) Everybody, is there an ē on the end of this word? (Signal.) *Yes.*

b. (Point to **a** in **rate**.) So tell me what you say for this letter. (Signal.) *ā.*

c. (Touch the ball for **rate**.) Yes, this word is **rate**. Everybody, read this word the fast way and remember to say **ā**. Get ready. (Signal.) *Rate.* Yes, **rate.**

d. (Touch the ball for **rat**.) Everybody, is there an ē on the end of this word? (Signal.) *No.*

e. (Point to **a** in **rat**.) So tell me what you say for this letter. (Signal.) *aaa.*

f. (Touch the ball for **rat**.) Everybody, read this word the fast way and remember to say **ă**. Get ready. (Signal.) *Rat.* Yes, **rat.**

g. (Repeat *a* through *f* until firm.)

EXERCISE 5

Listen, sound out

a. (Point to **magic**.) I'll tell you this word. (Pause.) **Magic.** What word? (Signal.) *Magic.* Yes, **magic.**

b. (Touch the ball for **magic**.) Sound it out. Get ready. (Quickly touch **m, a, g, i, c** as the children say:) *mmmaaagiiic.*

c. What word? (Signal.) *Magic.* Yes, **magic.**

d. (Repeat *b* and *c* until firm.)

EXERCISE 6

Listen, sound out with me

a. (Point to **eyes**.) I'll tell you this word. (Pause.) **Eyes.** What word? (Signal.) *Eyes.* Yes, **eyes.**

b. (Touch the ball for **eyes**.) Sound it out with me. Get ready. (Quickly touch **e, y, e, s** as you and the children say:) *eeeyyyeeesss.*

c. What word? (Signal.) *Eyes.* Yes, **eyes.**

d. (Repeat *b* and *c* until firm.)

rate

rat

magic

eyes

(Repeat any troublesome words.)

Individual test

(Call on individual children. Each child reads a different word.)

EXERCISE 3

Read the fast way

a. You're going to read all the words in this column the fast way.

b. (Touch the ball for **house**. Pause.) Get ready. (Slash.) *House.*

c. (Repeat step *b* until firm.)

d. (Repeat steps *b* and *c* for each remaining word in the column.)

e. (Repeat the column until the children read all the words in order without making mistakes.)

house

heap

mean

There

where

hear

near

EXERCISE 4

Children spell, then read

a. First you're going to spell each word. Then you're going to read that word the fast way.

b. (Touch the ball for **games**.) Spell it. Get ready. (Tap under each letter as the children say:) *G-A-M-E-S.*

• (Return to the ball.) Read it. Get ready. (Slash.) *Games.*

c. (Repeat step *b* for each remaining word in the column.)

d. (Repeat steps *b* and *c* until firm.)

games

spell

people

night

afraid

laugh

scare

Individual test

a. (Call on individual children to read one column of words from the lesson.)

b. (Praise children who read all words with no errors.)

Do not touch small letters.

Get ready to read all the words on this page without making a mistake.

EXERCISE 7

Read the fast way

a. Read these words the fast way.

b. (Touch the ball for **there**. Pause two seconds.) Get ready. (Signal.) *There.* Yes, **there.**

c. (Repeat *b* for **alwāys, where, what, who, stēēp, very,** and **any.**)

what

who

ther_e

stēēp

alwāys

very

wher_e

any

(Repeat any troublesome words.)

Individual test

(Call on individual children. Each child reads a different word.)

once

EXERCISE 8

Listen, sound out

a. (Point to **once.**) I'll tell you this word. (Pause.) **Once.** What word? (Signal.) *Once.* Yes, **once.**

b. (Touch the ball for **once.**) Sound it out. Get ready. (Quickly touch **o, n, c, e** as the children say:) *ooonnnceee.*

To Correct

(If the children do not say the sounds you point to:)

1. (Say:) You've got to say the sounds I point to.
2. (Repeat *b* until firm.)

c. What word? (Signal.) *Once.* Yes, **once.**

d. (Repeat *b* and *c* until firm.)

father

EXERCISE 9

Listen, sound out with me

a. (Point to **father.**) I'll tell you this word. (Pause.) **Father.** What word? (Signal.) *Father.* Yes, **father.**

b. (Touch the ball for **father.**) Sound it out with me. Get ready. (Quickly touch each sound as you and the children say:) *fffaaathththerrr.*

c. What word? (Signal.) *Father.* Yes, **father.**

d. (Repeat *b* and *c* until firm.)

READING VOCABULARY

EXERCISE 1

Teacher reads the words in red

a. I'll read each word in red. Then you'll spell each word.

b. (Touch the ball for **Boo**.) My turn. (Slash as you say:) Boo. What word? (Signal.) *Boo.*

c. (Return to the ball.) Spell it. Get ready. (Tap under each letter as the children say:) *B-O-O.*

- What word did you spell? (Signal.) *Boo.*

d. (Repeat steps *b* and *c* for each word in red.)

e. Your turn to read all the words in this column.

f. (Touch the ball for **Boo**. Pause.) Get ready. (Slash.) *Boo.*

g. (Repeat step *f* for each remaining word in the column.)

h. (Repeat steps *f* and *g* until firm.)

Boo

Ghost

right

stream

everybody

read

were

EXERCISE 2

Words with underlined parts

a. First you're going to read the underlined part of each word in this column. Then you're going to read the whole word.

b. (Touch the ball for **didn't**.) Read the underlined part. Get ready. (Tap the ball.) *Did.*

- Read the whole word. (Pause.) Get ready. (Slash.) *Didn't.*

c. (Repeat step *b* until firm.)

d. (Repeat steps *b* and *c* for each remaining word in the column.)

e. (Repeat the column until children read all the words in order without making a mistake.)

didn't

horses

tricks

sometimes

happened

leave

reading

Do not touch small letters.

Get ready to read all the words on this page without making a mistake.

herself

EXERCISE 10

Two-part word

a. (Cover **self.** Point to **her.**) Everybody, tell me what this part of the word says. Get ready. (Signal.) *Her.* Yes, **her.**

b. (Uncover **self.** Touch the ball for **herself.**) Now tell me what the whole word says. Get ready. (Signal.) *Herself.* Yes, **herself.**

c. (Repeat exercise until firm.)

house

EXERCISE 11

Read **ou** word the fast way

a. (Touch the ball for **house.**) Read this word the fast way. (Pause two seconds.) Get ready. (Signal.) *House.* Yes, **house.**

b. (Point to **ou** in **house.**) Everybody, what do these letters say? (Signal.) *ou.* Yes, **ou.**

c. (Touch the ball for **house.**) Sound it out. Get ready. (Quickly touch **h, ou, s** as the children say:) *housss.*

d. What word? (Signal.) *House.* Yes, **house.**

e. (Repeat *c* and *d* until firm.)

tall

EXERCISE 12

al word

a. (Point to **al** in **tall.**) What do these letters say? (Signal.) *All.* Yes, **all.**

b. (Touch the ball for **tall.**) Read this word the fast way. Get ready. (Signal.) *Tall.* Yes, **tall.**

far

EXERCISE 13

ar word

a. (Point to **ar** in **far.**) What do these letters say? (Signal.) *Are.* Yes, **are.**

b. (Touch the ball for **far.**) Read this word the fast way. Get ready. (Signal.) *Far.* Yes, **far.**

EXERCISE 14

Read the fast way

a. Read these words the fast way.

b. (Touch the ball for **about.** Pause two seconds.) Get ready. (Signal.) *About.* Yes, **about.**

c. (Repeat *b* for **ground, sound, shouted, clouds,** and **pouch.**)

about

ground

sound

shouted

clouds

pouch

Individual test

(Call on individual children to read a column of words from this lesson. If the column contains only one or two words, direct the child to read additional words from an adjacent column. Praise children who read all words with no errors.)

EXERCISE 6

Picture comprehension

a. Look at the picture.

b. (Ask these questions:)

1. Where are the girl and the kitten in this picture? (Signal.) *On a farm.*
2. How do you know that they are on a farm? (Let the children comment for ten seconds. Then comment briefly.)
3. What is the girl doing? (Signal.) *Holding the kitten.*
4. How does the girl feel? (The children respond.)
 • Look at her face. How can you tell that she looks happy? (The children respond.)
5. (Point to the freckles.) Those little dots on her face are freckles. Do you know anyone who has freckles? (The children respond.)

STORY-ITEMS REVIEW

The children will need pencils.

EXERCISE 7

Children read and do story-items review

a. (Pass out Worksheet 102 to each child.)

b. (Hold up side 1 of your worksheet and point to the row of stars below story item 7.)

c. Everybody, touch this row of stars on your worksheet. ✔

d. The items below the stars are about an old story. You didn't read that story today.

e. Everybody, get ready to read item 1. First word. ✔
 • Get ready. (Tap for each word as the children read:) *What did the tame tiger like to eat?*

f. What's the answer to item 1? (Signal.) *Ice cream.* Yes, **ice cream.**

g. Everybody, write the answer in the blank. ✔

h. Read item 2 to yourself and raise your hand when you know the answer.

i. (When all the hands are raised, say:) Everybody, what's the answer to item 2? (Signal.) *Stones.*

j. Everybody, write the answer in the blank. ✔

k. Everybody, you'll do the other item later.

INDEPENDENT ACTIVITIES

EXERCISE 8

Summary of independent activities

Everybody, now you'll do your worksheet. Remember to do all parts of the worksheet and to read all the parts carefully.

END OF LESSON 102

STORYBOOK

STORY 51

EXERCISE 15

First reading—title and three sentences

a. (Pass out Storybook 1.)

b. Everybody, open your reader to page 128.

c. Everybody, touch the title of the story and get ready to read the words in the title.

d. First word. ✔
- Get ready. (Tap.) *The.*

e. (Tap for each remaining word in the title.)

f. Everybody, say the title. (Signal.)
The magic pouch.
- Yes, we're going to read part one of this story. Tomorrow we'll read part two.

g. Everybody, get ready to read this story.

h. First word. ✔
- Get ready. (Tap.) *There.*

i. Next word. ✔
- Get ready. (Tap.) *Was.*

j. (Repeat *i* for the remaining words in the first three sentences. Have the children reread the first three sentences until firm.)

EXERCISE 16

Remaining sentences

a. I'm going to call on individual children to read a sentence. Everybody, follow along and point to the words. If you hear a mistake, raise your hand.

b. (Call on a child.) Read the next sentence.

To Correct

word-identification errors (**from,** for example)
1. That word is **from.** What word? *From.*
2. Go back to the beginning of the sentence and read the sentence again.

c. (Call on another child.) Read the next sentence.

d. (Repeat *c* for most of the remaining sentences in the story.)

e. (Occasionally have the group read a sentence. When the group is to read, say:) Everybody, read the next sentence. (Tap for each word in the sentence.)

1

the magic pouch[1]

ther̲e̲ was a little girl wh̲o̲ live̲d̲

nēar a tall mountain.[2] the mountain

was so tall that the top was alwāys

in the clou̲d̲s. the girl wanted to

go to the top of the mountain, but

her mother tōld her, "no."[3] she said,

"that mountain is stēĕp.[4] you would

fĪnd it very hard to get to the top."

but one dāy the little girl was

sittiñg and lookiñg at the mountain.

she said to herself, "I would lĪke to

see wha̲t̲ is in thōs̲e̲ clouds at the

top of the mountain. I think I

will go up and see."

EXERCISE 17

Second reading—sentences and questions

a. You're going to read the story again. This time I'm going to ask questions.

b. Starting with the first word of the title. ✔
- Get ready. (Tap as the children read the title.)

c. (Call on a child.) Read the first sentence.

To Correct

word-identification errors (**from,** for example)
1. That word is **from.** What word? *From.*
2. Go back to the beginning of the sentence and read the sentence again.

d. (Call on another child.) Read the next sentence.

e. (Repeat *d* for most of the remaining sentences in the story.)

f. (Occasionally have the group read a sentence.)

g. (After each underlined sentence has been read, present each comprehension question specified below to the entire group.)

[1] What's the title of this story? (Signal.) *The magic pouch.*
- A pouch is like a purse. And this pouch is going to be very special.

[2] Where did the little girl live? (Signal.) *Near a tall mountain.*
- What is a mountain? (The children respond.) Yes, like a very, very high hill.

[3] Where did she want to go? (Signal.) *To the top of the mountain.*
- Would her mother let her go? (Signal.) *No.*

[4] Why wouldn't she let her go? (Signal.) *The mountain was steep.*
- Maybe she was afraid because it was so tall that the girl might fall off.

STORY 102
EXERCISE 5

Reading—decoding

a. (Pass out Storybook 2.)

b. Everybody, open your reader to page 52.

c. Remember, if the group reads all the way to the red 5 without making more than five errors, we can go on.

d. Everybody, touch the title of the story. ✔

e. If you hear a mistake, raise your hand. Remember, children who do not have their place lose their turn. (Call on individual children to read two or three sentences. Do not ask comprehension questions. Tally all errors.)

To Correct

word-identification errors (**from**, for example)
1. That word is **from**. What word? *From.*
2. Go back to the beginning of the sentence and read the sentence again.

f. (If the children make more than five errors before they reach the red 5: when they reach the 5 return to the beginning of the story and have the children reread to the 5. Do not ask comprehension questions. Repeat step *f* until firm, and then go on to step *g*.)

g. (When the children read to the red 5 without making more than five errors: read the story to the children from the beginning to the 5. Ask the specified comprehension questions. When you reach the 5, call on individual children to continue reading the story. Have each child read two or three sentences. Ask the specified comprehension questions.)

The Kitten's New Home[1]

A kitten was sad because she did not have a home. She tried to live in a mail box and a nest and a fish bowl.[2] But she did not like these homes.

She started to cry. A small girl asked her, "Why are you crying?"

The kitten told the small girl about the mail box and the nest and the fish bowl. Then the kitten said, "I am sad because I have no home."[3]

The girl said, "I live on a farm. We have a big farm house. We have a barn. And it is fun to play in the barn. We have sheep and cows.[4] And the cows give lots of milk. We have everything but one thing."

"What is that?" the kitten asked.

The girl said, "We don't have a kitten and I love kittens."[5]

Then the small girl said, "Would you like to live on our farm?"(5)[6]

The kitten jumped into the girl's arms.[7] "I will be your kitten," the kitten said. She gave the girl one kiss and then another kiss.

So the girl and the kitten went to the farm. The kitten had a home and the girl had a kitten.[8] She loved that kitten.

This story is over.

---

[1] What's going to happen in this story? (The children respond.)

[2] Where did she try to live first? (Signal.) *In a mail box.*

• Then where did she try to live? (Signal.) *In a nest.*

• Then where did she try to live? (Signal.) *In a fish bowl.*

[3] Who said that? (Signal.) *The kitten.*

• What did she say? (Signal.) *I am sad because I have no home.*

• Who is the kitten talking to? (Signal.) *The girl.*

[4] Name some things they have on the girl's farm. (The children respond.)

[5] Does the girl like kittens? (Signal.) *Yes.*

[6] What did she ask? (Signal.) *Would you like to live on our farm?*

• What do you think the kitten will answer? (The children respond.)

[7] Why did she do that? (The children respond.)

[8] Did the kitten find a new home? (Signal.) *Yes.*

• Where? (The children respond.)

• What did the girl get? (Signal.) *A kitten.*

so the girl took her pet hound
and started up the tall mountain.[5]
they went up and up. the sIde of
the mountain was very stēēp. up
they went. the girl said to her
hound, "do not fall. it is very far
down to the ground."

soon the little girl and her
hound cāme to the clouds nēar the
top of the mountain. she said to her
hound, "now we will see what is on
the other sIde of thōse clouds."[6]

what do you think they will see
on the other sIde of the clouds?[7]

mōre to come

[5] What did the girl do? (The children respond.)
Why did she do that? (The children respond.)
[6] What did the girl want to see? (Signal.)
What is on the other side of those clouds.
• Who is she talking to? (Signal.) *Her hound.*
Yes, her hound dog.
[7] What do you think? (The children respond.)
• We'll read more next time and see what they saw.

EXERCISE 18
Picture comprehension

a. What do you think you'll see in the picture?
(The children respond.)
b. Turn the page and look at the picture.
c. (Ask these questions:)
  1. What is the girl doing? (Signal.)
     Looking at the mountain.
  2. (Point to the clouds.)
     What are those things at the top of the
     mountain? (Signal.) *Clouds.*
  3. Does the mountain look very far from her
     house? (Signal.) *Yes.*
  4. What could the girl be thinking about?
     (The children respond.)
  5. (Point to the dog.) I hope her hound helps
     her if they get in trouble.

SUMMARY OF INDEPENDENT ACTIVITY
EXERCISE 19

Introduction to independent activity

a. (Pass out Worksheet 51 to each child.)
b. (Hold up side 1 of your worksheet.)
Everybody, you're going to do this
worksheet on your own. (Tell the children
when they will work the items.)
• Let's go over the things you're going to do.

Story items

(Point to the story-items exercise.) Everybody,
remember to write your answers in the blanks.

Following instructions

a. (Touch the sentence in the box.)
b. Everybody, first you're going to read the
sentence in the box. Then you're going to
read the instructions below the box and do
what the instructions tell you to do.

Reading comprehension

(Point to the story on side 2.) You're going
to read this story and then do the items.
Remember to write the answers in the blanks.

Following instructions

(Point to the following-instructions exercise.)
Everybody, you're going to read the
instructions. Then you're going to do what the
instructions tell you to do.

END OF LESSON 51

EXERCISE 3

Children spell, then read

a. First you're going to spell each word. Then you're going to read that word the fast way.

b. (Touch the ball for **your.**) Spell it. Get ready. (Tap under each letter as the children say:) *Y-O-U-R.*

• (Return to the ball.) Read it. Get ready. (Slash.) *Your.*

c. (Repeat step *b* for each remaining word in the column.)

d. (Repeat steps *b* and *c* until firm.)

your

She

grew

care

scare

homes

would

EXERCISE 4

Words with underlined parts

a. First you're going to read the underlined part of each word in this column. Then you're going to read the whole word.

b. (Touch the ball for **mean.**) Read the underlined part. Get ready. (Tap the ball.) *ēēē.*

• Read the whole word. (Pause.) Get ready. (Slash.) *Mean.*

c. (Repeat step *b* until firm.)

d. (Repeat steps *b* and *c* for each remaining word in the column.)

e. (Repeat the column until children read all the words in order without making a mistake.)

mean

jumped

arms

everything

Kittens

another

asked

Individual test

a. (Call on individual children to read one column of words from the lesson.)

b. (Praise children who read all words with no errors.)

LESSON 52

LETTER NAMES
EXERCISE 1

Say vowel names

a. Everybody, say the names of these letters.

b. (Point to each letter. Pause.) Get ready. (Touch each letter.) (The children respond.)

c. Again. (Repeat *b* until firm.)

Individual test

(Call on individual children. Each child is to identify two letters.)

EXERCISE 2

Sound combination review

a. Here are some letters that go together. Get ready to tell me the sound they usually make.

b. (Point to **al**.) What sound do these letters usually make? (Signal.) *All.* Yes, **all.**

c. (Repeat *b* with **ou**.)

d. (Repeat both sound combinations until firm.)

al

ou

e u o

i a

READING VOCABULARY

EXERCISE 1

Teacher reads the words in red

a. I'll read each word in red. Then you'll spell each word.

b. (Touch the ball for **people.**) My turn. (Slash as you say:) People. What word? (Signal.) *People.*

c. (Return to the ball.) Spell it. Get ready. (Tap under each letter as the children say:) *P-E-O-P-L-E.*

• What word did you spell? (Signal.) *People.*

d. (Repeat steps *b* and *c* for each word in red.)

e. Your turn to read all the words in this column.

f. (Touch the ball for **people.** Pause.) Get ready. (Slash.) *People.*

g. (Repeat step *f* for each remaining word in the column.)

h. (Repeat steps *f* and *g* until firm.)

people

milk

ghost

laugh

New

king

sheep

EXERCISE 2

Words with underlined parts

a. First you're going to read the underlined part of each word in this column. Then you're going to read the whole word.

b. (Touch the ball for **bald.**) Read the underlined part. Get ready. (Tap the ball.) *All.* Read the whole word. (Pause.) Get ready. (Slash.) *Bald.*

c. (Repeat step *b* until firm.)

d. (Repeat steps *b* and *c* for each remaining word in the column.)

e. (Repeat the column until children read all the words in order without making a mistake.)

bald

farm

about

bean

small

What

near

READING VOCABULARY

Do not touch small letters.

Get ready to read all the words on this page without making a mistake.

rest

EXERCISE 3

Sound out first

a. (Touch the ball for **rest.**) Sound it out. Get ready. (Quickly touch **r, e, s, t** as the children say:) *rrreeessst.*

b. What word? (Signal.) *Rest.* Yes, **rest.**

c. (Repeat exercise until firm.)

ōpen

EXERCISE 4

Sound out first

a. (Touch the ball for **ōpen.**) Sound it out. Get ready. (Quickly touch **ō, p, e, n** as the children say:) *ōōōpeeennn.*

b. What word? (Signal.) *Open.* Yes, **open.**

c. (Repeat exercise until firm.)

bēfōre

EXERCISE 5

Sound out first

a. (Touch the ball for **bēfōre.**) Sound it out. Get ready. (Quickly touch **b, ē, f, ō, r** as the children say:) *bēēēfffōōōrrr.*

b. What word? (Signal.) *Before.* Yes, **before.**

c. (Repeat exercise until firm.)

EXERCISE 6

Practice final-e rule

a. (Touch the ball for **rode.**) Everybody, is there an **ē** on the end of this word? (Signal.) *Yes.*

b. (Point to **o** in **rode.**) So tell me what you say for this letter. (Signal.) *ō.*

c. (Touch the ball for **rode.**) Yes, this word is **rode.** Everybody, read this word the fast way and remember to say **ō.** Get ready. (Signal.) *Rode.* Yes, **rode.**

d. (Touch the ball for **rod.**) Everybody, is there an **ē** on the end of this word? (Signal.) *No.*

e. (Point to **o** in **rod.**) So tell me what you say for this letter. (Signal.) *ŏŏŏ.*

f. (Touch the ball for **rod.**) Everybody, read this word the fast way and remember to say **ŏŏŏ.** Get ready. (Signal.) *Rod.* Yes, **rod.**

g. (Repeat *a* through *f* until firm.)

EXERCISE 7

Sound out first

a. (Touch the ball for **grabbed.**) Sound it out. Get ready. (Quickly touch **g, r, a,** between the **b**'s, **d** as the children say:) *grrraaabd.*

b. What word? (Signal.) *Grabbed.* Yes, **grabbed.**

c. (Repeat exercise until firm.)

EXERCISE 8

Sound out first

a. (Touch the ball for **slammed.**) Sound it out. Get ready. (Quickly touch **s, l, a,** between the **m**'s, **d** as the children say:) *ssslllaaammmd.*

b. What word? (Signal.) *Slammed.* Yes, **slammed.**

c. (Repeat exercise until firm.)

rode

rod

grabbed

slammed

(Repeat any troublesome words.)

Individual test

(Call on individual children. Each child reads a different word.)

WORKSHEET 101

EXERCISE 6

Picture comprehension

a. Look at the picture.

b. (Ask these questions:)

1. Where is the kitten in this picture? (Signal.) *In a fish bowl.*
2. What else do you see in the fish bowl? (The children respond.)
3. Look at the kitten's face. Is that kitten happy? (Signal.) *No.*
   - What do you think the kitten is saying? (The children respond.)
4. What do you think the girl is saying to the kitten? (The children respond.)

STORY-ITEMS REVIEW

The children will need pencils.

EXERCISE 7

Children read and do story-items review

a. (Pass out Worksheet 101 to each child.)

b. (Hold up side 1 of your worksheet and point to the row of stars below story item 4.)

c. Everybody, touch this row of stars on your worksheet. ✔

d. The items below the stars are about an old story. You didn't read that story today.

e. Everybody, get ready to read item 1. First word. ✔
   - Get ready. (Tap for each word as the children read:) *Did Sid tap the oak tree or tape the oak tree?*

f. What's the answer to item 1? (Signal.) *Tap the oak tree.* Yes, **tap the oak tree.**

g. Everybody, write the answer in the blank. ✔

h. Read item 2 to yourself and raise your hand when you know the answer.

i. (When all the hands are raised, say:) Everybody, what's the answer to item 2? (Signal.) *The boss.*

j. Everybody, write the answer in the blank. ✔

k. Everybody, you'll do the other item later.

INDEPENDENT ACTIVITIES

EXERCISE 8

Summary of independent activities

Everybody, now you'll do your worksheet. Remember to do all parts of the worksheet and to read all the parts carefully.

END OF LESSON 101

Do not touch small letters.

Get ready to read all the words on this page without making a mistake.

come

EXERCISE 9

Read the fast way

a. Read this word the fast way.
b. (Touch the ball for **come**. Pause two seconds.) Get ready. (Signal.) *Come.* Yes, **come.**

coming

EXERCISE 10

Read the fast way first

a. (Touch the ball for **coming**.) Read this word the fast way. (Pause two seconds.) Get ready. (Signal.) *Coming.* Yes, **coming.**
b. (Return to the ball.) Sound it out. Get ready. (Quickly touch **c, o, m, ing** as the children say:) *cooommmiiing.*
c. What word? (Signal.) *Coming.* Yes, **coming.**
d. (Repeat *b* and *c* until firm.)

EXERCISE 11

Read the fast way

a. Read these words the fast way.
b. (Touch the ball for **once.** Pause two seconds.) Get ready. (Signal.) *Once.* Yes, **once.**
c. (Repeat *b* for remaining words.)

once

hanging

ōnly

her

hēre

eyes

who

charm

any

sound

from

out

called

(Repeat any troublesome words.)

Individual test

(Call on individual children. Each child reads a different word.)

STORYBOOK

STORY 101
EXERCISE 5

Reading—decoding

a. (Pass out Storybook 2.)

b. Everybody, open your reader to page 50.

c. Remember, if the group reads all the way to the red 5 without making more than five errors, we can go on.

d. Everybody, touch the title of the story. ✔

e. If you hear a mistake, raise your hand. Remember, children who do not have their place lose their turn. (Call on individual children to read two or three sentences. Do not ask comprehension questions. Tally all errors.)

To Correct

word-identification errors (**from,** for example)
1. That word is **from.** What word? *From.*
2. Go back to the beginning of the sentence and read the sentence again.

f. (If the children make more than five errors before they reach the red 5: when they reach the 5 return to the beginning of the story and have the children reread to the 5. Do not ask comprehension questions. Repeat step *f* until firm, and then go on to step *g*.)

g. (When the children read to the red 5 without making more than five errors: read the story to the children from the beginning to the 5. Ask the specified comprehension questions. When you reach the 5, call on individual children to continue reading the story. Have each child read two or three sentences. Ask the specified comprehension questions.)

The Kitten Needs a Home[1]

A little kitten was sad because she did not have a home. She said, "I must find a home."

She looked in a mail box. <u>She said, "This will be my home."</u>[2]And she went into the mail box.

It was very dark in that mail box. <u>The little kitten said, "I do not want to live in this mail box because it is too dark."</u>[3]

Then she looked at a nest in a tree. <u>She said, "This will be my home."</u>[4]She went up the tree and sat in the nest.

<u>Then it started to snow.</u>[5]

The kitten said, "I do not want to live in this nest because it is too cold." <u>She said, "I must find another home."</u>[6]

She began to walk from the nest. <u>Then she saw a fish bowl.</u>[7] She said, "This will be my home." ⑤ She went into the fish bowl, but she got wet. <u>She said, "I do not want to live in this fish bowl because I get too wet."</u>[8]

She started to cry. Just then a little girl came by. <u>The girl asked, "Why are you crying?"</u>[9]

The kitten answered, "Because I do not have a home."

More to come

---

[1] What is the title of this story? (Signal.) *The Kitten Needs a Home.*

[2] What place is she talking about? (Signal.) *A mail box.*

[3] Did the kitten want to live in the mail box? (Signal.) *No.*

• Why not? (Signal.) *Because it is too dark.*

[4] What place is she talking about now? (Signal.) *A nest in a tree.*

[5] Where was she when it started to snow? (Signal.) *In a nest in a tree.*

• How will she feel in the snow? (Signal.) *Cold.*

[6] What did she say? (Signal.) *I must find another home.*

• Why wasn't the nest a good place? (The children respond.)

[7] What did she see? (Signal.) *A fish bowl.*

• I wonder if there is water in that bowl. Let's read and find out.

[8] What was wrong with living in the fish bowl? (The children respond.)

[9] I wonder if the girl can help. Next time we'll find out.

Do not touch small letters.

Get ready to read all the words on this page without making a mistake.

EXERCISE 12

ou word

a. (Point to **ou** in **house**.) What do these letters say? (Signal.) *ou.* Yes, **ou.**

b. (Touch the ball for **house**.) Read this word the fast way. Get ready. (Signal.) *House.* Yes, **house.**

EXERCISE 13

ou word

a. (Point to **ou** in **ouch**.) What do these letters say? (Signal.) *ou.* Yes, **ou.**

b. (Touch the ball for **ouch**.) Read this word the fast way. Get ready. (Signal.) *Ouch.* Yes, **ouch.**

EXERCISE 14

ou word

a. (Touch the ball for **hounds**.) Read this word the fast way. (Pause two seconds.) Get ready. (Signal.) *Hounds.* Yes, **hounds.**

b. (Point to **ou** in **hounds**.) Everybody, what do these letters say? (Signal.) *ou.* Yes, **ou.**

c. (Touch the ball for **hounds**.) Sound it out. Get ready. (Quickly touch **h, ou, n, d, s** as the children say:) *hounnndsss.*

d. What word? (Signal.) *Hounds.* Yes, **hounds.**

e. (Repeat *c* and *d* until firm.)

hOUSe

ouch

hounds

Individual test

(Call on individual children to read a column of words from this lesson. If the column contains only one or two words, direct the child to read additional words from an adjacent column. Praise children who read all words with no errors.)

STORYBOOK

STORY 52

See first reading questions on next page.

EXERCISE 15

First reading—title and three sentences

a. (Pass out Storybook 1.)

b. Everybody, open your reader to page 131.

c. Everybody, touch the title of the story and get ready to read the words in the title.

d. First word. ✔

• Get ready. (Tap.) *The.*

e. (Tap for each remaining word in the title.)

f. Everybody, say the title. (Signal.) *The magic pouch.*

g. Yesterday we read part one. Today we're going to read part two.

h. Everybody, get ready to read this story.

i. First word. ✔

• Get ready. (Tap.) *Where.*

j. Next word. ✔

• Get ready. (Tap.) *Did.*

k. (Repeat *j* for the remaining words in the first three sentences. Have the children reread the first three sentences until firm.)

EXERCISE 3

Read the fast way

a. You're going to read all the words in this column the fast way.

b. (Touch the ball for **began.** Pause.) Get ready. (Slash.) *Began.*

c. (Repeat step *b* until firm.)

d. (Repeat steps *b* and *c* for each remaining word in the column.)

e. (Repeat the column until the children read all the words in order without making mistakes.)

began

read

who

grew

eat

Needs

wet

EXERCISE 4

Children spell, then read

a. First you're going to spell each word. Then you're going to read that word the fast way.

b. (Touch the ball for **saw.**) Spell it. Get ready. (Tap under each letter as the children say:) *S-A-W.*

• (Return to the ball.) Read it. Get ready. (Slash.) *Saw.*

c. (Repeat step *b* for each remaining word in the column.)

d. (Repeat steps *b* and *c* until firm.)

saw

how

Because

from

Home

must

begin

Individual test

a. (Call on individual children to read one column of words from the lesson.)

b. (Praise children who read all words with no errors.)

EXERCISE 16

Remaining sentences and questions

a. I'm going to call on individual children to read a sentence. Everybody, follow along and point to the words. If you hear a mistake, raise your hand.

b. (Call on a child.) Read the next sentence.

c. (Call on another child.) Read the next sentence.

To Correct

word-identification errors (**from,** for example)
1. That word is **from.** What word? *From.*
2. Go back to the beginning of the sentence and read the sentence again.

d. (Repeat *c* for most of the remaining sentences in the story.)

e. (Occasionally have the group read a sentence. When the group is to read, say:) Everybody, read the next sentence. (Tap for each word in the sentence.)

f. (After each underlined sentence has been read, present each comprehension question specified below to the entire group.)

[1] Everybody, say that question. (Signal.) *Where did the little girl live?*
• What's the answer? (Signal.) *Near a tall mountain.*
[2] Everybody, say that question. (Signal.) *What did the girl want to do?*
• What's the answer? (Signal.) *Go to the top of the mountain.*
[3] Everybody, say that question. (Signal.) *Who told her not to go up the mountain?*
• What's the answer? (Signal.) *Her mother.*
[4] Everybody, say that question. (Signal.) *Who did she take with her?*
• What's the answer? (Signal.) *Her hound.*
[5] Everybody, say that question. (Signal.) *Where did the girl go with her hound?*
• What's the answer? (The children respond.)

2

the magic pouch

where did the little girl live?[1]

what did the girl want to do?[2]

who told her not to go up the mountain?[3]

who did she take with her?[4]

where did the girl go with her hound?[5]

the little girl and her hound went into the clouds. she said, "I cannot see too well. these clouds make a fog."[6] but the girl and her hound kept going up and up.[7]

all at once they came out of the clouds. they could not see the ground any more. they could only see clouds under them. they were in the sun. the sun was in the girl's eyes, so she could not see well.[8] she sat down and said to her hound, "we must sit and rest."

all at once the little girl looked up and saw a funny little house. she said, "I didn't see that house before. let's go see who lives there."[9]

so the girl and her hound walked over to the funny little house.

all at once a loud sound came from the house.[10]

more to come

EXERCISE 17

Second reading—sentences and questions

a. You're going to read the story again. And I'm going to ask more questions.

b. Starting with the first word of the title. ✔
• Get ready. (Tap as the children read the title.)

c. (Call on a child.) Read the first sentence.

To Correct

word-identification errors (**from,** for example)
1. That word is **from.** What word? *From.*
2. Go back to the beginning of the sentence and read the sentence again.

d. (Call on another child.) Read the next sentence.

e. (Repeat *d* for most of the remaining sentences in the story.)

f. (Occasionally have the group read a sentence.)

g. (After each underlined sentence has been read, present each comprehension question specified below to the entire group.)

[6] Why couldn't the girl see too well? (Signal.) *The clouds made a fog.*
[7] Did they stop climbing? (Signal.) *No.*
[8] Why couldn't she see well this time? (Signal.) *The sun was in her eyes.*
[9] Where are they going? (Signal.) *To a funny little house.*
[10] What happened? (Signal.) *A loud sound came from the house.*
• Let's hear you make a loud sound. (The children respond.)
• I wonder what it could be. We'll read more next time.

READING VOCABULARY

EXERCISE 1

Teacher reads the words in red

a. I'll read each word in red. Then you'll spell each word.

b. (Touch the ball for **snow.**) My turn. (Slash as you say:) Snow. What word? (Signal.) *Snow.*

c. (Return to the ball.) Spell it. Get ready. (Tap under each letter as the children say:) *S-N-O-W.*

• What word did you spell? (Signal.) *Snow.*

d. (Repeat steps *b* and *c* for each word in red.)

e. Your turn to read all the words in this column.

f. (Touch the ball for **snow.** Pause.) Get ready. (Slash.) *Snow.*

g. (Repeat step *f* for each remaining word in the column.)

h. (Repeat steps *f* and *g* until firm.)

snow

nest

lunch

bowl

kitten

new

grew

EXERCISE 2

Words with underlined parts

a. First you're going to read the underlined part of each word in this column. Then you're going to read the whole word.

b. (Touch the ball for **dark.**) Read the underlined part. Get ready. (Tap the ball.) *ar.*

• Read the whole word. (Pause.) Get ready. (Slash.) *Dark.*

c. (Repeat step *b* until firm.)

d. (Repeat steps *b* and *c* for each remaining word in the column.)

e. (Repeat the column until children read all the words in order without making a mistake.)

dark

mouth

why

reach

crying

getting

seat

EXERCISE 18

Picture comprehension

a. Look at the picture.

b. (Ask these questions:)

1. Why are the girl and her hound sitting down? (The children respond.)

2. (Point to the clouds.) What are those? (Signal.) *Clouds.*

3. Everybody, look at the house. Tell me about it. (Let the children comment for ten seconds. Then comment briefly.)

4. Who do you think might live in that house? (The children respond.)

SUMMARY OF INDEPENDENT ACTIVITY

EXERCISE 19

Introduction to independent activity

a. (Pass out Worksheet 52 to each child.)

b. (Hold up side 1 of your worksheet.) Everybody, you're going to do this worksheet on your own. (Tell the children when they will work the items.)

- Let's go over the things you're going to do.

Story items

(Point to the story-items exercise.) Everybody, remember to write your answers in the blanks.

Following instructions

a. (Touch the sentence in the box.)

b. Everybody, first you're going to read the sentence in the box. Then you're going to read the instructions below the box and do what the instructions tell you to do.

Reading comprehension

(Point to the story on side 2.) You're going to read this story and then do the items. Remember to write the answers in the blanks.

Following instructions

(Point to the following-instructions exercise.) Everybody, you're going to read the instructions. Then you're going to do what the instructions tell you to do.

END OF LESSON 52

Look Ahead

In-Program Tests
Fluency Checkouts: Rate/Accuracy

Lessons 105, 110, 115, 120

- By lesson 120, children should be reading at least 75 words per minute with 97 percent accuracy. Provide extra practice on checkouts for those who are not at this level of mastery.

Lesson Number	Error Limit	Number of words read	Number of minutes	Words per minute
105	4	120	2	60
110	5	139	2	70
115	5	140	2	70
120	5	150	2	75

Worksheets

- Children should be able to complete all Workbook activities independently and with at least 90 percent accuracy.

Skills

	Lessons 101–120
Word Reading	157 regular words 39 irregular words
Comprehension	Answering review questions about stories previously read

Reading Activities

Help children develop decoding and comprehension skills by using the following activities.

Getting the Main Idea (Lessons 101–120)

Have children determine the main idea of a story in a story series by writing who or what the lesson story was about and the most important thing that happened in the story. An example from Lesson 113 is shown below.

Who or What	**Most Important Thing**	**Main Idea Sentence**
Boo	found castle	Boo found the monster
monster	saw magic gold rod	with the magic gold rod at the castle.

What Is Next? (Lessons 101–102, 103–111, 112–120)

List several story events on the board or on a sheet of paper. Have children number the sentences in the order in which they occurred. An example from the Ott and Carla story series (Lessons 112–120) is shown below.

(2) A teacher needed a genie for a yellow bottle.
(4) Carla rubbed the bottle.
(1) Ott made a pot of beans.
(5) Ott tells big lies.
(3) Ott is chosen for the yellow bottle.

Be the Teacher! (Lessons 101–120)

Make word cards using the words on which the children have made errors during the lessons. Then make a chart like the one below. Give these directions to the children: Take turns being the teacher. Show each card to your students. Say, "Read these words the fast way." Flip the word cards as children say the words. If the word is pronounced correctly, make a tally mark under the word on the smiley face row. If an error is made, tell children the word and make a tally mark under the word on the M row.

	tricks	heap	gold	casts	peach	puff	flip
M				I			
🙂	I	I	I		I		

READING VOCABULARY

Do not touch small letters.

Get ready to read all the words on this page without making a mistake.

EXERCISE 1

Practice final-e rule

a. (Touch the ball for **rat**.) Everybody, is there an ē on the end of this word? (Signal.) *No.*

b. (Point to **a** in **rat**.) So tell me what you say for this letter. (Signal.) *ăăă.*

c. (Touch the ball for **rat**.) Everybody, read this word the fast way and remember to say ăăă. Get ready. (Signal.) *Rat.* Yes, **rat.**

d. (Touch the ball for **rate**.) Everybody, is there an ē on the end of this word? (Signal.) *Yes.*

e. (Point to **a** in **rate**.) So tell me what you say for this letter. (Signal.) *ā.*

f. (Touch the ball for **rate**.) Everybody, read this word the fast way and remember to say ā. Get ready. (Signal.) *Rate.* Yes, **rate.**

g. (Repeat *a* through *f* until firm.)

EXERCISE 2

Two-part word

a. (Cover **one**. Point to **any**.) Everybody, tell me what this part of the word says. Get ready. (Signal.) *Any.* Yes, **any.**

b. (Uncover **one**. Touch the ball for **anyone**.) Now tell me what the whole word says. Get ready. (Signal.) *Anyone.* Yes, **anyone.**

c. (Repeat exercise until firm.)

rat

rate

anyone

insīde

EXERCISE 3

Two-part word

a. (Cover **sīde**. Point to **in**.) Everybody, tell me what this part of the word says. Get ready. (Signal.) *In.* Yes, **in.**

b. (Uncover **sīde**. Touch the ball for **insīde**.) Now tell me what the whole word says. Get ready. (Signal.) *Inside.* Yes, **inside.**

c. (Repeat exercise until firm.)

bēhīnd

EXERCISE 4

Two-part word

a. (Cover **hīnd**. Point to **bē**.) Everybody, tell me what this part of the word says. Get ready. (Signal.) *Be.* Yes, **be.**

b. (Uncover **hīnd**. Touch the ball for **bēhīnd**.) Now tell me what the whole word says. Get ready. (Signal.) *Behind.* Yes, **behind.**

c. (Repeat exercise until firm.)

(Repeat any troublesome words.)

Individual test

(Call on individual children. Each child reads a different word.)

Making Progress

	Since Lesson 1	Since Lesson 81
Word Reading	Sounds and 3 sound combinations 659 regular words 124 irregular words Reading high frequency hard words Discriminating long and short vowel words using final -*e* rule	2 sound combinations (ea, ee) 127 regular words 21 irregular words
Comprehension	**Picture Comprehension** Predicting what the picture will show Answering questions about the picture Answering written questions about specified pictures Completing picture deduction activities **Story Comprehension** Answering *who, what, when, where,* and *why* questions orally Making predictions about the story Answering questions about the story and other short passages in writing	Completing picture deduction activities

What to Use

Teacher	Students
Presentation Book B (pages 272–286) **Presentation Book C** (pages 1–64) **Teacher's Guide** (page 81) **Answer Key** **Spelling Presentation Book**	**Storybook 2** (pages 50–106) **Workbook B** **Workbook C** **Lined paper**

What's Ahead in Lessons 101–120

New Skills

- Children read stories of up to 15 parts in length.
- Children answer review questions about stories previously read (Lesson 101).

---

* At this point in the program, the emphasis is on reading and remembering a story over a period of time. This more closely approximates "real" reading, where it may take several weeks to complete a story. Now might be a good time to introduce appropriate level "chapter books" to the group.

New Vocabulary

- *Regular words:*

  (101) bowl, eat, kitten, lunch, needs, nest, reach, wet
  (102) arms, bald, bean, homes, king, kittens, milk, sheep
  (103) boo, games, heap, horses, tricks
  (104) biggest, cast, castle, frog, green, monster, planning, shopping
  (105) bead, howling, robbed, robed, stays, tickle, toad
  (106) bode, dress, dresses, fear, leaf, myself
  (107) caped, capped, eating, lead, meaner, themselves
  (108) bites, dart, flash, floating, he'll, heaved, plate, plopped, rammed, spells, telling
  (109) bin, cope, flower, hopper, scream
  (110) casts, feel, panes, pans, shy, sip, smiling, snake, we
  (111) bumpy, master, maybe, peek, rolled, shore, storm, wishes, year
  (112) alligator, apple, bottles, Ott, puff, rubs, smoke
  (113) beach, dimmed, dimmer, heel, peach, peaches, suddenly, takes, test
  (114) beat, bide, bunch, bust, coned, flies, junk, lies, melt, smash, step
  (115) able, banking, folded, forgot, middle, remember, Rome, sounded, spanking, thousands, waved
  (116) air, being, blushed, hater, hatter, poof, poorest, spin
  (117) filed, haven't, hears, streaming, we're, wished
  (118) closer, copper, fact, flow, formed, resting, splat, wise
  (119) broken, canes, cans, glass, spank, stick, windows
  (120) blanks, flip, flipped, parting, planed, planned, shade, yet

- *Irregular words:*

  (101) new
  (102) ghost, laugh, people
  (103) night, sometimes
  (104) laughing, turned, watched
  (105) animal, turn
  (106) laughed
  (107) knock, words
  (108) along, flew, knocked
  (109) anyhow, doesn't
  (110) might
  (111) appear, genie
  (112) disappear, strange
  (113) genies
  (114) alone, Carla, icebox
  (115) appears, city
  (116) face
  (117) appeared
  (118) across, believe, disappears, through
  (119) believed
  (120) few, wonderful

Do not touch small letters.

Get ready to read all the words on this page without making a mistake.

EXERCISE 5

Read the fast way

a. Read these words the fast way.
b. (Touch the ball for **loud.** Pause two seconds.) Get ready. (Signal.) *Loud.* Yes, **loud.**
c. (Repeat *b* for remaining words.)

any

slammed

hanging

who

loud

stopped

once

shouted

should

eyes

barn

opened

don't

slowly

touched

magic

(Repeat any troublesome words.)

Individual test

(Call on individual children. Each child reads a different word.)

They swam over to the swan and said, "Hello, pretty swan." And the swan said, "Hello."

Then one of the ducks said, "That is the ugly duckling."[12] And it was. The ugly duckling was not a duckling at all.[13] He had grown up to be a pretty swan.

So the swan and the ducks became good pals.[14] And the ducks never called the swan ugly again.[15]

This story is over.

[12] Who was that swan? (Signal.) *The ugly duckling.*

[13] Was the ugly duckling really a duckling? (Signal.) *No.*

- What was he? (Signal.) *A swan.*

[14] How did the swan and the ducks feel about each other? (The children respond.)

[15] Why not? (The children respond.) Yes, he grew up to be a pretty swan.

EXERCISE 6

Picture comprehension

a. Look at the picture.

b. (Ask these questions:)
   1. Show me the ducklings.
      (The children respond.)
   2. What is that swimming on the lake?
      (Signal.) *A swan.*
   3. Do you think that swan is pretty?
      (The children respond.)
   4. Who are the little ducks laughing at? (The children respond.) Yes, they are laughing at the ugly duckling and making fun of him.
   5. Why are they making fun of him?
      (The children respond.)
   6. Who do you think will grow up to be prettier, the ugly duckling or the other ducklings?
      (The children respond.)

WORKSHEET 100

INDEPENDENT ACTIVITIES
EXERCISE 7

Summary of independent activities

a. (Pass out Worksheet 100 to each child.)

b. Everybody, now you'll do your worksheet. Remember to do all parts of the worksheet and to read all the parts carefully.

INDIVIDUAL CHECKOUT
EXERCISE 8

2-minute individual fluency checkout: rate/accuracy

a. As you are doing your worksheet, I'll call on children one at a time to read to the star. Remember, you get two stars on the chart if you read to the star in less than two minutes and make no more than four errors.

b. (Call on each child. Tell the child:) Read to the star very carefully. Start with the title. Go. (Time the child. Tell the child any words the child misses. Stop the child as soon as the child makes the fifth error or exceeds the time limit.)

c. (If the child meets the rate-accuracy criterion, record two stars on your chart for lesson 100. Congratulate the child. Give children who do not earn two stars a chance to read to the star again before the next lesson is presented.)
   120 words/**2 min** = 60 wpm **[4 errors]**

END OF LESSON 100

Do not touch small letters.

Get ready to read all the words on this page without making a mistake.

plēaSe

EXERCISE 6

Sound out first

a. (Touch the ball for **plēase.**) Sound it out. Get ready. (Quickly touch **p, l, ē, s** as the children say:) *plllēēēsss.*
b. What word? (Signal.) *Please.* Yes, **please.**
c. (Repeat exercise until firm.)

lēaVe

EXERCISE 7

Sound out first

a. (Touch the ball for **lēave.**) Sound it out. Get ready. (Quickly touch **l, ē, v** as the children say:) *lllēēēvvv.*
b. What word? (Signal.) *Leave.* Yes, **leave.**
c. (Repeat exercise until firm.)

dōōr

EXERCISE 8

Sound out first

a. (Touch the ball for **dōōr.**) Sound it out. Get ready. (Quickly touch **d,** between the **ō's, r** as the children say:) *dōōōrrr.*
b. What word? (Signal.) *Door.* Yes, **door.**
c. (Repeat exercise until firm.)

thousand

EXERCISE 9

Sound out **ou** word with me

a. (Point to **ou** in **thousand.**) What do these letters say? (Signal.) *ou.* Yes, **ou.**
b. (Touch the ball for **thousand.**) Sound it out with me. Get ready. (Quickly touch **th, ou, s, a, n, d** as you and the children say:) *thththousssaaannnd.*
c. What word? (Signal.) *Thousand.* Yes, **thousand.**
d. (Repeat *b* and *c* until firm.)

found

EXERCISE 10

ou word

a. (Touch the ball for **found.**) Read this word the fast way. (Pause two seconds.) Get ready. (Signal.) *Found.* Yes, **found.**
b. (Point to **ou** in **found.**) Everybody, what do these letters say? (Signal.) *ou.* Yes, **ou.**
c. (Touch the ball for **found.**) Sound it out. Get ready. (Quickly touch **f, ou, n, d** as the children say:) *fffounnnd.*
d. What word? (Signal.) *Found.* Yes, **found.**
e. (Repeat *c* and *d* until firm.)

Individual test

(Call on individual children to read a column of words from this lesson. If the column contains only one or two words, direct the child to read additional words from an adjacent column.)

STORYBOOK

STORY 53

See first reading questions on next page.

EXERCISE 11

First reading—title and three sentences

a. (Pass out Storybook 1.)
b. Everybody, open your reader to page 134.
c. Everybody, touch the title of the story and get ready to read the words in the title.
d. First word. ✔
• Get ready. (Tap.) *The.*
e. (Tap for each remaining word in the title.)
f. Everybody, say the title. (Signal.) *The magic pouch.*
g. Yesterday we read part two. Today we're going to read part three.
h. Everybody, get ready to read this story.
i. First word. ✔
• Get ready. (Tap.) *Where.*
j. Next word. ✔
• Get ready. (Tap.) *Did.*
k. (Repeat *j* for the remaining words in the first three sentences. Have the children reread the first three sentences until firm.)

STORYBOOK 100

STORY 100

EXERCISE 5

Reading—decoding

a. (Pass out Storybook 2.)

b. Everybody, open your reader to page 47.

c. Remember, if the group reads all the way to the red 5 without making more than five errors, we can go on.

d. Everybody, touch the title of the story. ✔

e. If you hear a mistake, raise your hand. Remember, children who do not have their place lose their turn. (Call on individual children to read two or three sentences. Do not ask comprehension questions. Tally all errors.)

To Correct

word-identification errors (from, for example)

1. That word is **from.** What word? *From.*
2. Go back to the beginning of the sentence and read the sentence again.

---

f. (If the children make more than five errors before they reach the red 5: when they reach the 5 return to the beginning of the story and have the children reread to the 5. Do not ask comprehension questions. Repeat step *f* until firm, and then go on to step *g*.)

g. (When the children read to the red 5 without making more than five errors: read the story to the children from the beginning to the 5. Ask the specified comprehension questions. When you reach the 5, call on individual children to continue reading the story. Have each child read two or three sentences.

Ask the specified comprehension questions.)

The Ugly Duckling [1]

There once was a mother duck who found a big egg. She said, "I will put this egg with my other eggs." And so she did. [2]

Soon all of the eggs hatched. [3] The little eggs hatched and the big egg that she found hatched. What do you think came out of the big egg? A funny-looking duckling. [4] He was big, and he kept falling down when he tried to walk. [5]

The other ducklings called him names. "You are ugly," they said. "You are an ugly duckling." [6]

The ugly duckling was sad. None of the other ducklings would play with him. [7] They just called him names. "Boy, are you ever an ugly duckling," they would say.

The ★ ugly duckling said to himself, "I am so ugly and nobody likes me." [8]

The ducklings grew up. The little ducklings grew up to be pretty ducks, just like their mother and father. ⑤ [9] And what do you think happened to the big ugly duckling?

One day all of the ducklings saw a pretty swan swimming on the pond. [10] They all stopped and looked at the swan. "My, my," they said. "That swan is so pretty." [11]

---

[1] Who is the story going to be about? (Signal.) *The ugly duckling.*

[2] What did the mother duck do with the egg she found? (Signal.) *She put it with her other eggs.*

[3] What does that mean? (The children respond.) Yes, the ducklings come out of the eggs.

[4] What came out of the big egg? (Signal.) *A funny-looking duckling.*

[5] What happened when he tried to walk? (Signal.) *He kept falling down.*

[6] What did the other ducklings say? (Signal.) *You are an ugly duckling.*

• The other ducklings were mean to him.

[7] Did they play with him? (Signal.) *No.*

[8] What did he say to himself? (Signal.) *I am so ugly and nobody likes me.*

[9] Who did the little ducklings look like? (Signal.) *Their mother and father.*

[10] What did they see? (Signal.) *A pretty swan.*

• I wonder who that swan is? Let's read and find out.

[11] What did they say about the swan? (Signal.) *That swan is so pretty.*

EXERCISE 12

Remaining sentences and questions

a. I'm going to call on individual children to read a sentence. Everybody, follow along and point to the words. If you hear a mistake, raise your hand.

b. (Call on a child.) Read the next sentence.

c. (Call on another child.) Read the next sentence.

To Correct

word-identification errors (**from,** for example)
1. That word is **from.** What word? *From.*
2. Go back to the beginning of the sentence and read the sentence again.

d. (Repeat *c* for most of the remaining sentences in the story.)

e. (Occasionally have the group read a sentence. When the group is to read, say:) Everybody, read the next sentence. (Tap for each word in the sentence.)

f. (After each underlined sentence has been read, present each comprehension question specified below to the entire group.)

[1] Everybody, say that question. (Signal.) *Where did the little girl and her hound go?*

• What's the answer? (The children respond.)

[2] Everybody, say that question. (Signal.) *What did they see when they came out of the clouds?*

• What's the answer? (Signal.) *A funny little house.*

[3] Everybody, say that question. (Signal.) *What did they hear coming from the house?*

• What's the answer? (Signal.) *A loud sound.*

3

the magic pouch

<u>where did the little girl and her hound go?</u>[1]

<u>what did they see when they came out of the clouds?</u>[2]

<u>what did they hear coming from the house?</u>[3]

when the loud sound came from the house, the little girl stopped. <u>she looked all around, but she did not see anyone.</u>[4] the sound came from the house once more. the girl and her hound walked up to the house. <u>she called, "is anyone inside that house?"</u>[5]

all at once the door of the house opened. the girl looked inside the house, but she did not see anyone. slowly she walked inside. slowly her hound walked inside. then the door slammed behind them. the hound jumped. <u>the girl jumped.</u>[6] she said, "let's get out of here." she grabbed the door, but it would not open. the girl said, "I don't like this."

all at once <u>the girl looked at a funny pouch hanging on the wall.</u>[7] and a loud sound came out of the pouch. <u>it said, "open this pouch and let me out."</u>[8]

more to come

EXERCISE 13

Second reading—sentences and questions

a. You're going to read the story again. And I'm going to ask more questions.

b. Starting with the first word of the title. ✔
• Get ready. (Tap as the children read the title.)

c. (Call on a child.) Read the first sentence.

To Correct

word-identification errors (**from,** for example)
1. That word is **from.** What word? *From.*
2. Go back to the beginning of the sentence and read the sentence again.

d. (Call on another child.) Read the next sentence.

e. (Repeat *d* for most of the remaining sentences in the story.)

f. (Occasionally have the group read a sentence.)

g. (After each underlined sentence has been read, present each comprehension question specified below to the entire group.)

[4] Who did she see? (Signal.) *Nobody.*

[5] What did she say? (Signal.) *Is anyone inside that house?*

• (Repeat the question until the children give a firm response.)

[6] What did the girl and the hound do? (Signal.) *They jumped.*

• Why did they do that? (Signal.) *The door slammed behind them.*

[7] What was hanging there? (Signal.) *A funny pouch.*

• Do you think it will be a magic pouch? (The children respond.)

[8] Who said that? (The children respond.)

• We'll read more next time and see what's in the pouch.

EXERCISE 3

Read the fast way

a. You're going to read all the words in this column the fast way.

b. (Touch the ball for **wouldn't.** Pause.) Get ready. (Slash.) *Wouldn't.*

c. (Repeat step *b* until firm.)

d. (Repeat steps *b* and *c* for each remaining word in the column.)

e. (Repeat the column until the children read all the words in order without making mistakes.)

wouldn't

became

hello

were

become

egg

nobody

EXERCISE 4

Children spell, then read

a. First you're going to spell each word. Then you're going to read that word the fast way.

b. (Touch the ball for **pals.**) Spell it. Get ready. (Tap under each letter as the children say:) *P-A-L-S.*

• (Return to the ball.) Read it. Get ready. (Slash.) *Pals.*

c. (Repeat step *b* for each remaining word in the column.)

d. (Repeat steps *b* and *c* until firm.)

pals

falling

Boy

hopped

One

once

their

Individual test

a. (Call on individual children to read one column of words from the lesson.)

b. (Praise children who read all words with no errors.)

WORKSHEET 53

EXERCISE 14

Picture comprehension

a. What do you think you'll see in the picture? (The children respond.)

b. Turn the page and look at the picture.

c. (Ask these questions:)

1. How do the girl and her hound look? (The children respond.)
2. Why are they scared? (Let the children comment for ten seconds. Then comment briefly.)
3. What's that thing hanging on the wall? (Signal.) *A pouch.*
4. What would you do if you were that girl? (The children respond.)

SUMMARY OF INDEPENDENT ACTIVITY
EXERCISE 15

Introduction to independent activity

a. (Pass out Worksheet 53 to each child.)

b. (Hold up side 1 of your worksheet.) Everybody, you're going to do this worksheet on your own. (Tell the children when they will work the items.)

• Let's go over the things you're going to do.

Story items

(Point to the story-items exercise.) Everybody, remember to write your answers in the blanks.

Following instructions

a. (Touch the sentence in the box.)

b. Everybody, first you're going to read the sentence in the box. Then you're going to read the instructions below the box and do what the instructions tell you to do.

Reading comprehension

(Point to the story on side 2.) You're going to read this story and then do the items. Remember to write the answers in the blanks.

Following instructions

(Point to the following-instructions exercise.) Everybody, you're going to read the instructions. Then you're going to do what the instructions tell you to do.

END OF LESSON 53

READING VOCABULARY
EXERCISE 1

Teacher reads the words in red

a. I'll read each word in red. Then you'll spell each word.

b. (Touch the ball for **Title.**) My turn. (Slash as you say:) Title. What word? (Signal.) *Title.*

c. (Return to the ball.) Spell it. Get ready. (Tap under each letter as the children say:) *T-I-T-L-E.*

• What word did you spell? (Signal.) *Title.*

d. (Repeat steps *b* and *c* for each word in red.)

e. Your turn to read all the words in this column.

f. (Touch the ball for **Title.** Pause.) Get ready. (Slash.) *Title.*

g. (Repeat step *f* for each remaining word in the column.)

h. (Repeat steps *f* and *g* until firm.)

Title

None

Ugly

friend

grown

swan

swam

EXERCISE 2

Words with underlined parts

a. First you're going to read the underlined part of each word in this column. Then you're going to read the whole word.

b. (Touch the ball for **names.**) Read the underlined part. Get ready. (Tap the ball.) *Name.*

• Read the whole word. (Pause.) Get ready. (Slash.) *Names.*

c. (Repeat step *b* until firm.)

d. (Repeat steps *b* and *c* for each remaining word in the column.)

e. (Repeat the column until children read all the words in order without making a mistake.)

names

Duckling

hoped

hatched

hopped

swimming

himself

EXERCISE 1

Sound combination review

a. Here are some letters that go together. Get ready to tell me the sound they usually make.

b. (Point to **ar.**) What sound do these letters usually make? (Signal.) *Are.* Yes, **are.**

c. (Repeat *b* with **ou.**)

d. (Repeat both sound combinations until firm.)

ar   ou

READING VOCABULARY

Do not touch small letters.

Get ready to read all the words on this page without making a mistake.

full

EXERCISE 2

Listen, sound out

a. (Point to **full.**) I'll tell you this word. (Pause.) **Full.** What word? (Signal.) *Full.* Yes, **full.**

b. (Touch the ball for **full.**) Sound it out. Get ready. (Quickly touch **f, u,** between the **l**'s as the children say:) *fffuuulll.*

c. What word? (Signal.) *Full.* Yes, **full.**

d. (Repeat *b* and *c* until firm.)

EXERCISE 3

Two-part word

a. (Cover **ful.** Point to **care.**) Everybody, tell me what this part of the word says. Get ready. (Signal.) *Care.* Yes, **care.**

b. (Uncover **ful.** Touch the ball for **careful.**) Now tell me what the whole word says. Get ready. (Signal.) *Careful.* Yes, **careful.**

c. (Repeat exercise until firm.)

EXERCISE 4

Two-part word

a. (Cover **er.** Point to **bigg.**) Everybody, tell me what this part of the word says. Get ready. (Signal.) *Big.* Yes, **big.**

b. (Uncover **er.** Touch the ball for **bigger.**) Now tell me what the whole word says. Get ready. (Signal.) *Bigger.* Yes, **bigger.**

c. (Repeat exercise until firm.)

EXERCISE 5

Practice final-e rule

a. (Touch the ball for **fin.**) Everybody, is there an **ē** on the end of this word? (Signal.) *No.*

b. (Point to **i** in **fin.**) So tell me what you say for this letter. (Signal.) *iii.*

c. (Touch the ball for **fin.**) Everybody, read this word the fast way and remember to say **iii.** Get ready. (Signal.) *Fin.* Yes, **fin.**

d. (Touch the ball for **fine.**) Everybody, is there an **ē** on the end of this word? (Signal.) *Yes.*

e. (Point to **i** in **fine.**) So tell me what you say for this letter. (Signal.) *ī.*

f. (Touch the ball for **fine.**) Everybody, read this word the fast way and remember to say **ī.** Get ready. (Signal.) *Fine.* Yes, **fine.**

g. (Repeat *a* through *f* until firm.)

cāreful

bigger

fin

fine

(Repeat any troublesome words.)

Individual test

(Call on individual children. Each child reads a different word.)

WORKSHEET 99

EXERCISE 6

Picture comprehension

a. What do you think you'll see in the picture? (The children respond.)

b. Turn the page and look at the picture.

c. (Ask these questions:)
1. What do Spot and the pig have on their heads? (Signal.) *Wigs.*
2. What are they holding? (Signal.) *Mirrors.*
3. Why are they holding mirrors? (The children respond.)
4. Do they like the way they look? (The children respond.)
5. Do you think they look pretty? (The children respond.)

DEDUCTIONS

The children will need pencils.

EXERCISE 7

Picture deductions

a. (Pass out Worksheet 99 to each child.)

b. (Hold up side 2 of your worksheet and touch the sentence in the box in the deductions exercise.)

c. Everybody, touch this sentence on your worksheet. ✔

d. (Call on a child.) Read the sentence in the box. *Every little horse can run fast.*

e. Everybody, say that rule. (Signal.) *Every little horse can run fast.*

• (Repeat until firm.)

f. You know that some of the horses in the picture can run fast. What kind of horses are those? (Signal.) *Every little horse.*

• Everybody, touch a horse you know can run fast. ✔

g. You don't know about the horses that are not little. Everybody, touch a horse you don't know about. ✔

h. (Call on a child.) Read the instructions below the box. *Circle every horse that can run fast.*

i. Everybody, what are you going to do? (Signal.) *Circle every horse that can run fast.* Yes, circle every horse that you know can run fast.

j. Do it. ✔

INDEPENDENT ACTIVITIES

EXERCISE 8

Summary of independent activities

Everybody, now you'll do your worksheet. Remember to do all parts of the worksheet and to read all the parts carefully.

END OF LESSON 99

Get ready to read all the words on this page without making a mistake.

To Correct

1. (Touch the ball for the word the children missed.) Is there an **e** on the end of this word? (Signal.) (The children respond.)
2. (Point to the first vowel in the word.) So tell me what you say for this letter. (Signal.) (The children respond.)
3. (Touch the ball for the word.) Sound it out. Get ready. (Touch all sounds except the final **e**, if there is one, as the children sound out the word.)
4. What word? (Signal.) (The children respond.)
5. (Return to the first word in the column. Present all the words in order until firm.)

EXERCISE 6

Long vowel words

a. (Point to the words in this column.) Read these words the fast way.
b. (Touch the ball for **cape**. Pause two seconds.) Get ready. (Signal.) *Cape*. Yes, **cape**. (Repeat until firm.)
c. (Repeat *b* for **rate** and **note**.)

cape

rate

note

EXERCISE 7

Short vowel words

a. (Point to the words in this column.) Read these words the fast way.
b. (Touch the ball for **cap**. Pause two seconds.) Get ready. (Signal.) *Cap*. Yes, **cap**. *(Repeat until firm.)*
c. (Repeat *b* for **rat** and **not**.)

cap

rat

not

EXERCISE 8

Short and long vowel words

a. Everybody, read these words again. Remember what you say if there is an ē on the end of a word.
b. (Touch the ball for **note**. Pause two seconds.) Get ready. (Signal.) *Note*. Yes, **note**.
c. (Repeat *b* for **cape** and **rat**.)

note

cape

rat

(Repeat any troublesome words.)

Individual test

(Call on individual children. Each child reads a different word.)

STORY 99
EXERCISE 5

Reading—decoding

a. (Pass out Storybook 2.)

b. Everybody, open your reader to page 44.

c. Remember, if the group reads all the way to the red 5 without making more than five errors, we can go on.

d. Everybody, touch the title of the story. ✔

e. If you hear a mistake, raise your hand. Remember, children who do not have their place lose their turn. (Call on individual children to read two or three sentences. Do not ask comprehension questions. Tally all errors.)

To Correct

word-identification errors (**from**, for example)
1. That word is **from**. What word? *From.*
2. Go back to the beginning of the sentence and read the sentence again.

f. (If the children make more than five errors before they reach the red 5: when they reach the 5 return to the beginning of the story and have the children reread to the 5. Do not ask comprehension questions. Repeat step *f* until firm, and then go on to step *g*.)

g. (When the children read to the red 5 without making more than five errors: read the story to the children from the beginning to the 5. Ask the specified comprehension questions. When you reach the 5, call on individual children to continue reading the story. Have each child read two or three sentences.

Ask the specified comprehension questions.)

Spot Gets a Wig[1]

Spot and the tall girl were on their way to the mall when they met a fat pig.[2] That pig was crying. The tall girl asked the pig why he was crying. And the pig answered, "Because I cannot find my wig.[3] I had a big red wig. A big wind came up and took the wig with it."[4]

The girl said, "Well, come to the mall with us and I'll get you another wig."

So Spot and the girl and the fat pig went to the mall. The girl stopped in front of a wig shop. She said to the pig, "Look in that shop and see which wig you want."[5]

The fat pig looked and looked. Then he said, "I want that big yellow wig. That wig will make me look pretty."

"You wait here," the girl said. She went into the wig shop. ⑤Soon she came out of the shop with a big yellow wig. She gave it to the pig. He was very happy.[6] He said, "I love this wig."

But then what do you think happened? Spot began to cry.[7] The tall girl asked, "Why are you crying, Spot?"

"I don't have a pretty wig," she answered. "I want one too."[8]

The girl shook her head. "Wait here," the girl said.[9] When she came out of the shop, she was holding another yellow wig. She gave it to Spot.[10]

Spot said, "Now I am pretty too."

Do you think she looked very pretty in that big yellow wig?[11]

This story is over.

---

[1] What will happen in this story? (Signal.) *Spot will get a wig.*

• What is a wig? (The children respond.)

[2] Who met the fat pig? (Signal.) *Spot and the tall girl.*

[3] Why was the pig crying? (Signal.) *He could not find his wig.*

[4] What happened to the wig? (Signal.) *A big wind took it.* Yes, it blew away.

[5] What did she say? (Signal.) *Look in that shop and see which wig you want.*

• Do you think the tall girl will buy a wig for the pig? (The children respond.)

[6] Why was the pig happy? (The children respond.)

[7] What did Spot do? (Signal.) *She began to cry.*

• Let's find out why.

[8] Why was Spot crying? (Signal.) *She wanted a wig.*

[9] What do you think the girl will do? (The children respond.)

• Let's read and find out.

[10] What did she give to Spot? (Signal.) *A yellow wig.*

[11] What do you think? (The children respond.)

• We'll look at the picture and see if Spot looks pretty.

Do not touch small letters.

Get ready to read all the words on this page without making a mistake.

EXERCISE 9

Read the fast way

a. Read these words the fast way.

b. (Touch the ball for **magic**. Pause two seconds.) Get ready. (Signal.) *Magic.* Yes, **magic.**

c. (Repeat *b* for remaining words.)

magic

plēaSe

touched

any

many

would

could

ōpen

thousand

elf

EXERCISE 10

Sound out first

a. (Touch the ball for **elf**.) Sound it out. Get ready. (Quickly touch **e, l, f,** as the children say:) *eeelllfff.*

b. What word? (Signal.) *Elf.* Yes, **elf.**

c. (Repeat exercise until firm.)

cross

EXERCISE 11

Sound out first

a. (Touch the ball for **cross**.) Sound it out. Get ready. (Quickly touch **c, r, o,** between the **s**'s as the children say:) *crrrooosss.*

b. What word? (Signal.) *Cross.* Yes, **cross.**

c. (Repeat exercise until firm.)

Individual test

(Call on individual children to read a column of words from this lesson. If the column contains only one or two words, direct the child to read additional words from an adjacent column. Praise children who read all words with no errors.)

EXERCISE 3

Words with underlined parts

a. First you're going to read the underlined part of each word in this column. Then you're going to read the whole word.

b. (Touch the ball for **maker**.) Read the underlined part. Get ready. (Tap the ball.) *Make.*

• Read the whole word. (Pause.) Get ready. (Slash.) *Maker.*

c. (Repeat step *b* until firm.)

d. (Repeat steps *b* and *c* for each remaining word in the column.)

e. (Repeat the column until children read all the words in order without making a mistake.)

maker

happened

because

holding

began

thinking

crying

EXERCISE 4

Children spell, then read

a. First you're going to spell each word. Then you're going to read that word the fast way.

b. (Touch the ball for **where**.) Spell it. Get ready. (Tap under each letter as the children say:) *W-H-E-R-E.*

• (Return to the ball.) Read it. Get ready. (Slash.) *Where.*

c. (Repeat step *b* for each remaining word in the column.)

d. (Repeat steps *b* and *c* until firm.)

where

here

wig

even

every

ever

very

Individual test

a. (Call on individual children to read one column of words from the lesson.)

b. (Praise children who read all words with no errors.)

STORYBOOK

STORY 54

EXERCISE 12

First reading—title and three sentences

a. (Pass out Storybook 1.)

b. Everybody, open your reader to page 137.

c. Everybody, touch the title of the story and get ready to read the words in the title.

d. First word. ✔

• Get ready. (Tap.) *The.*

e. (Tap for each remaining word in the title.)

f. Everybody, say the title. (Signal.) *The magic pouch.*

g. Yesterday we read part three. Today we're going to read part four.

h. Everybody, get ready to read this story.

i. First word. ✔

• Get ready. (Tap.) *What.*

j. Next word. ✔

• Get ready. (Tap.) *Did.*

k. (Repeat *j* for the remaining words in the first three sentences. Have the children reread the first three sentences until firm.)

EXERCISE 13

Remaining sentences and questions

a. I'm going to call on individual children to read a sentence. Everybody, follow along and point to the words. If you hear a mistake, raise your hand.

b. (Call on a child.) Read the next sentence.

c. (Call on another child.) Read the next sentence.

d. (Repeat *c* for most of the remaining sentences in the story.)

4

the magic pouch

what did the little girl and her hound see on top of the mountain?[1]

why didn't they leave the funny house?[2]

what was hanging on the wall?[3]

the girl walked over to the pouch. she said, "is there some thing in that pouch?"[4]

"yes. I am a magic elf.[5] I have lived in this pouch for a thousand years. please, would you open the pouch and let me out?"

---

e. (Occasionally have the group read a sentence. When the group is to read, say:) Everybody, read the next sentence. (Tap for each word in the sentence.)

f. (After each underlined sentence has been read, present each comprehension question specified below to the entire group.)

[1] Everybody, say that question. (Signal.) *What did the little girl and her hound see on top of the mountain?*

• What's the answer? (Signal.) *A funny little house.*

[2] Everybody, say that question. (Signal.) *Why didn't they leave the funny house?*

• What's the answer? (Signal.) *The door slammed behind them.*

[3] Everybody, say that question. (Signal.) *What was hanging on the wall?*

• What's the answer? (Signal.) *A magic pouch.*

EXERCISE 14

Second reading—sentences and questions

a. You're going to read the story again. And I'm going to ask more questions.

b. Starting with the first word of the title. ✔

• Get ready. (Tap as the children read the title.)

c. (Call on a child.) Read the first sentence.

To Correct

word-identification errors (**from,** for example)
1. That word is **from.** What word? *From.*
2. Go back to the beginning of the sentence and read the sentence again.

d. (Call on another child.) Read the next sentence.

e. (Repeat *d* for most of the remaining sentences in the story.)

f. (Occasionally have the group read a sentence.)

g. (After each underlined sentence has been read, present each comprehension question specified below to the entire group.)

[4] What did the girl ask? (Signal.) *Is there something in that pouch?*

• (Repeat the question until the children give a firm response.)

[5] Who is in the pouch? (Signal.) *A magic elf.*

• Yes, we'll see a picture of the elf soon. An elf is a tiny little person.

READING VOCABULARY

EXERCISE 1

Teacher reads the words in red

a. I'll read each word in red. Then you'll spell each word.

b. (Touch the ball for **grew**.) My turn. (Slash as you say:) Grew. What word? (Signal.) *Grew.*

c. (Return to the ball.) Spell it. Get ready. (Tap under each letter as the children say:) *G-R-E-W.*

• What word did you spell? (Signal.) *Grew.*

d. (Repeat steps *b* and *c* for each word in red.)

e. Your turn to read all the words in this column.

f. (Touch the ball for **grew**. Pause.) Get ready. (Slash.) *Grew.*

g. (Repeat step *f* for each remaining word in the column.)

h. (Repeat steps *f* and *g* until firm.)

grew

hatched

front

swam

question

their

shook

EXERCISE 2

Words with underlined parts

a. First you're going to read the underlined part of each word in this column. Then you're going to read the whole word.

b. (Touch the ball for **leap**.) Read the underlined part. Get ready. (Tap the ball.) *ēēē.*

• Read the whole word. (Pause.) Get ready. (Slash.) *Leap.*

c. (Repeat step *b* until firm.)

d. (Repeat steps *b* and *c* for each remaining word in the column.)

e. (Repeat the column until children read all the words in order without making a mistake.)

leap

yellow

which

Then

why

mall

were

the little girl asked, "how many
years have you lived in that pouch?"
the elf said, "a thousand years."⁶
the girl started to open the
pouch. then she stopped. she said,
"elf, I don't think I should let you
out. this is not my house. I should
not be here."
the elf said, "this is my house.
so please open the pouch and let me
out.⁷ if you let me out, I will give
you the pouch.⁸ it is magic."
the girl touched the pouch. she
asked herself, "should I open this
pouch and let him out?"
more to come

---

⁶ How long? (Signal.) *A thousand years.*
• Could that really happen?
  (The children respond.)
• But in stories, all kinds of magic things can
  happen.
⁷ What does the elf want her to do? (Signal.)
  Let him out.
• Do you think she will? (The children respond.)
• Let's read some more and find out.
⁸ What did he say he'd give her? (Signal.)
  The pouch.
• Do you think she should let him out?
  (The children respond.)
• Next time we'll read part five and you'll be
  surprised at what happens.

EXERCISE 15
Picture comprehension

a. Look at the picture.
b. (Ask these questions:)
  1. Where is the pouch?
     (The children respond.)
  2. Why is that pouch moving?
     (The children respond.)
  • Yes, it's moving around because there's an
    elf in there.
  3. What do you think that elf in the pouch is
     thinking? (Let the children comment for
     ten seconds. Then comment briefly.)
  4. What do you think that girl is thinking?
     (The children respond.)
  5. Would you let that elf out if you were that
     girl? (The children respond.)

SUMMARY OF INDEPENDENT ACTIVITY
EXERCISE 16
Introduction to independent activity

a. (Pass out Worksheet 54 to each child.)
b. (Hold up side 1 of your worksheet.)
  Everybody, you're going to do this
  worksheet on your own. (Tell the children
  when they will work the items.)
• Let's go over the things you're going to do.

Story items

(Point to the story-items exercise.) Everybody,
remember to write your answers in the blanks.

Following instructions

a. (Touch the sentence in the box.)
b. Everybody, first you're going to read the
  sentence in the box. Then you're going to
  read the instructions below the box and do
  what the instructions tell you to do.

Reading comprehension

(Point to the story on side 2.) You're going
to read this story and then do the items.
Remember to write the answers in the blanks.

Following instructions

(Point to the following-instructions exercise.)
Everybody, you're going to read the
instructions. Then you're going to do what the
instructions tell you to do.

END OF LESSON 54

WORKSHEET 98

EXERCISE 7

Picture comprehension

a. Look at the picture.

b. (Ask these questions:)
1. What do you see in this picture? (The children respond.)
2. What is the pig doing? (Signal.) *Crying.*
3. What would you say to that pig if you were the girl? (The children respond.)

DEDUCTIONS

The children will need pencils.

EXERCISE 8

Picture deductions

a. (Pass out Worksheet 98 to each child.)

b. (Hold up side 2 of your worksheet and touch the sentence in the box in the deductions exercise.)

c. Everybody, touch this sentence on your worksheet. ✔

d. (Call on a child.) Read the sentence in the box. *All the fat pigs are happy.*

e. Everybody, say that rule. (Signal.) *All the fat pigs are happy.*

• (Repeat until firm.)

f. You know that some of the pigs in the picture are happy. What kind of pigs are those? (Signal.) *All the fat pigs.* Everybody, touch a pig you know is happy. ✔

g. You don't know about the pigs that are not fat. Everybody, touch a pig you don't know about. ✔

h. (Call on a child.) Read the instructions below the box. *Circle every pig that is happy.*

i. Everybody, what are you going to do? (Signal.) *Circle every pig that is happy.* Yes, circle every pig that you know is happy.

j. Do it. ✔

INDEPENDENT ACTIVITIES

EXERCISE 9

Summary of independent activities

Everybody, now you'll do your worksheet. Remember to do all parts of the worksheet and to read all the parts carefully.

END OF LESSON 98

READING VOCABULARY

Do not touch small letters.

Get ready to read all the words on this page without making a mistake.

EXERCISE 1

Sound out first

a. (Touch the ball for **r ēached.**) Sound it out. Get ready. (Quickly touch **r, ē, ch, d** as the children say:) *rrrēēēchd.*

b. What word? (Signal.) *Reached.* Yes, **reached.**

c. (Repeat exercise until firm.)

EXERCISE 2

Sound out first

a. (Touch the ball for **tīred.**) Sound it out. Get ready. (Quickly touch **t, ī, r, d** as the children say:) *tīīīrrrd.*

b. What word? (Signal.) *Tired.* Yes, **tired.**

c. (Repeat exercise until firm.)

EXERCISE 3

Sound out first

a. (Touch the ball for **wōke.**) Sound it out. Get ready. (Quickly touch **w, ō, k** as the children say:) *wwwōōōk.*

b. What word? (Signal.) *Woke.* Yes, **woke.**

c. (Repeat exercise until firm.)

EXERCISE 4

Sound out first.

a. (Touch the ball for **līe.**) Sound it out. Get ready. (Quickly touch **l, ī** as the children say:) *lllīīī.*

b. What word? (Signal.) *Lie.* Yes, **lie.**

c. (Repeat exercise until firm.)

EXERCISE 5

Practice final-e rule

a. (Touch the ball for **can.**) Everybody, is there an **ē** on the end of this word? (Signal.) *No.*

b. (Point to **a** in **can.**) So tell me what you say for this letter. (Signal.) *ăăă.*

c. (Touch the ball for **can.**) Everybody, read this word the fast way and remember to say **ăăă.** Get ready. (Signal.) *Can.* Yes, **can.**

d. (Touch the ball for **cane.**) Everybody, is there an **ē** on the end of this word? (Signal.) *Yes.*

e. (Point to **a** in **cane.**) So tell me what you say for this letter. (Signal.) *ā.*

f. (Touch the ball for **cane.**) Everybody, read this word the fast way and remember to say **ā.** Get ready. (Signal.) *Cane.* Yes, **cane.**

g. (Repeat *a* through *f* until firm.)

wōke

līe

can

cane

(Repeat any troublesome words.)

Individual test

(Call on individual children. Each child reads a different word.)

Spot Meets a Tall Girl[1]

One day Spot went for a walk. Soon she met a tall girl. The girl said, "How are you?"[2]

Spot did not hear that girl. She said to herself, "That girl wants to know who I am."[3]

So Spot said, "They call me Spot."

The tall girl shook her head. Then she shouted, "How are you?"

"I'm fine," Spot shouted back.

Then the tall girl began to walk away. Spot asked the question, "Where are you going?"[4]

"I am going to the mall in town," she answered.[5]

Spot said to herself, "That girl said that she will fall."[6]

Spot ran over to the girl. "Sit down," she said. "Then you won't fall down."

The girl smiled. Then she yelled, "I'm not going to fall. I'm going to the mall."

"Oh," Spot said. "You're going to the mall." Then Spot asked the question, "Can I go with you?" ⑤

"Yes," the tall girl said. "Come to the mall and we will have a ball."[7]

So Spot and the girl started to walk to the mall.

Soon they met a fat pig. That pig was crying.[8] The girl went over to the pig and asked, "Why are you crying?"

The pig told her why he was crying.[9] You will find out why when you read the next story.

More next time

1. Who is Spot going to meet? (Signal.) *A tall girl.*
2. What did the girl say? (Signal.) *How are you?*
- Does Spot hear well? (Signal.) *No.*
3. What did Spot say? (Signal.) *That girl wants to know who I am.*
- Did the girl ask who she was? (Signal.) *No.*
- What did the girl ask? (Signal.) *How are you?*
4. What's the question Spot asked? (Signal.) *Where are you going?*
5. Where is the girl going? (The children respond.) Right, she's going shopping at the mall.
6. What did Spot think the girl said? (Signal.) *She will fall.*
- Did the girl say she will fall? (Signal.) *No.*
- Where was she going? (Signal.) *To the mall.*
7. What will they do at the mall? (Signal.) *Have a ball.* Yes, they'll have a good time.
8. What was the fat pig doing? (Signal.) *Crying.*
9. Why do you think he was crying? (The children respond.)

Get ready to read all the words on this page without making a mistake.

To Correct

1. (Touch the ball for the word the children missed.) Is there an **ē** on the end of this word? (Signal.) (The children respond.)
2. (Point to the first vowel in the word.) So tell me what you say for this letter. (Signal.) (The children respond.)
3. (Touch the ball for the word.) Sound it out. Get ready. (Touch all sounds except the final **e**, if there is one, as the children sound out the word.)
4. What word? (Signal.) (The children respond.)
5. (Return to the first word in the column. Present all the words in order until firm.)

EXERCISE 6

Long vowel words

a. (Point to the words in this column.) Read these words the fast way.
b. (Touch the ball for **site**. Pause two seconds.) Get ready. (Signal.) *Site.* Yes, **site.** (Repeat until firm.)
c. (Repeat *b* for **fine.**)

site

fine

EXERCISE 7

Short vowel words

a. (Point to the words in this column.) Read these words the fast way.
b. (Touch the ball for **sit.** Pause two seconds.) Get ready. (Signal.) *Sit.* Yes, **sit.** (Repeat until firm.)
c. (Repeat *b* for **fin.**)

sit

fin

EXERCISE 8

Short and long vowel words

a. Everybody, read these words again. Remember what you say if there is an **ē** on the end of a word.
b. (Touch the ball for **site.** Pause two seconds.) Get ready. (Signal.) *Site.* Yes, **site.**
c. (Repeat *b* for **fin.**)

site

fin

(Repeat any troublesome words.)

Individual test

(Call on individual children. Each child reads a different word.)

EXERCISE 5

Children spell, then read

a. First you're going to spell each word. Then you're going to read that word the fast way.

b. (Touch the ball for **could.**) Spell it. Get ready. (Tap under each letter as the children say:) *C-O-U-L-D.*

• (Return to the ball.) Read it. Get ready. (Slash.) *Could.*

c. (Repeat step *b* for each remaining word in the column.)

d. (Repeat steps *b* and *c* until firm.)

could

noted

mopped

would

Spot

notes

head

Individual test

a. (Call on individual children to read one column of words from the lesson.)

b. (Praise children who read all words with no errors.)

STORY 98
EXERCISE 6

Reading—decoding

a. (Pass out Storybook 2.)

b. Everybody, open your reader to page 41.

c. Remember, if the group reads all the way to the red 5 without making more than five errors, we can go on.

d. Everybody, touch the title of the story. ✔

e. If you hear a mistake, raise your hand. Remember, children who do not have their place lose their turn. (Call on individual children to read two or three sentences. Do not ask comprehension questions. Tally all errors.)

To Correct

word-identification errors (**from,** for example)
1. That word is **from.** What word? *From.*
2. Go back to the beginning of the sentence and read the sentence again.

f. (If the children make more than five errors before they reach the red 5: when they reach the 5 return to the beginning of the story and have the children reread to the 5. Do not ask comprehension questions. Repeat step *f* until firm, and then go on to step *g.*)

g. (When the children read to the red 5 without making more than five errors: read the story to the children from the beginning to the 5. Ask the specified comprehension questions. When you reach the 5, call on individual children to continue reading the story. Have each child read two or three sentences. Ask the specified comprehension questions.)

Do not touch small letters.

Get ready to read all the words on this page without making a mistake.

been

EXERCISE 9

Listen, sound out

a. (Point to **been**.) I'll tell you this word. (Pause.) **Been.** What word? (Signal.) *Been.* Yes, **been.**

b. (Touch the ball for **been.**) Sound it out. Get ready. (Quickly touch **b,** between the **e**'s, **n** as the children say:) *beeennn.*

c. What word? (Signal.) *Been.* Yes, **been.**

d. (Repeat *b* and *c* until firm.)

setting

EXERCISE 10

Two-part word

a. (Cover **ing**. Point to **sett**.) Everybody, tell me what this part of the word says. Get ready. (Signal.) *Set.* Yes, **set.**

b. (Uncover **ing**. Touch the ball for **setting**.) Now tell me what the whole word says. Get ready. (Signal.) *Setting.* Yes, **setting.**

c. (Repeat exercise until firm.)

EXERCISE 11

Read the fast way

a. Read these words the fast way.

b. (Touch the ball for **any**. Pause two seconds.) Get ready. (Signal.) *Any.* Yes, **any.**

c. (Repeat b for **many, herself, slōwly, stall, shouted, pouch, bottom, very, cāreful,** and **I'm.**)

any

many

herself

slōwly

stall

shouted

pouch

bottom

very

cāreful

I'm

Individual test

(Call on individual children to read a column of words from this lesson. If the column contains only one or two words, direct the child to read additional words from an adjacent column.)

EXERCISE 3

Words with underlined parts

a. First you're going to read the underlined part of each word in this column. Then you're going to read the whole word.

b. (Touch the ball for **going.**) Read the underlined part. Get ready. (Tap the ball.) *ing.*

• Read the whole word. (Pause.) Get ready. (Slash.) *Going.*

c. (Repeat step *b* until firm.)

d. (Repeat steps *b* and *c* for each remaining word in the column.)

e. (Repeat the column until children read all the words in order without making a mistake.)

going

You're

crying

started

smiled

himself

herself

EXERCISE 4

Read the fast way

a. You're going to read all the words in this column the fast way.

b. (Touch the ball for **answered.** Pause.) Get ready. (Slash.) *Answered.*

c. (Repeat step *b* until firm.)

d. (Repeat steps *b* and *c* for each remaining word in the column.)

e. (Repeat the column until the children read all the words in order without making mistakes.)

answered

ate

know

began

question

yes

I'm

STORYBOOK

EXERCISE 12

First reading—title and three sentences

a. (Pass out Storybook 1.)

b. Everybody, open your reader to page 139.

c. Everybody, touch the title of the story and get ready to read the words in the title.

d. First word. ✔

• Get ready. (Tap.) *The.*

e. (Tap for each remaining word in the title.)

f. Everybody, say the title. (Signal.)
The magic pouch.

g. Yesterday we read part four. Today we're going to read part five.

h. Everybody, get ready to read this story.

i. First word. ✔

• Get ready. (Tap.) *What.*

j. Next word. ✔

• Get ready. (Tap.) *Was.*

k. (Repeat *j* for the remaining words in the first three sentences. Have the children reread the first three sentences until firm.)

5

the magic pouch

what was insīde the pouch?[1]

how many yēars had the elf lived in the pouch?[2]

the little girl said to herself, "should I ōpen this pouch?"[3] she looked at the pouch. then slōwly she ōpened it. out jumped a little elf, no bigger than your foot.[4] the girl's hound went, "owwwww."[5] then the elf jumped all around the room.[6] he jumped on the table and on the flŏŏr.[7] then he ran up one wall and down the other wall. he ēven ran around the hound.[8] "owwwww," the hound yelled.

"I'm out. I'm out," the elf shouted. "I lived in that pouch a thousand yēars and now I'm out."

at last the girl's hound stopped gōing "owwwww." the elf sat on the table and said, "I thank you very much. plēase tāke the magic pouch. but be cāreful. when you are good, the pouch will be good to you.[9] but when you are bad, the pouch will be bad to you.[10]

mōre to come

EXERCISE 13

Remaining sentences and questions

a. I'm going to call on individual children to read a sentence. Everybody, follow along and point to the words. If you hear a mistake, raise your hand.

b. (Call on a child.) Read the next sentence.

c. (Call on another child.) Read the next sentence.

To Correct

word-identification errors (**from,** for example)
1. That word is **from.** What word? *From.*
2. Go back to the beginning of the sentence and read the sentence again.

d. (Repeat *c* for most of the remaining sentences in the story.)

e. (Occasionally have the group read a sentence. When the group is to read, say:)
Everybody, read the next sentence.
(Tap for each word in the sentence.)

f. (After each underlined sentence has been read, present each comprehension question specified below to the entire group.)

[1] Everybody, say that question. (Signal.) *What was inside the pouch?*

• What's the answer? (Signal.) *A magic elf.*

• Turn the page and look at the picture for a second. See that little man? That's the elf. Now let's read some more.

[2] Everybody, say that question. (Signal.) *How many years had the elf lived in the pouch?*

• What's the answer? (Signal.)
A thousand years.

• Is that a long time?
(The children respond.)

READING VOCABULARY
EXERCISE 1

Teacher reads the words in red

a. I'll read each word in red. Then you'll spell each word.

b. (Touch the ball for **question.**) My turn. (Slash as you say:) Question. What word? (Signal.) *Question.*

c. (Return to the ball.) Spell it. Get ready. (Tap under each letter as the children say:) *Q-U-E-S-T-I-O-N.*

- What word did you spell? (Signal.) *Question.*

d. (Repeat steps *b* and *c* for each word in red.)

e. Your turn to read all the words in this column.

f. (Touch the ball for **question.** Pause.) Get ready. (Slash.) *Question.*

g. (Repeat step *f* for each remaining word in the column.)

h. (Repeat steps *f* and *g* until firm.)

question

why

who

oh

How

Girl

Because

EXERCISE 2

Words with underlined parts

a. First you're going to read the underlined part of each word in this column. Then you're going to read the whole word.

b. (Touch the ball for **she.**) Read the underlined part. Get ready. (Tap the ball.) *sh.* Read the whole word. (Pause.) Get ready. (Slash.) *She.*

c. (Repeat step *b* until firm.)

d. (Repeat steps *b* and *c* for each remaining word in the column.)

e. (Repeat the column until children read all the words in order without making a mistake.)

She

mall

That

small

hear

Soon

Then

5

the magic pouch

what was insIde the pouch?[1]

how many yēars had the elf lived in the pouch?[2]

the little girl said to herself, "should I ōpen this pouch?"[3] she looked at the pouch. then slōwly she ōpened it. out jumped a little elf, no bigger than your foot.[4] the girl's hound went, "owwwww."[5] then the elf jumped all around the room.[6] he jumped on the table and on the flōōr.[7] then he ran up one wall and down the other wall. he ēven ran around the hound.[8] "owwwww," the hound yelled.

"I'm out. I'm out," the elf shouted. "I lived in that pouch a thousand yēars and now I'm out."

at last the girl's hound stopped gōῑng "owwwww." the elf sat on the table and said, "I thank you very much. plēase tāke the magic pouch. but be cāreful. when you are good, the pouch will be good to you.[9] but when you are bad, the pouch will be bad to you.[10]

mōre to come

EXERCISE 14

Second reading—sentences and questions

a. You're going to read the story again. And I'm going to ask more questions.

b. Starting with the first word of the title. ✔
- Get ready. (Tap as the children read the title.)

c. (Call on a child.) Read the first sentence.

To Correct

word-identification errors (**from**, for example)
1. That word is **from**. What word? *From.*
2. Go back to the beginning of the sentence and read the sentence again.

d. (Call on another child.) Read the next sentence.

e. (Repeat *d* for most of the remaining sentences in the story.)

f. (Occasionally have the group read a sentence.)

g. (After each underlined sentence has been read, present each comprehension question specified below to the entire group.)

[3] What did she say? (Signal.) *Should I open this pouch?*

[4] Who jumped out? (Signal.) *A little elf.*
- How did he get out? (Signal.) *The girl opened the pouch.*
- Show me with your hands how big he was. (The children respond.)

[5] Let's hear how you think the hound sounded. (The children respond.)

[6] What did the elf do first? (Signal.) *Jumped all around the room.*

[7] Then what did he do? (Signal.) *Jumped on the table and on the floor.*

[8] Why did the elf do all that jumping and running around? (The children respond.)

[9] What happens when you are good? (Signal.) *The pouch will be good to you.*

[10] And what happens when you are bad? (Signal.) *The pouch will be bad to you.*

EXERCISE 15

Picture comprehension

a. Look at the picture.
b. (Ask these questions:)
1. What is the elf doing? (The children respond.)
2. What is the dog doing? (Signal.) *Howling and yelling.*
- What is that hound saying? (Signal.) *oww.*
3. Why is that hound howling? (The children respond.)
4. Look at the girl. What do you think she is thinking? (Let the children comment for ten seconds. Then comment briefly.)

WORSHEET 97

EXERCISE 6

Picture comprehension

a. What do you think you'll **see** in the picture? (The children respond.)

b. Turn the page and look at the picture.

c. (Ask these questions:)
   1. Show me the hat the tiger made. (The children respond.)
   2. What is his hat made of? (Signal.) *A cone.*
   3. What holds the hat on his head? (Signal.) *A string.*
   4. Why do you think the tiger has his tongue out like that? (The children respond.)
   5. Who is that man in the picture? (The children respond.)
   6. What does that sign say? (Signal.) *Ice cream.*

DEDUCTIONS

The children will need pencils.

EXERCISE 7

Picture deductions

a. (Pass out Worksheet 97 to each child.)

b. (Hold up side 2 of your worksheet and touch the sentence in the box in the deductions exercise.)

c. Everybody, touch this sentence on your worksheet. ✔

d. (Call on a child.) Read the sentence in the box. *All the big horses are tired.*

e. Everybody, say that rule. (Signal.) *All the big horses are tired.*

• (Repeat until firm.)

f. You know that some of the horses in the picture are tired. What kind of horses are those? (Signal.) *All the big horses.*

• Everybody, touch a horse you know is tired. ✔

g. You don't know about the horses that are not big. Everybody, touch a horse you don't know about. ✔

h. (Call on a child.) Read the instructions below the box. *Circle every horse that is tired.*

i. Everybody, what are you going to do? (Signal.) *Circle every horse that is tired.* Yes, circle every horse that you know is tired.

j. Do it. ✔

INDEPENDENT ACTIVITIES

EXERCISE 8

Summary of independent activities

Everybody, now you'll do your worksheet. Remember to do all parts of the worksheet and to read all the parts carefully.

END OF LESSON 97

WORKSHEET 55

SUMMARY OF INDEPENDENT ACTIVITY
EXERCISE 16

Summary of independent activities

a. (Pass out Worksheet 55 to each child.)

b. Everybody, now you'll do your worksheet. Remember to do all parts of the worksheet and to read all the parts carefully.

INDIVIDUAL CHECKOUT
EXERCISE 17

2-minute individual fluency checkout: rate/accuracy

a. As you are doing your worksheet, I'll call on children one at a time to read the **first page of the story.** Remember, you get two stars if you read the first page of the story in less than two minutes and make no more than three errors.

b. (Call on each child. Tell the child:) Start with the title and read the first page of the story very carefully. Go. (Time the child. Tell the child any words the child misses. Stop the child as soon as the child makes the fourth error or exceeds the time limit.)

c. (If the child meets the rate-accuracy criterion, record two stars on your chart for lesson 55. Congratulate the child. Give children who do not earn two stars a chance to read the first page of the story again before the next lesson is presented.)
105 words/**2 min** = 53 wpm **[3 errors]**

END OF LESSON 55

STORYBOOK

STORY 97
EXERCISE 5

Reading—decoding

a. (Pass out Storybook 2.)

b. Everybody, open your reader to page 38.

c. Remember, if the group reads all the way to the red 5 without making more than five errors, we can go on.

d. Everybody, touch the title of the story. ✔

e. If you hear a mistake, raise your hand. Remember, children who do not have their place lose their turn. (Call on individual children to read two or three sentences. Do not ask comprehension questions. Tally all errors.)

To Correct

word-identification errors (from, for example)
1. That word is **from**. What word? *From.*
2. Go back to the beginning of the sentence and read the sentence again.

f. (If the children make more than five errors before they reach the red 5: when they reach the 5 return to the beginning of the story and have the children reread to the 5. Do not ask comprehension questions. Repeat step *f* until firm, and then go on to step *g*.)

g. (When the children read to the red 5 without making more than five errors: read the story to the children from the beginning to the 5. Ask the specified comprehension questions. When you reach the 5, call on individual children to continue reading the story. Have each child read two or three sentences.
Ask the specified comprehension questions.)

The Tame Tiger Who Liked Ice Cream[1]

There once was a tame tiger. This tiger did not bite children.[2] He didn't eat goats or sheep.[3] He said, "I like ice cream.[4] So I will go to town and get some."

But the tiger didn't have any cash.[5] He said, "I will fill my pouch with round stones. I hope that the man at the ice cream store likes round stones."[6]

So the tiger filled his pouch with round stones. Then he walked to town. He went up to the man at the ice cream stand.

"I don't have any cash," the tiger said. "But I have a pouch filled with pretty round stones."[7]

"Let's see them," the man said.

So the tiger showed the man his stones. The man said, "I like those stones. They are pretty."[8]

The tiger gave the pouch to the man. ⑤ Then the tiger said, "I want a big cone, and I want some string."[9]

The man said, "What will you do with a big cone and some string?"

"Wait and see," the tiger said.

What do you think the tiger did?[10] He ate the ice cream from the cone.[11] Then he put the big cone on his head with a string.[12]

The tiger said, "I love ice cream and I love hats. I ate the ice cream and now I have the best hat in town."[13]

The man at the ice cream stand said, "That tiger is very tame. He is also very smart."

The end

---

[1] What is this story going to be about? (Signal.) *The tame tiger who liked ice cream.*
- A tiger is an animal with stripes.

[2] Did this tiger bite children? (Signal.) *No.* Right. He was tame.

[3] I wonder what he did eat? Let's read some more.

[4] Now we know. What does he eat? (Signal.) *Ice cream.*

[5] What didn't he have? (Signal.) *Cash.* What's cash? (The children respond.) Right. He didn't have any money.

[6] What does the tiger want to do with the round stones? (The children respond.)

[7] Does he have cash? (Signal.) *No.*
- What does he have? (Signal.) *Pretty round stones.*

[8] Did the man like those stones? (Signal.) *Yes.*

[9] What did the tiger say? (Signal.) *I want a big cone, and I want some string.*

[10] What do you think? (The children respond.)
- Let's keep reading.

[11] What's the first thing the tiger did? (Signal.) *He ate the ice cream.*

[12] What's the next thing he did? (Signal.) (The children respond.)

[13] How did he get that hat? (The children respond.) Right. He made it from the cone and string.

READING VOCABULARY

Do not touch small letters.

Get ready to read all the words on this page without making a mistake.

pick<small>ed</small>

EXERCISE 1

Sound out first.

a. (Touch the ball for **picked.**) Sound it out. Get ready. (Quickly touch **p, i,** between **c** and **k, d** as the children say:) *piiikd.*

b. What word? (Signal.) *Picked.* Yes, **picked.**

c. (Repeat exercise until firm.)

rē<small>a</small>ch<small>ed</small>

EXERCISE 2

Sound out first

a. (Touch the ball for **rēached.**) Sound it out. Get ready. (Quickly touch **r, ē, ch, d** as the children say:) *rrrēēēchd.*

b. What word? (Signal.) *Reached.* Yes, **reached.**

c. (Repeat exercise until firm.)

tīr<small>ed</small>

EXERCISE 3

Sound out first

a. (Touch the ball for **tīred.**) Sound it out. Get ready. (Quickly touch **t, ī, r, d** as the children say:) *tīīīrrrd.*

b. What word? (Signal.) *Tired.* Yes, **tired.**

c. (Repeat exercise until firm.)

rich

EXERCISE 4

Sound out first

a. (Touch the ball for **rich.**) Sound it out. Get ready. (Quickly touch **r, i, ch** as the children say:) *rrriiich.*

b. What word? (Signal.) *Rich.* Yes, **rich.**

c. (Repeat exercise until firm.)

wōk<small>e</small>

EXERCISE 5

Sound out first

a. (Touch the ball for **wōke.**) Sound it out. Get ready. (Quickly touch **w, ō, k** as the children say:) *wwwōōōk.*

b. What word? (Signal.) *Woke.* Yes, **woke.**

c. (Repeat exercise until firm.)

hop

hope

EXERCISE 6

Practice final-e rule

a. (Touch the ball for **hop.**) Everybody, is there an ē on the end of this word? (Signal.) *No.*

b. (Point to **o** in **hop.**) So tell me what you say for this letter. (Signal.) *ŏŏŏ.*

c. (Touch the ball for **hop.**) Everybody, read this word the fast way and remember to say **ŏŏŏ.** Get ready. (Signal.) *Hop.* Yes, **hop.**

d. (Touch the ball for **hope.**) Everybody, is there an ē on the end of this word? (Signal.) *Yes.*

e. (Point to **o** in **hope.**) So tell me what you say for this letter. (Signal.) *ō.*

f. (Touch the ball for **hope.**) Everybody, read this word the fast way and remember to say **ō.** Get ready. (Signal.) *Hope.* Yes, **hope.**

g. (Repeat *a* through *f* until firm.)

(Repeat any troublesome words.)

Individual test

(Call on individual children. Each child reads a different word.)

EXERCISE 3

Read the fast way

a. You're going to read all the words in this column the fast way.

b. (Touch the ball for **Let's.** Pause.) Get ready. (Slash.) *Let's.*

c. (Repeat step *b* until firm.)

d. (Repeat steps *b* and *c* for each remaining word in the column.)

e. (Repeat the column until the children read all the words in order without making mistakes.)

Let's

who

ice cream

didn't

hopping

But

Liked

EXERCISE 4

Children spell, then read

a. First you're going to spell each word. Then you're going to read that word the fast way.

b. (Touch the ball for **hoping.**) Spell it. Get ready. (Tap under each letter as the children say:) *H-O-P-I-N-G.*

• (Return to the ball.) Read it. Get ready. (Slash.) *Hoping.*

c. (Repeat step *b* for each remaining word in the column.)

d. (Repeat steps *b* and *c* until firm.)

hoping

tame

bite

then

cone

right

tiger

Individual test

a. (Call on individual children to read one column of words from the lesson.)

b. (Praise children who read all words with no errors.)

Get ready to read all the words on this page without making a mistake.

To Correct

1. (Touch the ball for the word the children missed.) Is there an ē on the end of this word? (Signal.) (The children respond.)
2. (Point to the first vowel in the word.) So tell me what you say for this letter. (Signal.) (The children respond.)
3. (Touch the ball for the word.) Sound it out. Get ready. (Touch all sounds except the final **e**, if there is one, as the children sound out the word.)
4. What word? (Signal.) (The children respond.)
5. (Return to the first word in the column. Present all the words in order until firm.)

EXERCISE 7

Long vowel words

a. (Point to the words in this column.) Read these words the fast way.
b. (Touch the ball for **cape.** Pause two seconds.) Get ready. (Signal.) *Cape.* Yes, **cape.** (Repeat until firm.)
c. (Repeat *b* for **came** and **hide.**)

cape

came

hide

EXERCISE 8

Short vowel words

a. (Point to the words in this column.) Read these words the fast way.
b. (Touch the ball for **cap.** Pause two seconds.) Get ready. (Signal.) *Cap.* Yes, **cap.** (Repeat until firm.)
c. (Repeat *b* for **cam** and **hid.**)

cap

cam

hid

EXERCISE 9

Short and long vowel words

a. Everybody, read these words again. Remember what you say if there is an ē on the end of a word.
b. (Touch the ball for **cape.** Pause two seconds.) Get ready. (Signal.) *Cape.* Yes, **cape.**
c. (Repeat *b* for **hide, hid,** and **cap.**)

cape

hide

hid

cap

(Repeat any troublesome words.)

Individual test

(Call on individual children. Each child reads a different word.)

READING VOCABULARY

EXERCISE 1

Teacher reads the words in red

a. I'll read each word in red. Then you'll spell each word.

b. (Touch the ball for **wait.**) My turn. (Slash as you say:) Wait. What word? (Signal.) *Wait.*

c. (Return to the ball.) Spell it. Get ready. (Tap under each letter as the children say:) *W-A-I-T.*

• What word did you spell? (Signal.) *Wait.*

d. (Repeat steps *b* and *c* for each word in red.)

e. Your turn to read all the words in this column.

f. (Touch the ball for **wait.** Pause.) Get ready. (Slash.) *Wait.*

g. (Repeat step *f* for each remaining word in the column.)

h. (Repeat steps *f* and *g* until firm.)

wait

know

Head

some

those

also

ate

EXERCISE 2

Words with underlined parts

a. First you're going to read the underlined part of each word in this column. Then you're going to read the whole word.

b. (Touch the ball for **string.**) Read the underlined part. Get ready. (Tap the ball.) *ing.*

• Read the whole word. (Pause.) Get ready. (Slash.) *String.*

c. (Repeat step *b* until firm.)

d. (Repeat steps *b* and *c* for each remaining word in the column.)

e. (Repeat the column until children read all the words in order without making a mistake.)

To Correct
word-identification errors
(**note,** for example)

1. That word is **note.** What word? (Signal.) *Note.*

2. Spell **note.** Get ready. (Tap under each letter.) *N-O-T-E.*

3. What word did you spell? (Signal.) *Note.*

4. (Repeat *2* and *3* until firm.)

5. (Return to the first word in the column and present all words in order.) Starting over.

string

stand

stones

cash

pouch

smart

likes

Do not touch small letters.

Get ready to read all the words on this page without making a mistake.

grass

EXERCISE 10

Sound out first

a. (Touch the ball for **grass**.) Sound it out. Get ready. (Quickly touch **g, r, a,** between the **s**'s as the children say:) *grrraaasss.*

b. What word? (Signal.) *Grass.* Yes, **grass.**

c. (Repeat exercise until firm.)

clēan

EXERCISE 11

Sound out first

a. (Touch the ball for **clēan**.) Sound it out. Get ready. (Quickly touch **c, l, ē, n** as the children say:) *clllēēēnnn.*

b. What word? (Signal.) *Clean.* Yes, **clean.**

c. (Repeat exercise until firm.)

dirty

EXERCISE 12

Listen, sound out with me

a. (Point to **dirty**.) I'll tell you this word. (Pause.) **Dirty.** What word? (Signal.) *Dirty.* Yes, **dirty.**

b. (Touch the ball for **dirty**.) Sound it out with me. Get ready. (Quickly touch each sound as you and the children say:) *diiirrrtyyy.*

c. What word? (Signal.) *Dirty.* Yes, **dirty.**

d. (Repeat *b* and *c* until firm.)

does

EXERCISE 13

Listen, sound out

a. (Point to **does**.) I'll tell you this word. (Pause.) **Does.** What word? (Signal.) *Does.* Yes, **does.**

b. (Touch the ball for **does**.) Sound it out. Get ready. (Quickly touch **d, o, e, s** as the children say:) *doooeeesss.*

c. What word? (Signal.) *Does.* Yes, **does.**

d. (Repeat *b* and *c* until firm.)

EXERCISE 14

Read the fast way

a. Read these words the fast way.

b. (Touch the ball for **rubbed.** Pause two seconds.) Get ready. (Signal.) *Rubbed.* Yes, **rubbed.**

c. (Repeat *b* for **thōse** and **been.**)

rubbed

thōse

been

(Repeat any troublesome words.)

Individual test

(Call on individual children. Each child reads a different word.)

WORKSHEET 96

EXERCISE 6

Picture comprehension

a. Look at the picture.

b. (Ask these questions:)

1. What is the little girl in the front row doing? **(The children respond.)**
2. **(Point to the woman.)** Who is that woman? **(Signal.)** *The teacher.*
3. What is Dan doing? **(The children respond.)** Yes, he's helping with the seat work.
4. Does the teacher look happy or sad? **(The children respond.)**

DEDUCTIONS

The children will need pencils.

EXERCISE 7

Picture deductions

a. (Pass out Worksheet 96 to each child.)

b. (Hold up side 2 of your worksheet and touch the sentence in the box in the deductions exercise.)

c. Everybody, touch this sentence on your worksheet. ✔

d. (Call on a child.) Read the sentence in the box. *All the little girls are smart.*

e. Everybody, say that rule. (Signal.) *All the little girls are smart.*

• (Repeat until firm.)

f. You know that some of the girls in the picture are smart. What kind of girls are those? (Signal.) *All the little girls.* Everybody, touch a girl you know is smart. ✔

g. You don't know about the girls who are not little. Everybody, touch a girl you don't know about. ✔

h. (Call on a child.) Read the instructions below the box. *Circle every girl who is smart.*

i. Everybody, what are you going to do? (Signal.) *Circle every girl who is smart.*

• Yes, circle every girl who you know is smart.

j. Do it. ✔

INDEPENDENT ACTIVITIES

EXERCISE 8

Summary of independent activities

Everybody, now you'll do your worksheet. Remember to do all parts of the worksheet and to read all the parts carefully.

END OF LESSON 96

Get ready to read all the words on this page without making a mistake.

into

EXERCISE 15

Two-part word

a. (Cover **to**. Point to **in**.) Everybody, tell me what this part of the word says. Get ready. (Signal.) *in*. Yes, **in**.

b. (Uncover **to**. Touch the ball for **into**.) Now tell me what the whole word says. Get ready. (Signal.) *Into*. Yes, **into**.

c. (Repeat exercise until firm.)

something

EXERCISE 16

Two-part word

a. (Cover **thing**. Point to **some**.) Everybody, tell me what this part of the word says. Get ready. (Signal.) *Some*. Yes, **some**.

b. (Uncover **thing**. Touch the ball for **something**.) Now tell me what the whole word says. Get ready. (Signal.) *Something*. Yes, **something**.

c. (Repeat exercise until firm.)

round

EXERCISE 17

ou word

a. (Touch the ball for **round**.) Read this word the fast way. (Pause two seconds.) Get ready. (Signal.) *Round*. Yes, **round**.

b. (Point to **ou** in **round**.) Everybody, what do these letters say? (Signal.) *ou*. Yes, **ou**.

c. (Touch the ball for **round**.) Sound it out. Get ready. (Quickly touch **r, ou, n, d** as the children say:) *rrrounnnd*.

d. What word? (Signal.) *Round*. Yes, **round**.

e. (Repeat *c* and *d* until firm.)

Individual test

(Call on individual children to read a column of words from this lesson. If the column contains only one or two words, direct the child to read additional words from an adjacent column. Praise children who read all words with no errors.)

STORYBOOK

STORY 56
EXERCISE 18

First reading—title and three sentences

a. (Pass out Storybook 1.)

b. Everybody, open your reader to page 141.

c. Everybody, touch the title of the story and get ready to read the words in the title.

d. First word. ✔

• Get ready. (Tap.) *The.*

e. (Tap for each remaining word in the title.)

f. Everybody, say the title. (Signal.) *The magic pouch.*

g. Yesterday we read part five. Today we're going to read part six.

h. Everybody, get ready to read this story.

i. First word. ✔

• Get ready. (Tap.) *The.*

j. Next word. ✔

• Get ready. (Tap.) *Elf.*

k. (Repeat *j* for the remaining words in the first three sentences. Have the children reread the first three sentences until firm.)

STORYBOOK

STORY 96
EXERCISE 5

Reading—decoding

a. (Pass out Storybook 2.)

b. Everybody, open your reader to page 36.

c. Remember, if the group reads all the way to the red 5 without making more than five errors, we can go on.

d. Everybody, touch the title of the story. ✔

e. If you hear a mistake, raise your hand. Remember, children who do not have their place lose their turn. (Call on individual children to read two or three sentences. Do not ask comprehension questions. Tally all errors.)

To Correct

word-identification errors (**from,** for example)
1. That word is **from.** What word? *From.*
2. Go back to the beginning of the sentence and read the sentence again.

f. (If the children make more than five errors before they reach the red 5: when they reach the 5 return to the beginning of the story and have the children reread to the 5. Do not ask comprehension questions. Repeat step *f* until firm, and then go on to step *g.*)

g. (When the children read to the red 5 without making more than five errors: read the story to the children from the beginning to the 5. Ask the specified comprehension questions. When you reach the 5, call on individual children to continue reading the story. Have each child read two or three sentences.

Ask the specified comprehension questions.)

Dan, the Teacher's Helper[1]

Dan was a dog that liked to read and liked to add. He went to school with a girl named Ann. When the teacher left the room, Dan became the teacher.[2] He did a fine job.

The next day Dan came to school. He sat in the back of the room and began to read his book. The teacher began to do work with the boys and girls. But some of the boys and girls said, "We want Dan to be our teacher."

That made the teacher sad.[3] She said, "I cannot let Dan be the teacher."

The boys and girls said, "Oh, that's too bad. He is a fine teacher."

The teacher said, "But I can let Dan be a teacher's helper. Dan can help you with your seat work."[4]

The boys and girls smiled. Dan wagged his tail.[5] He felt proud. Ann also felt very proud. ⑤[6]

So now the boys and girls in Ann's room come to school very early.[7] They say that they have the best room in town. They have a very smart teacher and that teacher has a fine helper. Do you think that the boys and girls in this room are lucky?[8]

This is the end.

---

[1] What's the title of the story? (Signal.) *Dan, the teacher's helper.*

• Is Dan going to be a teacher in this story? (Signal.) *No.*

[2] How did Dan get to be teacher? (Signal.) *The teacher left the room.*

[3] What made the teacher sad? (The children respond.)

[4] How will Dan be the teacher's helper? (Signal.) *Help the children with their seat work.*

[5] Why did he do that? (The children respond.)

[6] What does "feeling proud" mean? (The children respond.)

• Yes, Ann feels happy and lucky that her dog is teacher's helper.

[7] Why do you think they do that? (The children respond.)

[8] What do you think? (The children respond.)

6

the magic pouch

the elf tōld the little girl, "when you are bad, the pouch will be bad to you."[1]

the girl picked up the pouch. she said to the elf, "I have been good to you. let's see if this magic pouch will be good to me."

she rēached insIde the pouch and found ten round rocks that shIne. "thēse round rocks are gōld," she shouted.[2] "I'm rich."[3]

so the girl thanked the elf for the pouch.

then the girl and her hound started down the tall mountain. they went down and down. they went into the clouds. when they left the clouds, the girl could see the ground. down and down they went.[4]

when they rēached the bottom of the mountain, the sun was setting. it was getting lāte. the girl was tIred. but she ran to her house.

her mother met her at the dōōr. she said, "where were you? your father and I have looked all around for you."[5]

the little girl did not tell her mother where she went. she said, "I went to slēēp in the grass.[6] I just wōke up." she tōld a lIe, and that was bad.[7]

mōre to come

EXERCISE 19

Remaining sentences

a. I'm going to call on individual children to read a sentence. Everybody, follow along and point to the words. If you hear a mistake, raise your hand.

b. (Call on a child.) Read the next sentence.

To Correct

word-identification errors (**from,** for example)
1. That word is **from.** What word? *From.*
2. Go back to the beginning of the sentence and read the sentence again.

c. (Call on another child.) Read the next sentence.

d. (Repeat c for most of the remaining sentences in the story.)

e. (Occasionally have the group read a sentence. When the group is to read, say:) Everybody, read the next sentence. (Tap for each word in the sentence.)

EXERCISE 20

Second reading—sentences and questions

a. You're going to read the story again. This time I'm going to ask questions.

b. Starting with the first word of the title. ✔
• Get ready. (Tap as the children read the title.)

c. (Call on a child.) Read the first sentence.

To Correct

word-identification errors (**from,** for example)
1. That word is **from.** What word? *From.*
2. Go back to the beginning of the sentence and read the sentence again.

d. (Call on another child.) Read the next sentence.

e. (Repeat d for most of the remaining sentences in the story.)

f. (Occasionally have the group read a sentence.)

g. (After each underlined sentence has been read, present each comprehension question specified below to the entire group.)

[1] When would the pouch be bad? (The children respond.)

[2] What was in the pouch? (Signal.) *Gold.*

[3] Why was the pouch good to her? (The children respond.)

[4] Where were the girl and her hound going? (Signal.) *Home.*

• Did they take the elf with them? (Signal.) *No.*

[5] Why did her mother and father do that? (The children respond.)

[6] What did she say? (Signal.) *I went to sleep in the grass.*

• Was that the truth? (Signal.) *No.*

[7] What will the pouch do if she is bad? (The children respond.)

• Next time we'll see if the pouch does something bad.

EXERCISE 3

Read the fast way

a. You're going to read all the words in this column the fast way.

b. (Touch the ball for **begin.** Pause.) Get ready. (Slash.) *Begin.*

c. (Repeat step *b* until firm.)

d. (Repeat steps *b* and *c* for each remaining word in the column.)

e. (Repeat the column until the children read all the words in order without making mistakes.)

begin

began

left

string

tame

tone

with

EXERCISE 4

Children spell, then read

a. First you're going to spell each word. Then you're going to read that word the fast way.

b. (Touch the ball for **fine.**) Spell it. Get ready. (Tap under each letter as the children say:) *F-I-N-E.*

• (Return to the ball.) Read it. Get ready. (Slash.) *Fine.*

c. (Repeat step *b* for each remaining word in the column.)

d. (Repeat steps *b* and *c* until firm.)

fine

fin

lucky

tiger

seat

teacher

want

Individual test

a. (Call on individual children to read one column of words from the lesson.)

b. (Praise children who read all words with no errors.)

WORKSHEET 56

EXERCISE 21

Picture comprehension

a. Look at the picture.

b. (Ask these questions:)

1. What's that stuff on the table? (Signal.) *Gold.*
2. Why did the pouch give the girl so much gold? (Let the children comment for ten seconds. Then comment briefly.)
3. How does that girl look? (Signal.) *Happy.*
4. What would you do with all that gold? (Let the children comment for ten seconds. Then comment briefly.)

SUMMARY OF INDEPENDENT ACTIVITY

EXERCISE 22

Introduction to independent activity

a. (Pass out Worksheet 56 to each child.)

b. (Hold up side 1 of your worksheet.) Everybody, you're going to do this worksheet on your own. (Tell the children when they will work the items.)

• Let's go over the things you're going to do.

Story items

(Point to the story-items exercise.) Everybody, remember to write your answers in the blanks.

Following instructions

a. (Touch the sentence in the box on side 2.)

b. Everybody, first you're going to read the sentence in the box. Then you're going to read the instructions below the box and do what the instructions tell you to do.

Reading comprehension

(Point to the story.) You're going to read this story and then do the items. Remember to write the answers in the blanks.

Following instructions

(Point to the following-instructions exercise.) Everybody, you're going to read the instructions. Then you're going to do what the instructions tell you to do.

END OF LESSON 56

READING VOCABULARY

EXERCISE 1

Teacher reads the words in red

a. I'll read each word in red. Then you'll spell each word.

b. (Touch the ball for **Helper.**) My turn. (Slash as you say:) Helper. What word? (Signal.) *Helper.*

c. (Return to the ball.) Spell it. Get ready. (Tap under each letter as the children say:) *H-E-L-P-E-R.*

• What word did you spell? (Signal.) *Helper.*

d. (Repeat steps *b* and *c* for each word in red.)

e. Your turn to read all the words in this column.

f. (Touch the ball for **Helper.** Pause.) Get ready. (Slash.) *Helper.*

g. (Repeat step *f* for each remaining word in the column.)

h. (Repeat steps *f* and *g* until firm.)

Helper

Oh

early

smart

also

they

things

EXERCISE 2

Words with underlined parts

a. First you're going to read the underlined part of each word in this column. Then you're going to read the whole word.

b. (Touch the ball for **helper.**) Read the underlined part. Get ready. (Tap the ball.) *Help.*

• Read the whole word. (Pause.) Get ready. (Slash.) *Helper.*

c. (Repeat step *b* until firm.)

d. (Repeat steps *b* and *c* for each remaining word in the column.)

e. (Repeat the column until children read all the words in order without making a mistake.)

To Correct
word-identification errors
(**let,** for example)

1. That word is **let.** What word? (Signal.) *Let.*
2. Spell **let.** Get ready. (Tap under each letter.) *L-E-T.*
3. What word did you spell? (Signal.) *Let.*
4. (Repeat 2 and 3 until firm.)
5. (Return to the first word in the column and present all words in order.) Starting over.

helper

hoped

smiled

hopping

wagged

hopped

boys

READING VOCABULARY

Do not touch small letters.

Get ready to read all the words on this page without making a mistake.

EXERCISE 1

Read the fast way

a. Read these words the fast way.

b. (Touch the ball for **were.** Pause two seconds.) Get ready. (Signal.) *Were.* Yes, **were.**

c. (Repeat *b* for **hōlding, clēan, dirty, does,** and **who.**)

EXERCISE 2

Sound combination review

a. Here are some letters that go together. Get ready to tell me the sound they usually make.

b. (Point to **al.**) What sound do these letters usually make? (Signal.) *All.* Yes, **all.**

c. (Repeat *b* with **ou** and **ar.**)

d. (Repeat the series of sound combinations until firm.)

<u>al</u>

<u>ou</u>

<u>ar</u>

wer$_e$

hōlding

clēan

dirty

does

who

(Repeat any troublesome words.)

Individual test

(Call on individual children. Each child reads a different word.)

ate

at

EXERCISE 3

Practice final-e rule

a. (Point to **ate** and **at.**) You're going to say the name **ā** when you read one of these words.

b. (Point to **ate.**) Are you going to say the name **ā** when you read this word? (Signal.) *Yes.*

c. (Point to **at.**) Are you going to say the name **ā** when you read this word? (Signal.) *No.*

To Correct

1. You say the name **ā** in the word with the **ē** on the end.
2. (Point to the word.) Is there an **ē** on the end of this word? (Signal.) (The children respond.)
3. So are you going to say the name **ā** when you read this word? (Signal.) (The children respond.)
4. (Repeat *b* and *c*.)

d. (Repeat *b* and *c* until firm.)

e. Read these words the fast way.

f. (Touch the ball for **ate.** Pause two seconds.) Get ready. (Signal.) *Ate.* Yes, **ate.**

g. (Touch the ball for **at.** Pause two seconds.) Get ready. (Signal.) *At.* Yes, **at.**

h. (Repeat *f* and *g* until firm.)

EXERCISE 6

Picture comprehension

a. Look at the picture.

b. (Ask these questions:)

1. Show me who is the teacher in this picture. (The children respond.)
   - What's his name? *Dan.*
2. What words are on Dan's board? (The children respond.)
3. What's the little girl in the front row doing? (Signal.) *Raising her hand.* Why do you think she is raising her hand? (Let the children comment for ten seconds. Then comment briefly.)
4. What does Dan have on his eyes? (Signal.) *Glasses.*
5. Would you like to have Dan for a teacher? (The children respond.)

★ DEDUCTIONS

The children will need pencils.

EXERCISE 7

Picture deductions

a. (Pass out Worksheet 95 to each child.)

b. (Hold up side 2 of your worksheet and touch the sentence in the box in the deductions exercise.)

c. Everybody, touch this sentence on your worksheet. ✔

d. (Call on a child.) Read the sentence in the box. *All the big dogs are sleepy.*

e. Everybody, say that rule. (Signal.) *All the big dogs are sleepy.* (Repeat until firm.)

f. You know that some of the dogs in the picture are sleepy. What kind of dogs are those? (Signal.) *All the big dogs.* Everybody, touch a dog you know is sleepy. ✔

g. You don't know about the dogs that are not big. Everybody, touch a dog you don't know about. ✔

h. (Call on a child.) Read the instructions below the box. *Circle every dog that is sleepy.*

i. Everybody, what are you going to do? (Signal.) *Circle every dog that is sleepy.* Yes, circle every dog that you know is sleepy.

j. Do it. ✔

INDEPENDENT ACTIVITIES

EXERCISE 8

Summary of independent activities

Everybody, now you'll do your worksheet. Remember to do all parts of the worksheet and to read all the parts carefully.

INDIVIDUAL CHECKOUT

EXERCISE 9

2-minute individual fluency checkout: rate/accuracy

a. As you are doing your worksheet, I'll call on children one at a time to read to the star. Remember, you get two stars on the chart if you read to the star in less than two minutes and make no more than four errors.

b. (Call on each child. Tell the child:) Read to the star very carefully. Start with the title. Go. (Time the child. Tell the child any words the child misses. Stop the child as soon as the child makes the fifth error or exceeds the time limit.)

c. (If the child meets the rate-accuracy criterion, record two stars on your chart for lesson 95. Congratulate the child. Give children who do not earn two stars a chance to read to the star again before the next lesson is presented.)

120 words/**2 min** = 60 wpm **[4 errors]**

END OF LESSON 95

Get ready to read all the words on this page without making a mistake.

To Correct

1. (Touch the ball for the word the children missed.) Is there an ē on the end of this word? (Signal.) (The children respond.)
2. (Point to the first vowel in the word.) So tell me what you say for this letter. (Signal.) (The children respond.)
3. (Touch the ball for the word.) Sound it out. Get ready. (Touch all sounds except the final **e**, if there is one, as the children sound out the word.)
4. What word? (Signal.) (The children respond.)
5. (Return to the first word in the column. Present all the words in order until firm.)

EXERCISE 4

Short vowel words

a. (Point to the words in this column.) Read these words the fast way.
b. (Touch the ball for **pan.** Pause two seconds.) Get ready. (Signal.) *Pan.* Yes, **pan.** (Repeat until firm.)
c. (Repeat *b* for **cap** and **mad.**)

pan

cap

mad

EXERCISE 5

Long vowel words

a. (Point to the words in this column.) Read these words the fast way.
b. (Touch the ball for **pane.** Pause two seconds.) Get ready. (Signal.) *Pane.* Yes, **pane.** (Repeat until firm.)
c. (Repeat *b* for **cape** and **made.**)

pane

cape

made

EXERCISE 6

Short and long vowel words

a. Everybody, read these words again. Remember what you say if there is an ē on the end of a word.
b. (Touch the ball for **pane.** Pause two seconds.) Get ready. (Signal.) *Pane.* Yes, **pane.**
c. (Repeat *b* for **cap** and **mad.**)

pane

cap

mad

(Repeat any troublesome words.)

Individual test

(Call on individual children. Each child reads a different word.)

STORYBOOK

STORY 95

EXERCISE 5

Reading—decoding

a. (Pass out Storybook 2.)

b. Everybody, open your reader to page 34.

c. Remember, if the group reads all the way to the red 5 without making more than five errors, we can go on.

d. Everybody, touch the title of the story. ✔

e. If you hear a mistake, raise your hand. Remember, children who do not have their place lose their turn. (Call on individual children to read two or three sentences. Do not ask comprehension questions. Tally all errors.)

To Correct

word-identification errors (**from**, for example)
1. That word is **from.** What word? *From.*
2. Go back to the beginning of the sentence and read the sentence again.

f. (If the children make more than five errors before they reach the red 5: when they reach the 5 return to the beginning of the story and have the children reread to the 5. Do not ask comprehension questions. Repeat step *f* until firm, and then go on to step *g*.)

g. (When the children read to the red 5 without making more than five errors: read the story to the children from the beginning to the 5. Ask the specified comprehension questions. When you reach the 5, call on individual children to continue reading the story. Have each child read two or three sentences.

Ask the specified comprehension questions.)

Dan the Teacher[1]

A girl named Ann had a dog. The dog was named Dan.[2] One day Dan went to school with Ann.

The teacher said, "Ann, take that dog out of this school.[3] Schools are for boys and girls. Schools are not for dogs."

Ann said, "But this dog is very smart. He likes to read and he likes to add."[4]

The teacher said, "I will let that dog stay, but if he makes a sound, I will make him leave."

So the dog sat down to read a book to himself. The boys and girls worked with the teacher.

But then the teacher was called out of the room.

One boy said, "We do not have a teacher ★ now."[5]

Dan walked up and said, "I will be your teacher."

So he began to teach.[6] He was one of the best teachers the boys and girls had ever seen. ⑤ He helped the children read a very hard book. And he helped them spell hard words.[7]

At the end of the day, some of the children went up to the dog and gave him a big kiss. They said, "We hope that Dan will be our teacher from now on."[8]

More to come

---

[1] What's the title of this story? (Signal.) *Dan the teacher.*

[2] What was the name of the girl? (Signal.) *Ann.*

• What was the name of the dog? (Signal.) *Dan.*

[3] What did the teacher say? (Signal.) *Ann, take that dog out of this school.*

[4] What does Dan like to do? (Signal.) *Read and add.*

[5] What did the boy say? (Signal.) *We do not have a teacher now.*

• Why didn't they have a teacher? (The children respond.)

• Yes, the teacher was called out of the room.

[6] Who began to teach? (Signal.) *Dan the dog.*

[7] What did he help them do? (Signal.) *Spell hard words.*

• What else? *Read a very hard book.*

[8] Do you think Dan will keep on being their teacher? (The children respond.)

• Next time we'll find out.

Do not touch small letters.

Get ready to read all the words on this page without making a mistake.

ground

EXERCISE 7

ou word

a. (Touch the ball for **ground.**) Read this word the fast way. (Pause two seconds.) Get ready. (Signal.) *Ground.* Yes, **ground.**

b. (Point to **ou** in **ground.**) Everybody, what do these letters say? (Signal.) *ou.* Yes, **ou.**

c. (Touch the ball for **ground.**) Sound it out. Get ready. (Quickly touch **g, r, ou, n, d** as the children say:) *grrrounnnd.*

d. What word? (Signal.) *Ground.* Yes, **ground.**

e. (Repeat *c* and *d* until firm.)

stāyed

EXERCISE 8

Sound out first

a. (Touch the ball for **stāyed.**) Sound it out. Get ready. (Quickly touch **s, t, ā, y, d** as the children say:) *ssstāāāyyyd.*

b. What word? (Signal.) *Stayed.* Yes, **stayed.**

c. (Repeat exercise until firm.)

here

EXERCISE 9

Practice final-e rule

a. (Point to the first **e** in **here.**) Look at this letter and remember the rule about the **ē** at the end of a word.

b. (Touch the ball for **here.**) Read this word the fast way. (Pause two seconds.) Get ready. (Signal.) *Here.* Yes, **here.**

c. (Touch the ball for **here.**) Sound it out. Get ready. (Quickly touch **h, e, r** as the children say:) *hēēērrr.*

d. What word? (Signal.) *Here.* Yes, **here.**

e. (Repeat *b, c,* and *d* until firm.)

came

EXERCISE 10

Practice final-e rule

a. (Point to the **a** in **came.**) Look at this letter and remember the rule about the **ē** at the end of the word.

b. (Touch the ball for **came.**) Read this word the fast way. (Pause two seconds.) Get ready. (Signal.) *Came.* Yes, **came.**

c. (Touch the ball for **came.**) Sound it out. Get ready. (Quickly touch **c, ā, m** as the children say:) *cāāāmmm.*

d. What word? (Signal.) *Came.* Yes, **came.**

e. (Repeat *b, c,* and *d* until firm.)

Individual test

(Call on individual children to read a column of words from this lesson. If the column contains only one or two words, direct the child to read additional words from an adjacent column.)

like

EXERCISE 11

Practice final-e rule

a. Read this word the fast way. Remember to look at the end of the word.

b. (Touch the ball for **like.** Pause two seconds.) Get ready. (Signal.) *Like.* Yes, **like.**

lake

EXERCISE 12

Practice final-e rule

a. Read this word the fast way. Remember to look at the end of the word.

b. (Touch the ball for **lake.** Pause two seconds.) Get ready. (Signal.) *Lake.* Yes, **lake.**

these

EXERCISE 13

Practice final-e rule

a. Read this word the fast way. Remember to look at the end of the word.

b. (Touch the ball for **these.** Pause two seconds.) Get ready. (Signal.) *These.* Yes, **these.**

EXERCISE 3

Words with underlined parts

a. First you're going to read the underlined part of each word in this column. Then you're going to read the whole word.

b. (Touch the ball for **named.**) Read the underlined part. Get ready. (Tap the ball.) *Name.*

• Read the whole word. (Pause.) Get ready. (Slash.) *Named.*

c. (Repeat step *b* until firm.)

d. (Repeat steps *b* and *c* for each remaining word in the column.)

e. (Repeat the column until children read all the words in order without making a mistake.)

named

liked

makes

hoped

hopped

helped

called

EXERCISE 4

Children spell, then read

a. First you're going to spell each word. Then you're going to read that word the fast way.

b. (Touch the ball for **when.**) Spell it. Get ready. (Tap under each letter as the children say:) *W-H-E-N.*

• (Return to the ball.) Read it. Get ready. (Slash.) *When.*

c. (Repeat step *b* for each remaining word in the column.)

d. (Repeat steps *b* and *c* until firm.)

when

spell

gave

children

mopping

moping

seems

Individual test

a. (Call on individual children to read one column of words from the lesson.)

b. (Praise children who read all words with no errors.)

STORYBOOK

STORY 57
EXERCISE 14
First reading—title and three sentences

a. (Pass out Storybook 1.)

b. Everybody, open your reader to page 144.

c. Everybody, touch the title of the story and get ready to read the words in the title.

d. First word. ✔

* Get ready. (Tap.) *The.*

e. (Tap for each remaining word in the title.)

f. Everybody, say the title. (Signal.) *The magic pouch.*

g. Yesterday we read part six. Today we're going to read part seven.

h. Everybody, get ready to read this story.

i. First word. ✔

* Get ready. (Tap.) *Did.*

j. Next word. ✔

* Get ready. (Tap.) *The.*

k. (Repeat *j* for the remaining words in the first three sentences. Have the children reread the first three sentences until firm.)

EXERCISE 15
Remaining sentences and questions

a. I'm going to call on individual children to read a sentence. Everybody, follow along and point to the words. If you hear a mistake, raise your hand.

b. (Call on a child.) Read the next sentence.

c. (Call on another child.) Read the next sentence.

d. (Repeat *c* for most of the remaining sentences in the story.)

7

the magic pouch

<u>did the little girl tell her mother</u>
<u>where she was?</u>[1]

<u>what did she tell her mother?</u>[2]

<u>what does the pouch do when you</u>
<u>are bad?</u>[3]

the girl's mother looked at the pouch. she said, "where did you get that pouch?"

"I found it on the ground," the little girl said. <u>she told another lie.</u>[4]

"but mother, there are ten rocks of gold in this pouch. we are rich."

---

e. (Occasionally have the group read a sentence. When the group is to read, say:) Everybody, read the next sentence. (Tap for each word in the sentence.)

f. (After each underlined sentence has been read, present each comprehension question specified below to the entire group.)

[1] Everybody, say that question. (Signal.) *Did the little girl tell her mother where she was?*

* What's the answer? (Signal.) *No.*

* Why didn't she tell her? (The children respond.)

[2] Everybody, say that question. (Signal.) *What did she tell her mother?*

* What's the answer? (Signal.) *That she fell asleep in the grass.*

* Was that bad that she lied to her? (Signal.) *Yes.*

[3] Everybody, say that question. (Signal.) *What does the pouch do when you are bad?*

* What's the answer? (The children respond.)

EXERCISE 16
Second reading—sentences and questions

a. You're going to read the story again. And I'm going to ask more questions.

b. Starting with the first word of the title. ✔

* Get ready. (Tap as the children read the title.)

c. (Call on a child.) Read the first sentence.

To Correct

word-identification errors (**from,** for example)

1. That word is **from.** What word? *From.*
2. Go back to the beginning of the sentence and read the sentence again.

d. (Call on another child.) Read the next sentence.

e. (Repeat *d* for most of the remaining sentences in the story.)

f. (Occasionally have the group read a sentence.)

g. (After each underlined sentence has been read, present each comprehension question specified below to the entire group.)

[4] What was this lie? (Signal.) *That she found the pouch on the ground.*

* What was her first lie? (The children respond.)

READING VOCABULARY

EXERCISE 1

Teacher reads the words in red

a. I'll read each word in red. Then you'll spell each word.

b. (Touch the ball for **Ann.**) My turn. (Slash as you say:) Ann. What word? (Signal.) *Ann.*

c. (Return to the ball.) Spell it. Get ready. (Tap under each letter as the children say:) *A-N-N.*

- What word did you spell? (Signal.) *Ann.*

d. (Repeat steps *b* and *c* for each word in red.)

e. Your turn to read all the words in this column.

f. (Touch the ball for **Ann.** Pause.) Get ready. (Slash.) *Ann.*

g. (Repeat step *f* for each remaining word in the column.)

h. (Repeat steps *f* and *g* until firm.)

Ann

Dan

lucky

early

They

One

from

EXERCISE 2

Words with underlined parts

a. First you're going to read the underlined part of each word in this column. Then you're going to read the whole word.

b. (Touch the ball for **salt.**) Read the underlined part. Get ready. (Tap the ball.) *All.*

- Read the whole word. (Pause.) Get ready. (Slash.) *Salt.*

c. (Repeat step *b* until firm.)

d. (Repeat steps *b* and *c* for each remaining word in the column.)

e. (Repeat the column until children read all the words in order without making a mistake.)

To Correct

word-identification errors (**walking,** for example)

1. That word is **walking.** What word? (Signal.) *Walking.*
2. Spell **walking.** Get ready. (Tap under each letter.) *W-A-L-K-I-N-G.*
3. What word did you spell? (Signal.) *Walking.*
4. (Repeat *2* and *3* until firm.)
5. (Return to the first word in the column and present all words in order.) Starting over.

salt

began

leave

out

smart

with

schools

she reached in the pouch and took something out.⁵ but when she looked, she saw that she was not holding gold rocks. she was holding yellow mud.⁶ her mother said, "you are not funny. we are not rich. but you are dirty. go clean your hands."

the little girl got a rag and tried to rub the yellow mud from her hands. but it would not come from her hands. she rubbed and rubbed, but the yellow mud stayed on her hands.⁷ her mother tried to get the mud from her hands, but she could not do it.

then the girl started to cry.⁸

more to come

---

⁵ What was in the pouch when the elf gave it to her? (Signal.) *Gold.*

⁶ What is in the pouch now? (Signal.) *Yellow mud.*

• Why did that happen? (Signal.) *She was bad. (or She told a lie.)*

⁷ Why do you think that's happening? (The children respond.)

⁸ Why did she do that? (The children respond.)

• Do you think the mud will come off? (The children respond.)

• Next time we will read the last part of the story of the magic pouch.

EXERCISE 17
Picture comprehension

a. What do you think you'll see in the picture? (The children respond.)

b. Turn the page and look at the picture.

c. (Ask these questions:)

1. Who is that woman looking at the girl? (Signal.) *The girl's mother.*
2. What is in the girl's hand? (Signal.) *Mud.*
3. Why is she making a face? (The children respond.)
4. Do you think her mother is happy? (Signal.) *No.*
5. What do you think her mother is thinking? (The children respond.)

SUMMARY OF INDEPENDENT ACTIVITY
EXERCISE 18

Introduction to independent activity

a. (Pass out Worksheet 57 to each child.)

b. (Hold up side 1 of your worksheet.) Everybody, you're going to do this worksheet on your own. (Tell the children when they will work the items.)

• Let's go over the things you're going to do.

Story items

(Point to the story-items exercise.) Everybody, remember to write your answers in the blanks.

Following instructions

a. (Touch the sentence in the box.)

b. Everybody, first you're going to read the sentence in the box. Then you're going to read the instructions below the box and do what the instructions tell you to do.

Reading comprehension

(Point to the story on side 2.) You're going to read this story and then do the items. Remember to write the answers in the blanks.

Following instructions

(Point to the following-instructions exercise.) Everybody, you're going to read the instructions. Then you're going to do what the instructions tell you to do.

END OF LESSON 57

So the boss began to teach Sid how to read words like **pane** and **rode** and **tape** and **time**.[4] Sid sat at the side of the boss and the boss made notes for Sid to read. At first, Sid did not read the words like **hope** and **rob**. But every day, Sid would read a little better. ⑤ And before a week went by, Sid could read the words very well. The boss made up some hard notes. One note said, "Hide a bit of cheese near the mop."[5] Another note said, "Tape a cap to my cape."[6] But the boss could not fool Sid.[7]

Now, when the boss leaves the shop, she says, "Sid, read the notes on the table and do what the notes tell you to do." That's what Sid does. If a note tells him to fix a window pane, he does it.[8] If a note tells him to send a cone to a tree farm, he sends a cone, not a con.[9] Sid is very happy and so is the boss.[10]

The end

WORKSHEET 94

4 What words did Sid learn how to read? (Signal.) *Pane, rode, tape, time.*
5 What did one note say? (Signal.) *Hide a bit of cheese near the mop.*
6 What did that note say? (Signal.) *Tape a cap to my cape.*
7 Did Sid get fooled? (Signal.) *No.*
• Why not? (The children respond.)
• Yes, he's a good reader now.
8 What does he fix? (The children respond.)
9 What does he send to a tree farm? (Signal.) *A cone.*
10 How do Sid and the boss feel now? (Signal.) *Happy.*

EXERCISE 10

Picture comprehension

a. Look at the picture.
b. (Ask these questions:)
  1. Can you read the words the boss wrote? (Signal.) *Yes.*
  • Turn your book around and read the words. (The children respond.)
  2. Does Sid look sad? (Signal.) *No.*
  • How do you think he feels? (The children respond.)
  • Why does he feel that way? (The children respond.)

EXERCISE 11

Summary of independent activities

a. (Pass out Worksheet 94 to each child.)
b. Everybody, now you'll do your worksheet. Remember to do all parts of the worksheet and to read all the parts carefully.

END OF LESSON 94

READING VOCABULARY

Do not touch small letters.

Get ready to read all the words on this page without making a mistake.

EXERCISE 1

Read the fast way

a. Read these words the fast way.

b. (Touch the ball for **crīed.** Pause two seconds.) Get ready. (Signal.) *Cried.* Yes, **cried.**

c. (Repeat *b* for were, **clēan, rich, are, doing, kēēp,** and **līe.**)

rich

are

doing

crīed

were

kēēp

clēan

līe

at

ate

(Repeat any troublesome words.)

Individual test

(Call on individual children. Each child reads a different word.)

EXERCISE 2

Practice final-e rule

a. (Point to **at** and **ate.**) You're going to say the name ā when you read one of these words.

b. (Point to **at.**) Are you going to say the name ā when you read this word? (Signal.) *No.*

c. (Point to **ate.**) Are you going to say the name ā when you read this word? (Signal.) *Yes.*

To Correct

1. You say the name ā in the word with the ē on the end.
2. (Point to the word.) Is there an ē on the end of this word? (Signal.) (The children respond.)
3. So are you going to say the name ā when you read this word? (Signal.) (The children respond.)
4. (Repeat *b* and *c.*)

d. (Repeat *b* and *c* until firm.)

e. Read these words the fast way.

f. (Touch the ball for **at.** Pause two seconds.) Get ready. (Signal.) *At.* Yes, **at.**

g. (Touch the ball for **ate.** Pause two seconds.) Get ready. (Signal.) *Ate.* Yes, **ate.**

h. (Repeat *f* and *g* until firm.)

READ THE ITEMS 94
EXERCISE 7

Read the item

a. (Pass out Storybook 2.)

b. Open your reader to page 31. Get ready to read the item.

c. Finger under the first word of the item. ✔

- Get ready. (Tap.) *If.*

d. Next word. (Pause.) Get ready. (Tap.) *The.*

e. (Repeat step *d* for the remaining words in the item.)

f. (Repeat steps *c* through *e* until the item is firm.)

g. Everybody, say that item. (Pause. Signal.) *If the teacher says "Pin," say "Pine."*

h. Again. (Repeat step *g* until firm.)

i. What are you going to say if I say "**Pin**"? (Signal.) *Pine.*

- When are you going to say "**Pine**"? (Signal.) *When the teacher says "Pin."*

To Correct
(Have the children read the item aloud. Then repeat the questions.)

EXERCISE 8

Play the game

a. Read the item to yourself and think about what you're going to do and when you're going to do it. Raise your hand when you're ready.

b. (After the children raise their hands, say:) Get ready to play the game.

c. My turn. (Pause.) **Pin.** (Signal.) (The children are to say *Pine* immediately.)

To Correct
(Have the children read the item aloud. Then play the game again.)

The Boss Teaches Sid to Read[1]

Sid felt so sad that a tear ran down his cheek. The boss was so mad that she was sitting on the floor, tapping her cane and looking at Sid. The boss said, "You didn't plant seeds on the slope.[2] You planted seeds in the slop."

"Yes," Sid said. "I didn't mean to do a bad job. But I don't read very well."

The boss said, "Well, I will teach you how to read. If you are going to help me in this shop, you must be good at reading."[3]

STORY 94
EXERCISE 9

Reading—decoding

a. Everybody, get ready to read the story.

b. Remember, if the group reads all the way to the red 5 without making more than five errors, we can go on.

c. Everybody, touch the title of the story. ✔

d. If you hear a mistake, raise your hand. Remember, children who do not have their place lose their turn. (Call on individual children to read two or three sentences. Do not ask comprehension questions. Tally all errors.)

To Correct
word-identification errors (**from,** for example)
1. That word is **from.** What word? *From.*
2. Go back to the beginning of the sentence and read the sentence again.

e. (If the children make more than five errors: when they reach the 5, return to the beginning of the story and have the children reread to the 5. Do not ask comprehension questions. Repeat step *e* until firm, and then go on to step *f.*)

f. (If the children read to the number 5 without making more than five errors: read the story to the children from the beginning to the 5. Ask the specified comprehension questions. When you reach the 5, call on individual children to continue reading the story. Have each child read two or three sentences. Ask the specified comprehension questions.)

[1] What will happen in this story? (Signal.) *The boss will teach Sid to read.*

[2] Where did Sid plant seeds? (Signal.) *In the slop.*

[3] Why does Sid have to be a good reader? (The children respond.)

Get ready to read all the words on this page without making a mistake.

To Correct

1. (Touch the ball for the word the children missed.) Is there an ē on the end of this word? (Signal.) (The children respond.)
2. (Point to the first vowel in the word.) So tell me what you say for this letter. (Signal.) (The children respond.)
3. (Touch the ball for the word.) Sound it out. Get ready. (Touch all sounds except the final **e**, if there is one, as the children sound out the word.)
4. What word? (Signal.) (The children respond.)
5. (Return to the first word in the column. Present all the words in order until firm.)

EXERCISE 3

Short vowel words

a. (Point to the words in this column.) Read these words the fast way.
b. (Touch the ball for **fin.** Pause two seconds.) Get ready. (Signal.) *Fin.* Yes, **fin.** (Repeat until firm.)
c. (Repeat *b* for **sit** and **cam.**)

fin

sit

cam

EXERCISE 4

Long vowel words

a. (Point to the words in this column.) Read these words the fast way.
b. (Touch the ball for **fine.** Pause two seconds.) Get ready. (Signal.) *Fine.* Yes, **fine.** (Repeat until firm.)
c. (Repeat *b* for **site** and **came.**)

fine

site

came

EXERCISE 5

Short and long vowel words

a. Everybody, read these words again. Remember what you say if there is an ē on the end of a word.
b. (Touch the ball for **sit.** Pause two seconds.) Get ready. (Signal.) *Sit.* Yes, **sit.**
c. (Repeat *b* for **fine** and **cam.**)

sit

fine

cam

(Repeat any troublesome words.)

Individual test

(Call on individual children. Each child reads a different word.)

EXERCISE 5

Read the fast way

a. You're going to read all the words in this column the fast way.

b. (Touch the ball for **fixes.** Pause.) Get ready. (Slash.) *Fixes.*

c. (Repeat step *b* until firm.)

d. (Repeat steps *b* and *c* for each remaining word in the column.)

e. (Repeat the column until the children read all the words in order without making mistakes.)

fixes

don't

hide

slop

time

slope

spent

EXERCISE 6A

Rule for words with long and short vowels

a. (Touch the ball for **tapping.**) Look at this word. (Pause.) Is there only **one p** in this word? (Signal.) *No.*

b. So does the letter **a** say its name? (Signal.) *No.*

• Read this word. (Pause three seconds.) Get ready. (Signal.) *Tapping.*

c. (Touch the ball for **caned.**) Look at this word. (Pause.) Is there only **one n** in this word? (Signal.) *Yes.*

d. So does the letter **a** say its name? (Signal.) *Yes.*

• Read this word. (Pause three seconds.) Get ready. (Signal.) *Caned.*

To Correct

1. The **a** says its name. So the word is **caned.**
   OR
   The **a** does not say its name. So the word is **tapping.**

2. (Return to the first word in the column and present all words in order.) Starting over.

EXERCISE 6B

Children spell, then read

a. First you're going to spell each word. Then you're going to read the word the fast way.

b. (Touch the ball for **tapping.**) Spell it. Get ready. (Tap under each letter as the children say:) *T-A-P-P-I-N-G.*

• Return to the ball.) Read it. Get ready. (Slash.) *Tapping.*

c. (Repeat step *b* for each remaining word in the column.)

d. (Repeat steps *b* and *c* until firm.)

tapping

caned

hid

first

teaches

very

would

Individual test

a. (Call on individual children to read one column of words from the lesson.)

b. (Praise children who read all words with no errors.)

Do not touch small letters.

Get ready to read all the words on this page without making a mistake.

work

EXERCISE 6

Listen, sound out

a. (Point to **work**.) I'll tell you this word. (Pause.) **Work.** What word? (Signal.) *Work.* Yes, **work.**

b. (Touch the ball for **work**.) Sound it out. Get ready. (Quickly touch **w, o, r, k** as the children say:) *wwwooorrrk.*

c. What word? (Signal.) *Work.* Yes, **work.**

d. (Repeat *b* and *c* until firm.)

those

EXERCISE 7

Practice final-e rule

a. (Point to the **o** in **those**.) Look at this letter and remember the rule about the **ē** at the end of the word.

b. (Touch the ball for **those**.) Read this word the fast way. (Pause two seconds.) Get ready. (Signal.) *Those.* Yes, **those.**

c. (Touch the ball for **those**.) Sound it out. Get ready. (Quickly touch **th, o, s** as the children say:) *thththōōōsss.*

d. What word? (Signal.) *Those.* Yes, **those.**

e. (Repeat *b, c,* and *d* until firm.)

here

EXERCISE 8

Practice final-e rule

a. Read this word the fast way. Remember to look at the end of the word.

b. (Touch the ball for **here**. Pause two seconds.) Get ready. (Signal.) *Here.* Yes, **here.**

c. (Repeat *a* and *b* with **take, lake, like,** and **these**.)

take

lake

like

these

rēached

EXERCISE 9

Two-part word

a. (Cover **ed**. Point to **reach**.) Everybody, tell me what this part of the word says. Get ready. (Signal.) *Reach.* Yes, **reach.**

b. (Uncover **ed**. Touch the ball for **reached**.) Now tell me what the whole word says. Get ready. (Signal.) *Reached.* Yes, **reached.**

c. (Repeat exercise until firm.)

inside

EXERCISE 10

Two-part word

a. (Cover **side**. Point to **in**.) Everybody, tell me what this part of the word says. Get ready. (Signal.) *in.* Yes, **in.**

b. (Uncover **side**. Touch the ball for **inside**.) Now tell me what the whole word says. Get ready. (Signal.) *inside.* Yes, **inside.**

c. (Repeat exercise until firm.)

Individual test

(Call on individual children to read a column of words from this lesson. If the column contains only one or two words, direct the child to read additional words from an adjacent column. Praise children who read all words with no errors.)

EXERCISE 3

Words with underlined parts

a. First you're going to read the underlined part of each word in this column. Then you're going to read the whole word.

b. (Touch the ball for **each**.) Read the underlined part. Get ready. (Tap the ball.) ēēē
   • Read the whole word. (Pause.) Get ready. (Slash.) *Each.*

c. (Repeat step *b* until firm.)

d. (Repeat steps *b* and *c* for each remaining word in the column.)

e. (Repeat the column until children read all the words in order without making a mistake.)

each

farm

pouch

cheese

fool

hard

leaves

EXERCISE 4

Words with underlined parts

a. First you're going to read the underlined part of each word in this column. Then you're going to read the whole word.

b. (Touch the ball for **words**.) Read the underlined part. Get ready. (Tap the ball.) *Word.*
   • Read the whole word. (Pause.) Get ready. (Slash.) *Words.*

c. (Repeat step *b* until firm.)

d. (Repeat steps *b* and *c* for each remaining word in the column.)

e. (Repeat the column until children read all the words in order without making a mistake.)

words

before

hopped

hoped

began

planted

canner

STORY 58
EXERCISE 11

First reading—title and three sentences

a. (Pass out Storybook 1.)

b. Everybody, open your reader to page 147.

c. Everybody, touch the title of the story and get ready to read the words in the title.

d. First word. ✔

• Get ready. (Tap.) *The.*

e. (Tap for each remaining word in the title.)

f. Everybody, say the title. (Signal.)
The magic pouch.

g. Yesterday we read part seven. Today we're going to read part eight.

h. Everybody, get ready to read this story.

i. First word. ✔

• Get ready. (Tap.) *What.*

j. Next word. ✔

• Get ready. (Tap.) *Did.*

k. (Repeat *j* for the remaining words in the first three sentences. Have the children reread the first three sentences until firm.)

EXERCISE 12

Remaining sentences and questions

a. I'm going to call on individual children to read a sentence. Everybody, follow along and point to the words. If you hear a mistake, raise your hand.

b. (Call on a child.) Read the next sentence.

c. (Call on another child.)
Read the next sentence.

d. (Repeat *c* for most of the remaining sentences in the story.)

8

the magic pouch

what did the little girl take from the pouch?[1]

could she get the yellow mud from her hands?[2]

could her mother get the yellow mud from her hands?[3]

the girl crIed and crIed. then she said, "mother, I tōld you some lIes.[4] I did not slēep in the grass. I went to the top of the tall mountain. and I did not fInd the pouch on the ground. a funny elf gave it to me."

the girl tōld her mother all about the funny house and the elf.[5]

---

e. (Occasionally have the group read a sentence. Say:) Everybody, read the next sentence. *(Tap for each word in the sentence.)*

f. (After each underlined sentence has been read, present each comprehension question specified below to the entire group.)

[1] Everybody, say that question. (Signal.) *What did the little girl take from the pouch?*

• What's the answer? (Signal.) *Yellow mud.*

[2] Everybody, say that question. (Signal.) *Could she get the yellow mud from her hands?*

• What's the answer? (Signal.) *No.*

[3] Everybody, say that question. (Signal.) *Could her mother get the yellow mud from her hands?*

• What's the answer? (Signal.) *No.*

EXERCISE 13

Second reading—sentences and questions

a. You're going to read the story again. And I'm going to ask more questions.

b. Starting with the first word of the title. ✔

• Get ready. (Tap as the children read the title.)

c. (Call on a child.) Read the first sentence.

To Correct

word-identification errors (**from,** for example)
1. That word is **from.** What word? *From.*
2. Go back to the beginning of the sentence and read the sentence again.

d. (Call on another child.) Read the next sentence.

e. (Repeat *d* for most of the remaining sentences in the story.)

f. (Occasionally have the group read a sentence.)

g. (After each underlined sentence has been read, present each comprehension question specified below to the entire group.)

[4] Raise your hand if you remember the first lie. (Call on a child.) *That she fell asleep in the grass.*

• Raise your hand if you can tell us the second lie. (Call on a child.) *That she found the pouch on the ground.*

[5] Did she tell her the truth? (Signal.) *Yes.*

CAPITAL LETTERS

EXERCISE 1

Reviewing hard capitals

a. These are capital letters that you have seen before. See if you can tell me the letter name of each capital letter on this page.

b. (Point under capital **Q**.) What capital? (Signal.) *Q.*

c. (Repeat step *b* for each remaining capital.)

d. (Repeat steps *b* and *c* until firm.)

Q G R E

B L A H D

READING VOCABULARY

EXERCISE 2

Words beginning with capital letters

a. The words in this column begin with capital letters. First you're going to spell each word. Then you're going to read that word the fast way.

b. (Touch the ball for **If**.) Spell it. Get ready. (Tap under each letter as the children say:) *I-F.*

• (Return to the ball.) Read it. Get ready. (Slash.) *If.*

c. (Repeat step *b* for each remaining word in the column.)

d. (Repeat steps *b* and *c* until firm.)

To Correct
word-identification errors
(**note,** for example)

1. That word is **note.** What word? (Signal.) *Note.*
2. Spell **note.** Get ready. (Tap under each letter.) *N-O-T-E.*
3. What word did you spell? (Signal.) *Note.*
4. (Repeat *2* and *3* until firm.)
5. (Return to the first word in the column and present all words in order.) Starting over.

If

Tim

You

At

And

Hide

Does

and when she looked at her
hands, she saw that they were clean.[6]
her mother said, "where did the mud
go?"

"I don't see it any where," the
girl said. she looked to see if there
was more mud inside the pouch. and
what do you think was inside the
pouch? there were a thousand rocks
of gold.[7] her mother said, "we are
rich. we are very rich."

and the little girl said to herself,
"that pouch is good to me because I
was good. I will keep on doing good
things."[8] and she did. and every time
she was good, she reached in the
pouch and found something good.

no more to come[9]

---

[6] Why did her hands get clean?
(The children respond.)

[7] What was in the pouch? (Signal.)
A thousand rocks of gold.

• Why was the pouch so good to her?
(The children respond.)

[8] Why will she keep on doing good things?
(Signal.) *So the pouch will be good to her.*

[9] Is this the end of the story? (Signal.) *Yes.*

• How do you know? (Signal.)
Because it says "No more to come."

EXERCISE 14

Picture comprehension

a. Look at the picture.
b. (Ask these questions:)
   1. (Point to the rocks of gold.) What has
      come out of the magic pouch? (Signal.)
      Lots of gold.
   2. How does the girl feel about that?
      (The children respond.)
   3. Why was the pouch so good to her?
      (Let the children comment for ten
      seconds. Then comment briefly.)
   4. What would you like the pouch to do for
      you? (Let the children comment for ten
      seconds. Then comment briefly.)

WORKSHEET 58

SUMMARY OF INDEPENDENT ACTIVITY
EXERCISE 15

Introduction to independent activity

a. (Pass out Worksheet 58 to each child.)
b. (Hold up side 1 of your worksheet.)
Everybody, you're going to do this
worksheet on your own. (Tell the children
when they will work the items.)

• Let's go over the things you're going to do.

Story items

(Point to the story-items exercise.) Everybody,
remember to write your answers in the blanks.

Following instructions

a. (Touch the sentence in the box on side 2.)
b. Everybody, first you're going to read the
sentence in the box. Then you're going to
read the instructions below the box and do
what the instructions tell you to do.

Reading comprehension

(Point to the story.) You're going to read this
story and then do the items. Remember to
write the answers in the blanks.

Following instructions

(Point to the following-instructions exercise.)
Everybody, you're going to read the
instructions. Then you're going to do what the
instructions tell you to do.

END OF LESSON 58

So Sid and the boss went to the shop.[2] The boss dropped her cane into the can. She went to the table and picked up a note. Then she said, "Did you send out ten pine trees?"

"Pine trees?" Sid asked. "I sent out pin trees."

That made the boss mad.[3] She walked around the room. Then she said, "I hope that you did a better job with the other notes."

She picked up another note. Then she said, "Did you fix the window pane?"

"Window pane?" Sid asked. "I made a window pan."⑤

The boss got her cane from the can. She walked around the room. She yelled and yelled.[4] Then she said, "I hope you sent a cone to Sam's tree farm."[5]

"No," Sid said. "I sent a con from the jail."

The boss sat down on the floor. "This is a fine mess," she said. Then she asked, "Did you tape the oak tree?"[6]

"No," Sid said. "I tapped the oak tree." Sid was very, very sad. He wanted to do a good job, but he didn't read what the notes said.[7]

More to come[8]

[2] Why are they going to the shop? **(The children respond.)**
- Yes, to look at the notes and see if Sid did what the notes told him to do.

[3] What did Sid do that made the boss mad? **(Signal.)** *Sent out pin trees.*

[4] What did Sid do that made the boss yell? **(Signal.)** *Made a window pan.*

[5] What did Sid send to the tree farm? **(Signal.)** *A con.*

[6] What did Sid do to the oak tree? **(Signal.)** *Tapped it.*

[7] Did he want to do a good job? **(Signal.)** *Yes.*
- Why didn't he do a good job? **(Signal.)** *He didn't read what the notes said.*

[8] How do you think the story will end next time? **(The children respond.)** I think you'll be surprised.

EXERCISE 9

Picture comprehension

a. What do you think you'll see in the picture? **(The children respond.)**

b. Turn the page and look at the picture.

c. (Ask these questions:)

1. What's the boss holding in her hand? **(Signal.)** *A note.*
- What does the note say? **(Signal.)** *Fix the window pane.*
- Does the boss look happy? **(Signal.)** *No.*

2. What's that thing in the window? **(Signal.)** *A pan.*
- What was Sid supposed to put in the window? **(Signal.)** *A pane.*

3. How does Sid feel? **(Signal.)** *Sad.*

EXERCISE 10

Summary of independent activities

a. (Pass out Worksheet 93 to each child.)

b. Everybody, now you'll do your worksheet. Remember to do all parts of the worksheet and to read all the parts carefully.

END OF LESSON 93

READING VOCABULARY

Get ready to read all the words on this page without making a mistake.

elephant

EXERCISE 1

Listen, sound out with me

a. (Point to **elephant**.) I'll tell you this word. (Pause.) **Elephant.** What word? (Signal.) *Elephant.* Yes, **elephant.**

b. (Touch the ball for **elephant**.) Sound it out with me. Get ready. (Quickly touch each sound as you and the children say:) *eeellleeephaaannnt.*

c. What word? (Signal.) *Elephant.* Yes, **elephant.**

d. (Repeat *b* and *c* until firm.)

tall

EXERCISE 2

al word

a. (Point to **al** in **tall**.) What do these letters say? (Signal.) *All.* Yes, **all.**

b. (Touch the ball for **tall**.) Read this word the fast way. Get ready. (Signal.) *Tall.* Yes, **tall.**

ground

EXERCISE 3

ou word

a. (Touch the ball for **ground**.) Read this word the fast way. (Pause two seconds.) Get ready. (Signal.) *Ground.* Yes, **ground.**

b. (Point to **ou** in **ground**.) Everybody, what do these letters say? (Signal.) *ou.* Yes, **ou.**

c. (Touch the ball for **ground**.) Sound it out. Get ready. (Quickly touch **g, r, ou, n, d** as the children say:) *grrrounnnd.*

d. What word? (Signal.) *Ground.* Yes, **ground.**

e. (Repeat *c* and *d* until firm.)

cart

EXERCISE 4

ar word

a. (Touch the ball for **cart**.) Read this word the fast way. (Pause two seconds.) Get ready. (Signal.) *Cart.* Yes, **cart.**

b. (Point to **ar** in **cart**.) Everybody, what do these letters say? (Signal.) *Are.* Yes, **are.**

c. (Touch the ball for **cart**.) Sound it out. Get ready. (Quickly touch **c, ar, t** as the children say:) *Cart.*

d. What word? (Signal.) *Cart.* Yes, **cart.**

e. (Repeat *c* and *d* until firm.)

(Repeat any troublesome words.)

Individual test

(Call on individual children. Each child reads a different word.)

pine

pin

EXERCISE 5

Practice final-e rule

a. (Point to **pine** and **pin**.) You're going to say the name ī when you read one of these words.

b. (Point to **pine**.) Are you going to say the name ī when you read this word? (Signal.) *Yes.*

c. (Point to **pin**.) Are you going to say the name ī when you read this word? (Signal.) *No.*

To Correct

1. You say the name ī in the word with the ē on the end.
2. (Point to the word.) Is there an ē on the end of this word? (Signal.) (The children respond.)
3. So are you going to say the name ī when you read this word? (Signal.) (The children respond.)
4. (Repeat *b* and *c*.)

d. (Repeat *b* and *c* until firm.)

e. Read these words the fast way.

f. (Touch the ball for **pine**. Pause two seconds.) Get ready. (Signal.) *Pine.* Yes, **pine.**

g. (Touch the ball for **pin**. Pause two seconds.) Get ready. (Signal.) *Pin.* Yes, **pin.**

h. (Repeat *f* and *g* until firm.)

STORYBOOK

EXERCISE 6

Read the item

a. (Pass out Storybook 2.)

b. Open your reader to page 28. Get ready to read the item.

c. Finger under the first word of the item. ✔

• Get ready. (Tap.) *When.*

d. Next word. (Pause.) Get ready. (Tap.) *The.*

e. (Repeat step *d* for the remaining words in the item.)

f. (Repeat steps *c* through *e* until the item is firm.)

g. Everybody, say that item. (Pause. Signal.) *When the teacher says "Cone," say "Con."*

h. Again. (Repeat step *g* until firm.)

i. What are you going to say when I say "**Cone**"? (Signal.) *Con.*

• When are you going to say "**Con**"? (Signal.) *When the teacher says "Cone."*

To Correct

(Have the children read the item aloud. Then repeat the questions.)

EXERCISE 7

Play the game

a. Read the item to yourself and think about what you're going to do and when you're going to do it. Raise your hand when you're ready.

b. (After the children raise their hands, say:) Get ready to play the game.

c. My turn. (Pause.) **Cone.** (Signal.) (The children are to say *Con* immediately.)

To Correct

(Have the children read the item aloud. Then play the game again.)

The Boss Gets Mad[1]

Sid was sad and the boss was mad. The boss yelled at Sid for planting seeds in the slop. When the boss was tired of yelling, she said, "Let's go to the shop and see how well you did the other things the notes told you to do."

STORY 93

EXERCISE 8

Reading—decoding

a. Everybody, get ready to read the story.

b. Remember, if the group reads all the way to the red 5 without making more than five errors, we can go on.

c. Everybody, touch the title of the story. ✔

d. If you hear a mistake, raise your hand. Remember, children who do not have their place lose their turn. (Call on individual children to read two or three sentences. Do not ask comprehension questions. Tally all errors.)

To Correct

word-identification errors (**from,** for example)

1. That word is **from.** What word? *From.*

2. Go back to the beginning of the sentence and read the sentence again.

e. (If the children make more than five errors: when they reach the 5, return to the beginning of the story and have the children reread to the 5. Do not ask comprehension questions. Repeat step *e* until firm, and then go on to step *f.*)

f. (If the children read to the number 5 without making more than five errors: read the story to the children from the beginning to the 5. Ask the specified comprehension questions. When you reach the 5, call on individual children to continue reading the story. Have each child read two or three sentences.

Ask the specified comprehension questions.)

[1] What's the title of this story? (Signal.) *The boss gets mad.*

Get ready to read all the words on this page without making a mistake.

To Correct

1. (Touch the ball for the word the children missed.) Is there an ē on the end of this word? (Signal.) (The children respond.)
2. (Point to the first vowel in the word.) So tell me what you say for this letter. (Signal.) (The children respond.)
3. (Touch the ball for the word.) Sound it out. Get ready. (Touch all sounds except the final **e**, if there is one, as the children sound out the word.)
4. What word? (Signal.) (The children respond.)
5. (Return to the first word in the column. Present all the words in order until firm.)

EXERCISE 6

Long vowel words

a. (Point to the words in this column.) Read these words the fast way.
b. (Touch the ball for **made.** Pause two seconds.) Get ready. (Signal.) *Made.* Yes, **made.**
• (Repeat until firm.)
c. (Repeat *b* for **fine.**)

made

fine

EXERCISE 7

Short vowel words

a. (Point to the words in this column.) Read these words the fast way.
b. (Touch the ball for **mad.** Pause two seconds.) Get ready. (Signal.) *Mad.* Yes, **mad.**
• (Repeat until firm.)
c. (Repeat *b* for **fin.**)

mad

fin

EXERCISE 8

Short and long vowel words

a. Everybody, read these words again. Remember what you say if there is an ē on the end of a word.
b. (Touch the ball for **fine.** Pause two seconds.) Get ready. (Signal.) *Fine.* Yes, **fine.**
c. (Repeat *b* for **made.**)

fine

made

(Repeat any troublesome words.)

Individual test

(Call on individual children. Each child reads a different word.)

EXERCISE 4

Words with underlined parts

a. First you're going to read the underlined part of each word in this column. Then you're going to read the whole word.

b. (Touch the ball for **taped.**) Read the underlined part. Get ready. (Tap the ball.) *Tape.*

• Read the whole word. (Pause.) Get ready. (Slash.) *Taped.*

c. (Repeat step *b* until firm.)

d. (Repeat steps *b* and *c* for each remaining word in the column.)

e. (Repeat the column until children read all the words in order without making a mistake.)

To Correct

word-identification errors
(let, for example)

1. That word is **let.** What word? (Signal.) *Let.*
2. Spell **let.** Get ready. (Tap under each letter.) *L-E-T.*
3. What word did you spell? (Signal.) *Let.*
4. (Repeat 2 and 3 until firm.)
5. (Return to the first word in the column and present all words in order.) Starting over.

taped

pined

tapped

pinned

tired

hopped

yelling

EXERCISE 5

Words with underlined parts

a. First you're going to read the underlined part of each word in this column. Then you're going to read the whole word.

b. (Touch the ball for **planting.**) Read the underlined part. Get ready. (Tap the ball.) *ing.*

• Read the whole word. (Pause.) Get ready. (Slash.) *Planting.*

c. (Repeat step *b* until firm.)

d. (Repeat steps *b* and *c* for each remaining word in the column.)

e. (Repeat the column until children read all the words in order without making a mistake.)

planting

every

those

where

sound

these

when

Individual test

a. (Call on individual children to read one column of words from the lesson.)

b. (Praise children who read all words with no errors.)

Get ready to read all the words on this page without making a mistake.

here

EXERCISE 9

Practice final-e rule

a. Read this word the fast way. Remember to look at the end of the word.

b. (Touch the ball for **here.** Pause two seconds.) Get ready. (Signal.) *Here.* Yes, **here.**

c. (Repeat *a* and *b* with **take, lake, these, more, sore, came, smile,** and **like.**)

take

lake

these

more

sore

came

smile

like

Individual test

(Call on individual children to read a column of words from this lesson. If the column contains only one or two words, direct the child to read additional words from an adjacent column.)

fix

EXERCISE 10

Sound out first

a. (Touch the ball for **fix.**) Sound it out. Get ready. (Quickly touch **f, i, x** as the children say:) *fffiiix.*

b. What word? (Signal.) *Fix.* Yes, **fix.**

c. (Repeat exercise until firm.)

many

EXERCISE 11

Read the fast way

a. Read this word the fast way.

b. (Touch the ball for **many.** Pause two seconds.) Get ready. (Signal.) *Many.* Yes, **many.**

woke

EXERCISE 12

Practice final-e rule

a. (Point to the **o** in **woke.**) Look at this letter and remember the rule about the **ē** at the end of the word.

b. (Touch the ball for **woke.**) Read this word the fast way. (Pause two seconds.) Get ready. (Signal.) *Woke.* Yes, **woke.**

c. (Touch the ball for **woke.**) Sound it out. Get ready. (Quickly touch **w, o, k** as the children say:) *wwwōōōk.*

d. What word? (Signal.) *Woke.* Yes, **woke.**

e. (Repeat *b, c,* and *d* until firm.)

READING VOCABULARY

EXERCISE 2

Words beginning with capital letters

a. The words in this column begin with capital letters. First you're going to spell each word. Then you're going to read that word the fast way.

b. (Touch the ball for **Let.**) Spell it. Get ready. (Tap under each letter as the children say:) *L-E-T.*

• (Return to the ball.) Read it. Get ready. (Slash.) *Let.*

c. (Repeat step *b* for each remaining word in the column.)

d. (Repeat steps *b* and *c* until firm.)

To Correct

word-identification errors (let, for example)

1. That word is **let.** What word? (Signal.) *Let.*
2. Spell **let.** Get ready. (Tap under each letter.) *L-e-t.*
3. What word did you spell? (Signal.) *Let.*
4. (Repeat 2 and 3 until firm.)
5. (Return to the first word in the column and present all words in order.) Starting over.

Let

Did

Right

Because

Again

There

Hope

EXERCISE 3

Teacher reads the words in red

a. I'll read each word in red. Then you'll spell each word.

b. (Touch the ball for **swung.**) My turn. (Slash as you say:) Swung. What word? (Signal.) *Swung.*

c. (Return to the ball.) Spell it. Get ready.(Tap under each letter as the children say:) *S-W-U-N-G.*

• What word did you spell? (Signal.) *Swung.*

d. (Repeat steps *b* and *c* for each word in red.)

e. Your turn to read all the words in this column.

f. (Touch the ball for **swung.** Pause.) Get ready. (Slash.) *Swung.*

g. (Repeat step *f* for each remaining word in the column.)

h. (Repeat steps *f* and *g* until firm.)

swung

very

jail

cone

con

fine

fin

STORYBOOK

STORY 59

EXERCISE 13

First reading—title and three sentences

a. (Pass out Storybook 1.)

b. Everybody, open your reader to page 150.

c. Everybody, touch the title of the story and get ready to read the words in the title.

d. First word. ✔

• Get ready. (Tap.) *The.*

e. (Tap for each remaining word in the title.)

f. Everybody, say the title. (Signal.)
The bugs and the elephant.

g. Everybody, get ready to read this story.

h. First word. ✔

• Get ready. (Tap.) *Five.*

i. Next word. ✔

• Get ready. (Tap.) *Elephants.*

j. (Repeat *i* for the remaining words in the first three sentences. Have the children reread the first three sentences until firm.)

EXERCISE 14

Remaining sentences

a. I'm going to call on individual children to read a sentence. Everybody, follow along and point to the words. If you hear a mistake, raise your hand.

b. (Call on a child.) Read the next sentence.

To Correct
word-identification errors (**from,** for example)
1. That word is **from.** What word? *From.*
2. Go back to the beginning of the sentence and read the sentence again.

c. (Call on another child.) Read the next sentence.

d. (Repeat *c* for most of the remaining sentences in the story.)

e. (Occasionally have the group read a sentence. When the group is to read, say:) Everybody, read the next sentence. (Tap for each word in the sentence.)

---

the bugs and the elephant [1]

five elephants went for a walk.

one elephant was very tall. that

elephant said, "I must sit and rest.

I will look for a spot of ground

where I can sit." [2]

so she looked for a good site to

sit on the ground. at last she came to

a fine site that was in the sun. she

said, "this spot is fine." but a flȳ

was sitting in that spot. [3] the flȳ said,

"go awāy, elephant. this is mȳ spot." [4]

the elephant said, "hō, hō. you

cannot stop me if I want to sit in

the sun."

so the elephant sat down. that

flȳ got out of her wāy. then the

elephant said, "this is a fine site.

it is fun here."

the flȳ said, "you took mȳ spot.

so I will fix you." [5]

EXERCISE 15

Second reading—sentences and questions

a. You're going to read the story again. This time I'm going to ask questions.

b. Starting with the first word of the title. ✔

• Get ready. (Tap as the children read the title.)

c. (Call on a child.) Read the first sentence.

To Correct
word-identification errors (**from,** for example)
1. That word is **from.** What word? *From.*
2. Go back to the beginning of the sentence and read the sentence again.

d. (Call on another child.) Read the next sentence.

e. (Repeat *d* for most of the remaining sentences in the story.)

f. (Occasionally have the group read a sentence.)

g. (After each underlined sentence has been read, present each comprehension question specified below to the entire group.)

[1] What is this story about? (Signal.) *The bugs and the elephant.*

[2] Why was she looking for a spot of ground? (Signal.) *She wanted to sit.*

[3] Who was sitting there? (Signal.) *A fly.*

• What is a fly? (The children respond.)

• Yes, a fly is a bug.

[4] Who is talking? (Signal.) *The fly.*

• Who is the fly talking to? (Signal.) *The elephant.*

• What does he want the elephant to do? (Signal.) *Go away.*

[5] Why did the fly say that? (Signal.) *Because the elephant took his spot.*

CAPITAL LETTERS
EXERCISE 1

Reviewing hard capitals

a. These are capital letters that you have seen before. See if you can tell me the letter name of each capital letter on this page.

b. (Point under capital **D.**) What capital? (Signal.) *D.*

c. (Repeat step *b* for each remaining capital.)

d. (Repeat steps *b* and *c* until firm.)

D B H L R Q G A E

the fl̄y went awāy and the elephant went to slēep.[6]

when the elephant woke up, she saw that there were many bugs on the ground.[7] those bugs were all around her.

the elephant said, "how did these bugs get here?"

the little fl̄y said, "these bugs are with me. they are here to take you awāy."[8]

and they did. they picked up the elephant and took her to the lake. then they dropped her in the lake.

now the fl̄y is sittīng in the sun and the elephant is sittīng in the lake. the fl̄y thinks it is fun to sit in the sun. and the elephant thinks it is more fun to sit in the lake.[9]

this is the end.

[6] What did the elephant do? (Signal.)
Went to sleep.

[7] What did she see when she woke up?
(The children respond.)

[8] What are the bugs going to do? (Signal.)
Take the elephant away.

- Are bugs usually bigger than elephants?
(Signal.) *No.*
Those sure must be big monster bugs.

[9] Where did the elephant end up?
(Signal.) *In the lake.*

- Did she like it better in the sun or in the lake? (Signal.) *In the lake.*

EXERCISE 16

Picture comprehension

a. Look at the picture.

b. (Ask these questions:)

1. Tell me about those bugs.
(The children respond.)
Yes, they sure are big monster bugs.

2. (Point to the falling elephant.) What are they doing to that elephant? (Signal.)
Dropping her in the lake.

3. Why are they doing that?
(Let the children comment for ten seconds. Then comment briefly.)

4. Tell me some more things you see in this picture. (The children respond.)

SUMMARY OF INDEPENDENT ACTIVITY
EXERCISE 17

Introduction to independent activity

a. (Pass out Worksheet 59 to each child.)

b. (Hold up side 1 of your worksheet.)
Everybody, you're going to do this worksheet on your own. (Tell the children when they will work the items.)

- Let's go over the things you're going to do.

Story items

(Point to the story-items exercise.) Everybody, remember to write your answers in the blanks.

Following instructions

a. (Touch the sentence in the box on side 2.)

b. Everybody, first you're going to read the sentence in the box. Then you're going to read the instructions below the box and do what the instructions tell you to do.

Reading comprehension

(Point to the story.) You're going to read this story and then do the items. Remember to write the answers in the blanks.

Following instructions

(Point to the following-instructions exercise.) Everybody, you're going to read the instructions. Then you're going to do what the instructions tell you to do.

END OF LESSON 59

Now Sid went back to the pile of notes on the table. He picked up a note that said, "Plant seeds on the slope."[2]There was a slope in back of the shop. That is where the boss planted a lot of little plants.[3]But Sid did not read the note the right way. Here is what Sid said, "Plant seeds in the slop."[4]

Then he said, "These notes are very funny. But I will do what they say."⑤ So Sid grabbed some seeds and went outside. "Where is the slop?" he asked. He looked here and there. Then he saw a big pile of mud near the road. He said, "That must be the slop." So Sid dumped seeds in the mud.[5]

When he was near the side of the shop, a truck stopped in back of the shop. The boss got out of the truck.[6]She was walking with her cane. The boss said, "What are you doing out here?"

Sid said, "I just planted seeds in the slop."

The boss looked at Sid. Then the boss asked, "What did you do?"

Sid told her. The boss got mad.[7]"Not in the slop," the boss yelled. "On the slope. Plant the seeds on the slope."

Sid felt very sad.

More to come

[2] What did the note say? (Signal.)
Plant seeds on the slope.
• Remember that. What is a slope?
(The children respond.) Yes, a little hill.
[3] What did the boss do on the slope? (Signal.)
Planted little plants.
[4] What did Sid say? (Signal.)
Plant seeds in the slop.
• Oh, oh. Is that what the note said?
(Signal.) *No.*
• What did the note say? (Signal.)
Plant seeds on the slope.
[5] Where did he dump the seeds? (Signal.)
In the mud. Yes, in the slop pile of mud.
[6] Who came back to the shop?
(Signal.) *The boss.*
• Will she be proud of what Sid did?
(Signal.) *No.*
[7] Why did she get mad? (The children respond.)

EXERCISE 10

Picture comprehension

a. Look at the picture.
b. (Ask these questions:)
  1. Show me the note. (The children respond.)
  • Read what it says.
    (Signal.) *Plant seeds on the slope.*
  • That's where he should plant seeds.
  2. Show me the slop. (The children respond.)
  • What is Sid putting in the slop?
    (Signal.) *Seeds.*
  3. (Point to the boss.) Who is that woman?
    (Signal.) *Sid's boss.*
  • Why is she walking with a cane?
    (The children respond.)

EXERCISE 11

Summary of independent activities

a. (Pass out Worksheet 92 to each child.)
b. Everybody, now you'll do your worksheet. Remember to do all parts of the worksheet and to read all the parts carefully.

END OF LESSON 92

READING VOCABULARY

Get ready to read all the words on this page without making a mistake.

EXERCISE 1

ar word

a. (Touch the ball for **park.**) Read this word the fast way. (Pause two seconds.) Get ready. (Signal.) *Park.* Yes, **park.**

b. (Point to **ar** in **park.**) Everybody, what do these letters say? (Signal.) *Are.* Yes, **are.**

c. (Touch the ball for **park.**) Sound it out. Get ready. (Quickly touch **p, ar, k** as the children say:) *park.*

d. What word? (Signal.) *Park.* Yes, **park.**

e. (Repeat *c* and *d* until firm.)

EXERCISE 2

al word

a. (Point to **al** in **ball.**) What do these letters say? (Signal.) *All.* Yes, **all.**

b. (Touch the ball for **ball.**) Read this word the fast way. Get ready. (Signal.) *Ball.* Yes, **ball.**

EXERCISE 3

ou word

a. (Point to **ou** in **sound.**) What do these letters say? (Signal.) *ou.* Yes, **ou.**

b. (Touch the ball for **sound.**) Read this word the fast way. Get ready. (Signal.) *Sound.* Yes, **sound.**

park

ball

sound

> (Repeat any troublesome words.)

Individual test

(Call on individual children. Each child reads a different word.)

at

ate

EXERCISE 4

Practice final-e rule

a. (Point to **at** and **ate.**) You're going to say the name ā when you read one of these words.

b. (Point to **at.**) Are you going to say the name ā when you read this word? (Signal.) *No.*

c. (Point to **ate.**) Are you going to say the name ā when you read this word? (Signal.) *Yes.*

d. (Repeat *b* and *c* until firm.)

e. Read these words the fast way.

f. (Touch the ball for **at.** Pause two seconds.) Get ready. (Signal.) *At.* Yes, **at.**

g. (Touch the ball for **ate.** Pause two seconds.) Get ready. (Signal.) *Ate.* Yes, **ate.**

h. (Repeat *f* and *g* until firm.)

STORYBOOK

READ THE ITEMS 92
EXERCISE 7
Read the item

a. (Pass out Storybook 2.)

b. Open your reader to page 25. Get ready to read the item.

c. Finger under the first word of the item. ✔

• Get ready. (Tap.) *When.*

d. Next word. (Pause.) Get ready. (Tap.) *The.*

e. (Repeat step *d* for the remaining words in the item.)

f. (Repeat steps *c* through *e* until the item is firm.)

g. Everybody, say that item. (Pause. Signal.) *When the teacher says "Tap," say "Tape."*

h. Again. (Repeat step *g* until firm.)

i. What are you going to say when I say "**Tap**"? (Signal.) *Tape.*

• When are you going to say "**Tape**"? (Signal.) *When the teacher says "Tap."*

To Correct
(Have the children read the item aloud. Then repeat the questions.)

EXERCISE 8
Play the game

a. Read the item to yourself and think about what you're going to do and when you're going to do it. Raise your hand when you're ready.

b. (After the children raise their hands, say:) Get ready to play the game.

c. My turn. (Pause.) **Tap.** (Signal.) (The children are to say *Tape* immediately.)

To Correct
(Have the children read the item aloud. Then play the game again.)

Sid Plants Seeds in Slop[1]

Sid was reading notes that were on the table. But he was not reading these notes the right way. A note told him to send a cone to a tree farm. But Sid sent a con to the tree farm. Before that he tapped the oak tree near the door. But the note did not tell him to tap the tree. It told him to tape that tree.

STORY 92
EXERCISE 9
Reading—decoding

a. Everybody, get ready to read the story.

b. Remember, if the group reads all the way to the red 5 without making more than five errors, we can go on.

c. Everybody, touch the title of the story. ✔

d. If you hear a mistake, raise your hand. Remember, children who do not have their place lose their turn. (Call on individual children to read two or three sentences. Do not ask comprehension questions. Tally all errors.)

To Correct
word-identification errors (**from,** for example)
1. That word is **from.** What word? *From.*
2. Go back to the beginning of the sentence and read the sentence again.

e. (If the children make more than five errors: when they reach the 5, return to the beginning of the story and have the children reread to the 5. Do not ask comprehension questions. Repeat step *e* until firm, and then go on to step *f*.)

f. (If the children read to the number 5 without making more than five errors: read the story to the children from the beginning to the 5. Ask the specified comprehension questions. When you reach the 5, call on individual children to continue reading the story. Have each child read two or three sentences. Ask the specified comprehension questions.)

[1] What is Sid going to do? (Signal.) *Plant seeds in slop.*

• Yes, a pile of slop is a pile of mud.

Get ready to read all the words on this page without making a mistake.

To Correct

1. (Touch the ball for the word the children missed.) Is there an ē on the end of this word? (Signal.) (The children respond.)
2. (Point to the first vowel in the word.) So tell me what you say for this letter. (Signal.) (The children respond.)
3. (Touch the ball for the word.) Sound it out. Get ready. (Touch all sounds except the final **e**, if there is one, as the children sound out the word.)
4. What word? (Signal.) (The children respond.)
5. (Return to the first word in the column. Present all the words in order until firm.)

EXERCISE 5

Short vowel words

a. (Point to the words in this column.) Read these words the fast way.
b. (Touch the ball for **mad**. Pause two seconds.) Get ready. (Signal.) *Mad.* Yes, **mad.** (Repeat until firm.)
c. (Repeat *b* for **cap, can,** and **pan.**)

mad
cap
can
pan

EXERCISE 6

Long vowel words

a. (Point to the words in this column.) Read these words the fast way.
b. (Touch the ball for **made**. Pause two seconds.) Get ready. (Signal.) *Made.* Yes, **made.**
c. (Repeat *b* for **cape, cane,** and **pane.**)

made
cape
cane
pane

EXERCISE 7

Short and long vowel words

a. Everybody, read these words again. Remember what you say if there is an ē on the end of a word.
b. (Touch the ball for **cane.** Pause two seconds.) Get ready. (Signal.) *Cane.* Yes, **cane.**
c. (Repeat *b* for **can** and **made.**)

cane
can
made

(Repeat any troublesome words.)

Individual test

(Call on individual children. Each child reads a different word.)

EXERCISE 5

Words with underlined parts

a. First you're going to read the underlined part of each word in this column. Then you're going to read the whole word.

b. (Touch the ball for **notes.**) Read the underlined part. Get ready. (Tap the ball.) *Note.*

• Read the whole word. (Pause.) Get ready. (Slash.) *Notes.*

c. (Repeat step *b* until firm.)

d. (Repeat steps *b* and *c* for each remaining word in the column.)

e. (Repeat the column until children read all the words in order without making a mistake.)

To Correct

word-identification errors (walking, for example)

1. That word is **walking.** What word? (Signal.) *Walking.*
2. Spell **walking.** Get ready. (Tap under each letter.) *W-A-L-K-I-N-G.*
3. What word did you spell? (Signal.) *Walking.*
4. (Repeat *2* and *3* until firm.)
5. (Return to the first word in the column and present all words in order.) Starting over.

notes

noted

tapped

planted

plants

dumped

grabbed

EXERCISE 6

Words with underlined parts

a. First you're going to read the underlined part of each word in this column. Then you're going to read the whole word.

b. (Touch the ball for **outside.**) Read the underlined part. Get ready. (Tap the ball.) *ou.*

• Read the whole word. (Pause.) Get ready. (Slash.) *Outside.*

c. (Repeat step *b* until firm.)

d. (Repeat steps *b* and *c* for each remaining word in the column.)

e. (Repeat the column until children read all the words in order without making a mistake.)

outside

swing

these

part

tossed

where

proud

Individual test

a. (Call on individual children to read one column of words from the lesson.)

b. (Praise children who read all words with no errors.)

Get ready to read all the words on this page without making a mistake.

robber

EXERCISE 8

Two-part word

a. (Cover **er.** Point to **robb.**) Everybody, tell me what this part of the word says. Get ready. (Signal.) *Rob.* Yes, **rob.**

b. (Uncover **er.** Touch the ball for **robber.**) Now tell me what the whole word says. Get ready. (Signal.) *Robber.* Yes, **robber.**

c. (Repeat exercise until firm.)

running

EXERCISE 9

Two-part word

a. (Cover **ing.** Point to **runn.**) Everybody, tell me what this part of the word says. Get ready. (Signal.) *Run.* Yes, **run.**

b. (Uncover **ing.** Touch the ball for **running.**) Now tell me what the whole word says. Get ready. (Signal.) *Running.* Yes, **running.**

c. (Repeat exercise until firm.)

smile

EXERCISE 10

Practice final-e rule

a. Read this word the fast way. Remember to look at the end of the word.

b. (Touch the ball for **smile.** Pause two seconds.) Get ready. (Signal.) *Smile.* Yes, **smile.**

c. (Touch the ball for **smile.**) Sound it out. Get ready. (Quickly touch **s, m, i, l** as the children say:) *sssmmmiiilll.*

d. What word? (Signal.) *Smile.* Yes, **smile.**

e. (Repeat *b* through *d* until firm.)

EXERCISE 11

Read the fast way

a. Read these words the fast way.

b. (Touch the ball for **smiled.** Pause two seconds.) Get ready. (Signal.) *Smiled.* Yes, **smiled.**

c. (Repeat *b* for **more, like, liked, those,** and **here.**)

smiled

more

like

liked

those

here

(Repeat any troublesome words.)

Individual test

(Call on individual children. Each child reads a different word.)

EXERCISE 3

Teacher reads the words in red

a. I'll read each word in red. Then you'll spell each word.

b. (Touch the ball for **right.**) My turn. (Slash as you say:) Right. What word? (Signal.) *Right.*

c. (Return to the ball.) Spell it. Get ready. (Tap under each letter as the children say:) *R-I-G-H-T.*

• What word did you spell? (Signal.) *Right.*

d. (Repeat steps *b* and *c* for each word in red.)

e. Your turn to read all the words in this column.

f. (Touch the ball for **right.** Pause.) Get ready. (Slash.) *Right.*

g. (Repeat step *f* for each remaining word in the column.)

h. (Repeat steps *f* and *g* until firm.)

right

walking

jail

side

slope

felt

con

EXERCISE 4A

Rule for words with long and short vowels

a. (Touch the ball for **canned.**) Look at this word. (Pause.) Is there only **one n** in this word? (Signal.) *No.*

b. So does the letter **a** say its name? (Signal.) *No.*

• Read this word. (Pause three seconds.) Get ready. (Signal.) *Canned.*

c. (Touch the ball for **taped.**) Look at this word. (Pause.) Is there only **one p** in this word? (Signal.) *Yes.*

d. So does the letter **a** say its name? *(Signal.) Yes.*

• Read this word. (Pause three seconds.) Get ready. (Signal.) *Taped.*

To Correct

1. The **a** says its name. So the word is **taped.**

OR

The **a** does not say its name. So the word is **canned.**

2. (Return to the first word in the column and present all words in order.) Starting over.

EXERCISE 4B

Read the fast way

a. You're going to read all the words in this column the fast way.

b. (Touch the ball for **canned.** Pause.) Get ready. (Slash.) *Canned.*

c. (Repeat step *b* until firm.)

d. (Repeat steps *b* and *c* for each remaining word in the column.)

e. (Repeat the column until the children read all the words in order without making mistakes.)

canned

taped

slop

funny

pile

cone

picked

Do not touch small letters.

Get ready to read all the words on this page without making a mistake.

kite

EXERCISE 12

Practice final-e rule

a. (Point to the **i** in **kite**.) Look at this letter and remember the rule about the ē at the end of the word.

b. (Touch the ball for **kite**.) Read this word the fast way. (Pause two seconds.) Get ready. (Signal.) *Kite.* Yes, **kite**.

c. (Touch the ball for **kite**.) Sound it out. Get ready. (Quickly touch **k, i, t** as the children say:) *kīīīt.*

d. What word? (Signal.) *Kite.* Yes, **kite**.

e. (Repeat *b, c,* and *d* until firm.)

kit

EXERCISE 13

Sound out first

a. (Touch the ball for **kit**.) Sound it out. Get ready. (Quickly touch **k, i, t** as the children say:) *kiiit.*

b. What word? (Signal.) *Kit.* Yes, **kit**.

c. (Repeat exercise until firm.)

stēal

EXERCISE 14

Sound out first

a. (Touch the ball for **steal**.) Sound it out. Get ready. (Quickly touch **s, t, ē, l** as the children say:) *ssstēēēlll.*

b. What word? (Signal.) *Steal.* Yes, **steal**.

c. (Repeat exercise until firm.)

EXERCISE 15

Read the fast way

a. Read these words the fast way.

b. (Touch the ball for **plāying.** Pause two seconds.) Get ready. (Signal.) *Playing.* Yes, **playing**.

c. (Repeat *b* for **must**.)

plāying

must

Individual test

(Call on individual children to read a column of words from this lesson. If the column contains only one or two words, direct the child to read additional words from an adjacent column.)

STORY 60
EXERCISE 16

First reading—title and three sentences

a. (Pass out Storybook 1.)

b. Everybody, open your reader to page 153.

c. Everybody, touch the title of the story and get ready to read the words in the title.

d. First word. ✔

• Get ready. (Tap.) *The.*

e. (Tap for each remaining word in the title.)

f. Everybody, say the title. (Signal.) *The pet goat.*

CAPITAL LETTERS

EXERCISE 1

Reviewing hard capitals

a. These are capital letters that you have seen before. See if you can tell me the letter name of each capital letter in this row.

b. (Point under capital **H.**) What capital? (Signal.) *H.*

c. (Repeat step *b* for each remaining capital.)

d. (Repeat steps *b* and *c* until firm.)

H L G B

READING VOCABULARY

EXERCISE 2

Words beginning with capital letters

a. The words in this column begin with capital letters. First you're going to spell each word. Then you're going to read that word the fast way.

b. (Touch the ball for **He.**) Spell it. Get ready. (Tap under each letter as the children say:) *H-E.*

• Return to the ball.) Read it. Get ready. (Slash.) *He.*

c. (Repeat step *b* for each remaining word in the column.)

d. (Repeat steps *b* and *c* until firm.)

To Correct

word-identification errors (**walking,** for example)

1. That word is **walking.** What word? (Signal.) *Walking.*
2. Spell **walking.** Get ready. (Tap under each letter.) *W-A-L-K-I-N-G.*
3. What word did you spell? (Signal.) *Walking.*
4. (Repeat 2 and 3 until firm.)
5. (Return to the first word in the column and present all words in order.) Starting over.

He

Before

But

As

Have

Do

Each

g. Everybody, get ready to read this story.

h. First word. ✔
- Get ready. (Tap.) *A.*

i. Next word. ✔
- Get ready. (Tap.) *Girl.*

j. (Repeat *i* for the remaining words in the first three sentences. Have the children reread the first three sentences until firm.)

EXERCISE 17

Remaining sentences

a. I'm going to call on individual children to read a sentence. Everybody, follow along and point to the words. If you hear a mistake, raise your hand.

b. (Call on a child.) Read the next sentence.

To Correct

word-identification errors (**from,** for example)
1. That word is **from.** What word? *From.*
2. Go back to the beginning of the sentence and read the sentence again.

c. (Call on another child.) Read the next sentence.

d. (Repeat *c* for most of the remaining sentences in the story.)

e. (Occasionally have the group read a sentence. When the group is to read, say:) Everybody, read the next sentence. (Tap for each word in the sentence.)

EXERCISE 18

Second reading—sentences and questions

a. You're going to read the story again. This time I'm going to ask questions.

b. Starting with the first word of the title. ✔
- Get ready. (Tap as the children read the title.)

---

the pet goat[1]

a girl got a pet goat. she liked to go running with her pet goat. she played with her goat in her house. she played with the goat in her yard.[2]

but the goat did some things that made the girl's dad mad. the goat ate things. he ate cans and he ate canes.[3] he ate pans and he ate panes.[4] he even ate capes and caps.[5]

one day her dad said, "that goat must go.[6] he eats too many things."

the girl said, "dad, if you let the goat stay with us, I will see that he stops eating all those things."

her dad said, "we will try it."[7]

so the goat stayed and the girl made him stop eating cans and canes and caps and capes.[8]

but one day a car robber came to the girl's house. he saw a big red car near the house and said, "I will steal that car."[9]

he ran to the car and started to open the door.

the girl and the goat were playing in the back yard. they did not see the car robber.[10]

more to come

---

c. (Call on a child.) Read the first sentence.

To Correct

word-identification errors (**from,** for example)
1. That word is **from.** What word? *From.*
2. Go back to the beginning of the sentence and read the sentence again.

d. (Call on another child.) Read the next sentence.

e. (Repeat *d* for most of the remaining sentences in the story.)

f. (Occasionally have the group read a sentence.)

g. (After each underlined sentence has been read, present each comprehension question specified below to the entire group.)

[1] What's this story going to be about? (Signal.) *The pet goat.*

[2] What are some things she did with her goat? (The children respond.)

[3] What did he eat? (Signal.) *Cans and canes.*

[4] Name some more things he ate. (Signal.) *Pans and panes.*

[5] What else did he eat? (Signal.) *Capes and caps.*

[6] Why did he say that? (The children respond.)

[7] What are they going to try? (The children respond.)
- Let's see if the goat stops eating things.

[8] Did the goat get to stay? (Signal.) *Yes.*

[9] Who is talking? (Signal.) *A car robber.*

[10] Did the girl and the goat see him? (Signal.) *No.*
- Why not? (Signal.) *They were playing in the back yard.*
- What do you think will happen to that car robber? (The children respond.)
- We'll finish the story next time and find out.

but here is what Sid said when he looked at the words, "Send a con to Sam's tree farm." ⑤ [7]

Sid said to himself, "We don't have cons in this shop. Cons are in jail." So Sid called the jail and said to the jailer, "do you have a con that you can send to a tree farm?" [8]

The jailer said, "Yes, we have a fine con. he is getting out of jail today. he needs a job. I will be glad to send him to a tree farm."

"good," Sid said. "Send the con to Sam's tree farm." [9]

after Sid took care of the con, he said to himself, "I am really doing a good job. The boss will be proud of me."

do you think the boss will be proud of the things that Sid has done? [10]

more to come

---

[7] What did Sid say? (Signal.)
Send a con to Sam's tree farm.
- Were those the words on the note? (Signal.)
No. What did that note say? (Signal.) *Send a cone to Sam's tree farm.*

[8] Why did Sid call the jail? (Signal.)
To get a con.

[9] What is Sid sending? (Signal.) *A con.*
- What should he send? (Signal.) *A cone.*

[10] What do you think? (The children respond.)
- Right. Sid didn't read the notes and do what they said.

EXERCISE 11
Picture comprehension

a. What do you think you'll see in the picture? (The children respond.)
b. Turn the page and look at the picture.
c. (Ask these questions:)
   1. Show me the note. (The children respond.)
   - Read what the note says. (Signal.)
   Tape the oak tree near the door.
   2. Touch the oak tree. (The children respond.)
   - What is Sid doing to it? (Signal.) *Tapping it.*

EXERCISE 12
Summary of independent activities

a. (Pass out Worksheet 91 to each child.)
b. Everybody, now you'll do your worksheet. Remember to do all parts of the worksheet and to read all the parts carefully.

END OF LESSON 91

EXERCISE 19

Picture comprehension

a. Look at the picture.
b. (Ask these questions:)
  1. What is the girl doing?
     (Signal.) *Hugging her goat.*
  • Why is she doing that?
     (The children respond.)
  2. What is her father saying?
     (The children respond.)
  3. What does that goat have in his mouth?
     (The children respond.)

SUMMARY OF INDEPENDENT ACTIVITY
EXERCISE 20

Summary of independent activities

a. (Pass out Worksheet 60 to each child.)
b. Everybody, now you'll do your worksheet. Remember to do all parts of the worksheet and to read all the parts carefully.

INDIVIDUAL CHECKOUT
EXERCISE 21

2½-minute individual fluency checkout: rate/accuracy

a. As you are doing your worksheet, I'll call on children one at a time to read the **first page of the story.** Remember, you get two stars if you read the first page of the story in less than two and a half minutes and make no more than four errors.
b. (Call on each child. Tell the child:) Start with the title and read the first page of the story very carefully. Go. (Time the child. Tell the child any words the child misses. Stop the child as soon as the child makes the fifth error or exceeds the time limit.)
c. (If the child meets the rate-accuracy criterion, record two stars on your chart for lesson 60. Congratulate the child. Give children who do not earn two stars a chance to read the first page of the story again before the next lesson is presented.)
131 words/**2.5 min** = 52 wpm **[4 errors]**

END OF LESSON 60

EXERCISE 9

Play the game

a. Read the item to yourself and think about what you're going to do and when you're going to do it. Raise your hand when you're ready.

b. (After the children raise their hands, say:) Get ready to play the game.

c. My turn. (Pause.) Her. (Signal.) (The children are to say *Here* immediately.)

> **To Correct**
> (Have the children read the item aloud. Then play the game again.)

STORY 91
EXERCISE 10

Sid Sends a Con to the farm[1]

Sid did not read well. One note told him to send pine trees. but Sid sent pin trees. another note told him to fix the window pane. but Sid made a window pan.

now Sid went back to the table and picked up another note. The note said, "Tape the oak tree near the door."[2] but Sid did not read the words on the note. here is what Sid said, "Tap the oak tree near the door."[3]

he said, "That seems like a funny thing to do. but I will do it." So Sid went to the oak tree near the door.[4] he tapped it with his hand.[5] Then he went back to the table to read more notes.

here is what the next note said, "Send a cone to Sam's tree farm."[6]

Reading—decoding

a. Everybody, get ready to read the story.

b. Remember, if the group reads all the way to the red 5 without making more than five errors, we can go on.

c. Everybody, touch the title of the story. ✔

d. If you hear a mistake, raise your hand. Remember, children who do not have their place lose their turn. (Call on individual children to read two or three sentences. Do not ask comprehension questions. Tally all errors.)

> **To Correct**
> word-identification errors (**from**, for example)
> 1. That word is **from**. What word? *From.*
> 2. Go back to the beginning of the sentence and read the sentence again.

e. (If the children make more than five errors: when they reach the 5, return to the beginning of the story and have the children reread to the 5. Do not ask comprehension questions. Repeat step *e* until firm, and then go on to step *f*.)

f. (If the children read to the number 5 without making more than five errors: read the story to the children from the beginning to the 5. Ask the specified comprehension questions. When you reach the 5, call on individual children to continue reading the story. Have each child read two or three sentences. Ask the specified comprehension questions.)

[1] What will happen in this story? (Signal.) *Sid will send a con to the farm.*

• A con is a person who has been in jail.

[2] What did the note say? (Signal.) *Tape the oak tree near the door.*

• What is Sid supposed to do to the oak tree? (Signal.) *Tape it.*

[3] What did Sid say to do with the oak tree? (Signal.) *Tap it.*

• Oh, oh. Is that what the note said? (Signal.) *No.*

• What did the note tell him to do to the oak tree? (Signal.) *Tape it.*

[4] What do you think Sid will do to the tree? (Signal.) *Tap it.*

• What is he supposed to do? (Signal.) *Tape it.*

[5] What did he do? (Signal.) *Tapped it with his hand.*

[6] What did the note say? (Signal.) *Send a cone to Sam's tree farm.*

• Do you think Sid read what the note says? (Signal.) *No.*

• Let's read and find out.

Making Progress

	Since Lesson 1	Since Lesson 41
Word Reading	Sounds and 2 sound combinations (ar, al) 401 regular words 81 irregular words Reading high frequency hard words Discriminating long and short vowel words using final -e rule	1 sound combination (ou) 117 regular words 25 irregular words Discriminate long and short vowel words using final -e rule
Comprehension	**Picture Comprehension** Predicting what the picture will show Answering questions about the picture **Story Comprehension** Answering who, what, when, where, and why questions orally Answering questions about the story and other short passages in writing	

What to Use

Teacher	Students
Presentation Book B (pages 68–171) **Teacher's Guide** (pages 65–67) **Answer Key** **Spelling Presentation Book**	**Storybook 1** (pages 156–215) **Workbook B** lined paper

What's Ahead in Lessons 61–80

New Skills

- Story length will increase from 260 to 299 words.
- Children will answer written questions about pictures in the storybook (Lesson 61).
- Children review previously joined digraphs **th, sh, ing** in isolation and in review words (Lesson 68).
- * Beginning at Lesson 81, regular typeprint will be introduced. This twenty-lesson segment consolidates previously learned skills in preparation for this transition.

New Vocabulary

- *Regular words:*
  - (61) bending, bit, bite, hugged, save, sharp
  - (62) fate, kites, paper, starts, string, we'll, wind
  - (63) five, go, landed, lifted, no, shake, shaking, won't
  - (64) began, blowing, darker, grow, happen, happened, maker, makes, making, proud, thunder, Tim
  - (65) fire, float, forest, make, sadder, Sam, trapped, while
  - (66) became, fires, floated, hat, hate, or, plane, rail, scare, soaked, wade, wading
  - (67) beans, fifty, gave, hundred, hunting, meat, pile, train
  - (68) counted, counter, everything, home, missing, nine, Sandy, standing, tracks
  - (69) ninety, parked, Sid
  - (70) followed, outside, sets, shed
  - (71) load, seem, truck, waited
  - (72) lied, okay, scared, sorry
  - (73) check, dish, easy, tar, that's, wishing
  - (74) loading, lying, mark, mean, near, she's, shop
  - (75) finding, gift, I've, leaving, showed
  - (76) else, parts, care
  - (77) job, mixed, tent
  - (78) everybody, passed, snow, thing
  - (79) colder, deep, ears, show, slipped, stuck, window
  - (80) close, closed, con, cone, conned, cool, cream, drink, giving, mouth, sly
- *Irregular words:*
  - (62) wood, you'll
  - (63) again, know
  - (64) pretty, two
  - (65) someone, today
  - (66) first, shook, tv
  - (67) anything, bear, school, woman
  - (68) front
  - (71) crooks
  - (73) says
  - (74) their, what's
  - (77) worked
  - (78) done
  - (80) ice

EXERCISE 7

Words with underlined parts

a. First you're going to read the underlined part of each word in this column. Then you're going to read the whole word.

b. (Touch the ball for **proud.**) Read the underlined part. Get ready. (Tap the ball.) *ou.* Read the whole word. (Pause.) Get ready. (Slash.) *Proud.*

c. (Repeat step *b* until firm.)

d. (Repeat steps *b* and *c* for each remaining word in the column.)

e. (Repeat the column until children read all the words in order without making a mistake.)

proud →

found →

all →

jailer →

while →

reading →

really →

Individual test

a. (Call on individual children to read one column of words from the lesson.)

b. (Praise children who read all words with no errors.)

STORYBOOK

READ THE ITEMS 91

EXERCISE 8

Read the item

a. (Pass out Storybook 2.)

b. Open your reader to page 22. Get ready to read the item.

c. Finger under the first word of the item. ✔

• Get ready. (Tap.) *When.*

d. Next word. (Pause.) Get ready. (Tap.) *The.*

e. (Repeat step *d* for the remaining words in the item.)

f. (Repeat steps *c* through *e* until the item is firm.)

g. Everybody, say that item. (Pause. Signal.) *When the teacher says "Her," say "Here."*

h. Again. (Repeat step *g* until firm.)

i. What are you going to say when I say "Her"? (Signal.) *Here.*
When are you going to say "Here"? (Signal.) *When the teacher says "Her."*

To Correct

(Have the children read the item aloud. Then repeat the questions.)

Look Ahead

In-Program Tests
Fluency Checkouts: Rate/Accuracy

Lessons 65, 70, 75, 80

- By lesson 80, children should be reading at least 60 words per minute at 97 percent accuracy.

Lesson Number	Error Limit	Number of words read	Number of minutes	Words per minute
65	4	144	2.5	58
70	3	104	2.0	52
75	3	109	2.0	55
80	4	120	2.0	60

Skills

	Lessons 61–80
Word Reading	131 regular words 22 irregular words
Comprehension	Answering questions about specified pictures

Reading Activities

Help children develop decoding and comprehension skills by using the following reading activities.

Compound Words (Lessons 65, 67, 68, 70, 78)
Have children identify the two parts of a compound word by writing them separately as the "first part" and "next part" of the word. Use the words listed below from previous lessons and as the words are introduced, beginning with Lesson 65.

Words from previous lessons:

cannot
inside
himself
herself
anyone
something

New words:

someone (Lesson 65)
anything (Lesson 67)
everything (Lesson 68)
outside (Lesson 71)
everybody (Lesson 78)

Magic e! (Lessons 61–80)
Write the following list of words on the board: *hop, rat, cap, bit, fin, con, cam, dim, hat.* Then attach a star with the letter *e* on it to a tongue depressor. Have children take turns saying the short vowel words on the list and touching the word with their magic *e* star. Then have children say the new word with a long-vowel sound.

Memory Mastery (Lessons 61–80)
Using "final -e rule" words and their short-vowel counterparts (e.g., hop, hope), make two word cards for each word (approximately 20 words) on 3" x 5" index cards or construction paper. To play, place the cards face down on the floor. Each child, in turn, turns over two cards. If the two cards match and the child can read the words, the child keeps the pair and turns over two more cards. If the cards don't match, the next child takes a turn. Play continues until all the cards are off the floor. The child with the greatest number of cards is the winner.

EXERCISE 5

Read the fast way

a. You're going to read all the words in this column the fast way.

b. (Touch the ball for **note.** Pause.) Get ready. (Slash.) *Note.*

c. (Repeat step *b* until firm.)

d. (Repeat steps *b* and *c* for each remaining word in the column.)

e. (Repeat the column until the children read all the words in order without making mistakes.)

To Correct

word-identification errors (**note,** for example)

1. That word is **note.** What word? (Signal.) *Note.*

2. Spell **note.** Get ready. (Tap under each letter.) *N-O-T-E.*

3. What word did you spell? (Signal.) *Note.*

4. (Repeat *2* and *3* until firm.)

5. (Return to the first word in the column and present all words in order.) Starting over.

note

cane

pine

con

don't

looked

window

EXERCISE 6

Words with underlined parts

a. First you're going to read the underlined part of each word in this column. Then you're going to read the whole word.

b. (Touch the ball for **tapped.**) Read the underlined part. Get ready. (Tap the ball.) *Tapp.*

• Read the whole word. (Pause.) Get ready. (Slash.) *Tapped.*

c. (Repeat step *b* until firm.)

d. (Repeat steps *b* and *c* for each remaining word in the column.)

e. (Repeat the column until children read all the words in order without making a mistake.)

tapped

packed

times

notes

canned

caned

seems

READING VOCABULARY

Get ready to read all the words on this page without making a mistake.

EXERCISE 1

Read the fast way

a. Read these words the fast way.
b. (Touch the ball for **saved.** Pause two seconds.) Get ready. (Signal.) *Saved.* Yes, **saved.**
c. (Repeat *b* for **smiled** and **sore.**)

saved

smiled

sore

they

EXERCISE 2

Sound out first

a. (Touch the ball for **they.**) Sound it out Get ready. (Quickly touch **th, e, y** as the children say:) *thththeeeyyy.*
b. What word? (Signal.) *They.* Yes, **they.**
c. (Repeat exercise until firm.)

bending

EXERCISE 3

Sound out first

a. (Touch the ball for **bending.**) Sound it out. Get ready. (Quickly touch **b, e, n, d, ing** as the children say:) *beeennndiiing.*
b. What word? (Signal.) *Bending.* Yes, **bending.**
c. (Repeat exercise until firm.)

cross

EXERCISE 4

Sound out first

a. (Touch the ball for **cross.**) Sound it out. Get ready. (Quickly touch **c, r, o,** between the **s**'s as the children say:) *crrrooosss.*
b. What word? (Signal.) *Cross.* Yes, **cross.**
c. (Repeat exercise until firm.)

fin

fine

EXERCISE 5

Practice final-e rule

a. (Point to **fin** and **fine.**) You're going to say the name ī when you read one of these words.
b. (Point to **fin.**) Are you going to say the name ī when you read this word? (Signal.) *No.*
c. (Point to **fine.**) Are you going to say the name ī when you read this word? (Signal.) *Yes.*
d. (Repeat *b* and *c* until firm.)
e. Read these words the fast way.
f. (Touch the ball for **fin.** Pause two seconds.) Get ready. (Signal.) *Fin.* Yes, **fin.**
g. (Touch the ball for **fine.** Pause two seconds.) Get ready. (Signal.) *Fine.* Yes, **fine.**
h. (Repeat *f* and *g* until firm.)

(Repeat any troublesome words.)

Individual test

(Call on individual children. Each child reads a different word.)

READING VOCABULARY

EXERCISE 3

Words beginning with capital letters

a. The words in this column begin with capital letters. First you're going to spell each word. Then you're going to read that word the fast way.

b. (Touch the ball for **Another.**) Spell it. Get ready. (Tap under each letter as the children say:) *A-N-O-T-H-E-R.*

• (Return to the ball.) Read it. Get ready. (Slash.) *Another.*

c. (Repeat step *b* for each remaining word in the column.)

d. (Repeat steps *b* and *c* until firm.)

To Correct

word-identification errors (**note,** for example)

1. That word is **note.** What word? (Signal.) *Note.*

2. Spell **note.** Get ready. (Tap under each letter.) *N-O-T-E.*

3. What word did you spell? (Signal.) *Note.*

4. (Repeat *2* and *3* until firm.)

5. (Return to the first word in the column and present all words in order.) Starting over.

Another

After

There

Read

Each

Now

Walking

EXERCISE 4

Teacher reads the words in red

a. I'll read each word in red. Then you'll spell each word.

b. (Touch the ball for **oak.**) My turn. (Slash as you say:) Oak. What word? (Signal.) *Oak.*

c. (Return to the ball.) Spell it. Get ready. (Tap under each letter as the children say:) *O-A-K.*

• What word did you spell? (Signal.) *Oak.*

d. (Repeat steps *b* and *c* for each word in red.)

e. Your turn to read all the words in this column.

f. (Touch the ball for **oak.** Pause.) Get ready. (Slash.) *Oak.*

g. (Repeat step *f* for each remaining word in the column.)

h. (Repeat steps *f* and *g* until firm.)

oak

jail

jailer

sent

truck

more

send

Get ready to read all the words on this page without making a mistake.

To Correct

1. (Touch the ball for the word the children missed.) Is there an ē on the end of this word? (Signal.) (The children respond.)
2. (Point to the first vowel in the word.) So tell me what you say for this letter. (Signal.) (The children respond.)
3. (Touch the ball for the word.) Sound it out. Get ready. (Touch all sounds except the final **e**, if there is one, as the children sound out the word.)
4. What word? (Signal.) (The children respond.)
5. (Return to the first word in the column. Present all the words in order until firm.)

EXERCISE 6

Short vowel words

a. (Point to the words in this column.) Read these words the fast way.
b. (Touch the ball for **kit**. Pause two seconds.) Get ready. (Signal.) *Kit.* Yes, **kit.**
• (Repeat until firm.)
c. (Repeat *b* for **bit** and **can**.)

kit

bit

can

EXERCISE 7

Long vowel words

a. (Point to the words in this column.) Read these words the fast way.
b. (Touch the ball for **kite**. Pause two seconds.) Get ready. (Signal.) *Kite.* Yes, **kite.**
• (Repeat until firm.)
c. (Repeat *b* for **bite** and **cane**.)

kite

bite

cane

EXERCISE 8

Short and long vowel words

a. Everybody, read these words again. Remember what you say if there is an ē on the end of a word.
b. (Touch the ball for **bite**. Pause two seconds.) Get ready. (Signal.) *Bite.* Yes, **bite.**
c. (Repeat *b* for **kit**.)

bite

kit

(Repeat any troublesome words.)

Individual test

(Call on individual children. Each child reads a different word.)

CAPITAL LETTERS
EXERCISE 1

Reviewing hard capitals

a. These are capital letters that you have seen before. See if you can tell me the letter name of each capital letter in this row.

b. (Point under capital **E**.) What capital? (Signal.) *E.*

c. (Repeat step *b* for each remaining capital.)

d. (Repeat steps *b* and *c* until firm.)

E D R Q A

EXERCISE 2

Introducing hard capitals

a. These are capital letters that don't look like the letters you know. The letters you know are in the top row. The capitals are in the row below.

b. (Point under capital **B**.) This is capital **B**.

c. (Repeat step *b* for each remaining capital.)

d. Your turn. (Point under capital **B**.) What capital? (Signal.) *B.*

e. (Repeat step *d* for each remaining capital.)

f. (Repeat steps *d* and *e* until firm.)

b l h g
B L H G

Do not touch small letters.

Get ready to read all the words on this page without making a mistake.

EXERCISE 9

ar word

a. (Touch the ball for **sharp.**) Read this word the fast way. (Pause two seconds.) Get ready. (Signal.) *Sharp.* Yes, **sharp.**

b. (Point to **ar** in **sharp.**) Everybody, what do these letters say? (Signal.) *Are.* Yes, **are.**

c. (Touch the ball for **sharp.**) Sound it out. Get ready. (Quickly touch **sh, ar, p** as the children say:) *shshsharp.*

d. What word? (Signal.) *Sharp.* Yes, **sharp.**

e. (Repeat *c* and *d* until firm.)

called

EXERCISE 10

al word

a. (Touch the ball for **called.**) Read this word the fast way. (Pause two seconds.) Get ready. (Signal.) *Called.* Yes, **called.**

b. (Point to **al** in **called.**) Everybody, what do these letters say? (Signal.) *All.* Yes, **all.**

c. (Touch the ball for **called.**) Sound it out. Get ready. (Quickly touch **c, al, d** as the children say:) *cald.*

d. What word? (Signal.) *Called.* Yes, **called.**

e. (Repeat *c* and *d* until firm.)

those

EXERCISE 11

Practice final-e rule

a. Read this word the fast way. Remember to look at the end of the word.

b. (Touch the ball for **those.** Pause two seconds.) Get ready. (Signal.) *Those.* Yes, **those.**

c. (Touch the ball for **those.**) Sound it out. Get ready. (Quickly touch **th, o, s** as the children say:) *thththōōōsss.*

d. What word? (Signal.) *Those.* Yes, **those.**

e. (Repeat *b* through *d* until firm.)

these

EXERCISE 12

Practice final-e rule

a. Read this word the fast way. Remember to look at the end of the word.

b. (Touch the ball for **these.** Pause two seconds.) Get ready. (Signal.) *These.* Yes, **these.**

save

EXERCISE 13

Practice final-e rule

a. Read this word the fast way. Remember to look at the end of the word.

b. (Touch the ball for **save.** Pause two seconds.) Get ready. (Signal.) *Save.* Yes, **save.**

liked

EXERCISE 14

Two-part word

a. (Cover **d.** Point to **like.**) Everybody, tell me what this part of the word says. Get ready. (Signal.) *Like.* Yes, **like.**

b. (Uncover **d.** Touch the ball for **liked.**) Now tell me what the whole word says. Get ready. (Signal.) *Liked.* Yes, **liked.**

c. (Repeat exercise until firm.)

EXERCISE 15

Read the fast way

a. Read these words the fast way.

b. (Touch the ball for **trȳing.** Pause two seconds.) Get ready. (Signal.) *Trying.* Yes, **trying.**

c. (Repeat *b* for **hugged.**)

Individual test

(Call on individual children to read a column of words from this lesson. If the column contains only one or two words, direct the child to read additional words from an adjacent column.)

after the boss left, Sid went to the table and began to read those notes. here is what one note said. "Send ten pine trees."[7] but Sid did not read those words.⑤ here is what he said, "Send ten pin trees."[8]

Then he looked around the shop for pins. he stuck the pins in sticks.[9] he made ten little trees of pins. Then he said, "I don't know what anybody wants with pin trees, but I will send them out."[10]

and he did.

Then he picked up the next note. It said, "fix the window pane."[11] but here is what Sid said when he looked at the words. "fix the window pan."[12]

Sid looked around the shop for a window pan.[13] he said, "I can't see a window pan, so I will make one." and he did. he made a big tin pan. he nailed it over the window.[14] Then he said to himself, "I am doing a fine job."[15]

more to come

7 What did the note say? (Signal.)
Send ten pine trees.
8 What did Sid say? (Signal.) *Send ten pin trees.*
• Oh, oh. Is that what the note said? (Signal.)
No.
• What did it tell him to send? (Signal.)
Ten pine trees. Right, ten pine trees.
• He didn't read the words on the note.
9 What did he do? (Signal.)
He stuck the pins in sticks.
• Why did he do that?
(The children respond.)
• Yes, he was going to make pin trees.

10 What will he do with the pin trees?
(Signal.) *Send them out.*
• How will the boss feel about that?
(The children respond.)
11 What did that note say? (Signal.)
Fix the window pane.
• What is a window pane?
(The children respond.)
• Yes, a window pane is part of the glass in a window.
12 What did Sid say?
(Signal.) *Fix the window pan.*
• Oh, oh. Is that what the note said? (Signal.) *No.*
• What did it tell him to fix? (Signal.)
The window pane. Right, the window pane.
13 Why was he looking for a window pan?
(The children respond.)
• Yes, he didn't read the words right. What did the note tell him to fix?
(Signal.) *The window pane.*
14 Why did he do that? (The children respond.)
• He tried to fix a window pan.
15 What did he say?
(Signal.) *I am doing a fine job.*
• Was he doing a fine job? (Signal.) *No.*
• Next time we'll find out what other funny things Sid did.

EXERCISE 10

Picture comprehension

a. Look at the picture.
b. (Ask these questions:)
  1. Show me the note. (The children respond.)
  • What does it say? (Signal.)
  Send ten pine trees.
  2. What is Sid doing? (Signal.) *Making pin trees.*
  3. Show me the broken window pane.
  (The children respond.)
  • How is Sid going to fix it? (The children respond.) Yes, put a pan over it.

WORKSHEET 90

INDEPENDENT ACTIVITIES
EXERCISE 11

Summary of independent activities

a. (Pass out Worksheet 90 to each child.)
b. Everybody, now you'll do your worksheet. Remember to do all parts of the worksheet and to read all the parts carefully.

INDIVIDUAL CHECKOUT
EXERCISE 12

2-minute individual fluency checkout: rate/accuracy

a. As you are doing your worksheet, I'll call on children one at a time to read to the star. Remember, you get two stars on the chart if you read to the star in less than two minutes and make no more than four errors.
b. (Call on each child. Tell the child:) Read to the star very carefully. Start with the title. Go. (Time the child. Tell the child any words the child misses. Stop the child as soon as the child makes the fifth error or exceeds the time limit.)
c. (If the child meets the rate-accuracy criterion, record two stars on your chart for lesson 90. Congratulate the child. Give children who do not earn two stars a chance to read to the star again before the next lesson is presented.)
120 words/**2 min** = 60 wpm **[4 errors]**

END OF LESSON 90

STORYBOOK

STORY 61

EXERCISE 16

First reading—title and three sentences

a. (Pass out Storybook 1.)

b. Everybody, open your reader to page 156.

c. Everybody, touch the title of the story and get ready to read the words in the title.

d. First word. ✔

• Get ready. (Tap.) *The.*

e. (Tap for each remaining word in the title.)

f. Everybody, say the title. (Signal.)
  The goat stops the robber.

g. Everybody, get ready to read this story.

h. First word. ✔

• Get ready. (Tap *A.*)

i. Next word. ✔

• Get ready. (Tap.) *Girl.*

j. (Repeat *i* for the remaining words in the first three sentences. Have the children reread the first three sentences until firm.)

EXERCISE 17

Remaining sentences

a. I'm going to call on individual children to read a sentence. Everybody, follow along and point to the words. If you hear a mistake, raise your hand.

b. (Call on a child.) Read the next sentence.

To Correct

word-identification errors (**from**, for example)
1. That word is **from.** What word? *From.*
2. Go back to the beginning of the sentence and read the sentence again.

c. (Call on another child.) Read the next sentence.

d. (Repeat *c* for most of the remaining sentences in the story.)

e. (Occasionally have the group read a sentence. When the group is to read, say:) Everybody, read the next sentence. (Tap for each word in the sentence.)

> the gōat stops the robber[1]
>
>   a girl had a pet gōat. her dad
> had a red car.
>
>   a car robber was gŏing to stēal
> her dad's car.[2] the girl and her gōat
> werₑ plāyiñg in the back yard.
>
>   just then the gōat stoppₑd
> plāyiñg. he saw the robber. he bent
> his head down and started to run
> for the robber.[3] the robber was
> bendiñg ōver the sēat of the car. the
> gōat hit him with his sharp hōrns. the
> car robber went flÿiñg.[4]

EXERCISE 18

Second reading—sentences and questions

a. You're going to read the story again. This time I'm going to ask questions.

b. Starting with the first word of the title. ✔

• Get ready. (Tap as the children read the title.)

c. (Call on a child.) Read the first sentence.

To Correct

word-identification errors (**from**, for example)
1. That word is **from.** What word? *From.*
2. Go back to the beginning of the sentence and read the sentence again.

d. (Call on another child.) Read the next sentence.

e. (Repeat *d* for most of the remaining sentences in the story.)

f. (Occasionally have the group read a sentence.)

g. (After each underlined sentence has been read, present each comprehension question specified below to the entire group.)

[1] What's going to happen in this story? (Signal.) *The goat will stop the robber.*

[2] What was the robber going to do? (Signal.) *Steal her dad's car.*

[3] Who bent his head down? (Signal.) *The goat.*

• Then what did he do? (Signal.) *Started to run for the robber.*

[4] How did that happen? (Signal.) *The goat hit him with his sharp horns.*

READ THE ITEMS 90
EXERCISE 7
Read the item

a. (Pass out Storybook 2.)

b. Open your reader to page 19. Get ready to read the item.

c. Finger under the first word of the item. ✔

● Get ready. (Tap.) *When.*

d. Next word. (Pause.) Get ready. (Tap.) *The.*

e. (Repeat step *d* for the remaining words in the item.)

f. (Repeat steps *c* through *e* until the item is firm.)

g. Everybody, say that item. (Pause. Signal.) *When the teacher says "Dime," say "Dim."*

h. Again. (Repeat step *g* until firm.)

i. What are you going to say when I say "**Dime**"? (Signal.) *Dim.*

● When are you going to say "**Dim**"? (Signal.) *When the teacher says "Dime."*

To Correct

(Have the children read the item aloud. Then repeat the questions.)

EXERCISE 8
Play the game

a. Read the item to yourself and think about what you're going to do and when you're going to do it. Raise your hand when you're ready.

b. (After the children raise their hands, say:) Get ready to play the game.

c. My turn. (Pause.) **Dime.** (Signal.) The children are to say *Dim* immediately.

To Correct

(Have the children read the item aloud. Then play the game again.)

Sid Worked in a Seed Shop[1]

Sid had a job. he worked in a seed shop. That shop had lots of little plants.[2]

The boss of the shop had a bad leg. So she walked with a cane.[3] When she was not walking with her cane, she left her cane in a big can near the door.[4]

One day the boss said, "I must hop in the truck and go to the other side of town. You stay here and take care of the shop."[5]

So the boss got her cane from the can and went to the truck. When she got in her truck, she said, "There is a pile of notes on the table.[6] Take care of them." ★

EXERCISE 9
Reading—decoding

a. Everybody, look at the story on page 19.

b. Remember, if the group reads all the way to the red five without making more than five errors, we can go on.

c. Everybody, touch the title of the story. ✔

d. If you hear a mistake, raise your hand. Remember, children who do not have their place lose their turn. (Call on individual children to read two or three sentences. Do not ask comprehension questions. Tally all errors.)

To Correct

word-identification errors (**from**, for example)
1. That word is **from**. What word? *From.*
2. Go back to the beginning of the sentence and read the sentence again.

e. (If the children make more than five errors before they reach the red 5: when they reach the 5 return to the beginning of the story and have the children reread to the 5. Do not ask comprehension questions. Repeat step *e* until firm, and then go on to step *f*.)

f. (When the children read to the red 5 without making more than five errors: read the story to the children from the beginning to the 5. Ask the specified comprehension questions. When you reach the 5, call on individual children to continue reading the story. Have each child read two or three sentences. Ask the specified comprehension questions.)

[1] What is the title of this story? (Signal.) *Sid Worked in a Seed Shop.*

● What's a seed shop? (The children respond.)

[2] What kind of things were in that shop? (Signal.) *Plants.*

[3] Why did the boss use a cane? (Signal.) *She had a bad leg.*

[4] Where did she leave her cane when she wasn't using it? (Signal.) *In a big can near the door.*

[5] What was Sid supposed to do? (Signal.) *Stay there and take care of the shop.*

[6] What is a pile of notes? (The children respond.)

● Yes, papers with things on them for Sid to do.

the girl's dad ran out of the house. he grabbed the robber.[5] "you were trying to steal my car," he yelled.[6]

the girl said, "but my goat stopped him."

"yes," her dad said. "that goat saved my car."

the car robber said, "something hit me when I was trying to steal that car."

the girl said, "my goat hit you."

the girl hugged the goat. her dad said, "that goat can stay with us.[7] and he can eat all the cans and canes and caps and capes he wants."[8]

the girl smiled. her goat smiled. her dad smiled. but the car robber did not smile. he said, "I am sore."[9]

the end

[5] Who did? (Signal.) *The girl's dad.*
[6] What did he yell? (Signal.)
You were trying to steal my car.
[7] Can the goat stay with them? (Signal.) *Yes.*
[8] Name some things he can eat.
(The children respond.)
[9] Who said that? (Signal.) *The car robber.*
• Why is he sore? (Signal.)
Because the goat hit him with his sharp horns.

EXERCISE 19

Picture comprehension

a. What do you think you'll see in the picture?
b. Turn the page and look at the picture.
c. (Ask these questions:)
1. (Point to the robber.) Who is that man? (Signal.) *The car robber.*
2. What's the goat doing to him? (The children respond.)
• Yes, he's trying to hit him with his sharp horns.
3. How does the robber feel? (The children respond.)
4. What are the girl and her dad doing? (The children respond.)

WORKSHEET 61

FOLLOWING INSTRUCTIONS

The children will need pencils.

EXERCISE 20

Box items

a. (Pass out Worksheet 61 to each child.)
b. (Point to item 1 below the sentence in the box.) Everybody, touch item 1 below the sentence in the box. ✔
c. There are some new words on this part of your worksheet. I'll read item 1. (Read:) Make a box around the question mark.
d. Touch the word **question.** ✔
e. Touch the word **mark.** ✔
f. Your turn to read item 1. First word. ✔
• Get ready. (Tap for each word as the children read:) *Make a box around the question mark.*
g. What does this instruction tell you to do? (Signal.) *Make a box around the question mark.*
h. Point to the instructions. Everybody, read these instructions to yourselves. Then do what the instructions tell you to do. ✔

EXERCISE 5

Read the fast way

a. You're going to read all the words in this column the fast way.

b. (Touch the ball for **plant.** Pause.) Get ready. (Slash.) *Plant.*

c. (Repeat step *b* until firm.)

d. (Repeat steps *b* and *c* for each remaining word in the column.)

e. (Repeat the column until the children read all the words in order without making mistakes.)

plant

truck

stuck

window

note

seed

pile

EXERCISE 6

Words with underlined parts

a. First you're going to read the underlined part of each word in this column. Then you're going to read the whole word.

b. (Touch the ball for **shop.**) Read the underlined part. Get ready. (Tap the ball.) *shshsh.*

• Read the whole word. (Pause.) Get ready. (Slash.) *Shop.*

c. (Repeat step *b* until firm.)

d. (Repeat steps *b* and *c* for each remaining word in the column.)

e. (Repeat the column until children read all the words in order without making a mistake.)

shop

around

worked

sticks

packed

these

can't

Individual test

a. (Call on individual children to read one column of words from the lesson.)

b. (Praise children who read all their words with no errors.)

★ STORY-PICTURE ITEMS
EXERCISE 21

Story picture

a. (Point to the story-picture items exercise on side 2.)

b. Here's something new on your worksheet today. Everybody, touch the instructions. ✔

c. My turn to read the fast way. (Read:) Look at the picture on page 158 of your reader.

d. Your turn to read the instructions the fast way. First word. ✔

• Get ready. (Tap for each word as the children read:) *Look at the picture on page 158 of your reader.*

e. Everybody, what do the instructions tell you to do? (Signal.) *Look at the picture on page 158 of my reader.*

• Do it. (Check that the children look at the picture on page 158.)

f. Everybody, touch item 1 below the instructions. ✔

g. Read the fast way. First word. ✔

• Get ready. (Tap for each word as the children read:) *Does the girl look happy or sad?*

h. Look at the picture on page 158. Does the girl look happy or sad? (Signal.) *Happy.* Yes, she looks **happy.**

i. Write the answer in the blank. ✔

• (Accept phonetic spelling.)

SUMMARY OF INDEPENDENT ACTIVITY
EXERCISE 22

Introduction to independent activity

a. (Hold up side 1 of Worksheet 61.)

b. Everybody, you're going to finish this worksheet on your own. (Tell the children when they will work the remaining items.)

• Let's go over the things you're going to do.

Story items

(Point to the story-items exercise.) Everybody, remember to write your answers in the blanks.

Reading comprehension

(Point to the story on side 2.) You're going to read this story and then do the items. Remember to write the answers in the blanks.

END OF LESSON 61

EXERCISE 3A

Rule for words with long and short vowels

a. (Touch the ball for **cane.**) Look at this word. (Pause.) Is there only **one n** in this word? (Signal.) *Yes.*

b. So does the letter **a** say its name? (Signal.) *Yes.*

• Read this word. (Pause three seconds.) Get ready. (Signal.) *Cane.*

c. (Touch the ball for **pinned.**) Look at this word. (Pause.) Is there only **one n** in this word? (Signal.) *No.*

d. So does the letter **i** say its name? (Signal.) *No.*

• Read this word. (Pause three seconds.) Get ready. (Signal.) *Pinned.*

e. (Touch the ball for **pined.**) Look at this word. (Pause.) Is there only **one n** in this word? (Signal.) *Yes.*

f. So does the letter **i** say its name? (Signal.) *Yes.*

• Read this word. (Pause three seconds.) Get ready. (Signal.) *Pined.*

g. (Touch the ball for **moped.**) Look at this word. (Pause.) Is there only **one p** in this word? (Signal.) *Yes.*

h. So does the letter **o** say its name? (Signal.) *Yes.*

• Read this word. (Pause three seconds.) Get ready. (Signal.) *Moped.*

cane

pinned

pined

moped

mopped

send

sent

To Correct

1. The **a** says its name. So the word is **cane.**

   OR

   The **a** does not say its name. So the word is **pinned.**

2. (Return to the first word in the column and present all words in order.) Starting over.

EXERCISE 3B

Children spell, then read

a. First you're going to spell each word by letter names. Then you're going to read that word the fast way.

b. (Touch the ball for **cane.**) Spell by letter names. Get ready. (Tap under each letter as the children say:) *C-A-N-E.*

• Return to the ball.) Read it. Get ready. (Slash.) *Cane.*

c. (Repeat step *b* for each remaining word in the column.)

d. (Repeat steps *b* and *c* until firm.)

EXERCISE 4

Read the fast way

a. You're going to read all the words in this column the fast way.

b. (Touch the ball for **said.** Pause.) Get ready. (Slash.) *Said.*

c. (Repeat step *b* until firm.)

d. (Repeat steps *b* and *c* for each remaining word in the column.)

e. (Repeat the column until the children read all the words in order without making mistakes.)

said

hope

side

care

hop

car

sid

EXERCISE 1

Sound combination review

a. Here are some letters that go together. Get ready to tell me the sound they usually make.

b. (Point to **al**.) What sound do these letters usually make? (Signal.) *All.* Yes, **all.**

c. (Repeat *b* with **ou** and **ar**.)

d. (Repeat the series of sound combinations until firm.)

al

ou

ar

READING VOCABULARY

Get ready to read all the words on this page without making a mistake.

EXERCISE 2

Sound out first

a. (Touch the ball for **went**.) Sound it out. Get ready. (Quickly touch **w, e, n, t** as the children say:) *wwweeennnt.*

b. What word? (Signal.) *Went.* Yes, **went.**

c. (Repeat exercise until firm.)

EXERCISE 3

Sound out first

a. (Touch the ball for **very**.) Sound it out. Get ready. (Quickly touch **v, e, r, y** as the children say:) *vvveeerrryyy.*

b. What word? (Signal.) *Very.* Yes, **very.**

c. (Repeat exercise until firm.)

EXERCISE 4

Listen, sound out with me

a. (Point to **string**.) I'll tell you this word. (Pause.) **String.** What word? (Signal.) *String.* Yes, **string.**

b. (Touch the ball for **string**.) Sound it out with me. Get ready. (Quickly touch each sound as you and the children say:) *ssstrrriiing.*

c. What word? (Signal.) *String.* Yes, **string.**

d. (Repeat *b* and *c* until firm.)

(Repeat any troublesome words.)

Individual test

(Call on individual children. Each child reads a different word.)

CAPITAL LETTERS

EXERCISE 1

Reviewing hard capitals

a. These are capital letters that you have seen before. See if you can tell me the letter name of each capital letter on this page.

b. (Point under capital **R**.) What capital? (Signal.) *R.*

c. (Repeat step *b* for each remaining capital.)

d. (Repeat steps *b* and *c* until firm.)

R E A D Q

READING VOCABULARY

EXERCISE 2

Teacher reads the words in red

a. I'll read each word in red. Then you'll spell each word by letter names.

b. (Touch the ball for **plants**.) My turn. (Slash as you say:) Plants. What word? (Signal.) *Plants.*

c. (Return to the ball.) Spell by letter names. Get ready. (Tap under each letter as the children say:) *P-L-A-N-T-S.*

• What word did you spell? (Signal.) *Plants.*

d. (Repeat steps *b* and *c* for each word in red.)

e. Your turn to read all the words in this column.

f. (Touch the ball for **plants**. Pause.) Get ready. (Slash.) *Plants.*

g. (Repeat step *f* for each remaining word in the column.)

h. (Repeat steps *f* and *g* until firm.)

> **To Correct**
> **word-identification errors**
> (**hope,** for example)
> 1. That word is **hope.** What word? (Signal.) *Hope.*
> 2. (Return to the first word in the column and present all words in order.) Starting over.

plants

boss

key

pane

can

pan

words

Get ready to read all the words on this page without making a mistake.

To Correct

1. (Touch the ball for the word the children missed.) Is there an $\bar{e}$ on the end of this word? (Signal.) (The children respond.)
2. (Point to the first vowel in the word.) So tell me what you say for this letter. (Signal.) (The children respond.)
3. (Touch the ball for the word.) Sound it out. Get ready. (Touch all sounds except the final **e,** if there is one, as the children sound out the word.)
4. What word? (Signal.) (The children respond.)
5. (Return to the first word in the column. Present all the words in order until firm.)

EXERCISE 5

Long vowel words

a. (Point to the words in this column.) Read these words the fast way.
b. (Touch the ball for **fate.** Pause two seconds.) Get ready. (Signal.) *Fate.* Yes, **fate.**
• (Repeat until firm.)
c. (Repeat *b* for **kite.**)

fate

kite

EXERCISE 6

Short vowel words

a. (Point to the words in this column.) Read these words the fast way.
b. (Touch the ball for **fat.** Pause two seconds.) Get ready. (Signal.) *Fat.* Yes, **fat.**
• (Repeat until firm.)
c. (Repeat *b* for **kit.**)

fat

kit

EXERCISE 7

Short and long vowel words

a. Everybody, read these words again. Remember what you say if there is an $\bar{e}$ on the end of a word.
b. (Touch the ball for **kite.** Pause two seconds.) Get ready. (Signal.) *Kite.* Yes, **kite.**
c. (Repeat *b* for **fate** and **jane.**)

kite

fate

jane

(Repeat any troublesome words.)

Individual test

(Call on individual children. Each child reads a different word.)

Then he taped the dime to his arm. Then he began to tap the dime. When he had tapped the dime three times, "boooooommmmmm" came the sound of thunder. don looked down and saw that he had a cape. and there was a cap on his head. "I am super again," don said.[3]

When he was going out the door, he stopped and said, "I must do something good." he sat down and began to think. Then he said, "I've got it."[4]

he jumped up and began to fly.⑤ he went this way and that way. he was looking for a truck.[5] When he saw it, he dropped down to the street. he ran up to the truck. The little man was in the truck. don said, "get out of that truck."

The little man got out. "What do you want?" he asked don.

don handed the dime to the little man. "here," don said. "You need this dime more than I do."[6]Then don told the man how the dime works. "Tap the dime three times and you will be a super man. but you must be a good super man."

The man tapped the dime. "boooooommmmmm." he became a super man.[7] and he was the best super man there ever was. he did good things. he fixed things. he worked hard.[8] before long his baby got well, and he was very happy. but he wasn't as happy as don was.

don was no longer a super man.[9] but he did not care. he liked his job. he didn't mope. he was happy because he did the most super thing of all. he helped somebody else.[10]

The end[11]

---

[3] What happened when he tapped the dime three times? (Signal.) (The children respond.)
- Yes, he became super again.

[4] What do you think he's going to do? (The children respond.)
- Let's read and find out.

[5] What was he doing? (Signal.) *Looking for a truck.*
- Why was he looking for a truck? (The children respond.)

[6] What did Don do with the dime? (Signal.) *Gave it to the little man.*
- Why? (The children respond.)

[7] What happened to the little man? (Signal.) *He became a super man.*

[8] Why was he the best super man there ever was? (The children respond.)

[9] Was Don still a super man? (Signal.) *No.*

[10] What did Don do that was so super? (The children respond.)

[11] Will there be more Don stories? (Signal.) *No.*

EXERCISE 11

Picture comprehension

a. Look at the picture.

b. (Ask these questions:)
1. What is Don doing in this picture? (Signal.) *Flying.*
2. What is he looking for? (The children respond.)
3. Who is that in the truck? (Signal.) *The little man.*
4. What's going to happen to that little man? (The children respond.)

WORKSHEET 89

EXERCISE 12

Summary of independent activities

a. (Pass out Worksheet 89 to each child.)

b. Everybody, now you'll do your worksheet. Remember to do all parts of the worksheet and to read all the parts carefully.

END OF LESSON 89

Get ready to read all the words on this page without making a mistake.

EXERCISE 8

Read the fast way

a. Read these words the fast way.

b. (Touch the ball for **flying.** Pause two seconds.) Get ready. (Signal.) *Flying.* Yes, **flying.**

c. (Repeat *b* for **blōw, want,** and **wind.**)

blōw

want

wind

starts

EXERCISE 9

ar word

a. (Touch the ball for **starts.**) Read this word the fast way. (Pause two seconds.) Get ready. (Signal.) *Starts.* Yes, **starts.**

b. (Point to **ar** in **starts.**) Everybody, what do these letters say? (Signal.) *Are.* Yes, **are.**

c. (Touch the ball for **starts.**) Sound it out. Get ready. (Quickly touch **s, t, ar, t, s** as the children say:) *ssstartsss.*

d. What word? (Signal.) *Starts.* Yes, **starts.**

e. (Repeat *c* and *d* until firm.)

cloud

EXERCISE 10

ou word

a. (Point to **ou** in **cloud.**) What do these letters say? (Signal.) *ou.* Yes, **ou.**

b. (Touch the ball for **cloud.**) Read this word the fast way. Get ready. (Signal.) *Cloud.* Yes, **cloud.**

fall

EXERCISE 11

al word

a. (Point to **al** in **fall.**) What do these letters say? (Signal.) *All.* Yes, **all.**

b. (Touch the ball for **fall.**) Read this word the fast way. Get ready. (Signal.) *Fall.* Yes, **fall.**

time

EXERCISE 12

Practice final-e rule

a. Read this word the fast way. Remember to look at the end of the word.

b. (Touch the ball for **time.** Pause two seconds.) Get ready. (Signal.) *Time.* Yes, **time.**

kites

EXERCISE 13

Two-part word

a. (Cover **s.** Point to **kite.**) Everybody, tell me what this part of the word says. Get ready. (Signal.) *Kite.* Yes, **kite.**

b. (Uncover **s.** Touch the ball for **kites.** Now tell me what the whole word says. Get ready. (Signal.) *Kites.* Yes, **kites.**

c. (Repeat exercise until firm.)

(Repeat any troublesome words.)

Individual test

(Call on individual children. Each child reads a different word.)

READ THE ITEMS 89
EXERCISE 8

Read the item

a. (Pass out Storybook 2.)

b. Open your reader to page 16. Get ready to read the item.

c. Finger under the first word of the item. ✔
- Get ready. (Tap.) *When.*

d. Next word. (Pause.) Get ready. (Tap.) *The.*

e. (Repeat step *d* for the remaining words in the item.)

f. (Repeat steps *c* through *e* until the item is firm.)

g. Everybody, say that item. (Pause. Signal.) *When the teacher says "Here," say "Her."*

To Correct
1. Everybody, say the item with me. (Signal. Say the item with the children at a normal speaking rate. Repeat until firm.)
2. (Repeat step *g.* Then skip to step *i.*)

h. Again. (Repeat step *g* until firm.)

i. What are you going to say when I say "**Here**"? (Signal.) *Her.*
- When are you going to say "**Her**"? (Signal.) *When the teacher says "Here."*

To Correct
(Have the children read the item aloud. Then repeat the questions.)

EXERCISE 9

Play the game

a. Read the item to yourself and think about what you're going to do and when you're going to do it. Raise your hand when you're ready.

b. (After the children raise their hands, say:) Get ready to play the game.

c. My turn. (Pause.) **Here.** (Signal.) (The children are to say *Her* immediately.)

To Correct
(Have the children read the item aloud. Then play the game again.)

---

don does good Things[1]

don helped the little man take big bags from the truck. Then don went back to the store. The woman in the cape and cap was standing inside the store. She handed don the dime and said, "I think you will make a good super man."[2]

don took the dime and said, "Thank you."

STORY 89
EXERCISE 10

Reading—decoding

a. Everybody, look at the story on page 16.

b. Remember, if the group reads all the way to the red five without making more than five errors, we can go on.

c. Everybody, touch the title of the story. ✔

d. If you hear a mistake, raise your hand. Remember, children who do not have their place lose their turn. (Call on individual children to read two or three sentences. Do not ask comprehension questions. Tally all errors.)

To Correct
word-identification errors (**from,** for example)
1. That word is **from.** What word? *From.*
2. Go back to the beginning of the sentence and read the sentence again.

e. (If the children make more than five errors before they reach the red 5: when they reach the 5 return to the beginning of the story and have the children reread to the 5. Do not ask comprehension questions. Repeat step e until firm, and then go on to step *f.*)

f. (When the children read to the red 5 without making more than five errors: read the story to the children from the beginning to the 5. Ask the specified comprehension questions. When you reach the 5, call on individual children to continue reading the story. Have each child read two or three sentences. Ask the specified comprehension questions.)

[1] What is the title of this story? (Signal.) *Don does good things.*

[2] What did she say? (Signal.) *I think you will make a good super man.*
- Why did she think Don would be a good super man? (The children respond.)

Get ready to read all the words on this page without making a mistake.

EXERCISE 14

Read the fast way

a. Read these words the fast way.
b. (Touch the ball for **pāper.** Pause two seconds.) Get ready. (Signal.) *Paper.* Yes, **paper.**
c. (Repeat *b* for **name, more, wē'll, you'll, wood,** and **not.**)

wē'll

you'll

pāper

name

more

wood

not

Individual test

(Call on individual children to read a column of words from this lesson. If the column contains only one or two words, direct the child to read additional words from an adjacent column. Praise children who read all words with no errors.)

STORYBOOK

EXERCISE 15

First reading—title and three sentences

a. (Pass out Storybook 1.)
b. Everybody, open your reader to page 159.
c. Everybody, touch the title of the story and get ready to read the words in the title.
d. First word. ✔
• Get ready. (Tap.) *Jane.*
e. (Tap for each remaining word in the title.)
f. Everybody, say the title. (Signal.)
Jane wanted to fly, fly, fly.

EXERCISE 6

Words with underlined parts

a. First you're going to read the underlined part of each word in this column. Then you're going to read the whole word.

b. (Touch the ball for **inside.**) Read the underlined part. Get ready. (Tap the ball.) *In.*

• Read the whole word. (Pause.) Get ready. (Slash.) *Inside.*

c. (Repeat step *b* until firm.)

d. (Repeat steps *b* and *c* for each remaining word in the column.)

e. (Repeat the column until children read all the words in order without making a mistake.)

inside

fixed

moped

taped

became

somebody

things

EXERCISE 7

Words with underlined parts

a. First you're going to read the underlined part of each word in this column. Then you're going to read the whole word.

b. (Touch the ball for **hard.**) Read the underlined part. Get ready. (Tap the ball.) *ar.*

• Read the whole word. (Pause.) Get ready. (Slash.) *Hard.*

c. (Repeat step *b* until firm.)

d. (Repeat steps *b* and *c* for each remaining word in the column.)

e. (Repeat the column until children read all the words in order without making a mistake.)

hard

standing

longer

out

car

need

what

Individual test

a. (Call on individual children to read one column of words from the lesson.)

b. (Praise children who read all words with no errors.)

g. Everybody, get ready to read this story.

h. First word. ✔
- Get ready. (Tap.) *A.*

i. Next word. ✔
- Get ready. (Tap.) *Girl.*

j. (Repeat *i* for the remaining words in the first three sentences. Have the children reread the first three sentences until firm.)

EXERCISE 16

Remaining sentences

a. I'm going to call on individual children to read a sentence. Everybody, follow along and point to the words. If you hear a mistake, raise your hand.

b. (Call on a child.) Read the next sentence.

To Correct

word-identification errors (**from**, for example)
1. That word is **from.** What word? *From.*
2. Go back to the beginning of the sentence and read the sentence again.

c. (Call on another child.) Read the next sentence.

d. (Repeat *c* for most of the remaining sentences in the story.)

e. (Occasionally have the group read a sentence. When the group is to read, say:) Everybody, read the next sentence. (Tap for each word in the sentence.)

EXERCISE 17

Second reading—sentences and questions

a. You're going to read the story again. This time I'm going to ask questions.

b. Starting with the first word of the title. ✔
- Get ready. (Tap as the children read the title.)

---

jane wanted to fly, fly, fly [1]

a girl named jane said, "I want to fly, fly, fly in the sky, sky, sky." [2]
her father said, "but if you fall on your head, head, head, you'll end up in bed, bed, bed." [3]

but the girl did not stop talking about flying. one day she went to her dad and said, "if you help me make a big kite, I can fly in the sky like the birds."

her dad said, "I will help you make a kite, but I don't think you should try to fly."

jane said, "that is good, good, good. let's make a kite of wood, wood, wood." [4]

her dad said, "we'll need paper and string to make this thing."

jane and her dad got paper and string and wood. they made a kite that was very, very big.

jane said, "when the wind starts to blow, blow, blow, just see me go, go, go." [5]

her father said, "no, no, no." [6]

more to come

---

c. (Call on a child.) Read the first sentence.

To Correct

word-identification errors (**from**, for example)
1. That word is **from.** What word? *From.*
2. Go back to the beginning of the sentence and read the sentence again.

d. (Call on another child.) Read the next sentence.

e. (Repeat *d* for most of the remaining sentences in the story.)

f. (Occasionally have the group read a sentence.)

g. (After each underlined sentence has been read, present each comprehension question specified below to the entire group.)

[1] Can people really fly? (The children respond.)

[2] What did Jane say? (Signal.)
I want to fly, fly, fly in the sky, sky, sky.
- (Repeat the question until the children give a firm response.)

[3] Let's say that together. (Signal.) *But if you fall on your head, head, head, you'll end up in bed, bed, bed.*
- (Repeat the question until the children give a firm response.)

[4] What are they going to do? (Signal.) *Make a kite.*
- Why are they going to do that? (Signal.) *Because Jane wants to fly.*

[5] Let's say that together. (Signal.)
When the wind starts to blow, blow, blow, just see me go, go, go.

[6] What do you think will happen to Jane? (The children respond.)
- Next time we'll finish the story and find out.

EXERCISE 4A

Rule for words with long and short vowels

a. (Touch the ball for **taped.**) Look at this word. (Pause.) Is there only **one p** in this word? (Signal.) *Yes.*

b. So does the letter **a** say its name? (Signal.) *Yes.*

• Read this word. (Pause three seconds.) Get ready. (Signal.) *Taped.*

c. (Touch the ball for **tapped.**) Look at this word. (Pause.) Is there only **one p** in this word? (Signal.) *No.*

d. So does the letter **a** say its name? (Signal.) *No.*

• Read this word. (Pause three seconds.) Get ready. (Signal.) *Tapped.*

e. (Touch the ball for **dinner.**) Look at this word. (Pause.) Is there only **one n** in this word? (Signal.) *No.*

f. So does the letter **i** say its name? (Signal.) *No.*

• Read this word. (Pause three seconds.) Get ready. (Signal.) *Dinner.*

g. (Touch the ball for **diner.**) Look at this word. (Pause.) Is there only **one n** in this word? (Signal.) *Yes.*

h. So does the letter **i** say its name? (Signal.) *Yes.*

• Read this word. (Pause three seconds.) Get ready. (Signal.) *Diner.*

taped

tapped

dinner

diner

mopped

here

moping

To Correct

1. The **a** says its name. So the word is **taped.**
   OR
   The **a** does not say its name. So the word is **tapped.**

2. (Return to the first word in the column and present all words in order.) Starting over.

EXERCISE 4B

Children spell, then read

a. First you're going to spell each word by letter names. Then you're going to read that word the fast way.

b. (Touch the ball for **taped.**) Spell by letter names. Get ready. (Tap under each letter as the children say:) *T-A-P-E-D.*

• (Return to the ball.) Read it. Get ready. (Slash.) *Taped.*

c. (Repeat step *b* for each remaining word in the column.)

d. (Repeat steps *b* and *c* until firm.)

d. (Repeat steps *b* and *c* for each remaining word in the column.)

e. (Repeat the column until the children read all the words in order without making mistakes.)

I'll

from

thunder

are

else

Sid

I've

EXERCISE 5

Read the fast way

a. You're going to read all the words in this column the fast way.

b. (Touch the ball for **I'll.** Pause.) Get ready. (Slash.) *I'll.*

c. (Repeat step *b* until firm.)

WORKSHEET 62

EXERCISE 18

Picture comprehension

a. Look at the picture.

b. (Ask these questions:)

1. What are Jane and her dad doing? (Signal.) *Making a kite.*
2. Is Jane's kite big or small? (Signal.) *Big.*
3. (Point to the ball of string.) What is that? (Signal.) *String.*
4. (Point to the tail.) What do we call that part of the kite? (Signal.) *The tail.*
5. Show me the wooden parts of the kite. (The children respond.)
6. Show me the paper part of the kite. (The children respond.)
7. Is Jane's father sitting or standing? (Signal.) *Standing.*
8. What will he do with the hammer? (The children respond.)

• What will he do with the nails? (The children respond.)

• What does he have tucked in his belt? (Signal.) *A hammer.*

STORY-PICTURE ITEMS

The children will need pencils.

EXERCISE 19

Story picture

a. (Pass out Worksheet 62 to each child.)

b. (Point to the story-picture items exercise on side 2.)

c. Everybody, touch the instructions. ✔

d. My turn to read the fast way. (Read:) Look at the picture on page 160 of your reader.

e. Your turn to read the instructions the fast way. First word. ✔

• Get ready. (Tap for each word as the children read:) *Look at the picture on page 160 of your reader.*

f. Everybody, what does this instruction tell you to do? (Signal.) *Look at the picture on page 160 of your reader.*

• Do it. (Check that the children look at the picture on page 160.)

g. Everybody, touch item 1 below the instructions. ✔

h. Read the fast way. First word. ✔

• Get ready. (Tap for each word as the children read:) *Is Jane's kite big or small?*

i. Look at the picture on page 160. Is Jane's kite big or small? (Signal.) *Big.* Yes, her kite is **big.**

j. Write the answer in the blank. ✔

k. Everybody, touch item 2. ✔

• First word. Get ready. (Tap for each word as the children read:) *Is her father standing or sitting?*

l. What is her father doing, standing or sitting? (Signal.) *Standing.* Yes, **standing.**

m. Write the answer in the blank. ✔

• (Accept phonetic spelling.)

SUMMARY OF INDEPENDENT ACTIVITY

EXERCISE 20

Introduction to independent activity

a. (Hold up side 1 of Worksheet 62.)

b. Everybody, you're going to finish this worksheet on your own. (Tell the children when they will work the remaining items.)

• Let's go over the things you're going to do.

Story items

(Point to the story-items exercise.) Everybody, remember to write your answers in the blanks.

Following instructions

a. (Touch the sentence in the box.)

b. Everybody, first you're going to read the sentence in the box. Then you're going to read the instructions below the box and do what the instructions tell you to do.

Reading comprehension

(Point to the story on side 2.) You're going to read this story and then do the items. Remember to write the answers in the blanks.

END OF LESSON 62

EXERCISE 2

Introducing hard capitals

a. These are capital letters that don't look like the letters you know. The letters you know are in the top row. The capitals are in the row below.

b. (Point under capital **A.**) This is capital **A.**

c. (Repeat step *b* for each remaining capital.)

d. Your turn. (Point under capital **A.**) What capital? (Signal.) *A.*

e. (Repeat step *d* for each remaining capital.)

f. (Repeat steps *d* and *e* until firm.)

a r d e q

A R D E Q

READING VOCABULARY

EXERCISE 3

Teacher reads the words in red

a. I'll read each word in red. Then you'll spell each word by letter names.

b. (Touch the ball for **handed.**) My turn. (Slash as you say:) Handed. What word? (Signal.) *Handed.*

c. (Return to the ball.) Spell by letter names. Get ready. (Tap under each letter as the children say:) *H-A-N-D-E-D.*

• What word did you spell? (Signal.) *Handed.*

d. (Repeat steps *b* and *c* for each word in red.)

e. Your turn to read all the words in this column.

f. (Touch the ball for **handed.** Pause.) Get ready. (Slash.) *Handed.*

g. (Repeat step *f* for each remaining word in the column.)

h. (Repeat steps *f* and *g* until firm.)

To Correct
word-identification errors
(**hope,** for example)
1. That word is **hope.** What word? (Signal.) *Hope.*
2. (Return to the first word in the column and present all words in order.) Starting over.

handed
nailed
helped
side
must
most
you

EXERCISE 1

Sound combination review

a. Here are some letters that go together. Get ready to tell me the sound they usually make.

b. (Point to **ar.**) What sound do these letters usually make? (Signal.) *Are.* Yes, **are.**

c. (Repeat *b* with **ou** and **al.**)

d. (Repeat the series of sound combinations until firm.)

ar

ou

al

READING VOCABULARY

Get ready to read all the words on this page without making a mistake.

To Correct

1. (Touch the ball for the word the children missed.) Is there an **ē** on the end of this word? (Signal.) (The children respond.)

2. (Point to the first vowel in the word.) So tell me what you say for this letter. (Signal.) (The children respond.)

3. (Touch the ball for the word.) Sound it out. Get ready. (Touch all sounds except the final **e**, if there is one, as the children sound out the word.)

4. What word? (Signal.) (The children respond.)

5. (Return to the first word in the column. Present all the words in order until firm.)

EXERCISE 2

Long and short vowel words

a. Read these words the fast way. Remember what you say if there is an **ē** on the end of a word.

b. (Touch the ball for **kit.** Pause two seconds.) Get ready. (Signal.) *Kit.* Yes, **kit.**

c. (Repeat *b* for **pane, kite,** and **pan.**)

kit

pane

kite

pan

(Repeat any troublesome words.)

Individual test

(Call on individual children. Each child reads a different word.)

CAPITAL LETTERS

EXERCISE 1

Identifying capitals

a. See if you can tell me the letter name of each capital letter on this page.

b. (Point under **T**.) What capital? (Signal.) *T.*

c. (Repeat step *b* for each remaining capital.)

d. (Repeat steps *b* and *c* until firm.)

T K N J Z W U S Y C P I F X O V M

Get ready to read all the words on this page without making a mistake.

five

EXERCISE 3

Practice final-e rule

a. Read this word the fast way. Remember to look at the end of the word.

b. (Touch the ball for **five.** Pause two seconds.) Get ready. (Signal.) *Five.* Yes, **five.**

c. (Touch the ball for **five.**) Sound it out. Get ready. (Quickly touch **f, i, v** as the children say:) *fffiiivvv.*

d. What word? (Signal.) *Five.* Yes, **five.**

e. (Repeat *b* through *d* until firm.)

Jane

EXERCISE 4

Practice final-e rule

a. Read this word the fast way. Remember to look at the end of the word.

b. (Touch the ball for **jane.** Pause two seconds.) Get ready. (Signal.) *Jane.* Yes, **Jane.**

EXERCISE 5

Read the fast way

a. Read these words the fast way.

b. (Touch the ball for **came.** Pause two seconds.) Get ready. (Signal.) *Came.* Yes, **came.**

c. (Repeat *b* for **no, go, goes, like, shake,** and **shaking.**)

came

no

go

goes

like

shake

shaking

know

EXERCISE 6

Listen, sound out with me

a. (Point to **know.**) I'll tell you this word. (Pause.) **Know.** What word? (Signal.) *Know.* Yes, **know.**

b. (Touch the ball for **know.**) Sound it out with me. Get ready. (Quickly touch each sound as you and the children say:) *knnnooowww.*

c. What word? (Signal.) *Know.* Yes, **know.**

d. (Repeat *b* and *c* until firm.)

(Repeat any troublesome words.)

Individual test

(Call on individual children. Each child reads a different word.)

The woman said, "You did not do good. but I think you are sorry. So I will let you try to be a super man again."[3]

"Oh, thank you," don said. "I will try to be good."

The woman held up the dime. She said, "but before I give you the dime back, you must make up for all the bad things you did."[4]

"I will, I will," don said.

don looked at that dime. When he looked up, the woman was not around. don went up the stairs. he said, "I must clean up the mess I made."

So don began to work super hard.⑤[5] he fixed walls and doors and hats. Then he mopped up. Then he fixed a car and a bus. Then he went back to the school and began to fix the wall.[6]

When he was done with the wall, a truck stopped in front of the school. a little man began to carry big bags from the truck.[7] The bags were bigger than the man.[8] don jumped up and ran over to the man.

"let me help you," don said.[9] "You are too small for this job."

The man said, "This is the only job I can get. my baby is sick and I must work."[10]

"I will help you," don said.

This is almost the end.[11]

[3] Why is the woman giving him another chance? (Signal.) *Because she thinks Don is sorry.*

[4] What does Don have to do to get the dime? (Signal.) *Make up for all the bad things.*

[5] What did he do? (Signal.) *He began to work super hard.*

[6] Name some of the good things he did. (The children respond.)

[7] Who was carrying things from the truck? (Signal.) *A little man.*

[8] How big were the bags? (Signal.) *Bigger than the man.*

• Do you think Don will help? (Signal.) *Yes.*

[9] What did Don say? (Signal.) *Let me help you.*

• He sure is doing good now.

[10] Why does that man have to work? (Signal.) *His baby is sick.*

• Why doesn't he get a different job? (Signal.) *That's the only job he can get.*

[11] Next time we'll read the end of the Don stories.

EXERCISE 9

Picture comprehension

a. Look at the picture.

b. (Ask these questions:)

1. What's that little man doing? (The children respond.)

2. Does that bag look too heavy for him? (Signal.) *Yes.*

• Why do you think so? (The children respond.)

3. What's Don going to do? (The children respond.)

4. What would you do if you were Don? (The children respond.)

EXERCISE 10

Summary of independent activities

a. (Pass out Worksheet 88 to each child.)

b. Everybody, now you'll do your worksheet. Remember to do all parts of the worksheet and to read all the parts carefully.

END OF LESSON 88

Do not touch small letters.

Get ready to read all the words on this page without making a mistake.

EXERCISE 7

Listen, sound out

a. (Point to **again.**) I'll tell you this word. (Pause.) **Again.** What word? (Signal.) *Again.* Yes, **again.**

b. (Touch the ball for **again.**) Sound it out. Get ready. (Quickly touch **a, g, a, i, n** as the children say:) *aaagaaaiiinnn.*

c. What word? (Signal.) *Again.* Yes, **again.**

d. (Repeat *b* and *c* until firm.)

EXERCISE 8

ou word

a. (Touch the ball for **clouds.**) Read this word the fast way. (Pause two seconds.) Get ready. (Signal.) *Clouds.* Yes, **clouds.**

b. (Point to **ou** in **clouds.**) Everybody, what do these letters say? (Signal.) *ou.* Yes, **ou.**

c. (Touch the ball for **clouds.**) Sound it out. Get ready. (Quickly touch **c, l, ou, d, s** as the children say:) *cllloudsss.*

d. What word? (Signal.) *Clouds.* Yes, **clouds.**

e. (Repeat *c* and *d* until firm.)

EXERCISE 9

ar word

a. (Touch the ball for **started.**) Read this word the fast way. (Pause two seconds.) Get ready. (Signal.) *Started.* Yes, **started.**

b. (Point to **ar** in **started.**) Everybody, what do these letters say? (Signal.) *Are.* Yes, **are.**

c. (Touch the ball for **started.**) Sound it out. Get ready. (Quickly touch **s, t, ar, t, e, d** as the children say:) *sssstarted.*

d. What word? (Signal.) *Started.* Yes, **started.**

e. (Repeat *c* and *d* until firm.)

again

clouds

started

(Repeat any troublesome words.)

Individual test

(Call on individual children. Each child reads a different word.)

helped

EXERCISE 10

Sound out first

a. (Touch the ball for **helped.**) Sound it out. Get ready. (Quickly touch **h, e, l, p, d** as the children say:) *heeelllpd.*

b. What word? (Signal.) *Helped.* Yes, **helped.**

c. (Repeat exercise until firm.)

lifted

EXERCISE 11

Sound out first

a. (Touch the ball for **lifted.**) Sound it out. Get ready. (Quickly touch **l, i, f, t, e, d** as the children say:) *llliiifffteeed.*

b. What word? (Signal.) *Lifted.* Yes, **lifted.**

c. (Repeat exercise until firm.)

landed

EXERCISE 12

Two-part word

a. (Cover **ed.** Point to **land.**) Everybody, tell me what this part of the word says. Get ready. (Signal.) *Land.* Yes, **land.**

b. (Uncover **ed.** Touch the ball for **landed.**) Now tell me what the whole word says. Get ready. (Signal.) *Landed.* Yes, **landed.**

c. (Repeat exercise until firm.)

STORYBOOK

EXERCISE 6

Read the item

a. (Pass out Storybook 2.)

b. Open your reader to page 13. Get ready to read the item.

c. Finger under the first word of the item. ✔
- Get ready. (Tap.) *When.*

d. Next word. (Pause.) Get ready. (Tap.) *The.*

e. (Repeat step *d* for the remaining words in the item.)

f. (Repeat steps *c* through *e* until the item is firm.)

g. Everybody, say that item. (Pause. Signal.) *When the teacher says "Hate," say "Hat."*

To Correct
1. Everybody, say the item with me. (Signal. Say the item with the children at a normal speaking rate. Repeat until firm.)
2. (Repeat step *g*. Then skip to step *i*.)

h. Again. (Repeat step *g* until firm.)

i. What are you going to say when I say "**Hate**"? (Signal.) *Hat.*
- When are you going to say "**Hat**"? (Signal.) *When the teacher says "Hate."*

To Correct
(Have the children read the item aloud. Then repeat the questions.)

EXERCISE 7

Play the game

a. Read the item to yourself and think about what you're going to do and when you're going to do it. Raise your hand when you're ready.

b. (After the children raise their hands, say:) Get ready to play the game.

c. My turn. (Pause.) **Hate.** (Signal.) (The children are to say *Hat* immediately.)

To Correct
(Have the children read the item aloud. Then play the game again.)

---

don Works Super hard[1]

Somebody called don from the stairs. don went down the stairs. It was dim down there, but don could see the woman who gave him the dime.[2] The woman had a cap and a cape just like don's.

EXERCISE 8

Reading—decoding

a. Everybody, look at the story on page 13.

b. Remember, if the group reads all the way to the red five without making more than five errors, we can go on.

c. Everybody, touch the title of the story. ✔

d. If you hear a mistake, raise your hand. Remember, children who do not have their place lose their turn. (Call on individual children to read two or three sentences. Do not ask comprehension questions. Tally all errors.)

To Correct
word-identification errors (**from,** for example)
1. That word is **from.** What word? *From.*
2. Go back to the beginning of the sentence and read the sentence again.

e. (If the children make more than five errors before they reach the red 5: when they reach the 5 return to the beginning of the story and have the children reread to the 5. Do not ask comprehension questions. Repeat step e until firm, and then go on to step *f*.)

f. (When the children read to the red 5 without making more than five errors: read the story to the children from the beginning to the 5. Ask the specified comprehension questions. When you reach the 5, call on individual children to continue reading the story. Have each child read two or three sentences. Ask the specified comprehension questions.)

[1] What's the title of this story? (Signal.) *Don works super hard.*

[2] Who was down there? (Signal.) *The woman who gave him the dime.*

Get ready to read all the words on this page without making a mistake.

named

EXERCISE 13

Two-part word

a. (Cover **d.** Point to **name.**) Everybody, tell me what this part of the word says. Get ready. (Signal.) *Name.* Yes, **name.**

b. (Uncover **d.** Touch the ball for **named.**) Now tell me what the whole word says. Get ready. (Signal.) *Named.* Yes, **named.**

c. (Repeat exercise until firm.)

miles

EXERCISE 14

Two-part word

a. (Cover **s.** Point to **mile.**) Everybody, tell me what this part of the word says. Get ready. (Signal.) *Mile.* Yes, **mile.**

b. (Uncover **s.** Touch the ball for **miles.**) Now tell me what the whole word says. Get ready. (Signal.) *Miles.* Yes, **miles.**

c. (Repeat exercise until firm.)

EXERCISE 15

Read the fast way

a. Read these words the fast way.

b. (Touch the ball for **held.** Pause two seconds.) Get ready. (Signal.) *Held.* Yes, **held.**

c. (Repeat *b* for **does, didn't,** and **wōn't.**)

held

does

didn't

wōn't

Individual test

(Call on individual children to read a column of words from this lesson. If the column contains only one or two words, direct the child to read additional words from an adjacent column. Praise children who read all words with no errors.)

STORY 63
EXERCISE 16

First reading—title and three sentences

a. (Pass out Storybook 1.)

b. Everybody, open your reader to page 161.

c. Everybody, touch the title of the story and get ready to read the words in the title.

d. First word. ✔

• Get ready. (Tap.) *Jane.*

e. (Tap for each remaining word in the title.)

f. Everybody, say the title. (Signal.) *Jane goes up, up, up.*

EXERCISE 4

Words with underlined parts

a. First you're going to read the underlined part of each word in this column. Then you're going to read the whole word.

b. (Touch the ball for **called.**) Read the underlined part. Get ready. (Tap the ball.) *All.*

• Read the whole word. (Pause.) Get ready. (Slash.) *Called.*

c. (Repeat step *b* until firm.)

d. (Repeat steps *b* and *c* for each remaining word in the column.)

e. (Repeat the column until children read all the words in order without making a mistake.)

called

clean

then

almost

who

out

around

EXERCISE 5

Words with underlined parts

a. First you're going to read the underlined part of each word in this column. Then you're going to read the whole word.

b. (Touch the ball for **nobody.**) Read the underlined part. Get ready. (Tap the ball.) *No.*

• Read the whole word. (Pause.) Get ready. (Slash.) *Nobody.*

c. (Repeat step *b* until firm.)

d. (Repeat steps *b* and *c* for each remaining word in the column.)

e. (Repeat the column until children read all the words in order without making a mistake.)

nobody

somebody

anybody

bigger

before

jumped

thanked

Individual test

a. (Call on individual children to read one column of words from the lesson.)

b. (Praise children who read all words with no errors.)

g. Everybody, get ready to read this story.

h. First word. ✔
- Get ready. (Tap.) *A.*

i. Next word. ✔
- Get ready. (Tap.) *Girl.*

j. (Repeat *i* for the remaining words in the first three sentences. Have the children reread the first three sentences until firm.)

EXERCISE 17

Remaining sentences

a. I'm going to call on individual children to read a sentence. Everybody, follow along and point to the words. If you hear a mistake, raise your hand.

b. (Call on a child.) Read the next sentence.

To Correct

word-identification errors (**from,** for example)
1. That word is **from.** What word? *From.*
2. Go back to the beginning of the sentence and read the sentence again.

c. (Call on another child.) Read the next sentence.

d. (Repeat *c* for most of the remaining sentences in the story.)

e. (Occasionally have the group read a sentence. When the group is to read, say:) Everybody, read the next sentence. (Tap for each word in the sentence.)

EXERCISE 18

Second reading—sentences and questions

a. You're going to read the story again. This time I'm going to ask questions.

b. Starting with the first word of the title. ✔
- Get ready. (Tap as the children read the title.)

---

jane goes up, up, up[1]

a girl named jane wanted to fly, but her dad didn't want her to fly. he helped her make a big kite. but he told her that she could not fly with that kite.[2]

then one day, the wind started to blow. jane got her big kite. she said, "I don't know why, why, why dad won't let me fly, fly, fly."

as she was holding the kite, a big wind started to blow the kite away.[3] jane said, "I must hold on to that kite or it will go far away."

so she held on to the kite. but when the wind started to blow very hard, it lifted the kite into the sky.[4] she looked down and yelled, "I want my dad, dad, dad, because this is bad, bad, bad."[5]

the kite went up and up. soon it was near the clouds. jane yelled, "now I'm over the town, town, town, but I want to go down, down, down."

at last the kite came down. it landed in a farm five miles from town.[6] jane left the kite there and walked back to her home.[7] then she told her dad, "now I know why, why, why I should not fly, fly, fly."[8]

jane never tried flying again.

the end

---

c. (Call on a child.) Read the first sentence.

d. (Call on another child.) Read the next sentence.

e. (Repeat *d* for most of the remaining sentences in the story.)

f. (Occasionally have the group read a sentence.)

g. (After each underlined sentence has been read, present each comprehension question specified below to the entire group.)

[1] Why is she going up? (The children respond.)

[2] What did he tell her? (Signal.) *She could not fly with that kite.*
- Why didn't he want her to fly? (The children respond.)

[3] Why did the kite start to blow away? (Signal.) *Because of a big wind.*

[4] How did she get into the sky? (The children respond.)

[5] What did she yell? (Signal.) *I want my dad, dad, dad, because this is bad, bad, bad.*
- (Repeat the question until the children give a firm response.)
- Was she happy? (Signal.) *No.*
- How do you know? (The children respond.)

[6] Where did the kite come down? (Signal.) *In a farm.*
- How far was Jane from town? (Signal.) *Five miles.*

[7] How did she get home? (Signal.) *She walked.*

[8] Everybody, say what Jane said. (Signal.) *Now I know why, why, why I should not fly, fly, fly.*
- Why shouldn't she fly? (The children respond.)

EXERCISE 3A

Rule for words with long and short vowels

a. (Point to **moping** and **mopping**.) Here's a rule for reading these words: If there is only **one p**, the **o** says its name.

b. (Touch the ball for **moping**.) Read this word. (Pause three seconds.) Get ready. (Signal.) *Moping.*

c. (Point to the **p**'s in **mopping**.) This word does not have one **p**. It has **two.** So the **o** does not say its name.

d. (Touch the ball for **mopping**.) Read this word. (Pause three seconds.) Get ready. (Signal.) *Mopping.*

e. (Point to **canned** and **caned**.) Here's a rule for reading these words: If there is only **one n**, the **a** says its name.

f. (Point to the **n**'s in **canned**.) This word does **not** have one **n**. It has **two.** So the **a** does not say its name.

g. (Touch the ball for **canned**.) Read this word. (Pause three seconds.) Get ready. (Signal.) *Canned.*

h. (Point to the **n** in **caned**.) This word has **one n.** (Point to the **a**.) So the **a** says its name.

i. (Touch the ball for **caned**.) Read this word. (Pause three seconds.) Get ready. (Signal.) *Caned.*

To Correct
incorrect vowel sound (**moping,** for example)
1. There is one **p.** The **o** says its name. So the word is **moping.** What word? (Signal.) *Moping.*
   OR
   There are **two p**'s. The **o** does not say its name. So the word is **mopping.** What word? (Signal.) *Mopping.*
2. (Return to the first word in the column and present all words in order.) Starting over.

moping

mopping

canned

caned

you

tap

tape

j. (Touch the ball for **moping**.) Now you're going to read all of these words the fast way. (Pause two seconds.) Get ready. (Signal.) *Moping.*

k. (Repeat *j* for remaining words in exercise 3A.)

EXERCISE 3B

Children spell, then read

a. First you're going to spell each word by letter names. Then you're going to read that word the fast way.

b. (Touch the ball for **moping**.) Spell by letter names. Get ready. (Tap under each letter as the children say:) *M-O-P-I-N-G.*
- (Return to the ball.)
- Read it. Get ready. (Slash.) *Moping.*

c. (Repeat *b* for each remaining word in the column.)

d. (Repeat *b* and *c* until firm.)

EXERCISE 19

Picture comprehension

a. Look at the picture.

b. (Ask these questions:)

1. Where is Jane in this picture? (Signal.) *In the sky.*

2. How do you know she's in the sky? (Let the children comment for ten seconds. Then comment briefly.)

3. What part of the kite is she holding on to? (Signal.) *The string.*

4. Look at her face. How do you think she feels? (The children respond.)

5. What do you think she is thinking? (The children respond.)

SUMMARY OF INDEPENDENT ACTIVITY
EXERCISE 20

Introduction to independent activity

a. (Pass out Worksheet 63 to each child.)

b. (Hold up side 1 of your worksheet.) Everybody, you're going to do this worksheet on your own. (Tell the children when they will work the items.)

• Let's go over the things you're going to do.

Story items

(Point to the story-items exercise.) Everybody, remember to write your answer in the blanks.

Following instructions

a. (Touch the sentence in the box.)

b. Everybody, first you're going to read the sentence in the box. Then you're going to read the instructions below the box and do what the instructions tell you to do.

Story-picture items

(Point to the story-picture items on side 2.) Remember to follow these instructions and look at the picture when you work these items.

Reading comprehension

(Point to the story.) You're going to read this story and then do the items. Remember to write the answers in the blanks.

END OF LESSON 63

CAPITAL LETTERS

EXERCISE 1

Introducing capitals

a. These are capital letters. Capital letters are bigger than the other letters. In a few days, every sentence that you'll read will begin with a capital letter. See if you can tell me the letter name of each capital letter on this page.

b. (Point under **O**.) What capital? (Signal.) *O.*

c. (Repeat step *b* for each remaining capital.)

To Correct

(**W,** for example)
1. This is **double U.**
2. (Point under the capital.) What capital? (Signal.) *Double U.* Remember, **double U.**

d. (Repeat steps *b* and *c* until firm.)

O I Z V P J

N T C M U

F Y K X S W

READING VOCABULARY

EXERCISE 2

Teacher reads the words in red

a. I'll read each word in red. Then you'll spell each word by letter names.

b. (Touch the ball for **only.**) My turn. (Slash as you say:) Only. What word? (Signal.) *Only.*

c. (Return to the ball.) Spell by letter names. Get ready. (Tap under each letter as the children say:) *O-N-L-Y.* What word did you spell? (Signal.) *Only.*

d. (Repeat steps *b* and *c* for each word in red.)

e. Your turn to read all the words in this column.

f. (Touch the ball for **only.** Pause.) Get ready. (Slash.) *Only.*

g. (Repeat step *f* for each remaining word in the column.)

h. (Repeat steps *f* and *g* until firm.)

To Correct

word-identification errors (**hope,** for example)
1. That word is **hope.** What word? (Signal.) *Hope.*
2. (Return to the first word in the column and present all words in order.) Starting over.

only

fixed

carry

bags

baby

truck

saw

EXERCISE 1

Sound combination review

a. Here are some letters that go together. Get ready to tell me the sound they usually make.

b. (Point to **ar.**) What sound do these letters usually make? (Signal.) *Are.* Yes, **are.**

c. (Repeat *b* with **ou** and **al.**)

d. (Repeat the series of sound combinations until firm.)

ar
ou
al

READING VOCABULARY

Get ready to read all the words on this page without making a mistake.

To Correct

1. (Touch the ball for the word the children missed.) Is there an ē on the end of this word? (Signal.) (The children respond.)
2. (Point to the first vowel in the word.) So tell me what you say for this letter. (Signal.) (The children respond.)
3. (Touch the ball for the word.) Sound it out. Get ready. (Touch all sounds except the final **e**, if there is one, as the children sound out the word.)
4. What word? (Signal.) (The children respond.)
5. (Return to the first word in the column. Present all the words in order until firm.)

EXERCISE 2

Long and short vowel words

a. Read these words the fast way. Remember what you say if there is an ē on the end of a word.

b. (Touch the ball for **ate.** Pause two seconds.) Get ready. (Signal.) *Ate.* Yes, **ate.**

c. (Repeat *b* for **tim, at,** and **time.**)

ate
tim
at
time

(Repeat any troublesome words.)

Individual test

(Call on individual children. Each child reads a different word.)

all at once don looked down and saw that he did not have his cape. There was no cap on his head.[5]

don said, "I must see if I am still super."[6]

don ran to the street as fast as he could go. but he did not go very fast. he stopped at a parked car and tried to pick it up. he could not do that. ⑤[7]

"I am no longer super," he said. "I will tap the dime again." but the tape and the dime were not on his arm.[8]

Slowly, don walked back to the hat store. he was very sad. he said, "The woman who gave me the dime told me to be a good super man. but I did not do good."[9]It was dark inside the store, but don could see the holes in the walls and the holes in the doors and the holes in the hats.

don sat near the mop and began to mope. "I must fix up this store," he said.[10] he began to clean up the mess when a sound came from the stairs.

"Come down here, don," somebody called.[11]

To be continued[12]

---

[5] What happened to his cap and his cape? (The children respond.)
- Why are they gone? (The children respond.)

[6] Do you think he is still super? (The children respond.)
- Keep on reading. We'll find out.

[7] Was he still super? (Signal.) *No.*
- What happened when he tried to run fast? (The children respond.)
- And when he tried to pick up the parked car? (The children respond.)

[8] Why couldn't he tap the dime again? (The children respond.)

[9] Does he know he didn't do good? (Signal.) *Yes.*

[10] Is he sorry for what he has done? (Signal.) *Yes.*
- So what's he going to do about it? (Signal.) *Fix up the store.*

[11] Who could it be? (The children respond.)

[12] We'll read more about Don next time.

EXERCISE 9

Picture comprehension

a. What do you think you'll see in the picture? (The children respond.)

b. Turn the page and look at the picture.

c. (Ask these questions:)
1. Where is Don sitting? (The children respond.)
2. How do you know he is sad? (The children respond.)
3. What do you think he's saying to himself? (The children respond.)

WORKSHEET 87

EXERCISE 10

Summary of independent activities

a. (Pass out Worksheet 87 to each child.)

b. Everybody, now you'll do your worksheet. Remember to do all parts of the worksheet and to read all the parts carefully.

END OF LESSON 87

Do not touch small letters.

Get ready to read all the words on this page without making a mistake.

blōw

EXERCISE 3

Sound out first

a. (Touch the ball for **blōw.**) Sound it out. Get ready. (Quickly touch **b, l, ō, w** as the children say:) *blllōōōwww.*
b. What word? (Signal.) *Blow.* Yes, **blow.**
c. (Repeat exercise until firm.)

pretty

EXERCISE 4

Sound out first

a. (Touch the ball for **pretty.**) Sound it out. Get ready. (Quickly touch **p, r, e,** between the **t**'s, **y** as the children say:) *prrreeetyyy.*
b. What word? (Signal.) *Pretty.* Yes, **pretty.**
c. (Repeat exercise until firm.)

happened

EXERCISE 5

Sound out first

a. (Touch the ball for **happened.**) Sound it out. Get ready. (Quickly touch **h, a,** between the **p**'s, **e, n, d** as the children say:) *haaapeeennnd.*
b. What word? (Signal.) *Happened.* Yes, **happened.**
c. (Repeat exercise until firm.)

proud

EXERCISE 6

ou word

a. (Touch the ball for **proud.**) Read this word the fast way. (Pause two seconds.) Get ready. (Signal.) *Proud.* Yes, **proud.**
b. (Point to **ou** in **proud.**) Everybody, what do these letters say? (Signal.) *ou.* Yes, **ou.**
c. (Touch the ball for **proud.**) Sound it out. Get ready. (Quickly touch **p, r, ou, d** as the children say:) *prrroud.*
d. What word? (Signal.) *Proud.* Yes, **proud.**
e. (Repeat *c* and *d* until firm.)

darker

EXERCISE 7

ar word

a. (Touch the ball for **darker.**) Read this word the fast way. (Pause two seconds.) Get ready. (Signal.) *Darker.* Yes, **darker.**
b. (Point to **ar** in **darker.**) Everybody, what do these letters say? (Signal.) *Are.* Yes, **are.**
c. (Touch the ball for **darker.**) Sound it out. Get ready. (Quickly touch **d, ar, k, er** as the children say:) *darkerrr.*
d. What word? (Signal.) *Darker.* Yes, **darker.**
e. (Repeat *c* and *d* until firm.)

(Repeat any troublesome words.)

Individual test

(Call on individual children. Each child reads a different word.)

EXERCISE 8

Read the fast way

a. Read these words the fast way.
b. (Touch the ball for **once.** Pause two seconds.) Get ready. (Signal.) *Once.* Yes, **once.**
c. (Repeat *b* for **went, grōw, couldn't,** and **bēgan.**)

once

went

grōw

couldn't

bēgan

STORYBOOK

READ THE ITEMS 87
EXERCISE 6

Read the item

a. (Pass out Storybook 2.)

b. Open your reader to page 10. Get ready to read the item.

c. Finger under the first word of the item. ✔
- Get ready. (Tap.) *If.*

d. Next word. (Pause.) Get ready. (Tap.) *The.*

e. (Repeat step *d* for the remaining words in the item.)

f. (Repeat steps *c* through *e* until the item is firm.)

g. Everybody, say that item. (Pause. Signal.) *If the teacher says "When," say "Then."*

To Correct
1. Everybody, say the item with me. (Signal. Say the item with the children at a normal speaking rate. Repeat until firm.)
2. (Repeat step *g.* Then skip to step *i.*)

h. Again. (Repeat step *g* until firm.)

i. What are you going to say if I say "**When**"? (Signal.) *Then.*
- When are you going to say "**Then**"? (Signal.) *When the teacher says "When."*

To Correct
(Have the children read the item aloud. Then repeat the questions.)

EXERCISE 7

Play the game

a. Read the item to yourself and think about what you're going to do and when you're going to do it. Raise your hand when you're ready.

b. (After the children raise their hands, say:) Get ready to play the game.

c. My turn. (Pause.) **When.** (Signal.) (The children are to say *Then* immediately.)

To Correct
(Have the children read the item aloud. Then play the game again.)

---

don mopes[1]

The woman in the hat store told don to do good. but did don do what the woman said?[2]

don had made holes in walls. he crashed a car and a bus. he ran into the side of a school.[3] The boys and girls began to shout, "We hate you." Then they ran away.

don began to mope. he said, "I am a super man. but nobody likes me."[4] a tear ran down don's cheek. Then another tear ran down his cheek.

STORY 87
EXERCISE 8

Reading—decoding

a. Everybody, look at the story on page 10.

b. Remember, if the group reads all the way to the red five without making more than five errors, we can go on.

c. Everybody, touch the title of the story. ✔

d. If you hear a mistake, raise your hand. Remember, children who do not have their place lose their turn. (Call on individual children to read two or three sentences. Do not ask comprehension questions. Tally all errors.)

To Correct
word-identification errors (**from**, for example)
1. That word is **from.** What word? *From.*
2. Go back to the beginning of the sentence and read the sentence again.

e. (If the children make more than five errors before they reach the red 5: when they reach the 5 return to the beginning of the story and have the children reread to the 5. Do not ask comprehension questions. Repeat step *e* until firm, and then go on to step *f.*)

f. (When the children read to the red 5 without making more than five errors: read the story to the children from the beginning to the 5. Ask the specified comprehension questions. When you reach the 5, call on individual children to continue reading the story. Have each child read two or three sentences. Ask the specified comprehension questions.)

[1] What will he do? (Signal.) *Mope.*

[2] Did he? (Signal.) *No.*

[3] Name some bad things Don has done. (The children respond.)

[4] Why is he moping? (Signal.) *Nobody likes him.*

Do not touch small letters.

Get ready to read all the words on this page without making a mistake.

thunder

EXERCISE 9

Read the fast way first

a. (Touch the ball for **thunder.**) Read this word the fast way. (Pause two seconds.) Get ready. (Signal.) *Thunder.* Yes, **thunder.**

b. (Return to the ball.) Sound it out. Get ready. (Quickly touch **th, u, n, d, er** as the children say:) *thththuuunnnderrr.*

c. What word? (Signal.) *Thunder.* Yes, **thunder.**

d. (Repeat *b* and *c* until firm.)

e. (Repeat the exercise for **tried.**)

tried

EXERCISE 10

al word

a. (Point to **al** in **small.**) What do these letters say? (Signal.) *All.* Yes, **all.**

b. (Touch the ball for **small.**) Read this word the fast way. Get ready. (Signal.) *Small.* Yes, **small.**

EXERCISE 11

Listen, sound out

a. (Point to **two.**) I'll tell you this word. (Pause.) **Two.** What word? (Signal.) *Two.* Yes, **two.**

b. (Touch the ball for **two.**) Sound it out. Get ready. (Quickly touch **t, w, o** as the children say:) *twwwooo.*

c. What word? (Signal.) *Two.* Yes, **two.** This is the word for the **number** two.

d. (Repeat *b* and *c* until firm.)

EXERCISE 12

Two-part word

a. (Cover **s.** Point to **make.**) Everybody, tell me what this part of the word says. Get ready. (Signal.) *Make.* Yes, **make.**

b. (Uncover **s.** Touch the ball for **makes.**) Now tell me what the whole word says. Get ready. (Signal.) *Makes.* Yes, **makes.**

c. (Repeat exercise until firm.)

(Repeat any troublesome words.)

Individual test

(Call on individual children. Each child reads a different word.)

small

two

makes

EXERCISE 4

Words with underlined parts

a. First you're going to read the underlined part of each word in this column. Then you're going to read the whole word.

b. (Touch the ball for **clean**.) Read the underlined part. Get ready. (Tap the ball.) ē ē ē.

• Read the whole word. (Pause.) Get ready. (Slash.) *Clean.*

c. (Repeat step *b* until firm.)

d. (Repeat steps *b* and *c* for each remaining word in the column.)

e. (Repeat the column until children read all the words in order without making a mistake.)

clean

called

arm

dark

cheek

tear

school

EXERCISE 5

Words with underlined parts

a. First you're going to read the underlined part of each word in this column. Then you're going to read the whole word.

b. (Touch the ball for **longer**.) Read the underlined part. Get ready. (Tap the ball.) *Long.*

• Read the whole word. (Pause.) Get ready. (Slash.) *Longer.*

c. (Repeat step *b* until firm.)

d. (Repeat steps *b* and *c* for each remaining word in the column.)

e. (Repeat the column until children read all the words in order without making a mistake.)

longer

crashed

mopped

nobody

somebody

parked

slowly

Individual test

a. (Call on individual children to read one column of words from the lesson.)

b. (Praise children who read all words with no errors.)

Get ready to read all the words on this page without making a mistake.

shake

EXERCISE 13

Practice final-e rule

a. Read this word the fast way. Remember to look at the end of the word.

b. (Touch the ball for **shake.** Pause two seconds.) Get ready. (Signal.) *Shake.* Yes, **shake.**

c. (Touch the ball for **shake.**) Sound it out. Get ready. (Quickly touch **sh, a, k** as the children say:) *shshshaaak.*

d. What word? (Signal.) *Shake.* Yes, **shake.**

e. (Repeat *b* through *d* until firm.)

EXERCISE 14

Read the fast way

a. Read these words the fast way.

b. (Touch the ball for **shaking.** Pause two seconds.) Get ready. (Signal.) *Shaking.* Yes, **shaking.**

c. (Repeat *b* for **maker, making, blōwing, here, those,** and **more.**)

maker

making

blōwing

here

those

more

Individual test

(Call on individual children to read a column of words from this lesson. If the column contains only one or two words, direct the child to read additional words from an adjacent column.)

STORY 64
EXERCISE 15

First reading—title and three sentences

a. (Pass out Storybook 1.)

b. Everybody, open your reader to page 164.

c. Everybody, touch the title of the story and get ready to read the words in the title.

d. First word. ✔

• Get ready. (Tap.) *The.*

e. (Tap for each remaining word in the title.)

f. Everybody, say the title. (Signal.) *The little cloud.*

READING VOCABULARY

EXERCISE 2

Spelling by letter names

a. My turn to spell some of these words by saying the letter names.

b. (Touch the ball for **hate.**) My turn. (Tap under each letter as you say:) **H-A-T-E.**

c. (Touch the ball for **dim.**) My turn. (Tap under each letter as you say:) **D-I-M.**

d. (Touch the ball for **her.**) My turn. (Tap under each letter as you say:) **H-E-R.**

e. Your turn to spell all the words in this column by letter names.

f. (Touch the ball for **hate.**) Spell by letter names. Get ready. (Tap under each letter as children say:) *H-A-T-E.*

g. (Repeat step *f* for each remaining word in the column.)

h. (Repeat any words on which children make mistakes.)

i. Now you're going to read all the words in this column the fast way.

j. (Touch the ball for **hate.**) Get ready. (Slash.) *Hate.*

k. (Repeat step *j* for each remaining word in the column.)

l. (Repeat steps *j* and *k* until firm.)

hate

dim

her

here

again

cape

mope

To Correct

word-identification errors (**hope,** for example)

1. That word is **hope.** What word? (Signal.) *Hope.*
2. (Return to the first word in the column and present all words in order.) Starting over.

EXERCISE 3

Teacher reads the words in red

a. I'll read each word in red. Then you'll spell each word by letter names.

b. (Touch the ball for **could.**) My turn. (Slash as you say:) Could. What word? (Signal.) *Could.*

c. (Return to the ball.) Spell by letter names. Get ready. (Tap under each letter as the children say:) *C-O-U-L-D.*

• What word did you spell? (Signal.) *Could.*

d. (Repeat steps *b* and *c* for each word in red.)

e. Your turn to read all the words in this column.

f. (Touch the ball for **could.** Pause.) Get ready. (Slash.) *Could.*

g. (Repeat step *f* for each remaining word in the column.)

h. (Repeat steps *f* and *g* until firm.)

could

come

long

head

same

holes

tried

g. Everybody, get ready to read this story.

h. First word. ✔

• Get ready. (Tap.) *There.*

i. Next word. ✔

• Get ready. (Tap.) *Was.*

j. (Repeat *i* for the remaining words in the first three sentences. Have the children reread the first three sentences until firm.)

EXERCISE 16

Remaining sentences

a. I'm going to call on individual children to read a sentence. Everybody, follow along and point to the words. If you hear a mistake, raise your hand.

b. (Call on a child.) Read the next sentence.

To Correct

word-identification errors (**from,** for example)

1. That word is **from.** What word? *From.*
2. Go back to the beginning of the sentence and read the sentence again.

c. (Call on another child.) Read the next sentence.

d. (Repeat *c* for most of the remaining sentences in the story.)

e. (Occasionally have the group read a sentence. When the group is to read, say:) Everybody, read the next sentence. (Tap for each word in the sentence.)

---

the little cloud[1]

there was a little cloud. the little cloud lived in the sky with a mother cloud and a father cloud.[2]

the father cloud was very big and very dark. every now and then the father cloud would say, "it is time to make some rain."[3] the father cloud would shake and make loud thunder sounds—"boom, boom." then the rain would fall from the cloud. the father cloud was very proud. he was the best rain maker in the sky.[4]

but the mother cloud was pretty good at making rain too. every now and then she would say, "I think I'll make some rain." she would make some loud thunder sounds, and out would come the rain.[5]

but the little cloud could not make rain. he would say, "I think I'll make some rain." he would shake and shake. he would try as hard as he could, but no rain came from that small cloud.[6]

EXERCISE 17

Second reading—sentences and questions

a. You're going to read the story again. This time I'm going to ask questions.

b. Starting with the first word of the title. ✔

• Get ready. (Tap as the children read the title.)

c. (Call on a child.) Read the first sentence.

To Correct

word-identification errors (**from,** for example)

1. That word is **from.** What word? *From.*
2. Go back to the beginning of the sentence and read the sentence again.

d. (Call on another child.) Read the next sentence.

e. (Repeat *d* for most of the remaining sentences in the story.)

f. (Occasionally have the group read a sentence.)

g. (After each underlined sentence has been read, present each comprehension question specified below to the entire group.)

[1] What's this story going to be about? (Signal.) *The little cloud.*

[2] Who did the little cloud live with? (Signal.) *A mother cloud and a father cloud.*

[3] What did the father cloud say? (Signal.) *It is time to make some rain.*

[4] Why was the father cloud proud? (Signal.) *He was the best rain maker in the sky.*

[5] Was the mother cloud good at making rain? (Signal.) *Yes.*

• Do you think the little cloud can make rain? (The children respond.)

[6] What happened when the small cloud tried to make rain? (Signal.) *No rain came.*

★ **CAPITAL LETTERS**

EXERCISE 1

Introducing capitals

a. These are capital letters. Capital letters are bigger than the other letters. In a few days, every sentence that you'll read will begin with a capital letter. See if you can tell me the letter name of each capital letter on this page.

b. (Point under **P.**) What capital? (Signal.) *P.*

c. (Repeat step *b* for each remaining capital.)

To Correct
(W, for example)
1. This is **double U.**
2. (Point under the capital.) What capital? (Signal.) *Double U.*
• Remember, **double U.**

d. (Repeat steps *b* and *c* until firm.)

P C Y F W K I Z O J S M N T V X U

the mother cloud said, "don't feel bad. when you are bigger, you will make rain. you are too small now, but you will grow."[7]

and that small cloud did grow. every day he got a little bigger and a little darker. and every day he tried to make rain. but he couldn't even make loud sounds. and not one drop of rain came from that cloud. he felt very sad.[8]

then one day something happened.[9] the wind was blowing very hard. that wind began to blow the little cloud far away from his mother and father.[10] he called to them. but they were making loud sounds, so they couldn't hear him.[11]

more next time

EXERCISE 18
Picture comprehension
a. Look at the picture.
b. (Ask these questions:)
1. What are the mother and father cloud doing? (Signal.) *Making rain.*
2. Show me the little cloud. (The children respond.)
3. Which cloud is darker, the little cloud or the father cloud? (Signal.) *The father cloud.*
4. How do you think the little cloud feels? (Signal.) *Sad.*
5. Why is the little cloud sad? (Signal.) *Because he cannot make rain.*
6. Do you think he'll ever make rain? (The children respond.)

[7] Why couldn't the small cloud make rain? (Signal.) *He was too small.*
[8] Why did he feel sad? (Signal.) *He couldn't make rain.*
[9] What do you think happened? (The children respond.)
• Let's read some more and find out.
[10] What was making the cloud go so far away from his mother and father? (Signal.) *The wind.*
[11] Why didn't they hear him when he called? (Signal.) *They were making loud sounds.*

SUMMARY OF INDEPENDENT ACTIVITY
EXERCISE 19
Introduction to independent activity
a. (Pass out Worksheet 64 to each child.)
b. (Hold up side 1 of your worksheet.) Everybody, you're going to do this worksheet on your own. (Tell the children when they will work the items.)
• Let's go over the things you're going to do.

Story items
(Point to the story-items exercise.) Everybody, remember to write your answers in the blanks.

Following instructions
a. (Touch the sentence in the box.)
b. Everybody, first you're going to read the sentence in the box. Then you're going to read the instructions below the box and do what the instructions tell you to do.

Story-picture items
(Point to the story-picture items on side 2.) Remember to follow these instructions and look at the picture when you work these items.

Reading comprehension
(Point to the story.) You're going to read this story and then do the items. Remember to write the answers in the blanks.

END OF LESSON 64

don said, "When I worked in the hat store, I would mope and mop. but now I can have fun. I can fly. I can pick up cars and throw them around. I can do anything I want."

don walked down the street. a man said, "look at that funny man in the cap and cape."

That made don mad.[3] he stopped and said, "I have this cape and this cap because I am a super man."

The man said, "You don't look like a super man to me."

don walked over to a bus.[4] he picked up the bus. Then he gave it a heave. "Crash." The bus was bent.[5]

The man said, "let me out of here." and he ran down the street.

"Come back," don shouted, but the man kept on running.

don walked to a school. boys and girls were coming out of the school. don said, "boys and girls, I am a super man."

One girl said, "You look like a nut in that cap and cape."[6]

a boy said, "let's see how fast you can run."

"I will show you," don said.

he ran so fast that the boys and girls could not see him. "Crash." don ran into the school and made a big hole in the side of the school.[7]

One of the boys said, " Stop that. You are making a mess out of our school.[8] I don't like you."

"but you must like me," don said. "I am a super man, and the boys and girls love super men."

"We hate you," all the boys and girls said.[9] Then they ran away. don was sad. he sat down and began to mope.[10]

To be continued[11]

---

[3] Why did he get mad? **(The children respond.)**

[4] What do you think he'll do to it? **(The children respond.)**

• Let's read and find out.

[5] How did that happen? **(The children respond.)**

[6] Everybody say that. **(Signal.)** *You look like a nut in that cap and cape.*

[7] Where was the hole? **(Signal.)** *In the side of the school.*

[8] What did one of the boys say? **(Signal.)** *You are making a mess out of our school.*

[9] What did they say? **(Signal.)** *We hate you.*

[10] Why did he begin to mope? **(The children respond.)**

[11] Will there be more Don stories? **(Signal.)** *Yes.*

EXERCISE 10

Picture comprehension

a. Look at the picture.

b. (Ask these questions:)

1. What is Don crashing into? **(Signal.)** *The school.*
2. What do you think those children are saying to him? **(The children respond.)**
3. Is Don doing something good? **(Signal.)** *No.* He hasn't done anything good yet.

WORKSHEET 86

WORKSHEET 86
EXERCISE 11

Summary of independent activities

a. (Pass out Worksheet 86 to each child.)

b. Everybody, look at your worksheet for this lesson. ✔

• This whole worksheet is written the new way.

c. Everybody, now you'll do your worksheet. Remember to do all parts of the worksheet and read all the parts carefully.

END OF LESSON 86

EXERCISE 1

Sound combination review

a. Here are some letters that go together. Get ready to tell me the sound they usually make.

b. (Point to **ou.**) What sound do these letters usually make? (Signal.) *ou.* Yes, **ou.**

c. (Repeat *b* with **al** and **ar.**)

d. (Repeat the series of sound combinations until firm.)

ou

al

ar

READING VOCABULARY

Get ready to read all the words on this page without making a mistake.

EXERCISE 2

Long and short vowel words

a. Read these words the fast way. Remember what you say if there is an ē on the end of a word.

b. (Touch the ball for **time.** Pause two seconds.) Get ready. (Signal.) *Time.* Yes, **time.**

c. (Repeat *b* for **same, sam,** and **tim.**)

time

same

sam

tim

fire

EXERCISE 3

Practice final-e rule

a. Read this word the fast way. Remember to look at the end of the word.

b. (Touch the ball for **fire.** Pause two seconds.) Get ready. (Signal.) *Fire.* Yes, **fire.**

c. (Touch the ball for **fire.**) Sound it out. Get ready. (Quickly touch **f, i, r** as the children say:) *ffiiirrr.*

d. What word? (Signal.) *Fire.* Yes, **fire.**

e. (Repeat *b* through *d* until firm.)

while

EXERCISE 4

Practice final-e rule

a. Read this word the fast way. Remember to look at the end of the word.

b. (Touch the ball for **while.** Pause two seconds.) Get ready. (Signal.) *While.* Yes, **while.**

(Repeat any troublesome words.)

Individual test

(Call on individual children. Each child reads a different word.)

READ THE ITEMS 86

EXERCISE 7

Read the item

a. (Pass out Storybook 2.)

b. Open your reader to page 7. Get ready to read the item.

c. Finger under the first word of the item. ✔

• Get ready. (Tap.) *If.*

d. Next word. (Pause.) Get ready. (Tap.) *The.*

e. (Repeat step *d* for the remaining words in the item.)

f. (Repeat steps *c* through *e* until the item is firm.)

g. Everybody, say that item. (Pause. Signal.) *If the teacher says "Of," say "For."*

To Correct

1. Everybody, say the item with me. (Signal. Say the item with the children at a normal speaking rate. Repeat until firm.)

2. (Repeat step *g.* Then skip to step *i.*)

h. Again. (Repeat step *g* until firm.)

i. What are you going to say if I say "**Of**"? (Signal.) *For.*

• When are you going to say "**For**"? (Signal.) *When the teacher says "Of."*

To Correct

(Have the children read the item aloud. Then repeat the questions.)

EXERCISE 8

Play the game

a. Read the item to yourself and think about what you're going to do and when you're going to do it. Raise your hand when you're ready.

b. (After the children raise their hands, say:) Get ready to play the game.

c. My turn. (Pause.) **Of.** (Signal.) (The children are to say *For* immediately.)

To Correct

(Have the children read the item aloud. Then play the game again.)

EXERCISE 9

Reading—decoding

a. Everybody, look at the story on page 7. ✔

• You're going to read this story today. But before you read the story, turn to page 8. ✔

b. Everybody, in the middle of the story there's a big red number 5 in a circle. Touch that number 5. ✔

• That 5 tells you that, if the group reads all the way to the 5 without making more than five errors, we can go on in the story. But if the group makes more than five errors, you have to go back and read the first part again. You have to keep reading it until you can read it without making more than five errors. I'll count the errors. Now turn back to page 7. ✔

c. Everybody, touch the title of the story. ✔

---

don makes a mess[1]

The woman who gave don the dime told him that he was to do good. <u>but was don doing good?</u>[2]

---

d. I'm going to call on individual children to read two or three sentences. Everybody, follow along. If you hear a mistake, raise your hand. Children who do not have their place lose their turn. (Call on individual children to read two or three sentences. Do not ask comprehension questions.)

To Correct

word-identification errors (from, for example)

1. That word is **from.** What word? *From.*

2. Go back to the beginning of the sentence and read the sentence again.

3. (Tally all errors.)

e. (If the children make more than five errors: when they reach the 5 say:) You made too many errors. Go back to the beginning of the story and we'll try again. Try to read more carefully this time. (Call on individual children to read two or three sentences. Do not ask comprehension questions. Repeat step e until firm, and then go on to step *f.*)

f. (When the children read to the number 5 without making more than five errors: say:) Good reading. I'll read the story from the beginning to the 5 and ask you some questions. (Read the story, starting with the title. Stop at the end of each underlined sentence and ask the specified question. When you reach the 5, call on individual children to continue reading the story. Have each child read two or three sentences. Ask the specified questions at the end of each underlined sentence.)

[1] What's Don going to do? (Signal.) *Make a mess.*

• He's made a big mess already.

[2] What's the answer? (Signal.) *No.*

• Name some bad thngs he has done. (The children respond.)

Get ready to read all the words on this page without making a mistake.

EXERCISE 5

Read the fast way

a. Read these words the fast way.

b. (Touch the ball for **shake.** Pause two seconds.) Get ready. (Signal.) *Shake.* Yes, **shake.**

c. (Repeat *b* for **here, those, make,** and **making.**)

shake

here

those

make

making

someone

EXERCISE 6

Two-part word

a. (Cover **one.** Point to **some.**) Everybody, tell me what this part of the word says. Get ready. (Signal.) *Some.* Yes, **some.**

b. (Uncover **one.** Touch the ball for **someone.**) Now tell me what the whole word says. Get ready. (Signal.) *Someone.* Yes, **someone.**

c. (Repeat exercise until firm.)

todāy

EXERCISE 7

Two-part word

a. (Cover **dāy.** Point to **to.**) Everybody, tell me what this part of the word says. Get ready. (Signal.) *To.* Yes, **to.**

b. (Uncover **dāy.** Touch the ball for **todāy.**) Now tell me what the whole word says. Get ready. (Signal.) *Today.* Yes, **today.**

c. (Repeat exercise until firm.)

forest

EXERCISE 8

Two-part word

a. (Cover **est.** Point to **for.**) Everybody, tell me what this part of the word says. Get ready. (Signal.) *For.* Yes, **for.**

b. (Uncover **est.** Touch the ball for **forest.**) Now tell me what the whole word says. Get ready. (Signal.) *Forest.* Yes, **forest.**

c. (Repeat exercise until firm.)

sadder

EXERCISE 9

Sound out first

a. (Touch the ball for **sadder.**) Sound it out. Get ready. (Quickly touch **s, a,** between the **d**'s, **er** as the children say:) *sssaaaderrr.*

b. What word? (Signal.) *Sadder.* Yes, **sadder.**

c. (Repeat exercise until firm.)

(Repeat any troublesome words.)

Individual test

(Call on individual children. Each child reads a different word.)

EXERCISE 5

Teacher reads the words in red

a. I'll read the words in red to you.

b. (Touch the ball for **don't.** Slash as you say:) Don't. What word? (Signal.) *Don't.*

c. (Repeat step *b* for the words in red.)

d. Your turn to read all the words in this column the fast way.

e. (Touch the ball for **don't.** Pause.) Get ready. (Slash.) *Don't.*

f. (Repeat step *e* for each remaining word in the column.)

don't

throw

bent

men

side

heave

tent

EXERCISE 6

Words with underlined parts

a. First you're going to read the underlined part of each word in this column. Then you're going to read the whole word.

b. (Touch the ball for **anything.**) Read the underlined part. Get ready. (Tap the ball.) *Thing.*

• Read the whole word. (Pause.) Get ready. (Slash.) *Anything.*

c. (Repeat step *b* until firm.)

d. (Repeat steps *b* and *c* for each remaining word in the column.)

e. (Repeat the column until children read all the words in order without making a mistake.)

anything

doing

worked

inside

running

slowly

began

Individual test

a. (Call on individual children to read one column of words from the lesson.)

b. (Praise children who read all words with no errors.)

EXERCISE 10

Read the fast way

a. Read these words the fast way.

b. (Touch the ball for **once.** Pause two seconds.) Get ready. (Signal.) *Once.* Yes, **once.**

c. (Repeat *b* for **two, around,** and **more.**)

once

two

around

more

small

EXERCISE 11

al word

a. (Point to **al** in **small.**) What do these letters say? (Signal.) *All.* Yes, **all.**

b. (Touch the ball for **small.**) Read this word the fast way. Get ready. (Signal.) *Small.* Yes, **small.**

trapped

EXERCISE 12

Sound out first

a. (Touch the ball for **trapped.**) Sound it out. Get ready. (Quickly touch **t, r, a,** between the **p**'s, **d** as the children say:) *trrraaapd.*

b. What word? (Signal.) *Trapped.* Yes, **trapped.**

c. (Repeat exercise until firm.)

blōwing

EXERCISE 13

Sound out first

a. (Touch the ball for **blōwing.**) Sound it out. Get ready. (Quickly touch **b, l, ō, w, ing** as the children say:) *blllōōōwwwiiing.*

b. What word? (Signal.) *Blowing.* Yes, **blowing.**

c. (Repeat exercise until firm.)

flōat

EXERCISE 14

Sound out first

a. (Touch the ball for **flōat.**) Sound it out. Get ready. (Quickly touch **f, l, ō, t** as the children say:) *ffflllōōōt.*

b. What word? (Signal.) *Float.* Yes, **float.**

c. (Repeat exercise until firm.)

darker

EXERCISE 15

ar word

a. (Touch the ball for **darker.**) Read this word the fast way. (Pause two seconds.)

• Get ready. (Signal.) *Darker.* Yes, **darker.**

b. (Point to **ar** in **darker.**) Everybody, what do these letters say? (Signal.) *Are.* Yes, **are.**

c. (Touch the ball for **darker.**) Sound it out. Get ready. (Quickly touch **d, ar, k, er** as the children say:) *darkerrr.*

d. What word? (Signal.) *Darker.* Yes, **darker.**

e. (Repeat *c* and *d* until firm.)

out

EXERCISE 16

ou word

a. (Point to **ou** in **out.**) What do these letters say? (Signal.) *ou.* Yes, **ou.**

b. (Touch the ball for **out.**) Read this word the fast way. Get ready. (Signal.) *Out.* Yes, **out.**

Individual test

(Call on individual children to read a column of words from this lesson. If the column contains only one or two words, direct the child to read additional words from an adjacent column. Praise children who read all words with no errors.)

READING VOCABULARY

EXERCISE 3

Spelling by letter names

a. My turn to spell some of these words by saying the letter names.

b. (Touch the ball for **gave.**) My turn. (Tap under each letter as you say:) **G-A-V-E.**

c. (Touch the ball for **here.**) My turn. (Tap under each letter as you say:) **H-E-R-E.**

d. (Touch the ball for **when.**) My turn. (Tap under each letter as you say:) **W-H-E-N.**

e. Your turn to spell all the words in this column by letter names.

f. (Touch the ball for **gave.**) Spell by letter names. Get ready. (Tap under each letter as children say:) *G-A-V-E.*

g. (Repeat step *f* for each remaining word in the column.)

h. (Repeat any words on which children make mistakes.)

i. Now you're going to read all the words in this column the fast way.

j. (Touch the ball for **gave.**) Get ready. (Slash.) *Gave.*

k. (Repeat step *j* for each remaining word in the column.)

l. (Repeat steps *j* and *k* until firm.)

gave

here

when

bug

because

doing

came

To Correct

word-identification errors (**hope,** for example)

1. That word is **hope.** What word? (Signal.) *Hope.*

2. (Return to the first word in the column and present all words in order.) Starting over.

EXERCISE 4

Teacher reads the words in red

a. I'll read each word in red. Then you'll spell each word by letter names.

b. (Touch the ball for **hat.**) My turn. (Slash as you say:) Hat. What word? (Signal.) *Hat.*

c. (Return to the ball.) Spell by letter names. Get ready. (Tap under each letter as the children say:) *H-A-T.* What word did you spell? (Signal.) *Hat.*

d. (Repeat steps *b* and *c* for each word in red.)

e. Your turn to read all the words in this column.

f. (Touch the ball for **hat.** Pause.) Get ready. (Slash.) *Hat.*

g. (Repeat step *f* for each remaining word in the column.)

h. (Repeat steps *f* and *g* until firm.)

hat

hate

hole

said

nothing

mess

saw

STORY 65
EXERCISE 17

First reading—title and three sentences

a. (Pass out Storybook 1.)

b. Everybody, open your reader to page 167.

c. Everybody, touch the title of the story and get ready to read the words in the title.

d. First word. ✔

• Get ready. (Tap.) *The.*

e. (Tap for each remaining word in the title.)

f. Everybody, say the title. (Signal.)
The small cloud must help.

g. Everybody, get ready to read this story.

h. First word. ✔

• Get ready. (Tap.) *The.*

i. Next word. ✔

• Get ready. (Tap.) *Wind.*

j. (Repeat *i* for the remaining words in the first three sentences. Have the children reread the first three sentences until firm.)

EXERCISE 18

Remaining sentences

a. I'm going to call on individual children to read a sentence. Everybody, follow along and point to the words. If you hear a mistake, raise your hand.

b. (Call on a child.) Read the next sentence.

To Correct

word-identification errors (**from,** for example)
1. That word is **from.** What word? *From.*
2. Go back to the beginning of the sentence and read the sentence again.

c. (Call on another child.) Read the next sentence.

d. (Repeat *c* for most of the remaining sentences in the story.)

e. (Occasionally have the group read a sentence. When the group is to read, say:)
Everybody, read the next sentence.
(Tap for each word in the sentence.)

> the small cloud must help [1]
>
> the wind was blowing the small cloud away from his father and mother. the small cloud couldn't even see them any more. [2] "I am so sad that I will cry," the cloud said. but what do you think happened? when the cloud tried to cry, no tears came out. [3] that made the cloud even sadder.
>
> he said, "I am so small that I can't even make tears." [4]

EXERCISE 19

Second reading—sentences and questions

a. You're going to read the story again. This time I'm going to ask questions.

b. Starting with the first word of the title. ✔

• Get ready. (Tap as the children read the title.)

c. (Call on a child.) Read the first sentence.

To Correct

word-identification errors (**from,** for example)
1. That word is **from.** What word? *From.*
2. Go back to the beginning of the sentence and read the sentence again.

d. (Call on another child.) Read the next sentence.

e. (Repeat *d* for most of the remaining sentences in the story.)

f. (Occasionally have the group read a sentence.)

g. (After each underlined sentence has been read, present each comprehension question specified below to the entire group.)

[1] What's the small cloud going to do in this story? (Signal.) *Help.*

• Let's see who he helps.

[2] How far was the small cloud from his mother and father? (The children respond.)

• Yes, he was so far he couldn't even see them any more.

[3] Could he cry? (Signal.) *No.*

• Why not? (Signal.) *No tears came out.*

[4] What did he say? (Signal.)
I am so small that I can't even make tears.

LETTER NAMES

EXERCISE 1

Letter names

a. Here are letters that are all mixed up. Tell me the name of each letter.

b. (Point to each letter.) Get ready. (Tap.) (The children respond.)

c. (Repeat step *b* until firm.)

EXERCISE 2

Individual test

a. See how many letter names you can say.

b. (Call on individual children. Immediately say the correct letter name if a child makes a mistake.)

eqvhkarfiybtwnzjdxmusocglp

just then someone called, "help, help."

the little cloud looked down. there was a small deer and a mother deer.[5] and near them was a big forest fire.[6] that small deer and the mother deer were trapped. "help, help," they called.

the little cloud said to himself, "I must get help." then he called, "mom and dad, come over here and make some rain on the forest." but the mother cloud and the father cloud were too far away. they couldn't hear the little cloud.[7]

"what will I do?" the little cloud asked himself. "if I could make rain, I could help those deer. but I am too small."

the fire was getting bigger all the time. now it was all around the two deer. the small cloud said, "I must get my mother and father."

but every time the small cloud started to float one way, the wind took him back.[8] the small cloud looked down at the two deer. then the cloud said, "I am the only one who can help those deer. so I will do what I can."[9]

more to come[10]

---

[5] Who called for help? (Signal.)
A small deer and a mother deer.

[6] Why did they need help? (Signal.)
There was a forest fire.

• How could clouds help them?
(The children respond.)

• Yes, rain would help. But could the small cloud make rain? (Signal.) *No.*

[7] Did the mother or father cloud help?
(Signal.) *No.*

• Why? (Signal.) (The children respond.)

• Yes, they were too far away.

[8] Why couldn't the cloud get his mother and father? (Signal.) *The wind took him back.*

[9] Who's going to have to help the deer?
(Signal.) *The small cloud.*

• Do you think he will? (The children respond.)

[10] Next time we'll find out if the small cloud can help.

EXERCISE 20

Picture comprehension

a. Look at the picture.

b. (Ask these questions:)
   1. Where are the deer in this picture?
      (Signal.) *In the forest.*
   2. What is happening in that forest?
      (The children respond.)
   • Yes, two deer are trapped in a big fire.
   3. Do you think the deer feel hot or cold?
      (The children respond.)
   4. What do you think the cloud is saying to himself? (Let the children comment for ten seconds. Then comment briefly.)

SUMMARY OF INDEPENDENT ACTIVITY
EXERCISE 21

Summary of independent activities

a. (Pass out Worksheet 65 to each child.)

b. Everybody, now you'll do your worksheet. Remember to do all parts of the worksheet and to read all the parts carefully.

INDIVIDUAL CHECKOUT
EXERCISE 22

2½-minute individual fluency checkout: rate/accuracy

a. As you are doing your worksheet, I'll call on children one at a time to read **part of the story.** Remember, you get two stars if you read part of the story in less than two and a half minutes and make no more than four errors.

b. (Call on each child. Tell the child:) Read the second page of the story very carefully, and keep reading to the end of the story. Go. (Time the child. Tell the child any words the child misses. Stop the child as soon as the child makes the fourth error or exceeds the time limit.)

c. (If the child meets the rate-accuracy criterion, record two stars on your chart for lesson 65. Congratulate the child. Give children who do not earn two stars a chance to read part of the story again before the next lesson is presented.)
144 words/**2.5 min** = 58 wpm **[4 errors]**

END OF LESSON 65

WORKSHEET 85

did don mope after he became a super man?[5]

don was hopping around the store in his cap and his cape. he was hitting the walls and making holes. he was having a lot of fun.

all at once he stopped. he said, "I will go outside and show what a super man I am."[6]

When don left the store, he didn't open the door. he ran into the door. "Crash."[7]

Some boys were standing outside the store. They said, "look at that funny man in a cap and a cape."

don said, "I am no funny man. I am ★ a super man."

don ran to a car that was parked near the store.[8] he picked the car up and gave it a big heave.[9] The car crashed into another car. ⑤

The boys yelled, "let's get out of here. That man is a nut."

"Come back," don shouted. "let me show you how super I am."

but the boys did not come back. They ran as fast as they could go.[10]

don said, "I think I will fly to the top of this store." So he did.[11] Then he said, "I think I will dive down to the street." So he did. he took a dive. "Crash." he made a big hole in the street.[12]

"This is a lot of fun," don said.[13]

To be continued[14]

- What's the answer? (Signal.) *No.*
[5] What's the answer? (Signal.) *No.*
[6] What's he going to do? (Signal.) *Go outside and show what a super man he is.*
[7] What went crash? (Signal.) *The door.*
- Why? (The children respond.)
[8] What do you think he'll do to that car? (The children respond.)
- Let's find out.
[9] What did he do to the car? (The children respond.)
[10] Who ran? (Signal.) *The boys.*
- Why did they run? (The children respond.)
- I don't blame them. I'd run away, too.
[11] What did he do? (Signal.) *Fly to the top of the store.*
[12] How did the hole get in the street? (The children respond.)

[13] What did he say? (Signal.) *This is a lot of fun.*
[14] Will there be more Don stories? (Signal.) *Yes.*

EXERCISE 12

Picture comprehension

a. What do you think you'll see in the picture? (The children respond.)
b. Turn the page and look at the picture.
c. (Ask these questions:)
   1. What's Don doing in this picture? (The children respond.)
   - What's going to happen to that car? (The children respond.)
   2. Why are those boys running? (The children respond.)
   3. What would you do if you were near Don? (The children respond.)

INDEPENDENT ACTIVITIES
EXERCISE 13

Summary of independent activities

a. (Pass out Worksheet 85 to each child.)
b. Everybody, now you'll do your worksheet. Remember to do all parts of the worksheet and to read all the parts carefully.

INDIVIDUAL CHECKOUT
EXERCISE 14

2-minute individual fluency checkout: rate/accuracy

a. As you are doing your worksheet, I'll call on children one at a time to read part of the story. Turn back to page 5 in your reader. ✔
- Touch the big star. ✔
- I'll call on children one at a time to read to that star. Remember, you get two stars on the chart if you read to the star in less than two minutes and make no more than four errors.
b. (Call on each child. Tell the child:) Read to the star very carefully. Start with the title. Go. (Time the child. Tell the child any words the child misses. Stop the child as soon as the child makes the fifth error or exceeds the time limit.)
c. (If the child meets the rate-accuracy criterion, record two stars on your chart for lesson 85. Congratulate the child. Give children who do not earn two stars a chance to read to the star again before the next lesson is presented.)
120 words/**2 min** = 60 wpm **[4 errors]**

END OF LESSON 85

EXERCISE 1

Sound combination review

a. Here are some letters that go together. Get ready to tell me the sound they usually make.

b. (Point to **ar.**) What sound do these letters usually make? (Signal.) *Are.* Yes, **are.**

c. (Repeat *b* with **al** and **ou.**)

d. (Repeat the series of sound combinations until firm.)

ar

al

ou

READING VOCABULARY

Get ready to read all the words on this page without making a mistake.

EXERCISE 2

Long and short vowel words

a. Read these words the fast way. Remember what you say if there is an **ē** on the end of a word.

b. (Touch the ball for **hat.** Pause two seconds.) Get ready. (Signal.) *Hat.* Yes, **hat.**

c. (Repeat *b* for **time, hate,** and **tim.**)

hat

time

hate

tim

(Repeat any troublesome words.)

almōst

EXERCISE 3

al word

a. (Point to **al** in **almōst.**) What do these letters say? (Signal.) *All.* Yes, **all.**

b. (Touch the ball for **almōst.**) Read this word the fast way. Get ready. (Signal.) *Almost.* Yes, **almost.**

proud

EXERCISE 4

ou word

a. (Point to **ou** in **proud.**) What do these letters say? (Signal.) *ou.* Yes, **ou.**

b. (Touch the ball for **proud.**) Read this word the fast way. Get ready. (Signal.) *Proud.* Yes, **proud.**

hard

EXERCISE 5

ar word

a. (Point to **ar** in **hard.**) What do these letters say? (Signal.) *Are.* Yes, **are.**

b. (Touch the ball for **hard.**) Read this word the fast way. Get ready. (Signal.) *Hard.* Yes, **hard.**

Individual test

(Call on individual children. Each child reads a different word.)

READ THE ITEMS 85
EXERCISE 9

Read the item

a. (Pass out Storybook 2.)

b. Open your reader to page 4. Get ready to read the item.

c. Finger under the first word of the item. ✔

• Get ready. (Tap.) *When.*

d. Next word. (Pause.) Get ready. (Tap.) *The.*

e. (Repeat step *d* for the remaining words in the item.)

f. (Repeat steps *c* through *e* until the item is firm.)

g. Everybody, say that item. (Pause. Signal.) *When the teacher says "Saw," say "Was."*

To Correct
1. Everybody, say the item with me. (Signal. Say the item with the children at a normal speaking rate. Repeat until firm.)
2. (Repeat step *g*. Then skip to step *i*.)

h. Again. (Repeat step *g* until firm.)

i. What are you going to say when I say "**Saw**"? (Signal.) *Was.*

• When are you going to say "**Was**"? (Signal.) *When the teacher says "Saw."*

To Correct
(Have the children read the item aloud. Then repeat the questions.)

EXERCISE 10

Play the game

a. Read the item to yourself and think about what you're going to do and when you're going to do it. Raise your hand when you're ready.

b. (After the children raise their hands, say:) Get ready to play the game.

c. My turn. (Pause.) **Saw.** (Signal.) (The children are to say *Was* immediately.)

To Correct
(Have the children read the item aloud. Then play the game again.)

EXERCISE 11

Reading—decoding

a. Everybody, look at the story on page 4.

b. Everybody, in the middle of the story there's a big red number 5 in a circle. Touch that number 5. ✔

• That 5 tells you that, if the group reads all the way to the 5 without making more than five errors, we can go on in the story. But if the group makes more than five errors, you have to go back and read the first part again. You have to keep reading it until you can read it without making more than five errors. I'll count the errors. I'll tell you about the big star later.

c. Everybody, touch the title of the story. ✔

> **don has Super fun**[1]
>
> Who gave don the dime?[2]
>
> Where did he tape the dime?[3]
>
> Was he doing good things?[4]

d. I'm going to call on individual children to read two or three sentences. Everybody, follow along. If you hear a mistake, raise your hand. Children who do not have their place lose their turn. (Call on individual children to read two or three sentences. Do not ask comprehension questions.)

To Correct
word-identification errors (from, for example)
1. That word is **from.** What word? *From.*
2. Go back to the beginning of the sentence and read the sentence again.
3. (Tally all errors.)

e. (If the children make more than five errors: when they reach the 5, say:) You made too many errors. Go back to the beginning of the story and we'll try again. Try to read more carefully this time. (Call on individual children to read two or three sentences. Do not ask comprehension questions. Repeat step *e* until firm, and then go on to step *f*.)

f. (When the children read to the number 5 without making more than five errors: say:) Good reading. I'll read the story from the beginning to the 5 and ask you some questions. (Read the story, starting with the title. Stop at the end of each underlined sentence and ask the specified question. When you reach the 5, call on individual children to continue reading the story. Have each child read two or three sentences. Ask the specified questions at the end of each underlined sentence.)

[1] What's Don going to do in this story? (Signal.) *Have super fun.*

[2] Everybody, say that question. (Signal.) *Who gave Don the dime?*

• What's the answer? (Signal.) *The woman.*

[3] What's the answer? (Signal.) *To his arm.*

[4] Say that question. (Signal.) *Was he doing good things?*

Do not touch small letters.

Get ready to read all the words on this page without making a mistake.

first

EXERCISE 6

Listen, sound out

a. (Point to **first.**) I'll tell you this word. (Pause.) **First.** What word? (Signal.) *First.* Yes, **first.**

b. (Touch the ball for **first.**) Sound it out. Get ready. (Quickly touch **f, i, r, s, t** as the children say:) *fffiiirrrssst.*

c. What word? (Signal.) *First.* Yes, **first.**

d. (Repeat *b* and *c* until firm.)

water

EXERCISE 7

Listen, sound out with me

a. (Point to **water.**) I'll tell you this word. (Pause.) **Water.** What word? (Signal.) *Water.* Yes, **water.**

b. (Touch the ball for **water.**) Sound it out with me. Get ready. (Quickly touch each sound as you and the children say:) *wwwaaaterrr.*

c. What word? (Signal.) *Water.* Yes, **water.**

d. (Repeat *b* and *c* until firm.)

flōₐted

EXERCISE 8

Sound out first

a. (Touch the ball for **flōated.**) Sound it out. Get ready. (Quickly touch **f, l, ō, t, e, d** as the children say:) *ffflllōōōteeed.*

b. What word? (Signal.) *Floated.* Yes, **floated.**

c. (Repeat exercise until firm.)

EXERCISE 9

Read the fast way

a. Read these words the fast way.

b. (Touch the ball for **again.** Pause two seconds.) Get ready. (Signal.) *Again.* Yes, **again.**

c. (Repeat *b* for **took, plane, shook, sōaked, thank, when,** and **then.**)

again

took

plane

shook

sōaked

thank

when

then

(Repeat any troublesome words.)

Individual test

(Call on individual children. Each child reads a different word.)

EXERCISE 7

Read the fast way

a. You're going to read all the words in this column the fast way.

b. (Touch the ball for **dime.** Pause.) Get ready. (Slash.) *Dime.*

c. (Repeat step *b* until firm.)

d. (Repeat step *b* and *c* for each remaining word in the column.)

e. (Repeat the column until the children read all the words in order without making mistakes.)

dime

tape

dim

let's

don't

saw

store

dive

EXERCISE 8

Words with underlined parts

a. First you're going to read the underlined part of each word in this column. Then you're going to read the whole word.

b. (Touch the ball for **crashed.**) Read the underlined part. Get ready. (Tap the ball.) *Crash.*

• Read the whole word. (Pause.) Get ready. (Slash.) *Crashed.*

c. (Repeat step *b* until firm.)

d. (Repeat steps *b* and *c* for each remaining word in the column.)

e. (Repeat the column until children read all the words in order without making a mistake.)

crashed

didn't

outside

shouted

picked

became

holes

Individual test

a. I'm going to call on individual children to read one column of words the fast way. Raise your hand if you hear a mistake.

b. (Call on individual children to read one column of words from this lesson.)

c. (Praise children who read all words with no errors.)

Get ready to read all the words on this page without making a mistake.

faster

EXERCISE 10

Two-part word

a. (Cover **er.** Point to **fast.**) Everybody, tell me what this part of the word says. Get ready. (Signal.) *Fast.* Yes, **fast.**

b. (Uncover **er.** Touch the ball for **faster.**) Now tell me what the whole word says. Get ready. (Signal.) *Faster.* Yes, **faster.**

c. (Repeat exercise until firm.)

fires

EXERCISE 11

Two-part word

a. (Cover **s.** Point to **fire.**) Everybody, tell me what this part of the word says. Get ready. (Signal.) *Fire.* Yes, **fire.**

b. (Uncover **s.** Touch the ball for **fires.**) Now tell me what the whole word says. Get ready. (Signal.) *Fires.* Yes, **fires.**

c. (Repeat exercise until firm.)

EXERCISE 12

Two-part word

a. (Cover **came.** Point to **be.**) Everybody, tell me what this part of the word says. Get ready. (Signal.) *Be.* Yes, **be.**

b. (Uncover **came.** Touch the ball for **became.**) Now tell me what the whole word says. Get ready. (Signal.) *Became.* Yes, **became.**

c. (Repeat exercise until firm.)

EXERCISE 13

Listen, sound out

a. (Point to **woman.**) I'll tell you this word. (Pause.) **Woman.** What word? (Signal.) *Woman.* Yes, **woman.**

b. (Touch the ball for **woman.**) Sound it out. Get ready. (Quickly touch **w, o, m, a, n** as the children say:) *wwwooommmaaannn.*

c. What word? (Signal.) *Woman.* Yes, **woman.**

d. (Repeat *b* and *c* until firm.)

EXERCISE 14

Last part, first part

a. (Cover **s.** Point to **care.**) Read this part of the word the fast way. (Pause two seconds.) Get ready. (Signal.) *Care.* Yes, **care.**

b. (Uncover **s.** Point to **s.**) First you say **sss.** (Move your finger quickly under **care.**) Then you say (pause) **care.**

c. (Touch the ball for **scare.**) Get ready. (Move to **s,** then quickly along the arrow.) *Ssscare.*

d. Say it fast. (Signal.) *Scare.*

• Yes, what word? (Signal.) *Scare.* Yes, **scare.**

e. (Repeat exercise until firm.)

became

woman

scare

(Repeat any troublesome words.)

Individual test

(Call on individual children. Each child reads a different word.)

READING VOCABULARY
EXERCISE 5

Words with underlined parts

a. First you're going to read the underlined part of each word in this column. Then you're going to read the whole word.

b. (Touch the ball for **crash.**) Read the underlined part. Get ready. (Tap the ball.) *shshsh.*

• Read the whole word. (Pause.) Get ready. (Slash.) *Crash.*

c. (Repeat step *b* until firm.)

d. (Repeat steps *b* and *c* for each remaining word in the column.)

e. (Repeat the column until children read all the words in order without making a mistake.)

┌─ **To Correct** ───────────
│ **word-identification errors**
│ (**hope,** for example)
│
│ 1. That word is **hope.**
│   What word? (Signal.)
│   *Hope.*
│ 2. (Return to the first word
│   in the column and
│   present all words in
│   order.) Starting over.
└──────────────────────────

crash

out

who

parked

where

walls

why

EXERCISE 6

Teacher reads the words in red

a. I'll read the words in red to you.

b. (Touch the ball for **heave.** Slash as you say:) Heave. What word? (Signal.) *Heave.*

c. (Repeat step *b* for the words in red.)

d. Your turn to read all the words in this column the fast way.

e. (Touch the ball for **heave.** Pause.) Get ready. (Slash.) *Heave.*

f. (Repeat step *e* for each remaining word in the column.)

heave

having

making

again

when

what

tap

Get ready to read all the words on this page without making a mistake.

EXERCISE 15

Practice final-e rule

a. Read this word the fast way. Remember to look at the end of the word.

b. (Touch the ball for **wade.** Pause two seconds.) Get ready. (Signal.) *Wade.* Yes, **wade.**

EXERCISE 16

Read the fast way

a. Read these words the fast way.

b. (Touch the ball for **wading.** Pause two seconds.) Get ready. (Signal.) *Wading.* Yes, **wading.**

c. (Repeat *b* for **or, shake,** and **lake.**)

Individual test

(Call on individual children to read a column of words from this lesson. If the column contains only one or two words, direct the child to read additional words from an adjacent column. Praise children who read all words with no errors.)

wade

wading

or

shake

lake

tv

EXERCISE 17

Listen, I'll tell you this word

a. Listen, I'll tell you this word. (Point to **tv.**) This says tee vee.

b. What does this say? (Signal.) *Tee vee.* Yes, we can watch **TV.**

c. (Repeat exercise until firm.)

STORYBOOK

STORY 66

EXERCISE 18

First reading—title and three sentences

a. (Pass out Storybook 1.)

b. Everybody, open your reader to page 170.

c. Everybody, touch the title of the story and get ready to read the words in the title.

d. First word. ✔

• Get ready. (Tap.) *The.*

e. (Tap for each remaining word in the title.)

f. Everybody, say the title. (Signal.) *The small cloud is happy.*

EXERCISE 3

Letter names

a. Here are letters that are all mixed up. Tell me the name of each letter.

b. (Point to each letter.) Get ready. (Tap.) (The children respond.)

c. (Repeat step *b* until firm.)

EXERCISE 4

Individual test

a. See how many letter names you can say.

b. (Call on individual children. Immediately say the correct letter name if a child makes a mistake.)

ortglzbhuskvajfcmeqxdnypiw

the small cloud is happy[1]

the little cloud was the only one who could help the two deer.[2] the small cloud said, "I will try to rain. I will try as hard as I can."

the cloud began to shake. he shook and shook and shook. and each time he shook, he became a little bigger and a little darker.[3] he shook some more. and he became even bigger and darker.

then he began to make loud sounds.[4] "boom, boom," he said. the sounds he made were almost as loud as his father's sounds. "boom, boom."

and all at once rain started to fall from the little cloud.[5] two or three drops fell. then more drops began to fall. again the cloud made a

loud sound. "boom." the rain was falling faster and faster. it started to fall so fast that it soaked the forest.[6] it soaked the trees that were on fire. and it soaked the two deer. "thank you, thank you," they called to the cloud.[7] the cloud kept making rain. when that cloud stopped, the forest looked like a lake.[8] all of the fires were out, and the deer were standing in the water.

all at once the mother cloud and the father cloud floated up to the little cloud. the father cloud said, "we see what you did. you are a good cloud."

the mother cloud said, "I am so proud. today my little cloud became a real rain cloud."[9]

this is the end.

g. Everybody, get ready to read this story.
h. First word. ✔
• Get ready. (Tap.) *The.*
i. Next word. ✔
• Get ready. (Tap.) *Little.*
j. (Repeat *i* for the remaining words in the first three sentences. Have the children reread the first three sentences until firm.)

EXERCISE 19

Remaining sentences

a. I'm going to call on individual children to read a sentence. Everybody, follow along and point to the words. If you hear a mistake, raise your hand.

b. (Call on a child.) Read the next sentence.

┌─ **To Correct** ─────────────────────
word-identification errors (**from,** for example)
1. That word is **from.** What word? *From.*
2. Go back to the beginning of the sentence and read the sentence again.
└──────────────────────────────────────

c. (Call on another child.) Read the next sentence.

d. (Repeat *c* for most of the remaining sentences in the story.)

e. (Occasionally have the group read a sentence. When the group is to read, say:) Everybody, read the next sentence. (Tap for each word in the sentence.)

EXERCISE 20

Second reading—sentences and questions

a. You're going to read the story again. This time I'm going to ask questions.

b. Starting with the first word of the title. ✔
• Get ready. (Tap as the children read the title.)

c. (Call on a child.) Read the first sentence.

d. (Call on another child.) Read the next sentence.

e. (Repeat *d* for most of the remaining sentences in the story.)

f. (Occasionally have the group read a sentence.)

g. (After each underlined sentence has been read, present each comprehension question specified below to the entire group.)

[1] What's the title of this story? (Signal.) *The small cloud is happy.*

[2] What is the matter with the deer? (The children respond.)
• Right, they are trapped in a forest fire.

[3] What happened each time he shook? (Signal.) *He became a little bigger and a little darker.*

[4] What sounds do you think he'll make? (Signal.) *Boom, boom.*

[5] What happened? (Signal.) *Rain started to fall from the little cloud.*

[6] What happened when the rain fell? (Signal.) *It soaked the forest.*
• What does that mean? (The children respond.)
• Yes, the fire will go out.

[7] Who is speaking? (Signal.) *The two deer.*

[8] How much rain did he make? (The children respond.)
• Yes, enough to make a lake.
• Did it put the fire out? (Signal.) *Yes.*

[9] Why did she say that? (The children respond.)

LETTER NAMES
EXERCISE 1

Letter names

a. (Use transparency and crayon.)
b. Your turn. See how many letter names you can say.
c. (Point under **a.**) Get ready. (Tap.) *A.*
d. (Tap under each remaining letter as the children say each name. Circle all letters that are missed. Immediately say the correct letter name if the children make a mistake.)
e. (If any letters are circled, say:) Everybody, get ready to tell me the names of all the circled letters. (**Point to each circled letter.**) Get ready. (**Tap.**)

EXERCISE 2

Individual test

a. See how many letter names you can say.
b. (Call on individual children. Immediately say the correct letter name if the child makes a mistake.)

abcdefghijklmnopqrstuvwxyz

WORKSHEET 66

EXERCISE 21

Picture comprehension

a. Look at the picture.

b. (Ask these questions:)

1. Is there still a fire in that forest? (Signal.) *No.*

2. What happened to the fire? **(Let the children comment for ten seconds. Then comment briefly.)**

3. Which cloud is making the rain? (Signal.) *The small cloud.*

4. How does the small cloud feel? (Signal.) *Happy.*

5. Why are the father and mother clouds smiling? **(The children respond.)**

SUMMARY OF INDEPENDENT ACTIVITY
EXERCISE 22

Introduction to independent activity

a. (Pass out Worksheet 66 to each child.)

b. (Hold up side 1 of your worksheet.) Everybody, you're going to do this worksheet on your own. **(Tell the children when they will work the items.)**

• Let's go over the things you're going to do.

Story items

(Point to the story-items exercise.) Everybody, remember to write your answers in the blanks.

Following instructions

a. (Touch the sentence in the box.)

b. Everybody, first you're going to read the sentence in the box. Then you're going to read the instructions below the box and do what the instructions tell you to do.

Story-picture items

(Point to the story-picture items on side 2.) Remember to follow these instructions and look at the picture when you work these items.

Reading comprehension

(Point to the story.) You're going to read this story and then do the items. Remember to write the answers in the blanks.

END OF LESSON 66

he hit the wall again. "Pow." he made another hole in the wall. now there were two holes in the wall.

don hopped around the hat shop hitting things. he said, "I hate hats."

"Pow." he hit a hat box and made a hole in it.[9] Then he said, "I hate mops." So he broke the mop.[10]

"This is fun," he said. by now the store was a mess. There were holes in the wall. The hats had holes in them. The doors had holes in them.[11]

don said, "no one can stop me now. I am a super man."[12]

To be continued[13]

---

[9] Why did he do that? (Signal.) *He hated hats.*

[10] Why did he do that? (Signal.)
He hated mops.

[11] Name some things that had holes in them.
(The children respond.) Yes, the walls, the hats, and the doors.

• How did those holes get there?
(The children respond.)

[12] Is he a super man? (Signal.) *Yes.* Is he a good super man? (Signal.) *No.*

[13] Is this the end of the Don stories? (Signal.)
No. Right, the story will be continued next time. There is more to come.

EXERCISE 11

Picture comprehension

a. Look at the picture.

b. (Ask these questions:)

1. What is Don breaking? (Signal.) *A mop.*

• Why is he breaking it? (Signal.)
He hates mops.

2. What happened to the wall? (Signal.)
Don kicked a hole in it.

3. How many holes are in the wall?
(Signal.) *Two.*

4. How does that place look?
(The children respond.)

• It sure is a mess.

5. What does Don have on his shoulders?
(Signal.) *A cape.*

• And on his head? (Signal.) *A cap.*

6. Would you make a mess like that if you were a super man?
(The children respond.)

EXERCISE 12

Summary of independent activities

a. (Pass out Worksheet 84 to each child.)

b. Everybody, now you'll do your worksheet. Remember to do all parts of the worksheet and to read all the parts carefully.

END OF LESSON 84

READING VOCABULARY

Do not touch small letters.

Get ready to read all the words on this page without making a mistake.

school

EXERCISE 1

Listen, sound out with me

a. (Point to **school.**) I'll tell you this word. (Pause.) **School.** What word? (Signal.) *School.* Yes, **school.**

b. (Touch the ball for **school.**) Sound it out with me. Get ready. (Quickly touch each sound as you and the children say:) *ssschoooolll.*

c. What word? (Signal.) *School.* Yes, **school.**

d. (Repeat *b* and *c* until firm.)

gave

EXERCISE 2

Practice final-e rule

a. Read this word the fast way. Remember to look at the end of the word.

b. (Touch the ball for **gave.** Pause two seconds.) Get ready. (Signal.) *Gave.* Yes, **gave.**

c. (Touch the ball for **gave.**) Sound it out. Get ready. (Quickly touch **g, a, v** as the children say:) *gāāāvvv.*

d. What word? (Signal.) *Gave.* Yes, **gave.**

e. (Repeat *b* through *d* until firm.)

EXERCISE 3

Long and short vowel words

a. Read these words the fast way. Remember what you say if there is an **ē** on the end of a word.

b. (Touch the ball for **bit.** Pause two seconds.) Get ready. (Signal.) *Bit.* Yes, **bit.**

c. (Repeat *b* for **hat, hate,** and **bite.**)

bit

hat

hate

bite

(Repeat any troublesome words.)

Individual test

(Call on individual children. Each child reads a different word.)

be͟ar

EXERCISE 4

Sound out first

a. (Touch the ball for **bear.**) Sound it out. Get ready. (Quickly touch **b, e, r** as the children say:) *beeerrr.*

b. What word? (Signal.) *Bear.* Yes, **bear.**

c. (Repeat exercise until firm.)

tr͞ain

EXERCISE 5

Sound out first

a. (Touch the ball for **train.**) Sound it out. Get ready. (Quickly touch **t, r, ā, n** as the children say:) *trrrāāānnn.*

b. What word? (Signal.) *Train.* Yes, **train.**

c. (Repeat exercise until firm.)

hundred

EXERCISE 6

Sound out first

a. (Touch the ball for **hundred.**) Sound it out. Get ready. (Quickly touch **h, u, n, d, r, e, d** as the children say:) *huuunnndrrreeed.*

b. What word? (Signal.) *Hundred.* Yes, **hundred.**

c. (Repeat exercise until firm.)

EXERCISE 9

Play the game

a. Read the item to yourself and think about what you're going to do and when you're going to do it. Raise your hand when you're ready.

b. (After the children raise their hands, say:) Get ready to play the game.

c. My turn. (Pause.) **For.** (Signal.) (The children are to say *Of* immediately.)

To Correct
(Have the children read the item aloud. Then play the game again.)

---

don Is a Super man[1]

Who gave don a dime?[2]

Where was the woman with the cape and the cap?

how could don be a super man?[3]

don said, "I hope this works." Then he tapped the dime one time, two times, three times. There was the sound of thunder.[4]

"boooooommmmmm."

"What was that?" don asked. he looked at his hand. The dime was still there. Then don saw that he had a cape and a cap.[5]

"Wow," don said. "When I tapped that dime, I became a super man."

don said, "I must keep this dime. I will tape it to my arm."[6]and he did. Then he said, "now I will see if I am a super man."[7]

don kicked the wall. "Pow." he made a big hole in the wall.[8]don smiled. "Wow," he said. "I am a super man." he hopped around the store.⑤

STORY 84

EXERCISE 10

Reading—decoding

a. Everybody, look at the story on page 1. ✔
- This whole story is written the new way. This is the way all adult stories are written. You're going to read this story today. But before you read the story, turn to page 2. ✔

b. Everybody, in the middle of the story there's a big red number 5 in a circle. Touch that number 5. ✔
- That 5 tells you that, if the group reads all the way to the 5 without making more than five errors, we can go on in the story. But if the group makes more than five errors, you have to go back and read the first part again. You have to keep reading it until you can read it without making more than five errors. I'll count the errors. Now turn back to page 1. ✔

c. Everybody, touch the title of the story. ✔

d. I'm going to call on individual children to read two or three sentences. Everybody, follow along. If you hear a mistake, raise your hand. Children who do not have their place lose their turn. (Call on individual children to read two or three sentences. Do not ask comprehension questions.)

To Correct
word-identification errors (**from**, for example)
1. That word is **from.** What word? *From.*
2. Go back to the beginning of the sentence and read the sentence again.
3. (Tally all errors.)

---

e. (If the children make more than five errors: when they reach the 5, say:) You made too many errors. Go back to the beginning of the story and we'll try again. Try to read more carefully this time. (Call on individual children to read two or three sentences. Do not ask comprehension questions.) (Repeat step e until firm, and then go on to step f.)

f. (When the children read to the number 5 without making more than five errors: say:) Good reading. I'll read the story from the beginning to the 5 and ask you some questions. (Read the story, starting with the title. Stop at the end of each underlined sentence and ask the specified question. When you reach the 5, call on individual children to continue reading the story. Have each child read two or three sentences. Ask the specified questions at the end of each underlined sentence.)

[1] What will happen to Don in this story? (Signal.) *He will be a super man.*

[2] What's the answer? (Signal.) *The woman.*

[3] What's the answer? (Signal.) *Tap the dime three times.*

[4] What happened after Don tapped the dime three times? (Signal.) *There was the sound of thunder.*

[5] What did Don get? (Signal.) *A cape and a cap.*

[6] What is Don going to do with the dime? (Signal.) *Tape it to his arm.*

[7] Do you think he is a super man? (The children respond.)
- Let's read and find out.

[8] What did he do? (Signal.) *He made a big hole in the wall.*
- Was that a good thing to do? (Signal.) *No.*

Do not touch small letters.

Get ready to read all the words on this page without making a mistake.

bēans

EXERCISE 7

Read the fast way first

a. (Touch the ball for **bēans.**) Read this word the fast way. (Pause two seconds.) Get ready. (Signal.) *Beans.* Yes, **beans.**

b. (Return to the ball.) Sound it out. Get ready. (Quickly touch **b, ē, n, s** as the children say:) *bēēēnnnsss.*

c. What word? (Signal.) *Beans.* Yes, **beans.**

d. (Repeat *b* and *c* until firm.)

e. (Repeat the exercise for **mēat, fifty,** and **hunting.**)

mēat

fifty

hunting

EXERCISE 8

Read the fast way

a. Read these words the fast way.

b. (Touch the ball for **scare.** Pause two seconds.) Get ready. (Signal.) *Scare.* Yes, **scare.**

c. (Repeat *b* for **pile, ground, work, wood,** and **woman.**)

scare

pile

ground

work

wood

woman

stāyed

EXERCISE 9

Two-part word

a. (Cover **ed.** Point to **stāy.**) Everybody, tell me what this part of the word says. Get ready. (Signal.) *Stay.* Yes, **stay.**

b. (Uncover **ed.** Touch the ball for **stāyed.**) Now tell me what the whole word says. Get ready. (Signal.) *Stayed.* Yes, **stayed.**

c. (Repeat exercise until firm.)

swimming

EXERCISE 10

Two-part word

a. (Cover **ing.** Point to **swimm.**) Everybody, tell me what this part of the word says. Get ready. (Signal.) *Swim.* Yes, **swim.**

b. (Uncover **ing.** Touch the ball for **swimming.**) Now tell me what the whole word says. Get ready. (Signal.) *Swimming.* Yes, **swimming.**

c. (Repeat exercise until firm.)

(Repeat any troublesome words.)

Individual test

(Call on individual children. Each child reads a different word.)

EXERCISE 7

Read the fast way

a. You're going to read all the words in this column the fast way.

b. (Touch the ball for **miles.** Pause.) Get ready. (Slash.) *Miles.*

c. (Repeat step *b* until firm.)

d. (Repeat steps *b* and *c* for each remaining word in the column.)

e. (Repeat the column until the children read all the words in order without making mistakes.)

miles

hole

broke

store

pow

again

were

Individual test

a. I'm going to call on individual children to read one column of words the fast way. Raise your hand if you hear a mistake.

b. (Call on individual children to read one column of words from this lesson.)

c. (Praise children who read all words with no errors.)

READ THE ITEMS 84
EXERCISE 8

Read the item

a. (Pass out Storybook 2.)

b. Open your reader to page 1. Get ready to read the item.

c. Finger under the first word of the item. ✔
- Get ready. (Tap.) *If.*

d. Next word. (Pause.) Get ready. (Tap.) *The.*

e. (Repeat step *d* for the remaining words in the item.)

f. (Repeat steps *c* through *e* until the item is firm.)

g. Everybody, say that item. (Pause. Signal.) *If the teacher says "For," say "Of."*

To Correct
1. Everybody, say the item with me. (Signal. Say the item with the children at a normal speaking rate. Repeat until firm.)
2. (Repeat step *g.* Then skip to step *i.*)

h. Again. (Repeat step *g* until firm.)

i. What are you going to say if I say "**For**"? (Signal.) *Of.*
- When are you going to say "**Of**"? (Signal.) *When the teacher says "For."*

To Correct
(Have the children read the item aloud. Then repeat the questions.)

Do not touch small letters.

Get ready to read all the words on this page without making a mistake.

EXERCISE 11

th words

a. (Point to **th.**) When these letters are together, they usually say **ththth.**

b. What do these letters usually say? (Signal.) *ththth.* Yes, **ththth.**

• (Repeat until firm.)

c. (Point to the words.) These are words you already know. See if you can read them when they look this way.

d. (Point to **th** in **the.**) What do these letters say? (Signal.) *ththth.*

e. (Touch the ball for **the.**) Read the fast way. Get ready. (Signal.) *The.* Yes, **the.**

f. (Repeat *d* and *e* for **them, that,** and **there.**)

g. (Repeat the series of words until firm.)

Individual test

(Call on individual children to read a column of words from this lesson. If the column contains only one or two words, direct the child to read additional words from an adjacent column. Praise children who read all words with no errors.)

the

them

that

there

EXERCISE 12

Two-part word

a. (Cover **thing.** Point to **any.**) Everybody, tell me what this part of the word says. Get ready. (Signal.) *Any.* Yes, **any.**

b. (Uncover **thing.** Touch the ball for **anything.**) Now tell me what the whole word says. Get ready. (Signal.) *Anything.* Yes, **anything.**

c. (Repeat exercise until firm.)

STORYBOOK

STORY 67
EXERCISE 13

First reading—title and three sentences

a. (Pass out Storybook 1.)

b. Everybody, open your reader to page 173.

c. Everybody, touch the title of the story and get ready to read the words in the title.

d. First word. ✔

• Get ready. (Tap.) *The.*

e. (Tap for each remaining word in the title.)

f. Everybody, say the title. (Signal.) *The tall man gets a scare.*

EXERCISE 5

Read the fast way

a. You're going to read all the words in this column the fast way.

b. (Touch the ball for **hate**. Pause.) Get ready. (Slash.) *Hate.*

c. (Repeat step *b* until firm.)

d. (Repeat steps *b* and *c* for each remaining word in the column.)

e. (Repeat the column until the children read all the words in order without making mistakes.)

hate

tap

hat

hop

when

hitting

who

EXERCISE 6

Words with underlined parts

a. First you're going to read the underlined part of each word in this column. Then you're going to read the whole word.

b. (Touch the ball for **another**.) Read the underlined part. Get ready. (Tap the ball.) *Other.* Read the whole word. (Pause.) Get ready. (Slash.) *Another.*

c. (Repeat step *b* until firm.)

d. (Repeat steps *b* and *c* for each remaining word in the column.)

e. (Repeat the column until children read all the words in order without making a mistake.)

another

walked

smiles

hopped

tapped

became

smiled

g. Everybody, get ready to read this story.

h. First word. ✔

- Get ready. (Tap.) *One.*

i. Next word. ✔

- Get ready. (Tap.) *Day.*

j. (Repeat *i* for the remaining words in the first three sentences. Have the children reread the first three sentences until firm.)

EXERCISE 14

Remaining sentences

a. I'm going to call on individual children to read a sentence. Everybody, follow along and point to the words. If you hear a mistake, raise your hand.

b. (Call on a child.) Read the next sentence.

To Correct

word-identification errors (**from,** for example)
1. That word is **from.** What word? *From.*
2. Go back to the beginning of the sentence and read the sentence again.

c. (Call on another child.) Read the next sentence.

d. (Repeat *c* for most of the remaining sentences in the story.)

e. (Occasionally have the group read a sentence. When the group is to read, say:) Everybody, read the next sentence. (Tap for each word in the sentence.)

---

the tall man gets a scare[1]

one dāy the tall man and his dog went for a walk to the lake. the dog said, "I hate to walk, walk, walk, but I love to talk, talk, talk."[2]

the tall man said, "go jump in the lake."[3]

the dog sat down. then she said, "you can swim around, around, around. I'll stāy on the ground, ground, ground."[4]

the tall man became very mad. he said, "dogs love to swim. so let's go for a swim."

the dog said, "you can swim if you wish, wish, wish. but I dōn't like to be with fish, fish, fish."[5]

so the tall man went swimming and the dog stāyed on the ground. soon the tall man came out of the lake. he said, "now let's have something to ēat. look around for some fire wood."[6]

the dog said, "I love to ēat things that are good, good, good. but I hate to go hunting for wood, wood, wood."

the tall man said, "if you dōn't get wood, you can't have anything to ēat."

EXERCISE 15

Second reading—sentences and questions

a. You're going to read the story again. This time I'm going to ask questions.

b. Starting with the first word of the title. ✔

- Get ready. (Tap as the children read the title.)

c. (Call on a child.) Read the first sentence.

To Correct

word-identification errors (**from,** for example)
1. That word is **from.** What word? *From.*
2. Go back to the beginning of the sentence and read the sentence again.

d. (Call on another child.) Read the next sentence.

e. (Repeat *d* for most of the remaining sentences in the story.)

f. (Occasionally have the group read a sentence.)

g. (After each underlined sentence has been read, present each comprehension question specified below to the entire group.)

[1] What's going to happen to the tall man in this story? (The children respond.)

- Let's read and see why he gets scared.

[2] Let's hear you say it the way the dog did. (Signal.) *I hate to walk, walk, walk, but I love to talk, talk, talk.*

[3] What did the tall man want her to do? (Signal.) *Go jump in the lake.*

[4] Is the dog going in the lake? (Signal.) *No.*

- Where is she going to stay? (Signal.) *On the ground.*

[5] Why wouldn't the dog go for a swim? (Signal.) *She didn't like to be with fish.*

[6] What does the tall man want her to do now? (Signal.) *Look around for some fire wood.*

- Why do they need fire wood? (The children respond.)

READING VOCABULARY

EXERCISE 3

Words with underlined parts

a. First you're going to read the underlined part of each word in this column. Then you're going to read the whole word.

b. (Touch the ball for **them.**) Read the underlined part. Get ready. (Tap the ball.) *ththth.*

• Read the whole word. (Pause.) Get ready. (Slash.) *Them.*

c. (Repeat step *b* until firm.)

d. (Repeat steps *b* and *c* for each remaining word in the column.)

e. (Repeat the column until children read all the words in order without making a mistake.)

To Correct

word-identification errors (**cone,** for example)

1. That word is **hope.** What word? (Signal.) *Hope.*
2. (Return to the first word in the column and present all words in order.) Starting over.

them

why

what

wall

where

around

arm

EXERCISE 4

Teacher reads the words in red

a. I'll read the words in red to you.

b. (Touch the ball for **two.** Slash as you say:) Two. What word? (Signal.) *Two.*

c. (Repeat step *b* for the words in red.)

d. Your turn to read all the words in this column the fast way.

e. (Touch the ball for **two.** Pause.) Get ready. (Slash.) *Two.*

f. (Repeat step *e* for each remaining word in the column.)

two

thunder

tape

cap

hope

gave

cape

mess

so the dog looked for wood.[7] when she found a big pile of wood, she called the tall man. the tall man took the wood and made a big fire. then the tall man bēgan to cook bēans and mēat.[8] the dog sat and looked at the food.

then all at once, the dog yelled, "ōver there, there, there. I see a bear, bear, bear."[9]

the tall man jumped into the lake.[10] the dog ate all of the bēans and mēat.

the dog said, "I gave the tall man a scare, scare, scare. there was no bear ōver there, there, there.[11] hō, hō."[12]

the end

[7] Did the dog look around for some fire wood? (Signal.) *Yes.*

[8] What did he cook? (Signal.) *Beans and meat.*

[9] Who is talking? (Signal.) *The dog.*
   • What did she say she saw? (Signal.) *A bear.*

[10] So what did the tall man do? (Signal.) *He jumped into the lake.*

[11] How did the tall man get scared? (The children respond.)
   • Was there really a bear over there? (Signal.) *No.*

[12] Why is she laughing? (The children respond.)

EXERCISE 16
Picture comprehension

a. Look at the picture.
b. (Ask these questions:)
   1. Does the tall man look scared? (Signal.) *Yes.*
   2. Why is he scared? (Let the children comment for ten seconds. Then comment briefly.)
   3. What is the tall man doing? (Signal.) *Jumping in the lake.*
   • Why is he doing that? (The children respond.)
   4. What is that cooking on the fire? (The children respond.)
   5. What do you think the dog is going to do? (Signal.) *Eat the food.*
   • I think the tall man won't get any of that food.

WORKSHEET 67

SUMMARY OF INDEPENDENT ACTIVITY
EXERCISE 17

Introduction to independent activity

a. (Pass out Worksheet 67 to each child.)
b. (Hold up side 1 of your worksheet.) Everybody, you're going to do this worksheet on your own. (Tell the children when they will work the items.)
   • Let's go over the things you're going to do.

Story items

(Point to the story-items exercise.) Everybody, remember to write your answers in the blanks.

Following instructions

a. (Touch the sentence in the box.)
b. Everybody, first you're going to read the sentence in the box. Then you're going to read the instructions below the box and do what the instructions tell you to do.

Story-picture items

(Point to the story-picture items on side 2.) Remember to follow these instructions and look at the picture when you work these items.

Reading comprehension

(Point to the story.) You're going to read this story and then do the items. Remember to write the answers in the blanks.

END OF LESSON 67

LETTER NAMES
EXERCISE 1

Letter names

a. (Use transparency and crayon.)

b. Look at these letters. You know the names of the letters that are in red. Get ready to tell me those letter names.

c. (Point under **a.**) Get ready. (Tap.) *A.*

d. (Repeat step *c* for **e, i, o,** and **u.**)

e. My turn to say the names of all the letters. (Point to each letter and say its name.)

f. Your turn. See how many letter names you can say. (Point under **a.**) Get ready. (Tap.) *A.*

• (Tap under each remaining letter as the children say its name.)

To Correct

1. (Immediately say the letter name.)
2. What name? (Tap.) (The children respond.)
3. (Circle the letter.)
4. (Continue to the next letter.)

g. (If any letters are circled, say:) Everybody, get ready to tell me the names of all the circled letters. (Point to each circled letter.) Get ready. (Tap.) (The children respond.)

EXERCISE 2

Individual test

a. See how many letter names you can say.

b. (Call on individual children. Immediately say the correct letter name if the child makes a mistake.)

abcdefghijklmnopqrstuvwxyz

READING VOCABULARY

Get ready to read all the words on this page without making a mistake.

everything

EXERCISE 1

Two-part word

a. (Cover **thing.** Point to **every.**) Everybody, tell me what this part of the word says. Get ready. (Signal.) *Every.* Yes, **every.**

b. (Uncover **thing.** Touch the ball for **everything.**) Now tell me what the whole word says. Get ready. (Signal.) *Everything.* Yes, **everything.**

c. (Repeat exercise until firm.)

began

EXERCISE 2

Two-part word

a. (Cover **gan.** Point to **be.**) Everybody, tell me what this part of the word says. Get ready. (Signal.) *Be.* Yes, **be.**

b. (Uncover **gan.** Touch the ball for **began.**) Now tell me what the whole word says. Get ready. (Signal.) *Began.* Yes, **began.**

c. (Repeat exercise until firm.)

counted

EXERCISE 3

ou word

a. (Touch the ball for **counted.**) Read this word the fast way. (Pause two seconds.) Get ready. (Signal.) *Counted.*

b. (Point to **ou** in **counted.**) Everybody, what do these letters say? (Signal.) *ou.* Yes, **ou.**

c. (Touch the ball for **counted.**) Sound it out. Get ready. (Quickly touch **c, ou, n, t, e, d** as the children say:) *counnnteeed.*

d. What word? (Signal.) *Counted.* Yes, **counted.**

e. (Repeat c and d until firm.)

counter

EXERCISE 4

Two-part word

a. (Cover **er.** Point to **count.**) Everybody, tell me what this part of the word says. Get ready. (Signal.) *Count.* Yes, **count.**

b. (Uncover **er.** Touch the ball for **counter.**) Now tell me what the whole word says. Get ready. (Signal.) *Counter.* Yes, **counter.**

c. (Repeat exercise until firm.)

(Repeat any troublesome words.)

Individual test

(Call on individual children. Each child reads a different word.)

EXERCISE 5

Long and short vowel words

a. Read these words the fast way. Remember what you say if there is an $\bar{e}$ on the end of a word.

b. (Touch the ball for **time.** Pause two seconds.) Get ready. (Signal.) *Time.* Yes, **time.**

c. (Repeat b for **mad, tim,** and **made.**)

time

mad

tim

made

"I will do good," don said.[8]

then the woman handed don a dime.

that dime looked dim in the dark.

the woman said, "keep that dime.

when you want to be a super man, tap

the dime three times."[9]

don looked at the dime, but when he

looked up, he did not see the woman.

"where are you?" don asked.

there was no answer. don called again,

but there was no answer.[10]**then don took**

the dime and went up the dim stairs. he

said to himself, "I must be having a

dream."[11]**but then he looked at the dime**

and said, "if I am dreaming, how did I

get this dime?"[12]

don picked up his mop and began to

mop again. then he said, "I think I will

tap that dime three times and see what

happens. I hope it works."

so don dropped his mop and tapped

his dime one time, two times, three times.[13]

to be continued[14]

---

[8] What did Don say? (Signal.) *I will do good.*

[9] What's Don supposed to do when he wants to be a super man? (Signal.) *Tap the dime three times.*

• Show me how you'd do that. (The children respond.)

[10] What happened to the woman? (The children respond.)

• She disappeared.

[11] Why did he say that? (The children respond.)

[12] Was he dreaming? (Signal.) *No.*

• How do you know? *He had a dime.*

[13] Why is he tapping the dime? (The children respond.)

• Do you think he will be a super man? (The children respond.)

[14] We'll find out more next time.

EXERCISE 13

Picture comprehension

a. What do you think you'll see in the picture? (The children respond.)

b. Turn the page and look at the picture.

c. (Ask these questions:)

1. Who is with Don? *A woman.*

2. Show me the woman's cap. (The children respond.)

• Show me her cape. (The children respond.)

3. How do you know that Don and the woman are downstairs in a basement? (The children respond.)

4. What is the woman giving Don? (Signal.) *A dime.*

5. What do you think she's telling Don about that dime? (The children respond.)

EXERCISE 14

Summary of independent activities

a. (Pass out Worksheet 83 to each child.)

b. Everybody, now you'll do your worksheet. Remember to do all parts of the worksheet and read all the parts carefully.

END OF LESSON 83

Starting with lesson 84, present stories from Storybook 2.

Do not touch small letters.

Get ready to read all the words on this page without making a mistake.

EXERCISE 6

Read the fast way

a. Read these words the fast way.
b. (Touch the ball for **home.** Pause two seconds.) Get ready. (Signal.) *Home.* Yes, **home.**
c. (Repeat *b* for remaining words.)

nine

tracks

side

fifty

home

hundred

tv

before

thrēē

school

liked

standing

trāin

(Repeat any troublesome words.)

Individual test

(Call on individual children. Each child reads a different word.)

STORYBOOK

READ THE ITEMS 83

EXERCISE 9

Read the item

a. (Pass out Storybook 1.)

b. Open your reader to page 222. Get ready to read the item.

c. Finger under the first word of the item. ✔
- Get ready. (Tap.) *When.*

d. Next word. (Pause.) Get ready. (Tap.) *The.*

e. (Repeat step *d* for the remaining words in the item.)

f. (Repeat steps *c* through *e* until the item is firm.)

g. Everybody, say that item. (Pause. Signal.) *When the teacher says "What," say "That."*

To Correct

1. Everybody, say the item with me. (Signal. Say the item with the children at a normal speaking rate. Repeat until firm.)
2. (Repeat step *g*. Then skip to step *i*.)

h. Again. (Repeat step *g* until firm.)

i. What are you going to say when I say "**What**"? (Signal.) *That.*
- When are you going to say "**That**"? (Signal.) *When the teacher says "What."*

To Correct

(Have the children read the item aloud. Then repeat the questions.)

EXERCISE 10

Play the game

a. Read the item to yourself and think about what you're going to do and when you're going to do it. Raise your hand when you're ready.

b. (After the children raise their hands, say:) Get ready to play the game.

c. My turn. (Pause.) **What.** (Signal.) (The children are to say *That* immediately.)

To Correct

(Have the children read the item aloud. Then play the game again.)

STORY 83

EXERCISE 11

First reading

a. Everybody, get ready to read the story. Touch the title of the story. ✔
- We're going to read this story two times. The second time, I'll ask everybody the questions.

b. I'm going to call on individual children to read two or three sentences. Everybody, follow along. If you hear a mistake, raise your hand. Children who do not have their place lose their turn. (Call on individual children to read two or three sentences. Do not ask comprehension questions.)

To Correct

word-identification errors (**from,** for example)
1. That word is **from.** What word? *From.*
2. Go back to the beginning of the sentence and read the sentence again.

---

don mēēts a woman[1]

wherₑ did don work?[2]

whȳ did don mope?[3]

somebody tōld don to come down the stāirs. so don dropped his mop and went down the stāirs. it was very dim down therₑ.[4] but don could see a woman in the dark. the woman had a cap and a cape.[5] she said, "don, do you want to be a super man?"[6]

"yes, I do," don said.

the woman said, "I will help you be a super man if you tell me that you will do good."[7]

EXERCISE 12

Second reading

a. Everybody, you're going to read the story again. This time, I'm going to ask questions. Touch the title of the story. ✔

b. (Call on individual children to read two or three sentences. Ask the specified questions at the end of each underlined sentence.)

[1] Who is Don going to meet? (Signal.) *A woman.*

[2] What's the answer? (Signal.) *In a hat store.*

[3] What's the answer? (The children respond.)

[4] What did it look like downstairs? (Signal.) *Dim.* Yes, there was not much light.

[5] Tell me about the woman Don met. (The children respond.)

[6] What did she say? (Signal.) *Don, do you want to be a super man?*

[7] What did Don have to promise? (Signal.) *To do good.*

Do not touch small letters.

Get ready to read all the words on this page without making a mistake.

ēven

EXERCISE 7

Read the fast way first

a. (Touch the ball for **ēven.**) Read this word the fast way. (Pause two seconds.) Get ready. (Signal.) *Even.* Yes, **even.**

b. (Return to the ball.) Sound it out. Get ready. (Quickly touch **ē, v, e, n** as the children say:) *ēēēvvveeennn.*

c. What word? (Signal.) *Even.* Yes, **even.**

d. (Repeat *b* and *c* until firm.)

e. (Repeat the exercise for **very, sandy,** and **missing.**)

very

sandy

missing

front

EXERCISE 8

Listen, sound out

a. (Point to **front.**) I'll tell you this word. (Pause.) **Front.** What word? (Signal.) *Front.* Yes, **front.**

b. (Touch the ball for **front.**) Sound it out. Get ready. (Quickly touch **f, r, o, n, t** as the children say:) *fffrrrooonnnt.*

c. What word? (Signal.) *Front.* Yes, **front.**

d. (Repeat *b* and *c* until firm.)

th

EXERCISE 9

th words

a. (Point to **th.**) When these letters are together, they usually say **ththth.**

b. What do these letters usually say? (Signal.) *ththth.* Yes, **ththth.**

• (Repeat until firm.)

c. (Point to the words.) These are words you already know. See if you can read them when they look this way.

d. (Point to **th** in **there.**) What do these letters say? (Signal.) *ththth.*

e. (Touch the ball for **there.**) Read the fast way. Get ready. (Signal.) *There.* Yes, **there.**

f. (Repeat *d* and *e* for **they, the,** and **this.**)

g. (Repeat the series of words until firm.)

there

they

the

this

Individual test

(Call on individual children to read a column of words from this lesson. If the column contains only one or two words, direct the child to read additional words from an adjacent column. Praise children who read all words with no errors.)

EXERCISE 7

Teacher reads the words in red

a. I'll read the words in red to you.

b. (Touch the ball for **broke.** Slash as you say:) Broke. What word? (Signal.) *Broke.*

c. (Repeat step *b* for the words in red.)

d. Your turn to read all the words in this column the fast way.

e. (Touch the ball for **broke.** Pause.) Get ready. (Slash.) *Broke.*

f. (Repeat step *e* for each remaining word in the column.)

To Correct

word-identification errors (**somebody,** for example)

1. That word is **somebody.** What word? (Signal.) *Somebody.*
2. (Return to the first word in the column and present all words in order.) Starting over.

broke

holes

dimes

cap

dime

hat

stairs

EXERCISE 8

Read the fast way

a. You're going to read all the words in this column the fast way.

b. (Touch the ball for **mop.** Pause.) Get ready. (Slash.) *Mop.*

c. (Repeat step *b* until firm.)

d. (Repeat steps *b* and *c* for each remaining word in the column.)

e. (Repeat the column until the children read all the words in order without making mistakes.)

mop

when

mope

times

why

two

answer

Criterion

(If the children make any mistakes in the column, say:) Do this column again without making any mistakes. (Repeat the column.)

(If the children make no mistakes in the column, say:) Good reading. You made no mistakes in this column. (Proceed to the next column.)

Individual test

a. I'm going to call on individual children to read one column of words the fast way. Raise your hand if you hear a mistake.

b. (Call on individual children to read one column of words from this lesson.)

c. (Praise children who read all words with no errors.)

STORYBOOK

STORY 68
EXERCISE 10

First reading—title and three sentences

a. (Pass out Storybook 1.)

b. Everybody, open your reader to page 176.

c. Everybody, touch the title of the story and get ready to read the words in the title.

d. First word. ✔
- Get ready. (Tap.) *Sandy.*

e. (Tap for each remaining word in the title.)

f. Everybody, say the title. (Signal.)
Sandy counted everything.

g. Everybody, get ready to read this story.

h. First word. ✔
- Get ready. (Tap.) *Sandy.*

i. Next word. ✔
- Get ready. (Tap.) *Was.*

j. (Repeat *i* for the remaining words in the first three sentences. Have the children reread the first three sentences until firm.)

EXERCISE 11

Remaining sentences

a. I'm going to call on individual children to read a sentence. Everybody, follow along and point to the words. If you hear a mistake, raise your hand.

b. (Call on a child.) Read the next sentence.

To Correct

word-identification errors (**from**, for example)
1. That word is **from.** What word? *From.*
2. Go back to the beginning of the sentence and read the sentence again.

c. (Call on another child.) Read the next sentence.

d. (Repeat *c* for most of the remaining sentences in the story.)

e. (Occasionally have the group read a sentence. When the group is to read, say:) Everybody, read the next sentence. (Tap for each word in the sentence.)

---

sandy counted everything[1]

sandy was a girl who liked to count. she counted things all the time. on her way to school, she would count trees and dogs and cats.[2] she would count boys and girls. she even counted the steps she took.

sandy liked school. the part she liked best was when the teacher said, "now we will work on counting." sandy was the best counter in the school.

one day sandy was walking to school and she was counting things. she was walking near the rail road tracks.[3] and a train went by. so sandy counted the train cars. there were one hundred cars in that train.[4] there were fifty red cars and fifty yellow cars.[5]

EXERCISE 12

Second reading—sentences and questions

a. You're going to read the story again. This time I'm going to ask questions.

b. Starting with the first word of the title. ✔
- Get ready. (Tap as the children read the title.)

c. (Call on a child.) Read the first sentence.

To Correct word-identification errors
(**from,** for example)
1. That word is **from.** What word? *From.*
2. Go back to the beginning of the sentence and read the sentence again.

d. (Call on another child.) Read the next sentence.

e. (Repeat *d* for most of the remaining sentences in the story.)

f. (Occasionally have the group read a sentence.)

g. (After each underlined sentence has been read, present each comprehension question specified below to the entire group.)

[1] What does the title say Sandy counts? (Signal.) *Everything.*
- Can you count? (Signal.) *Yes.*
- Let's hear you count to five. (Signal.) (The children respond.)

[2] Name some things she would count. (The children respond.)

[3] What do you usually find on railroad tracks? (Signal.) *Trains.* Yes, trains.

[4] How many cars? (Signal.) *One hundred.*
- That's a lot of train cars.

[5] Tell me about the cars. (The children respond.)

EXERCISE 5

Teacher reads the words in red

a. I'll read the words in red to you.

b. (Touch the ball for **were.** Slash as you say:) Were. What word? (Signal.) *Were.*

c. (Repeat step *b* for the words in red.)

d. Your turn to read all the words in this column the fast way.

e. (Touch the ball for **were.** Pause.) Get ready. (Slash.) *Were.*

f. (Repeat step *e* for each remaining word in the column.)

> **To Correct**
> word-identification errors
> (**somebody,** for example)
> 1. That word is **somebody.** What word? (Signal.) *Somebody.*
> 2. (Return to the first word in the column and present all words in order.) Starting over.

were

them

good

cape

dim

hate

tap

EXERCISE 6

Words with underlined parts

a. First you're going to read the underlined part of each word in this column. Then you're going to read the whole word.

b. (Touch the ball for **mopping.**) Read the underlined part. Get ready. (Tap the ball.) *Mopp.*

• Read the whole word. (Pause.) Get ready. (Slash.) *Mopping.*

c. (Repeat step *b* until firm.)

d. (Repeat steps *b* and *c* for each remaining word in the column.)

mopping

picked

somebody

handed

dreaming

dropped

tapped

Criterion

(If the children make any mistakes in the column, say:) Do this column again without making any mistakes. (Repeat the column.)

(If the children make no mistakes in the column, say:) Good reading. You made no mistakes in this column. (Proceed to the next column.)

Criterion

(If the children make any mistakes in the column, say:) Do this column again without making any mistakes. (Repeat the column.)

(If the children make no mistakes in the column, say:) Good reading. You made no mistakes in this column. (Proceed to the next column.)

after school was over, sandy began to walk home. she walked near the rail road tracks. and there was <u>the same train she had seen before.</u>[6] the train was standing on the track. <u>there were two men and one woman in front of the train.</u>[7]

one of the men was saying, "where are the tv sets? they should <u>be on this train. but they are missing."</u>[8]

the woman said, "how could they be missing? this train has been standing here all day. the tv sets were on this train before, so they must be on this train now."

more to come

---

[6] What did she see on her way home? (Signal.)
The same train she had seen before.

[7] Who did she see? (Signal.)
Two men and one woman.

[8] What are missing? (Signal.) *TV sets.*

• Where should they be? (Signal.) *On the train.*

• Where do you think they are?
(The children respond.)

EXERCISE 13
Picture comprehension

a. What do you think you'll see in the picture?
(The children respond.)

b. Turn the page and look at the picture.

c. (Ask these questions:)

1. Where is Sandy in this picture?
(The children respond for ten seconds. Then comment briefly.)

2. What is Sandy holding? (Signal.) *A book.*

3. Why is her finger out like that? (Signal.)
She is counting.

4. What is she counting? (Signal.) *Train cars.*

5. How many train cars can you count in this picture? (Signal.) (The children respond.)

6. Show me the railroad tracks.
(The children respond.)

SUMMARY OF INDEPENDENT ACTIVITY
EXERCISE 14
Introduction to independent activity

a. (Pass out Worksheet 68 to each child.)

b. (Hold up side 1 of your worksheet.)
Everybody, you're going to do this worksheet on your own. (Tell the children when they will work the items.)

• Let's go over the things you're going to do.

Story items

(Point to the story-items exercise.) Everybody, remember to write your answers in the blanks.

Following instructions

a. (Touch the sentence in the box.)

b. Everybody, first you're going to read the sentence in the box. Then you're going to read the instructions below the box and do what the instructions tell you to do.

Story-picture items

(Point to the story-picture items on side 2.) Remember to follow these instructions and look at the picture when you work these items.

Reading comprehension

(Point to the story.) You're going to read this story and then do the items. Remember to write the answers in the blanks.

END OF LESSON 68

READING VOCABULARY
EXERCISE 3

Teacher introduces reading vocabulary

Everybody, you're going to read columns of words. If you make a mistake in a column, you'll do the column again until you can do it without making a mistake. If you don't make any mistakes in a column, we'll go to the next column.

> ┌─ **To Correct** ──────────────────────────
> **word-identification errors**
> **(somebody,** for example)
> 1. That word is **somebody.** What word? (Signal.) *Somebody.*
> 2. (Return to the first word in the column and present all words in order.) Starting over.

EXERCISE 4

Words with underlined parts

a. First you're going to read the underlined part of each word in this column. Then you're going to read the whole word.

b. (Touch the ball for **where.**) Read the underlined part. Get ready. (Tap the ball.) *whwhwh.*

- Read the whole word. (Pause.) Get ready. (Slash.) *Where.*

c. (Repeat step *b* until firm.)

d. (Repeat steps *b* and *c* for each remaining word in the column.)

where

are

called

there

dark

dream

three

Criterion

(If the children make any mistakes in the column, say:) Do this column again without making any mistakes. (Repeat the column.)

(If the children make no mistakes in the column, say:) Good reading. You made no mistakes in this column. (Proceed to the next column.)

READING VOCABULARY

Get ready to read all the words on this page without making a mistake.

EXERCISE 1

Long and short vowel words

a. Read these words the fast way. Remember what you say if there is an ē on the end of a word.

b. (Touch the ball for **side.** Pause two seconds.) Get ready. (Signal.) *Side.* Yes, **side.**

c. (Repeat *b* for **fine, fin,** and **sid.**)

side

fine

fin

sid

began

EXERCISE 2

Two-part word

a. (Cover **gan.** Point to **be.**) Everybody, tell me what this part of the word says. Get ready. (Signal.) *Be.* Yes, **be.**

b. (Uncover **gan.** Touch the ball for **began.**) Now tell me what the whole word says. Get ready. (Signal.) *Began.* Yes, **began.**

c. (Repeat exercise until firm.)

herself

EXERCISE 3

Two-part word

a. (Cover **self.** Point to **her.**) Everybody, tell me what this part of the word says. Get ready. (Signal.) *Her.* Yes, **her.**

b. (Uncover **self.** Touch the ball for **herself.**) Now tell me what the whole word says. Get ready. (Signal.) *Herself.* Yes, **herself.**

c. (Repeat exercise until firm.)

inside

EXERCISE 4

Two-part word

a. (Cover **side.** Point to **in.**) Everybody, tell me what this part of the word says. Get ready. (Signal.) *In.* Yes, **in.**

b. (Uncover **side.** Touch the ball for **inside.**) Now tell me what the whole word says. Get ready. (Signal.) *Inside.* Yes, **inside.**

c. (Repeat exercise until firm.)

home

EXERCISE 5

Practice final-e rule

a. Read this word the fast way. Remember to look at the end of the word.

b. (Touch the ball for **home.** Pause two seconds.) Get ready. (Signal.) *Home.* Yes, **home.**

c. (Touch the ball for **home.**) Sound it out. Get ready. (Quickly touch **h, o, m** as the children say:) *hooommm.*

d. What word? (Signal.) *Home.* Yes, **home.**

e. (Repeat *b* through *d* until firm.)

(Repeat any troublesome words.)

Individual test

(Call on individual children. Each child reads a different word.)

★ LETTER NAMES
EXERCISE 1

Letter names

a. (Use transparency and crayon.)

b. Look at these letters. You know the names of the letters that are in red. Get ready to tell me those letter names.

c. (Point under **a.**) Get ready. (Tap.) *A.*

d. (Repeat step *c* for **e, i, o,** and **u.**)

e. My turn to say the names of all the letters. (Point to each letter and say its name.)

f. Your turn. See how many letter names you can say. (Point under **a.**) Get ready. (Tap.) *A.*

• (Tap under each remaining letter as the children say its name.)

To Correct
1. (Immediately say the letter name.)
2. What name? (Tap.) (The children respond.)
3. (Circle the letter.)
4. (Continue to the next letter.)

g. (If any letters are circled, say:) Everybody, get ready to tell me the names of all the circled letters. (Point to each circled letter.) Get ready. (Tap.) (The children respond.)

EXERCISE 2

Individual test

a. See how many letter names you can say.

b. (Call on individual children. Immediately say the correct letter name if the child makes a mistake.)

abcdefghijklmnopqrstuvwxyz

Do not touch small letters.

Get ready to read all the words on this page without making a mistake.

EXERCISE 6

Read the fast way

a. Read these words the fast way.

b. (Touch the ball for **one.** Pause two seconds.) Get ready. (Signal.) *One.* Yes, **one.**

c. (Repeat *b* for remaining words.)

one

standing

many

work

ninety

calling

where

left

counter

next

were

parked

EXERCISE 7

ar word

a. (Touch the ball for **parked.**) Read this word the fast way. (Pause two seconds.) Get ready. (Signal.) *Parked.* Yes, **parked.**

b. (Point to **ar** in **parked.**) Everybody, what do these letters say? (Signal.) *Are.* Yes, **are.**

c. (Touch the ball for **parked.**) Sound it out. Get ready. (Quickly touch **p, ar, k, d** as the children say:) *parkd.*

d. What word? (Signal.) *Parked.* Yes, **parked.**

e. (Repeat *c* and *d* until firm.)

about

EXERCISE 8

ou word

a. (Point to **ou** in **about.**) What do these letters say? (Signal.) *ou.* Yes, **ou.**

b. (Touch the ball for **about.**) Read this word the fast way. Get ready. (Signal.) *About.* Yes, **about.**

(Repeat any troublesome words.)

Individual test

(Call on individual children. Each child reads a different word.)

WORKSHEET 82

when the store was mopped, don would sit and mope.[6] he would think of the things he would do if he was a super man.

"I would fInd crooks," he said. "they would shoot at me, but I would not feel a thing."

every dāy was the same. don would mop and mop. then he would mope and mope.[7] when he mopped, he would think about being a super man. when he would mope, he would think about that too.

then one dāy something happened. don was mopping in the back of the store. all at once, he stopped mopping. "I think I hēar something," he said.[8]

the sound came from the dōōr that led down the stāirs.[9] somebody was sāying, "come down the stāirs." don ōpened the dōōr and went down the stāirs.[10]

to be continued[11]

[6] After he mopped, he would sit and … (Signal.) *Mope.*
- Yes, he felt sad and complained. He moped.

[7] What happened after he mopped? (The children respond.)

[8] Why did he stop mopping? (Signal.) *He heard something.*

[9] Where did the sound come from? (The children respond.)
- This is a little scary.

[10] What did Don do? (Signal.) *He opened the door and went down the stairs.*

[11] That means more of the story next time. Next time the story will be continued.

EXERCISE 12

Picture comprehension

a. Look at the picture.

b. (Ask these questions:)

1. Who is that in the picture? (Signal.) *Don.*
2. How many hats do you see? (Signal.) *Three.*
3. What is Don holding? (Signal.) *A mop.*
4. Where do you think he's going? *(Signal.) Downstairs.*
- Why? (The children respond.)
5. What do you think he's going to find downstairs? (The children respond.)

EXERCISE 13

Summary of independent activities

a. (Pass out Worksheet 82 to each child.)

b. Everybody, now you'll do your worksheet. Remember to do all parts of the worksheet and to read all the parts carefully.

END OF LESSON 82

Do not touch small letters.

Get ready to read all the words on this page without making a mistake.

found

EXERCISE 9

Read the fast way

a. Read this word the fast way.

b. (Touch the ball for **found.** Pause two seconds.) Get ready. (Signal.) *Found.* Yes, **found.**

EXERCISE 10

Read the fast way

a. Read these words the fast way.

b. (Touch the ball for **made.** Pause two seconds.) Get ready. (Signal.) *Made.* Yes, **made.**

c. (Repeat b for **here.**)

made

here

this

EXERCISE 11

Read the fast way first

a. (Touch the ball for **this.**) Read this word the fast way. (Pause two seconds.) Get ready. (Signal.) *This.* Yes, **this.**

b. (Return to the ball.) Sound it out. Get ready. (Quickly touch **th, i, s** as the children say:) *thththiiisss.*

c. What word? (Signal.) *This.* Yes, **this.**

d. (Repeat b and c until firm.)

e. (Repeat the exercise for **they.**)

they

EXERCISE 12

Read the fast way

a. Read these words the fast way.

b. (Touch the ball for **there.** Pause two seconds.) Get ready. (Signal.) *There.* Yes, **there.**

c. (Repeat b for **that** and **the.**)

there

that

the

Individual test

(Call on individual children to read a column of words from this lesson. If the column contains only one or two words, direct the child to read additional words from an adjacent column. Praise children who read all words with no errors.)

READ THE ITEMS 82
EXERCISE 8

Read the item

a. (Pass out Storybook 1.)

b. Open your reader to page 219. Get ready to read the item.

c. Finger under the first word of the item. ✔
- Get ready. (Tap.) *Say.*

d. Next word. (Pause.) Get ready. (Tap.) *Spot.*

e. (Repeat step *d* for the remaining words in the item.)

f. (Repeat steps *c* through *e* until the item is firm.)

g. Everybody, say that item. (Pause. Signal.) *Say "Spot" if the teacher says "Stop."*

To Correct
1. Everybody, say the item with me. (Signal. Say the item with the children at a normal speaking rate. Repeat until firm.)
2. (Repeat step *g*. Then skip to step *i*.)

h. (Again. Repeat step *g* until firm.)

i. What are you going to say if I say **"Stop"**? (Signal.) *Spot.*
- When are you going to say **"Spot"**? (Signal.) *When the teacher says "Stop."*

To Correct
(Have the children read the item aloud. Then repeat the questions.)

EXERCISE 9

Play the game

a. Read the item to yourself and think about what you're going to do and when you're going to do it. Raise your hand when you're ready.

b. (After the children raise their hands, say:) Get ready to play the game.

c. My turn. (Pause.) **Stop.** (Signal.) (The children are to say *Spot* immediately.)

To Correct
(Have the children read the item aloud. Then play the game again.)

STORY 82
EXERCISE 10

First reading

a. Everybody, get ready to read the story. Touch the title of the story. ✔
- We're going to read this story two times. The second time, I'll ask everybody the questions.

b. I'm going to call on individual children to read two or three sentences. Everybody, follow along. If you hear a mistake, raise your hand. Children who do not have their place lose their turn. (Call on individual children to read two or three sentences. Do not ask comprehension questions.)

To Correct
word-identification errors (from, for example)
1. That word is **from.** What word? *From.*
2. Go back to the beginning of the sentence and read the sentence again.

---

don was sad[1]

don had a job that he did not like.[2] he worked in a hat store. he mopped up in that store at the end of ēach dāy. every dāy he mopped and mopped.[3] when he mopped, he talked to himself. he would sāy, "I hate to work in this hat store.[4] I hate to mop."

then he would think of things that he would like to do. he said, "I wish I was big. I wish I could flȳ. I would like to be a super man.[5] but I am just a mopper. I am not big. I cannot flȳ."

EXERCISE 11

Second reading

a. Everybody, you're going to read the story again. This time, I'm going to ask questions. Touch the title of the story. ✔

b. (Call on individual children to read two or three sentences. Ask the specified questions at the end of each underlined sentence.)
[1] Who is this story about? (Signal.) *Don.*
- And how did Don feel in the story? (Signal.) *Sad.*
- Let's read. We'll find out what he's sad about.
[2] Why was Don sad? (Signal.) *He had a job that he did not like.*
[3] What was his job? (Signal.) *Mopping.*
[4] Where does he do his mopping? (Signal.) *In a hat store.*
[5] What does he want to be? (Signal.) *A super man.*
- What could he do if he were a super man? (The children respond.)

STORYBOOK

STORY 69

EXERCISE 13

First reading—title and three sentences

a. (Pass out Storybook 1.)

b. Everybody, open your reader to page 179.

c. Everybody, touch the title of the story and get ready to read the words in the title.

d. First word. ✔

• Get ready. (Tap.) *A.*

e. (Tap for each remaining word in the title.)

f. Everybody, say the title. (Signal.)
A train car was missing.

g. Everybody, get ready to read this story.

h. First word. ✔

• Get ready. (Tap.) *What.*

i. Next word. ✔

• Get ready. (Tap.) *Did.*

j. (Repeat *i* for the remaining words in the first three sentences. Have the children reread the first three sentences until firm.)

EXERCISE 14

Remaining sentences and questions

a. I'm going to call on individual children to read a sentence. Everybody, follow along and point to the words. If you hear a mistake, raise your hand.

b. (Call on a child.) Read the next sentence.

c. (Call on another child.) Read the next sentence.

To Correct

word-identification errors (**from,** for example)

1. That word is **from.** What word? *From.*
2. Go back to the beginning of the sentence and read the sentence again.

---

a trāin car was missing[1]

what did sandy like to do?[2]

how many cars werₑ in the trāin?[3]

how many red cars werₑ in the trāin?[4]

sandy was standing nēₐr the woman and the men. they werₑ talking about the trāin and the missing tv sets.

one man said, "how many cars arₑ in this trāin?"[5]

the other man said, "therₑ arₑ ninety-nine cars in this trāin."[6]

---

d. (Repeat *c* for most of the remaining sentences in the story.)

e. (Occasionally have the group read a sentence. When the group is to read, say:) Everybody, read the next sentence. (Tap for each word in the sentence.)

f. (After each underlined sentence has been read, present each comprehension question specified below to the entire group.)

[1] What does the title tell us about one of the train cars? (Signal.) *It was missing.*

[2] Everybody, say that question. (Signal.) *What did Sandy like to do?*

• What's the answer? (Signal.) *Count things.*

[3] Everybody, say that question. (Signal.) *How many cars were in the train?*

• What's the answer? (Signal.) *One hundred.*

[4] Everybody, say that question. (Signal.) *How many red cars were in the train?*

• What's the answer? (Signal.) *Fifty.*

EXERCISE 15

Second reading—sentences and questions

a. You're going to read the story again. And I'm going to ask more questions.

b. Starting with the first word of the title. ✔

• Get ready. (Tap as the children read the title.)

c. (Call on a child.) Read the first sentence.

To Correct

word-identification errors (**from,** for example)

1. That word is **from.** What word? *From.*
2. Go back to the beginning of the sentence and read the sentence again.

d. (Call on another child.) Read the next sentence.

e. (Repeat *d* for most of the remaining sentences in the story.)

f. (Occasionally have the group read a sentence.)

g. (After each underlined sentence has been read, present each comprehension question specified below to the entire group.)

[5] What's the answer? (Signal.) *One hundred.*

[6] How many did he say there were? (Signal.) *Ninety-nine.*

EXERCISE 6

Read the fast way

a. You're going to read all the words in this column the fast way.

b. (Touch the ball for **store**. Pause.) Get ready. (Slash.) *Store.*

c. (Repeat step *b* until firm.)

d. (Repeat steps *b* and *c* for each remaining word in the column.)

To Correct

word-identification errors
(**dig,** for example)

1. That word is **dig.** What word? (Signal.) *Dig.*

2. (Return to the first word in the column and present all words in order.) Starting over.

store

happened

day

same

would

hear

mope

Criterion

(If the children make any mistakes in the column, say:) Do this column again without making any mistakes. (Repeat the column.)

(If the children make no mistakes in the column, say:) Good reading. You made no mistakes in this column. (Proceed to the next column.)

EXERCISE 7

Read the fast way

a. You're going to read all the words in this column the fast way.

b. (Touch the ball for **hat**. Pause.) Get ready. (Slash.) *Hat.*

c. (Repeat step *b* until firm.)

d. (Repeat steps *b* and *c* for each remaining word in the column.)

hat

mop

crooks

mope

dim

hate

dime

Individual test

a. I'm going to call on individual children to read one column of words the fast way. Raise your hand if you hear a mistake.

b. (Call on individual children to read one column of words from this lesson.)

c. (Praise children who read all words with no errors.)

sandy said, "no, there are one hundred cars in this train."

the woman said, "get out of here, little girl.[7] can't you see that we are talking?"

sandy said, "but I counted the cars in this train when I went to school. there are one hundred cars in this train."

"go home, little girl," the woman said. "there are ninety-nine cars in this train."

so sandy left. she began to count the cars in the train. she found out that there were not one hundred cars. there were only ninety-nine cars.[8]

sandy said to herself, "I am the best counter there is. and I counted one hundred cars. so now I must fInd out where one of the cars went."[9]

more to come

---

[7] Who said that? (Signal.) *The woman.*
[8] How did she find that out? (Signal.) *She counted them.*
• Is a train car missing? (Signal.) *Yes.*
[9] How many cars are missing? (Signal.) *One.*
• Next time we'll see if Sandy can find the missing train car.

EXERCISE 16

Picture comprehension

a. Look at the picture.
b. (Ask these questions:)
1. Where is everyone standing? (Signal.) *In front of the train.*
2. How many people are in front of the train? (Signal.) *Four.*
3. How many people are wearing hats? (Signal.) *Two.*
4. What do you think Sandy is telling them? (The children respond.)
5. What is in the missing train car? (Signal.) *TV sets.*

SUMMARY OF INDEPENDENT ACTIVITY
EXERCISE 17

Introduction to independent activity

a. (Pass out Worksheet 69 to each child.)
b. (Hold up side 1 of your worksheet.) Everybody, you're going to do this worksheet on your own. (Tell the children when they will work the items.)
• Let's go over the things you're going to do.

Story items

(Point to the story-items exercise.) Everybody, remember to write your answers in the blanks.

Following instructions

a. (Touch the sentence in the box.)
b. Everybody, first you're going to read the sentence in the box. Then you're going to read the instructions below the box and do what the instructions tell you to do.

Story-picture items

(Point to the story-picture items on side 2.) Remember to follow these instructions and look at the picture when you work these items.

Reading comprehension

(Point to the story.) You're going to read this story and then do the items. Remember to write the answers in the blanks.

END OF LESSON 69

EXERCISE 4

Sound out **g** words

a. The words in red have a funny-looking letter for the sound **g**.

b. (Touch the ball for **gas**.) My turn to sound it out. Get ready. (Touch under each sound as you say:) *gaaasss.*

c. (Touch the ball for **gas**.) Your turn. Sound it out. Get ready. (Touch under each sound as the children say:) *gaaasss.* What word? (Signal.) *Gas.*

d. (Touch the ball for **dig**.) Sound it out. Get ready. (Touch under each sound as the children say:) *diiig.*
  • What word? (Signal.) *Dig.*

e. Your turn to read all the words in this column the fast way.

f. (Touch the ball for **gas**. Pause.) Get ready. (Slash.) *Gas.*

g. (Repeat step *f* for each remaining word in the column.)

gas

dig

something

once

tried

saying

thing

Criterion

(If the children make any mistakes in the column, say:) Do this column again without making any mistakes. (Repeat the column.)

(If the children make no mistakes in the column, say:) Good reading. You made no mistakes in this column. (Proceed to the next column.)

> **To Correct**
> word-identification errors
> (**dig**, for example)
> 1. That word is **dig**. What word? (Signal.) *Dig.*
> 2. (Return to the first word in the column and present all words in order.) Starting over.

EXERCISE 5

Words with underlined parts

a. First you're going to read the underlined part of each word in this column. Then you're going to read the whole word.

b. (Touch the ball for **mopped**.) Read the underlined part. Get ready. (Tap the ball.) *Mopp.*
  • Read the whole word. (Pause.) Get ready. (Slash.) *Mopped.*

c. (Repeat step *b* until firm.)

d. (Repeat steps *b* and *c* for each remaining word in the column.)

mopped

liked

talked

mopper

cannot

worked

opened

Criterion

(If the children make any mistakes in the column, say:) Do this column again without making any mistakes. (Repeat the column.)

(If the children make no mistakes in the column, say:) Good reading. You made no mistakes in this column. (Proceed to the next column.)

READING VOCABULARY

Get ready to read all the words on this page without making a mistake.

To Correct

1. (Touch the ball for the word the children missed.) Is there an **ē** on the end of this word? (Signal.) (The children respond.)
2. (Point to the first vowel in the word.) So tell me what you say for this letter. (Signal.) (The children respond.)
3. (Touch the ball for the word.) Sound it out. Get ready. (Touch all sounds except the final **e**, if there is one, as the children sound out the word.)
4. What word? (Signal.) (The children respond.)
5. (Return to the first word in the column. Present all the words in order until firm.)

EXERCISE 1

Long vowel words

a. (Point to the words in this column.) Read these words the fast way.

b. (Touch the ball for **hide.** Pause two seconds.) Get ready. (Signal.) *Hide.* Yes, **hide.**

• (Repeat until firm.)

c. (Repeat *b* for **here** and **bite.**)

hide

here

bite

EXERCISE 2

Short vowel words

a. (Point to the words in this column.) Read these words the fast way.

b. (Touch the ball for **hid.** Pause two seconds.) Get ready. (Signal.) *Hid.* Yes, **hid.**

• (Repeat until firm.)

c. (Repeat *b* for **her** and **bit.**)

hid

her

bit

EXERCISE 3

Short and long vowel words

a. Everybody, read these words again. Remember what you say if there is an **ē** on the end of a word.

b. (Touch the ball for **bite.** Pause two seconds.) Get ready. (Signal.) *Bite.* Yes, **bite.**

c. (Repeat *b* for **hid, here,** and **her.**)

bite

hid

here

her

(Repeat any troublesome words.)

Individual test

(Call on individual children. Each child reads a different word.)

READING VOCABULARY

EXERCISE 1

Teacher introduces reading vocabulary

Everybody, you're going to read columns of words. If you make a mistake in a column, you'll do the column again until you can do it without making a mistake. If you don't make any mistakes in a column, we'll go to the next column.

EXERCISE 2

Words with underlined parts

a. First you're going to read the underlined part of each word in this column. Then you're going to read the whole word.

b. (Touch the ball for **read.**) The underlined letters are **e-a**. The letters **e-a** make the sound $\bar{e}\bar{e}\bar{e}$ in this word. What sound? (Tap the ball.) $\bar{e}\bar{e}\bar{e}$.

• Read the whole word. (Pause.) Get ready. (Slash.) *Read.*

c. (Repeat step *b* until firm.)

d. (Touch the ball for **dream.**) Read the underlined part. Get ready. (Tap the ball.) $\bar{e}\bar{e}\bar{e}$.

• Read the whole word. (Pause.) Get ready. (Slash.) *Dream.*

e. (Repeat step *d* until firm.)

f. (Repeat steps *d* and *e* for each remaining word.)

read

dream

shoot

every

when

super

sound

To Correct

word-identification errors (**dig,** for example)

1. That word is **dig.** What word? (Signal.) *Dig.*
2. (Return to the first word in the column and present all words in order.) Starting over.

EXERCISE 3

Teacher reads the words in red

a. I'll read the words in red to you.

b. (Touch the ball for **stairs.** Slash as you say:) Stairs. What word? (Signal.) *Stairs.*

c. (Repeat step *b* for the words in red.)

d. Your turn to read all the words in this column the fast way.

e. (Touch the ball for **stairs.** Pause.) Get ready. (Slash.) *Stairs.*

f. (Repeat step *e* for each remaining word in the column.)

Criterion

(If the children make any mistakes in the column, say:) Do this column again without making any mistakes. (Repeat the column.)

(If the children make no mistakes in the column, say:) Good reading. You made no mistakes in this column. (Proceed to the next column.)

stairs

say

says

continued

from

each

very

Do not touch small letters.

Get ready to read all the words on this page without making a mistake.

EXERCISE 4

Read the fast way

a. Read these words the fast way.

b. (Touch the ball for **those**. Pause two seconds.) Get ready. (Signal.) *Those.* Yes, **those.**

c. (Repeat *b* for remaining words.)

those

next

follōwed

inside

shed

steps

sets

just

missing

came

found

car

sound

ninety

nine

think

these

(Repeat any troublesome words.)

Individual test

(Call on individual children. Each child reads a different word.)

the fox said, "but I gave you a dime."[5]

the man said, "no, you did not give me a dime. I think you are trying to con me."

"I dōn't con men," the fox said. "I came here for a cone. and I gave you a dime for that cone."

the man looked at that sly fox. then the man said, "if this is not a trick, I will give you the cone."[6]

the fox said, "I am not lȳing. I am not trȳing to con you."[7]

just then a little girl came up to the ice crēam stand. it was the girl that the fox had met in the woods.[8] the girl said to the fox, "you are the fox that trIed to con me out of mȳ cone. I am glad to see that you are buȳing a cone."[9]

the man at the stand said, "so you are a con fox."[10]

the fox was so mad that he ran back to the woods. he never trIed to con the man at the cone stand again.[11]

this is the end.

[5] Did he really do that? (Signal.) *No.*
• So why did he say he did? (The children respond.)
• He's trying to con the man.
[6] Everybody, what did the man say? (Signal.) *If this is not a trick, I will give you the cone.*
• Is it a trick? (Signal.) *Yes.*
[7] Is the fox lying? (Signal.) *Yes.*
• He's not telling the truth.
[8] Who came up to the ice cream stand? (Signal.) *The girl.*
• Oh, oh. She'll tell on him.
[9] What did she think he was doing? (Signal.) *Buying a cone.*
• And was he really? (Signal.) *No.*
[10] What does the man know about that fox now? (Signal.) *That he is a con fox.*
[11] Why didn't he try to con the man again? (The children respond.)

EXERCISE 12

Picture comprehension

a. What do you think you'll see in the picture? (The children respond.)
b. Turn the page and look at the picture.
c. (Ask these questions:)
  1. What is the man holding? (Signal.) *An ice cream cone.*
  2. Does the fox look as if he wants the cone? (The children respond.)
  • How can you tell? (The children respond.)
  3. Who do you see walking up to the stand? (Signal.) *The little girl.*
  4. Will the fox be glad to see her? (Signal.) *No.*
  5. What kind of ice cream cone do you like best? (The children respond.)

WORKSHEET 81

EXERCISE 13

Summary of independent activities

a. (Pass out Worksheet 81 to each child.)
b. Everybody, now you'll do your worksheet. Remember to do all parts of the worksheet and to read all the parts carefully.

END OF LESSON 81

Do not touch small letters.

Get ready to read all the words on this page without making a mistake.

inside

EXERCISE 5

Two-part word

a. (Cover **side.** Point to **in.**) Everybody, tell me what this part of the word says. Get ready. (Signal.) *In.* Yes, **in.**

b. (Uncover **side.** Touch the ball for **inside.**) Now tell me what the whole word says. Get ready. (Signal.) *Inside.* Yes, **inside.**

c. (Repeat exercise until firm.)

outside

EXERCISE 6

Two-part word

a. (Cover **side.** Point to **out.**) Everybody, tell me what this part of the word says. Get ready. (Signal.) *Out.* Yes, **out.**

b. (Uncover **side.** Touch the ball for **outside.**) Now tell me what the whole word says. Get ready. (Signal.) *Outside.* Yes, **outside.**

c. (Repeat exercise until firm.)

scare

EXERCISE 7

Last part, first part

a. (Cover **s.** Point to **care.**) Read this part of the word the fast way. (Pause two seconds.) Get ready. (Signal.) *Care.* Yes, **care.**

b. (Uncover **s.** Point to **s.**) First you say **sss.** (Move your finger quickly under **care.**)

• Then you say (pause) **care.**

c. (Touch the ball for **scare.**) Get ready. (Move to **s,** then quickly along the arrow.) *Ssscare.*

d. Say it fast. (Signal.) *Scare.*

• Yes, what word? (Signal.) *Scare.* Yes, **scare.**

e. (Repeat exercise until firm.)

rāil

EXERCISE 8

Sound out first

a. (Touch the ball for **rāil.**) Sound it out. Get ready. (Quickly touch **r, ā, l** as the children say:) *rrrāāālll.*

b. What word? (Signal.) *Rail.* Yes, **rail.**

c. (Repeat exercise until firm.)

Individual test

(Call on individual children to read a column of words from this lesson. If the column contains only one or two words, direct the child to read additional words from an adjacent column. Praise children who read all words with no errors.)

STORYBOOK

STORY 70

EXERCISE 9

First reading—title and three sentences

a. (Pass out Storybook 1.)

b. Everybody, open your reader to page 182.

c. Everybody, touch the title of the story and get ready to read the words in the title.

d. First word. ✔

• Get ready. (Tap.) *Sandy.*

e. (Tap for each remaining word in the title.)

f. Everybody, say the title. (Signal.) *Sandy finds the train car.*

STORYBOOK

READ THE ITEMS 81

EXERCISE 8

Read the item

a. (Pass out Storybook 1.)

b. Open your reader to page 216. Get ready to read the item.

c. Finger under the first word of the item. ✔

• Get ready. (Tap.) *Say.*

d. Next word. (Pause.) Get ready. (Tap.) *What.*

e. (Repeat step *d* for the remaining words in the item.)

f. (Repeat steps *c* through *e* until the item is firm.)

g. Everybody, say that item. (Pause. Signal.) *Say "What" when the teacher says "That."*

To Correct

1. Everybody, say the item with me. (Signal. Say the item with the children at a normal speaking rate. Repeat until firm.)
2. (Repeat step *g.* Then skip to step *i.*)

h. Again. (Repeat *g* until firm.)

i. What are you going to say when I say "**That**"? (Signal.) *What.* When are you going to say "**What**"? (Signal.) *When the teacher says "That."*

To Correct

(Have the children read the item aloud. Then repeat the questions.)

EXERCISE 9

Play the game

a. Read the item to yourself and think about what you're going to do and when you're going to do it. Raise your hand when you're ready.

b. (After the children raise their hands, say:) Get ready to play the game.

c. My turn. (Pause.) **That.** (Signal.) (The children are to say *What* immediately.)

To Correct

(Have the children read the item aloud. Then play the game again.)

STORY 81

EXERCISE 10

First reading

a. Everybody, get ready to read the story. Touch the title of the story. ✔

• We're going to read this story two times. The second time, I'll ask questions.

b. I'm going to call on individual children to read two or three sentences. Everybody, follow along. If you hear a mistake, raise your hand. Children who do not have their place lose their turn. (Call on individual children to read two or three sentences. Do not ask comprehension questions.)

To Correct

word-identification errors (**from,** for example)
1. That word is **from.** What word? *From.*
2. Go back to the beginning of the sentence and read the sentence again.

---

the con fox[1]

the sly fox wanted an ice cream cone. he couldn't con the girl out of her cone, but he had a plan. he said, "I will go to the ice cream stand. when I get there, I will con somebody out of a cone."[2]

so that fox went to town. when he came to the ice cream stand, he said, "hand me a cone."[3]

the man at the stand made up a big cone. then the man said, "that will be one dime."[4]

EXERCISE 11

Second reading

a. Everybody, you're going to read the story again. This time, I'm going to ask questions. Touch the title of the story. ✔

b. (Call on individual children to read two or three sentences. Ask the specified questions at the end of each underlined sentence.)

[1] What kind of fox? (Signal.) *The con fox.*

• What does con mean? (The children respond.)

• It means to trick. A con fox will try to trick somebody.

[2] Where is he going to go? (Signal.) *To an ice cream stand.*

• And what does he want to do there? (Signal.) *Con somebody out of a cone.*

• Do you think he will con somebody? (The children respond.)

• Let's read and find out.

[3] What did he say? (Signal.) *Hand me a cone.*

[4] What's the dime for? (Signal.) *The ice cream cone.*

sandy fInds the trāin car[1]

when sandy counted the cars on her wāy to school, there were one hundred cars in the trāin. when she counted the cars after school, there were ninety-nine cars.[2] one car was missing.

sandy said, "I must think about this. there were fifty red cars and fifty yellōw cars. but now there are not fifty red cars. one red car is missing."[3]

sandy walked next to the rāil rōad track.

soon she came to a shed. there were rāil rōad tracks that led to the shed.[4] sandy said to herself, "I will fInd out what is in that shed."

so sandy follōwed the tracks to the shed.[5]

she looked inside the shed and saw a red trāin car standing on the tracks. the car dōōr was ōpen. sandy looked around. no one was around. so sandy ran ōver to the dōōr of the red car and looked inside. the car was filled with tv sets.[6]

she said to herself, "I found the car with the tv sets."

sandy was all set to run back to tell someone that she had found the missing car. but just then there was a sound nēar her.[7] it was the sound of foot steps.[8]

more to come

g. Everybody, get ready to read this story.

h. First word. ✔

• Get ready. (Tap.) *When.*

i. Next word. ✔

• Get ready. (Tap.) *Sandy.*

j. (Repeat *i* for the remaining words in the first three sentences. Have the children reread the first three sentences until firm.)

EXERCISE 10

Remaining sentences

a. I'm going to call on individual children to read a sentence. Everybody, follow along and point to the words. If you hear a mistake, raise your hand.

b. (Call on a child.) Read the next sentence.

To Correct

word-identification errors (**from,** for example)

1. That word is **from.** What word? *From.*
2. Go back to the beginning of the sentence and read the sentence again.

c. (Call on another child.) Read the next sentence.

d. (Repeat *c* for most of the remaining sentences in the story.)

e. (Occasionally have the group read a sentence. When the group is to read, say:) Everybody, read the next sentence. (Tap for each word in the sentence.)

EXERCISE 11

Second reading—sentences and questions

a. You're going to read the story again. This time I'm going to ask questions.

b. Starting with the first word of the title. ✔

• Get ready. (Tap as the children read the title.)

c. (Call on a child.) Read the first sentence.

d. (Call on another child.) Read the next sentence.

e. (Repeat *d* for most of the remaining sentences in the story.)

f. (Occasionally have the group read a sentence.)

g. (After each underlined sentence has been read, present each comprehension question specified below to the entire group.)

[1] What is Sandy going to do in this story? (Signal.) *Find the train car.*

[2] How many cars should there have been? (Signal.) *One hundred.*

• How many were missing? (Signal.) *One.*

[3] What's the color of the missing car? (Signal.) *Red.*

[4] Where did the tracks go? (Signal.) *To the shed.*

• What's a shed? (The children respond.)

• Yes, it's a place where you can put things.

[5] Do you think she'll find something in the shed? (The children respond.)

• What? (Signal.) *The missing train car.*

[6] The train car was in the shed. And what was in the train car? (Signal.) *TV sets.*

[7] What did she hear? (Signal.) *A sound.*

• What could it be? (The children respond.)

• Let's find out.

[8] What was the sound? (Signal.) *Footsteps.*

• Let's hear you make footsteps. (The children respond.)

• How do you think Sandy feels? (The children respond.)

EXERCISE 6

Sound out **g** words

a. The words in red have a funny-looking letter for the sound **g**.

b. (Touch the ball for **got**.) My turn to sound it out. Get ready. (Touch under each sound as you say:) gooot.

c. (Touch the ball for **got**.) Your turn. Sound it out. Get ready. (Touch under each sound as the children say:) *gooot.* What word? (Signal.) *Got.*

d. (Touch the ball for **bug**.) Sound it out. Get ready. (Touch under each sound as the children say:) *buuug.* What word? (Signal.) *Bug.*

e. Your turn to read all the words in this column the fast way.

f. (Touch the ball for **got**. Pause.) Get ready. (Slash.) *Got.*

g. (Repeat step *f* for each remaining word in the column.)

got

bug

gave

again

lying

trying

fox

Criterion

(If the children make any mistakes in the column, say:) Do this column again without making any mistakes. (Repeat the column.)

(If the children make no mistakes in the column, say:) Good reading. You made no mistakes in this column. (Proceed to the next column.)

To Correct

word-identification errors (**cone**, for example)

1. That word is **cone**. What word? (Signal.) *Cone.*
2. (Return to the first word in the column and present all words in order.) Starting over.

EXERCISE 7

Read the fast way

a. You're going to read all the words in this column the fast way.

b. (Touch the ball for **dim**. Pause.) Get ready. (Slash.) *Dim.*

c. (Repeat step *b* until firm.)

d. (Repeat steps *b* and *c* for each remaining word in the column.)

dim

dime

glad

mope

cone

stand

con

Individual test

a. I'm going to call on individual children to read one column of words the fast way. Raise your hand if you hear a mistake.

b. (Call on individual children to read one column of words from this lesson.)

c. (Praise children who read all words with no errors.)

EXERCISE 12

Picture comprehension

a. What do you think you'll see in the picture? (The children respond.)

b. Turn the page and look at the picture.

c. (Ask these questions:)
1. What's that building where Sandy is? (Signal.) *A shed.*
2. Why do you think the train car is in the shed? (The children respond.)
3. What is Sandy doing in the picture? (Let the children comment for ten seconds. Then comment briefly.)
4. We'll read more of the story next time and see if Sandy has trouble.

SUMMARY OF INDEPENDENT ACTIVITY
EXERCISE 13

Summary of independent activities

a. (Pass out Worksheet 70 to each child.)

b. Everybody, now you'll do your worksheet. Remember to do all parts of the worksheet and to read all the parts carefully.

INDIVIDUAL CHECKOUT
EXERCISE 14

2-minute individual fluency checkout: rate/accuracy

a. As you are doing your worksheet, I'll call on children one at a time to read the **second page of the story.** Remember, you get two stars if you read the second page of the story in less than two minutes and make no more than three errors.

b. (Call on each child. Tell the child:) Read the second page of the story very carefully. Go. (Time the child. Tell the child any words the child misses. Stop the child as soon as the child makes the fourth error or exceeds the time limit.)

c. (If the child meets the rate-accuracy criterion, record two stars on your chart for lesson 70. Congratulate the child. Give children who do not earn two stars a chance to read the second page of the story again before the next lesson is presented.)

104 words/**2 min** = 52 wpm **[3 errors]**

END OF LESSON 70

EXERCISE 4

Words with underlined parts

a. First you're going to read the underlined part of each word in this column. Then you're going to read the whole word.

b. (Touch the ball for **cream.**) The underlined letters are **e-a.** The letters **e-a** make the sound ēēē in this word. What sound? (Tap the ball.) ēēē.

• Read the whole word. (Pause.) Get ready. (Slash.) *Cream.*

c. (Repeat step *b* until firm.)

d. (Touch the ball for **teacher.**) Read the underlined part. Get ready. (Tap the ball.) ēēē.

• Read the whole word. (Pause.) Get ready. (Slash.) *Teacher.*

e. (Repeat step *d* until firm.)

f. (Repeat steps *d* and *e* for each remaining word in the column.)

cream

teacher

then

what

when

are

out

To Correct

word-identification errors (**cone,** for example)

1. That word is **cone.** What word? (Signal.) *Cone.*
2. (Return to the first word in the column and present all words in order.) Starting over.

EXERCISE 5

Teacher reads the words in red

a. I'll read the words in red to you.

b. (Touch the ball for **super.** Slash as you say:) Super. What word? (Signal.) *Super.*

c. (Repeat step *b* for the words in red.)

d. Your turn to read all the words in this column the fast way.

e. (Touch the ball for **super.** Pause.) Get ready. (Slash.) *Super.*

f. (Repeat step *e* for each remaining word in the column.)

super

buying

plan

trick

woods

somebody

tried

Criterion

(If the children make any mistakes in the column, say:) Do this column again without making any mistakes. (Repeat the column.)

(If the children make no mistakes in the column, say:) Good reading. You made no mistakes in this column. (Proceed to the next column.)

Criterion

(If the children make any mistakes in the column, say:) Do this column again without making any mistakes. (Repeat the column.)

(If the children make no mistakes in the column, say:) Good reading. You made no mistakes in this column. (Proceed to the next column.)

READING VOCABULARY

Do not touch small letters.

Get ready to read all the words on this page without making a mistake.

EXERCISE 1

Long and short vowel words

a. Read these words the fast way. Remember to look at the end of the word.

b. (Touch the ball for **sid.** Pause two seconds.) Get ready. (Signal.) *Sid.* Yes, **sid.**

c. (Repeat *b* for **hide, hid,** and **side.**)

sid

hide

hid

side

(Repeat any troublesome words.)

behīnd

EXERCISE 2

Two-part word

a. (Cover **hīnd.** Point to **be.**) Everybody, tell me what this part of the word says. Get ready. (Signal.) *Be.* Yes, **be.**

b. (Uncover **hīnd.** Touch the ball for **behīnd.**) Now tell me what the whole word says. Get ready. (Signal.) *Behind.* Yes, **behind.**

c. (Repeat exercise until firm.)

outside

EXERCISE 3

Two-part word

a. (Cover **side.** Point to **out.**) Everybody, tell me what this part of the word says. Get ready. (Signal.) *Out.* Yes, **out.**

b. (Uncover **side.** Touch the ball for **outside.**) Now tell me what the whole word says. Get ready. (Signal.) *Outside.* Yes, **outside.**

c. (Repeat exercise until firm.)

inside

EXERCISE 4

Two-part word

a. (Cover **side.** Point to **in.**) Everybody, tell me what this part of the word says. Get ready. (Signal.) *in.* Yes, **in.**

b. (Uncover **side.** Touch the ball for **inside.**) Now tell me what the whole word says. Get ready. (Signal.) *Inside.* Yes, **inside.**

c. (Repeat exercise until firm.)

truck

EXERCISE 5

Sound out first

a. (Touch the ball for **truck.**) Sound it out. Get ready. (Quickly touch **t, r, u,** between **c** and **k** as the children say:) *trrruuuk.*

b. What word? (Signal.) *Truck.* Yes, **truck.**

c. (Repeat exercise until firm.)

wāited

EXERCISE 6

Sound out first

a. (Touch the ball for **wāited.**) Sound it out. Get ready. (Quickly touch **w, ā, t, e, d** as the children say:) *wwwāāāteeed.*

b. What word? (Signal.) *Waited.* Yes, **waited.**

c. (Repeat exercise until firm.)

missing

EXERCISE 7

Sound out first

a. (Touch the ball for **missing.**) Sound it out. Get ready. (Quickly touch **m, i,** between the **s**'s, **ing** as the children say:) *mmmiiisssiiing.*

b. What word? (Signal.) *Missing.* Yes, **missing.**

c. (Repeat exercise until firm.)

Individual test

(Call on individual children. Each child reads a different word.)

READING VOCABULARY

EXERCISE 1

Teacher introduces reading vocabulary

Everybody, you're going to read columns of words. If you make a mistake in a column, you'll do the column again until you can do it without making a mistake. If you don't make any mistakes in a column, we'll go to the next column.

> **To Correct**
>
> word-identification errors
> (**cone,** for example)
> 1. That word is **cone.** What word? (Signal.) *Cone.*
> 2. (Return to the first word in the column and present all words in order.) Starting over.

EXERCISE 2

Teacher reads the fast way

a. The words in this column have letters that look a little different. Also, there are no lines over any letters. I'll read the words in the column. Then you'll read them.

b. (Touch the ball for **that.**) My turn. (Slash as you say:) That. What word? (Signal.) *That.*

c. (Repeat step *b* for each remaining word in the column.)

EXERCISE 3

Children read the fast way

a. Your turn to read all the words in this column the fast way.

b. (Touch the ball for **that.**) Get ready. (Slash.) *That.*

c. (Repeat step b for each remaining word in the column.)

that

mad

sly

crooks

cone

here

like

Criterion

(If the children make any mistakes in the column, say:) Do this column again without making any mistakes. (Repeat the column.)

(If the children make no mistakes in the column, say:) Good reading. You made no mistakes in this column. (Proceed to the next column.)

Do not touch small letters.

Get ready to read all the words on this page without making a mistake.

EXERCISE 8

Read the fast way

a. Read these words the fast way.

b. (Touch the ball for **books.** Pause two seconds.) Get ready. (Signal.) *Books.* Yes, **books.**

c. (Repeat *b* for remaining words.)

books

crooks

what

here

shed

there

couldn't

of

sēēm

from

front

these

those

talking

standing

doing

something

lōad

Individual test

(Call on individual children to read a column of words from this lesson.)

Look Ahead

In-Program Tests

Fluency Checkouts: Rate/Accuracy

Lessons 85, 90, 95, 100

- Children should be reading at least 60 words per minute at 97 percent accuracy.

Lesson Number	Error Limit	Number of words read	Number of minutes	Words per minute
85	4	120	2	60
90	4	120	2	60
95	4	120	2	60
100	4	120	2	60

Group Reading

- Story reading procedure changes at Lesson 84:
  - —Children read from the beginning of the story to the red 5. During this reading, the teacher counts the number of errors made.
  - —If the group makes more than 5 errors, they reread that portion of the story. If the group cannot read within the error limit on the second try, they may need review of the vocabulary.
  - —When the group reads within the error limit, *you* read the first part of the story to them, asking comprehension questions at specified points. Model expression, and read a little faster than the children usually do but not so fast that they cannot follow.
  - —After the red 5, the children continue taking turns reading, and you ask comprehension questions.

Skills

	Lessons 81–100
Word Reading	2 sound combinations (ea, ee) 127 regular words 21 irregular words Reading words the fast way
Comprehension	Completing picture deduction activities

Spelling

- By lesson 86 in the reading program, the children have been introduced to all the letter names and have made the transition from spelling by sounds to spelling by letter names. This is reflected in the Spelling Presentation Book.

Reading Activities

Help children develop decoding and comprehension skills by using the following activities.

Real or Not? (Lessons 81–100)

List several story events on the board. Have children determine if each story event is something that could actually happen (fact) or something that could not actually happen (fantasy). Sample items from the Don story series (Lessons 82–89) are shown below.

1. Don mopped the store. (fact)
2. Don walked down the stairs to a dim basement. (fact)
3. Don kicked a hole through the school wall. (fantasy)
4. Don moped because he was sad. (fact)
5. Don flew to the top of the store. (fantasy)
6. Don had a magic dime. (fantasy)
7. Don picked up a bus and heaved it. (fantasy)
8. Don helped others. (fact)

Word Pair Matching (Lessons 90–94)

After children have completed Lessons 90–94, select several word pairs with endings for a matching exercise. Write each word on a 3" x 5" index card. Have children match the short-vowel word with its long-vowel counterpart. Check children's work by having them say each pair of words aloud. A sample matching exercise is shown below.

Match

tapped	hopping
mopping	pinned
pined	diner
hoping	moping
dinner	taped

Alphabet Match

Write a lowercase letter of the alphabet on each of 26 library book pockets. Attach the pockets to a poster board. On 3" x 5" index cards, write each capital letter. Have children match each uppercase and lowercase letter by putting each index card into the correct pocket.

LESSONS 81–100

STORYBOOK

STORY 71
EXERCISE 9

First reading—title and three sentences

a. (Pass out Storybook 1.)
b. Everybody, open your reader to page 185.
c. Everybody, touch the title of the story and get ready to read the words in the title.
d. First word. ✔
• Get ready. (Tap.) *A.*
e. (Tap for each remaining word in the title.)
f. Everybody, say the title. (Signal.)
   A crook stops Sandy.
g. Everybody, get ready to read this story.
h. First word. ✔
• Get ready. (Tap.) *Sandy.*
i. Next word. ✔
• Get ready. (Tap.) *Had.*
j. (Repeat *i* for the remaining words in the first three sentences. Have the children reread the first three sentences until firm.)

EXERCISE 10

Remaining sentences

a. I'm going to call on individual children to read a sentence. Everybody, follow along and point to the words. If you hear a mistake, raise your hand.
b. (Call on a child.) Read the next sentence.

To Correct
word-identification errors (**from,** for example)
1. That word is **from.** What word? *From.*
2. Go back to the beginning of the sentence and read the sentence again.

c. (Call on another child.) Read the next sentence.
d. (Repeat *c* for most of the remaining sentences in the story.)
e. (Occasionally have the group read a sentence. When the group is to read, say:) Everybody, read the next sentence. (Tap for each word in the sentence.)

---

a crook stops sandy[1]

sandy had found the missing train car. but now there was a sound behind her. it was the sound of foot steps.

"I must hide," sandy said.

then she jumped into the red train car and hid behind a big tv set.[2] then she looked out. a big man came into the shed. then another man came in.

one man said, "back your truck up to the end of the shed. we will load the tv sets into the truck.[3] but we must load them fast."

the other man said, "yes." then the men left the shed. sandy said to herself, "these men are crooks.[4] they are stealing the tv sets."

EXERCISE 11

Second reading—sentences and questions

a. You're going to read the story again. This time I'm going to ask questions.
b. Starting with the first word of the title. ✔
• Get ready. (Tap as the children read the title.)
c. (Call on a child.) Read the first sentence.

To Correct
word-identification errors (**from,** for example)
1. That word is **from.** What word? *From.*
2. Go back to the beginning of the sentence and read the sentence again.

d. (Call on another child.) Read the next sentence.
e. (Repeat *d* for most of the remaining sentences in the story.)
f. (Occasionally have the group read a sentence.)
g. (After each underlined sentence has been read, present each comprehension question specified below to the entire group.)

[1] What is a crook? (The children respond.)
• Yes, a bad person who steals things.
[2] Why did she do that? (The children respond.)
[3] What are the men going to do? (Signal.) *Load the TV sets into the truck.*
• Why are they going to do that? (The children respond.)
[4] Why did she say that? (Signal.) *Because the men are going to steal the TV sets.*

Making Progress

	Since Lesson 1	Since Lesson 61
Word Reading	Sounds and 3 sound combinations 532 regular words 103 irregular words Reading high frequency hard words Discriminating long and short vowel words using the final *-e* rule	131 regular words 22 irregular words
Comprehension	**Picture Comprehension** Predicting what the picture will show Answering questions about the picture Answering written questions about specified pictures **Story Comprehension** Answering *who, what, when, where,* and *why* questions orally Making predictions about the story Answering questions about the story and other short passages in writing	Answering written questions about specified pictures

What to Use

Teacher	Students
Presentation Book B (pages 172–271) **Teacher's Guide** (pages 60, 67–75, 77–78) **Answer Key** **Spelling Presentation Book**	**Storybook 1** (pages 216–224) **Storybook 2** (pages 1–48) **Workbook B** **Lined paper**

What's Ahead in Lessons 81–100

New Skills

- Children will read words (Lesson 81) and stories (Lesson 84) in regular typeprint. Previously joined sounds **wh, ch, oo, qu,** and **er** appear separated.
- All letter names are introduced (Lesson 86).
- Children spell words by letter names (Lesson 86).
- Children learn capital letters beginning with "easy capitals"— those that look like the lowercase letters (Lesson 87)—and then harder capitals (Lesson 89).
- Children learn a rule for long and short vowel words when the word ends with a suffix, such as **hopping, hoping** (Lesson 88). These words can be difficult because children don't see the *e* at the end of the word. Provide extra practice for children who may need it.
- On Worksheets, picture deduction activities are introduced.

New Sound Combinations

Lesson 81 — **ea** as in *eat*
Lesson 83 — **ee** as in *three*

New Vocabulary

- *Regular words:*
  - (81) fox, got, mope, plan, super, trick
  - (82) day, gas, mop, mopped, mopper, say, saying, stairs
  - (83) broke, dark, dimes, handed, holes, mopping, shoot, tap, tapped, times
  - (84) hitting, hopped, mess, pow, smiles, tape
  - (85) crash, crashed, dive, having, heave, walls
  - (86) men, throw
  - (87) cheek, long, longer, nobody, tear
  - (88) baby, carry, fixed, moping, taped, thanked
  - (89) diner, moped, most, nailed, need
  - (90) boss, key, packed, pined, pinned, plant, plants, seed, send, sent, sticks
  - (91) caned, canned, jail, jailer, notes, now, oak, seems
  - (92) as, dumped, have, noted, planted, slop, slope, swing, tossed
  - (93) let, planting, swung, yelling
  - (94) and, canner, cheese, fixes, fool, hoped, if, leaves, spent, tapping, teaches
  - (95) Ann, Dan, lucky, smart, spell
  - (96) begin, boys, helper, hopping, seat, tame, tiger, tone, wagged
  - (97) cash, hoping, stones, wait
  - (99) hatched, leap, which, wig
  - (100) duckling, egg, grown, hello, names, pals, title, ugly
- *Irregular words:*
  - (81) buying, somebody, woods
  - (82) continued, talked
  - (83) answer
  - (86) nothing, said
  - (88) anybody, you
  - (90) words
  - (92) right
  - (95) early, schools
  - (98) question, you're
  - (99) grew
  - (100) become, friend, none, swan

sandy waited. she could hear the men talking outside. then she could hear the sound of the truck.

she said to herself, "I must get out of here."[5] she jumped from the train car and began to run as fast as she could go. she ran out of the shed. and then she stopped. the big man was standing in front of her.

he said, "what are you doing here?"

sandy looked at the man. she wanted to run, but she didn't think that she could run faster than the man.[6] she had to think of something to say. but she couldn't seem to talk.[7] she looked at the big man and the big man looked at her.[8]

more to come

---

[5] What did she say? (Signal.)
I must get out of here.
• Why did she say that?
(The children respond.)

[6] Why didn't she run? (The children respond.)

[7] Why do you suppose she couldn't talk?
(The children respond.)

[8] How does this part of the story end?
(The children respond.)
• Yes, Sandy and the big man are looking at each other. Next time we'll read some more.

WORKSHEET 71

EXERCISE 12
Picture comprehension

a. Look at the picture.
b. (Ask these questions:)
  1. Where is Sandy in this picture? (Signal.) *In the train car.*
  2. Do you think the men can see her? (The children respond.)
  3. What do you think the men are talking about? (The children respond.)
  4. Do those men look like crooks? (Let the children comment for ten seconds. Then comment briefly.)
  5. What is inside the train? (Signal.) *TV sets.*
  6. How do you think Sandy feels? (The children respond.)

SUMMARY OF INDEPENDENT ACTIVITY
EXERCISE 13
Introduction to independent activity

a. (Pass out Worksheet 71 to each child.)
b. (Hold up side 1 of your worksheet.) Everybody, you're going to do this worksheet on your own. (Tell the children when they will work the items.)
• Let's go over the things you're going to do.

Story items

(Point to the story-items exercise.) Everybody, remember to write your answers in the blanks.

Following instructions

a. (Touch the sentence in the box.)
b. Everybody, first you're going to read the sentence in the box. Then you're going to read the instructions below the box and do what the instructions tell you to do.

Story-picture items

(Point to the story-picture items on side 2.) Remember to follow these instructions and look at the picture when you work these items.

Reading comprehension

(Point to the story.) You're going to read this story and then do the items. Remember to write the answers in the blanks.

END OF LESSON 71

"close your eyes and ōpen your mouth," the girl said.[5]

the slȳ fox was thinking, "hō, hō, I conned that girl out of her cone."

when the fox closed his eyes, he did not get a cone in his mouth. he got a drink of cōld water.[6]

"there," the girl said. "that should make your mouth cool."

"no, no," the fox shouted. "mȳ mouth nēēds something cōlder than that water."

the girl said, "close your eyes and ōpen your mouth."

the fox said to himself, "this time I will con her out of her cone."[7]

but he did not con her out of a cone. he conned her out of a bit of ice. she dropped the ice into his mouth.[8] then she said, "now your mouth must fēēl cool."

"no, no," the fox yelled. "I nēēd a cone."

the girl said, "you can have the cone, but I ate all the ice crēam."

but the fox did not take the cone.[9] she had made him so mad that he ran back into the woods. he never trīed to con her again.

more to come[10]

[5] Do you think she'll put ice cream into his mouth? (The children respond.)
- Let's keep reading.

[6] Did he get the ice cream? (Signal.) *No.*
- What did he get? (Signal.)
A drink of cold water.
- He didn't con her that time.

[7] Everybody, say that. (Signal.)
This time I will con her out of her cone.
- Will he do it? Let's read more.

[8] What did he get? (Signal.) *Ice.*

[9] Why not? (Signal.)
The girl had eaten all the ice cream.

[10] Is this the end of the story? (Signal.) *No.*
- Right. Next time we'll see if he cons somebody out of a cone.

EXERCISE 16
Picture comprehension

a. Look at the picture.
b. (Ask these questions:)
1. What is the fox sitting on? (Signal.) *A log.*
2. What's the girl doing to the fox? (Signal.) (The children respond.)
- She's giving him a drink of cold water.
3. Is that what he wants? (Signal.) *No.*
- What does he want? (Signal.)
Her ice cream cone.
4. Is he conning her out of her cone in this picture? (Signal.) *No.*
- It doesn't look like he can trick her.

SUMMARY OF INDEPENDENT ACTIVITY
EXERCISE 17
Summary of independent activities

a. (Pass out Worksheet 80 to each child.)
b. Everybody, now you'll do your worksheet. Remember to do all parts of the worksheet and to read all the parts carefully.

INDIVIDUAL CHECKOUT
EXERCISE 18
2-minute individual fluency checkout: rate/accuracy

a. As you are doing your worksheet, I'll call on children one at a time to read the **first page of the story.** Remember, you get two stars if you read the first page of the story in less than two minutes and make no more than four errors.
b. (Call on each child. Tell the child:) Start with the title and read the first page of the story very carefully. Go. (Time the child. Tell the child any words the child misses. Stop the child as soon as the child makes the fifth error or exceeds the time limit.)
c. (If the child meets the rate-accuracy criterion, record two stars on your chart for lesson 80. Congratulate the child. Give children who do not earn two stars a chance to read the first page of the story again before the next lesson is presented.)
120 words/**2 min** = 60 wpm **[4 errors]**

END OF LESSON 80

READING VOCABULARY

Do not touch small letters.

Get ready to read all the words on this page without making a mistake.

EXERCISE 1

sh words

a. (Point to **sh.**) When these letters are together, they usually say **shshsh.**

b. What do these letters usually say? (Signal.) *shshsh.* Yes, **shshsh.**

• (Repeat until firm.)

c. (Point to the words.) These are words that you already know. See if you can read them when they look this way.

d. (Point to **sh** in **shed.**) What do these letters say? (Signal.) *shshsh.*

e. (Touch the ball for **shed.**) Read the fast way. Get ready. (Signal.) *Shed.* Yes, **shed.**

f. (Repeat *d* and *e* for **she.**)

g. (Repeat both words until firm.)

sh

shed

she

(Repeat any troublesome words.)

Individual test

(Call on individual children. Each child reads a different word.)

must

EXERCISE 2

Sound out first

a. (Touch the ball for **must.**) Sound it out. Get ready. (Quickly touch **m, u, s, t** as the children say:) *mmmuuussst.*

b. What word? (Signal.) *Must.* Yes, **must.**

c. (Repeat exercise until firm.)

sorry

EXERCISE 3

Sound out first

a. (Touch the ball for **sorry.**) Sound it out. Get ready. (Quickly touch **s, o,** between the **r**'s, **y** as the children say:) *sssooorrryyy.*

b. What word? (Signal.) *Sorry.* Yes, **sorry.**

c. (Repeat exercise until firm.)

līed

EXERCISE 4

Sound out first

a. (Touch the ball for **līed.**) Sound it out. Get ready. (Quickly touch **l, ī, d** as the children say:) *lllīīīd.*

b. What word? (Signal.) *Lied.* Yes, **lied.**

c. (Repeat exercise until firm.)

STORYBOOK

STORY 80
EXERCISE 13

First reading—title and three sentences

a. (Pass out Storybook 1.)

b. Everybody, open your reader to page 213.

c. Everybody, touch the title of the story and get ready to read the words in the title.

d. First word. ✔

• Get ready. (Tap.) *The.*

e. (Tap for each remaining word in the title.)

f. Everybody, say the title. (Signal.)
The fox wants a cone.

g. Everybody, get ready to read this story.

h. First word. ✔

• Get ready. (Tap.) *A.*

i. Next word. ✔

• Get ready. (Tap.) *Little.*

j. (Repeat *i* for the remaining words in the first three sentences. Have the children reread the first three sentences until firm.)

EXERCISE 14

Remaining sentences

a. I'm going to call on individual children to read a sentence. Everybody, follow along and point to the words. If you hear a mistake, raise your hand.

b. (Call on a child.) Read the next sentence.

To Correct

word-identification errors (**from,** for example)
1. That word is **from.** What word? *From.*
2. Go back to the beginning of the sentence and read the sentence again.

c. (Call on another child.) Read the next sentence.

d. (Repeat *c* for most of the remaining sentences in the story.)

e. (Occasionally have the group read a sentence. When the group is to read, say:) Everybody, read the next sentence. (Tap for each word in the sentence.)

> the fox wants a cone[1]
> a little girl was sitting in the woods. she had an ice crēam cone.
> she was sitting on a log, ēating her ice crēam cone.[2]
> a slȳ fox was looking at her. that fox was thinking. "I will con that girl. I will con her into giving me her cone."[3]
> so the slȳ fox ran up to the girl. then he fell ōver and began to shout, "help me, help me. mȳ mouth is on fire.[4] give me something cool for mȳ mouth."

EXERCISE 15

Second reading—sentences and questions

a. You're going to read the story again. This time I'm going to ask questions.

b. Starting with the first word of the title. ✔

• Get ready. (Tap as the children read the title.)

c. (Call on a child.) Read the first sentence.

To Correct

word-identification errors (**from,** for example)
1. That word is **from.** What word? *From.*
2. Go back to the beginning of the sentence and read the sentence again.

d. (Call on another child.) Read the next sentence.

e. (Repeat *d* for most of the remaining sentences in the story.)

f. (Occasionally have the group read a sentence.)

g. (After each underlined sentence has been read, present each comprehension question specified below to the entire group.)

[1] What will this story be about? (Signal.) *The fox wants a cone.*

[2] What was the girl sitting on? (Signal.) *A log.*

• What was she doing? (Signal.) *Eating her ice cream cone.*

[3] Everybody, say that. (Signal.) *I will con her into giving me her cone.*

• What does the sly fox want? (Signal.) *The ice cream cone.*

• He's going to try to con her or trick her into giving him the cone.

[4] Who is shouting? (Signal.) *The fox.*

• Is his mouth really on fire? (Signal.) *No.*

• So why is he saying that? (The children respond.)

Get ready to read all the words on this page without making a mistake.

standing

EXERCISE 5

Sound out first

a. (Touch the ball for **standing.**) Sound it out. Get ready. (Quickly touch **s, t, a, n, d, ing** as the children say:) *ssstaaannndiiing.*

b. What word? (Signal.) *Standing.* Yes, **standing.**

c. (Repeat exercise until firm.)

something

EXERCISE 6

Two-part word

a. (Cover **thing.** Point to **some.**) Everybody, tell me what this part of the word says. Get ready. (Signal.) *Some.* Yes, **some.**

b. (Uncover **thing.** Touch the ball for **something.**) Now tell me what the whole word says. Get ready. (Signal.) *Something.* Yes, **something.**

c. (Repeat exercise until firm.)

scared

EXERCISE 7

Two-part word

a. (Cover **d.** Point to **scare.**) Everybody, tell me what this part of the word says. Get ready. (Signal.) *Scare.* Yes, **scare.**

b. (Uncover **d.** Touch the ball for **scared.**) Now tell me what the whole word says. Get ready. (Signal.) *Scared.* Yes, **scared.**

c. (Repeat exercise until firm.)

EXERCISE 8

Long and short vowel words

a. Read these words the fast way. Remember to look at the end of the word.

b. (Touch the ball for **here.** Pause two seconds.) Get ready. (Signal.) *Here.* Yes, **here.**

c. (Repeat *b* for **cam, hide, came, her,** and **hid.**)

here

(Repeat any troublesome words.)

Individual test

(Call on individual children. Each child reads a different word.)

cam

hide

came

her

hid

Do not touch small letters.

Get ready to read all the words on this page without making a mistake.

EXERCISE 12

Read the fast way

a. Read these words the fast way.

b. (Touch the ball for **closed.** Pause two seconds.) Get ready. (Signal.) *Closed.* Yes, **closed.**

c. (Repeat *b* for remaining words.)

closed

take

made

fire

dropped

thinking

something

giving

again

conned

crīed

cool

cōlder

ōpen

Do not touch small letters.

Get ready to read all the words on this page without making a mistake.

EXERCISE 9

Read the fast way

a. Read these words the fast way.
b. (Touch the ball for **plāying.** Pause two seconds.) Get ready. (Signal.) *Playing.* Yes, **playing.**
c. (Repeat *b* for remaining words.)

plāyiṇg

ōkāy

rāil

can't

shouted

you'll

with

trīed

doiṇg

missiṇg

runniṇg

lookiṇg

whȳ

parked

also

more

nine

Individual test

(Call on individual children to read a column of words from this lesson. If the column contains only one or two words, direct the child to read additional words from an adjacent column. Praise children who read all words with no errors.)

Do not touch small letters.

Get ready to read all the words on this page without making a mistake.

hall

EXERCISE 6

al word

a. (Touch the ball for **hall.**) Read this word the fast way. (Pause two seconds.) Get ready. (Signal.) *Hall.* Yes, **hall.**

b. (Point to **al** in **hall.**) Everybody, what do these letters say? (Signal.) *All.* Yes, **all.**

c. (Touch the ball for **hall.**) Sound it out. Get ready. (Quickly touch **h, al** as the children say:) *hall.*

d. What word? (Signal.) *Hall.* Yes, **hall.**

e. (Repeat *c* and *d* until firm.)

barked

EXERCISE 7

ar word

a. (Touch the ball for **barked.**) Read this word the fast way. (Pause two seconds.) Get ready. (Signal.) *Barked.* Yes, **barked.**

b. (Point to **ar** in **barked.**) Everybody, what do these letters say? (Signal.) *Are.* Yes, **are.**

c. (Touch the ball for **barked.**) Sound it out. Get ready. (Quickly touch **b, ar, k, d** as the children say:) *barkd.*

d. What word? (Signal.) *Barked.* Yes, **barked.**

e. (Repeat *c* and *d* until firm.)

EXERCISE 8

ou word

a. (Touch the ball for **mouth.**) Read this word the fast way. (Pause two seconds.) Get ready. (Signal.) *Mouth.* Yes, **mouth.**

b. (Point to **ou** in **mouth.**) Everybody, what do these letters say? (Signal.) *ou.* Yes, **ou.**

c. (Touch the ball for **mouth.**) Sound it out. Get ready. (Quickly touch **m, ou, th** as the children say:) *mmmouththth.*

d. What word? (Signal.) *Mouth.* Yes, **mouth.**

e. (Repeat *c* and *d* until firm.)

EXERCISE 9

ou word

a. (Point to **ou** in **out.**) What do these letters say? (Signal.) *ou.* Yes, **ou.**

b. (Touch the ball for **out.**) Read this word the fast way. Get ready. (Signal.) *Out.* Yes, **out.**

EXERCISE 10

Read the fast way

a. Read this word the fast way.

b. (Touch the ball for **shouted.** Pause two seconds.) Get ready. (Signal.) *Shouted.* Yes, **shouted.**

EXERCISE 11

Listen, sound out with me

a. (Point to **close.**) I'll tell you this word. (Pause.) **Close (clōz).** What word? (Signal.) *Close.* Yes, **close.**

b. (Touch the ball for **close.**) Sound it out with me. Get ready. (Quickly touch **c, l, o, s** as you and the children say:) *clllōōōsss.*

c. What word? (Signal.) *Close.* Yes, **close.**

d. (Repeat *b* and *c* until firm.)

mouth

out

shouted

close

(Repeat any troublesome words.)

Individual test

(Call on individual children. Each child reads a different word.)

STORY 72
EXERCISE 10

First reading—title and three sentences

a. (Pass out Storybook 1.)
b. Everybody, open your reader to page 188.
c. Everybody, touch the title of the story and get ready to read the words in the title.
d. First word. ✔
• Get ready. (Tap.) *Sandy.*
e. (Tap for each remaining word in the title.)
f. Everybody, say the title. (Signal.) *Sandy tells what she found.*
g. Everybody, get ready to read this story.
h. First word. ✔
• Get ready. (Tap.) *Sandy.*
i. Next word. ✔
• Get ready. (Tap.) *Tried.*
j. (Repeat *i* for the remaining words in the first three sentences. Have the children reread the first three sentences until firm.)

EXERCISE 11

Remaining sentences

a. I'm going to call on individual children to read a sentence. Everybody, follow along and point to the words. If you hear a mistake, raise your hand.
b. (Call on a child.) Read the next sentence.

To Correct
word-identification errors (**from,** for example)
1. That word is **from.** What word? *From.*
2. Go back to the beginning of the sentence and read the sentence again.

c. (Call on another child.) Read the next sentence.
d. (Repeat *c* for most of the remaining sentences in the story.)
e. (Occasionally have the group read a sentence. When the group is to read, say:) Everybody, read the next sentence. (Tap for each word in the sentence.)

sandy tells what she found[1]

sandy trIed to run from the shed but the big man stopped her.[2]

he asked her, "what are you doing here?"

sandy wanted to sāy something. but she couldn't think of a thing to say.

the big man said, "can't you hēar me? I asked you what you are doing here?"[3]

sandy said, "mȳ hound dog."[4]

"what about your hound dog?" the man asked.

EXERCISE 12

Second reading—sentences and questions

a. You're going to read the story again. This time I'm going to ask questions.
b. Starting with the first word of the title. ✔
• Get ready. (Tap as the children read the title.)
c. (Call on a child.) Read the first sentence.

To Correct
word-identification errors (**from,** for example)
1. That word is **from.** What word? *From.*
2. Go back to the beginning of the sentence and read the sentence again.

d. (Call on another child.) Read the next sentence.
e. (Repeat *d* for most of the remaining sentences in the story.)
f. (Occasionally have the group read a sentence.)
g. (After each underlined sentence has been read, present each comprehension question specified below to the entire group.)
[1] What is Sandy going to do in this part of the story? (Signal.) *Tell what she found.*
• And what did she find? (The children respond.)
[2] Why didn't Sandy get out of the shed? (Signal.) *The big man stopped her.*
[3] Why did the big man repeat the question? (The children respond.)
• Right, she couldn't think of anything to say.
[4] What did she finally say? (Signal.) *My hound dog.*
• Does she really have a dog with her? (Signal.) *No.*

READING VOCABULARY

Do not touch small letters.

Get ready to read all the words on this page without making a mistake.

drink

EXERCISE 1

Sound it out

a. (Touch the ball for **drink.**) Sound it out. Get ready. (Quickly touch **d, r, i, n, k** as the children say:) *drrriiinnnk.*

b. What word? (Signal.) *Drink.* Yes, **drink.**

c. (Repeat exercise until firm.)

slȳ

EXERCISE 2

Sound out first

a. (Touch the ball for **slȳ.**) Sound it out. Get ready. (Quickly touch **s, l, ȳ** as the children say:) *ssslllȳȳȳ.*

b. What word? (Signal.) *Sly.* Yes, **sly.**

c. (Repeat exercise until firm.)

EXERCISE 3

Long and short vowel words

a. Read these words the fast way. Remember to look at the end of the word.

b. (Touch the ball for **con.** Pause two seconds.) Get ready. (Signal.) *Con.* Yes, **con.**

c. (Repeat *b* for **dime, ate, dim, cone,** and **at.**)

con

dime

ate

dim

cone

at

ice

EXERCISE 4

Listen, sound out

a. (Point to **ice.**) I'll tell you this word. (Pause.) **Ice.** What word? (Signal.) *Ice.* Yes, **ice.**

b. (Touch the ball for **ice.**) Sound it out. Get ready. (Quickly touch **i, c, e** as the children say:) *iiikeee.*

> **To Correct**
> (If the children do not say the sounds you point to:)
> 1. (Say:) You've got to say the sounds I point to.
> 2. (Repeat *b* until firm.)

c. What word? (Signal.) *Ice.* Yes, **ice.**

d. (Repeat *b* and *c* until firm.)

crēₐm

EXERCISE 5

Sound out first

a. (Touch the ball for **crēam.**) Sound it out. Get ready. (Quickly touch **c, r, ē, m** as the children say:) *crrrēēēmmm.*

b. What word? (Signal.) *Cream.* Yes, **cream.**

c. (Repeat exercise until firm.)

> (Repeat any troublesome words.)

Individual test

(Call on individual children. Each child reads a different word.)

---

sandy said, "I can't fInd him. he ran awāy and I was lookiñg for him."

sandy had tōld a big lIe.⁵ but she didn't want to tell the big man whȳ she had come to the shed.

the man said, "well, get out of here, and dōn't come back. if I fInd you plāyiñg around this shed any more, you'll be sorry."

sandy said, "ōkāy. I wōn't come back." she ran awāy from the big man as fast as she could go.⁶ she said, "I must tell someone what I found out."⁷

sandy ran back to the trāin that had a car missiñg. the men and the woman werₑ still standiñg nēₐr the trāin. a cop was with them now. sandy ran up to the cop. she yellₑd, "I found the car with the tv sets."⁸

more to come

---

⁵ What lie did she tell? (The children respond.)
- Why did she tell the lie? (The children respond.)

⁶ Why did the man let her go? (The children respond.)
- Right, I don't think he knows that she found the TV sets.

⁷ What is she going to tell someone? (The children respond.)

⁸ What did she yell? (Signal.) *I found the car with the TV sets.*

EXERCISE 13

Picture comprehension

a. What do you think you'll see in the picture? (The children respond.)

b. Turn the page and look at the picture.

c. (Ask these questions:)
1. Who is that man? (The children respond.)
2. Does he look mean? (Signal.) *Yes.*
- Look at him. How do you know he's mean? (Let the children comment for ten seconds. Then comment briefly.)
3. What is he saying to Sandy? (The children respond.)
4. What's she going to do when he finishes talking to her? (The children respond.)

SUMMARY OF INDEPENDENT ACTIVITY
EXERCISE 14

Introduction to independent activity

a. (Pass out Worksheet 72 to each child.)

b. (Hold up side 1 of your worksheet.) Everybody, you're going to do this worksheet on your own. (Tell the children when they will work the items.)
- Let's go over the things you're going to do.

Story items

(Point to the story-items exercise.) Everybody, remember to write your answers in the blanks.

Following instructions

a. (Touch the sentence in the box.)

b. Everybody, first you're going to read the sentence in the box. Then you're going to read the instructions below the box and do what the instructions tell you to do.

Story-picture items

(Point to the story-picture items on side 2.) Remember to follow these instructions and look at the picture when you work these items.

Reading comprehension

(Point to the story.) You're going to read this story and then do the items. Remember to write the answers in the blanks.

END OF LESSON 72

when school was ōver, the snōw was very dēēp. tim walked outside. then he said, "mȳ ēars are getting cōld.⁶ I had better run home." so tim began to run. he ran as fast as he could go, but the snōw was very dēēp and it was hard to run in that snōw. the other boys and girls were plāying in the snōw, but tim did not have time to plāy. he said, "I must get home before mȳ ēars get too cōld."

at last, tim came to the ōld trēē. he grabbed his red and white hat. he slipped the hat ōver his ēars. then he said, "I dōn't hate this hat. I like this hat now."⁷

tim did not hate his hat after that dāy. and he did not hide his hat in trēēs. now tim has time to plāy with the other boys and girls when the snōw gets dēēp.

this stōry is ōver.

⁶ Everybody, say that. (Signal.) *My ears are getting cold.*
• Why are they cold? (The children respond.)
• Where's his hat? (The children respond.)
⁷ Why did Tim say that?
(The children respond.)

EXERCISE 14

Picture comprehension

a. Look at the picture.
b. (Ask these questions:)
  1. What is Tim doing?
     (The children respond.)
  2. Why is his hat in the hole in that tree?
     (Signal.) *Tim hid it there.*
  3. What's the weather like in this scene?
     (The children respond.)
  4. Is Tim hot or cold? (Signal.) *Cold.*
  5. Have you ever been in a snowstorm without a hat? (The children respond.)

SUMMARY OF INDEPENDENT ACTIVITY
EXERCISE 15

Introduction to independent activity

a. (Pass out Worksheet 79 to each child.)
b. (Hold up side 1 of your worksheet.) Everybody, you're going to do this worksheet on your own. (Tell the children when they will work the items.)
• Let's go over the things you're going to do.

Story items

(Point to the story-items exercise.) Everybody, remember to write your answers in the blanks.

Following instructions

a. (Touch the sentence in the box.)
b. Everybody, first you're going to read the sentence in the box. Then you're going to read the instructions below the box and do what the instructions tell you to do.

Story-picture items

(Point to the story-picture items on side 2.) Remember to follow these instructions and look at the picture when you work these items.

Reading comprehension

(Point to the story.) You're going to read this story and then do the items. Remember to write the answers in the blanks.

END OF LESSON 79

READING VOCABULARY

Get ready to read all the words on this page without making a mistake.

sh

EXERCISE 1

sh words

a. (Point to **sh**.) When these letters are together, they usually say **shshsh**.

b. What do these letters usually say? (Signal.) *shshsh.* Yes, **shshsh**.

• (Repeat until firm.)

c. (Point to the words.) These are words you already know. See if you can read them when they look this way.

d. (Point to **sh** in **she**.) What do these letters say? (Signal.) *shshsh.*

e. (Touch the ball for **she**.) Read the fast way. Get ready. (Signal.) *She.* Yes, **she**.

f. (Repeat *d* and *e* for **shouted, shed, dish,** and **wishing**.)

g. (Repeat the series of words until firm.)

she

shouted

shed

dish

wishing

(Repeat any troublesome words.)

Individual test

(Call on individual children. Each child reads a different word.)

EXERCISE 2

Long and short vowel words

a. Read these words the fast way. Remember to look at the end of the word.

b. (Touch the ball for **ate**. Pause two seconds.) Get ready. (Signal.) *Ate.* Yes, **ate**.

c. (Repeat *b* for **sid, at,** and **side**.)

ate

sid

at

side

STORY 79
EXERCISE 11

First reading—title and three sentences

a. (Pass out Storybook 1.)

b. Everybody, open your reader to page 210.

c. Everybody, touch the title of the story and get ready to read the words in the title.

d. First word. ✔

- Get ready. (Tap.) *Tim.*

e. (Tap for each remaining word in the title.)

f. Everybody, say the title. (Signal.) *Tim and his hat.*

g. Everybody, get ready to read this story.

h. First word. ✔

- Get ready. (Tap.) *Tim.*

i. Next word. ✔

- Get ready. (Tap.) *Had.*

j. (Repeat *i* for the remaining words in the first three sentences. Have the children reread the first three sentences until firm.)

EXERCISE 12

Remaining sentences

a. I'm going to call on individual children to read a sentence. Everybody, follow along and point to the words. If you hear a mistake, raise your hand.

b. (Call on a child.) Read the next sentence.

To Correct
word-identification errors (**from,** for example)
1. That word is **from.** What word? *From.*
2. Go back to the beginning of the sentence and read the sentence again.

c. (Call on another child.) Read the next sentence.

d. (Repeat *c* for most of the remaining sentences in the story.)

e. (Occasionally have the group read a sentence. When the group is to read, say:) Everybody, read the next sentence. (Tap for each word in the sentence.)

---

tim and his hat[1]

tim had a hat. it was red and white. tim said, "I hate this hat." but his mother said, "it is cold outside. so you must have a hat."[2]

  when tim was outside, he said, "I will take this hat and hide it." <u>so he did.</u>[3] he found an old tree with a hole in it. <u>he stuck the hat in the hole.</u>[4] then he said, "when I come back from school, I will get my hat from the tree."

  tim got to school on time. he began reading his book. then he looked out the window. what do you think was falling from the sky? <u>snow was falling.</u>[5] when tim saw the snow, he said, "wow, it is getting cold out there." and it was. it was getting colder and colder.

EXERCISE 13

Second reading—sentences and questions

a. You're going to read the story again. This time I'm going to ask questions.

b. Starting with the first word of the title. ✔

- Get ready. (Tap as the children read the title.)

c. (Call on a child.) Read the first sentence.

To Correct
word-identification errors (**from,** for example)
1. That word is **from.** What word? *From.*
2. Go back to the beginning of the sentence and read the sentence again.

d. (Call on another child.) Read the next sentence.

e. (Repeat *d* for most of the remaining sentences in the story.)

f. (Occasionally have the group read a sentence.)

g. (After each underlined sentence has been read, present each comprehension question specified below to the entire group.)

[1] Who will this story be about? (Signal.) *Tim.*

- What does Tim have? (Signal.) *A hat.*

[2] Why does he need a hat? (Signal.) *It is cold outside.*

[3] What did he do? (Signal.) *He hid his hat.*

- Why did he hide his hat? (The children respond.)

- Right, he hated his hat.

[4] Where did he hide his hat? (The children respond.)

[5] What was happening? (The children respond.)

- Was it cold outside? (Signal.) *Yes.*

- I'll bet Tim's ears get really cold. Let's read more and find out.

Do not touch small letters.

Get ready to read all the words on this page without making a mistake.

EXERCISE 3

Read the fast way

a. Read these words the fast way.

b. (Touch the ball for **there**. Pause two seconds.)

Get ready. (Signal.) *There*. Yes, **there**.

c. (Repeat *b* for remaining words.)

there

were

came

outside

ninety

talking

saw

what

who

that's

please

game

before

white

says

(Repeat any troublesome words.)

Individual test

(Call on individual children. Each child reads a different word.)

Do not touch small letters.

Get ready to read all the words on this page without making a mistake.

EXERCISE 10

Read the fast way

a. Read these words the fast way.

b. (Touch the ball for **hole.** Pause two seconds.) Get ready. (Signal.) *Hole.* Yes, **hole.**

c. (Repeat *b* for remaining words.)

hole

white

take

thing

came

when

school

all

after

ēars

windōw

from

began

shōw

could

dēēp

Individual test

(Call on individual children to read a column of words from this lesson. If the column contains only one or two words, direct the child to read additional words from an adjacent column.)

Do not touch small letters.

Get ready to read all the words on this page without making a mistake.

ēaSy

EXERCISE 4

Read the fast way first

a. (Touch the ball for **ēasy.**) Read this word the fast way. (Pause two seconds.) Get ready. (Signal.) *Easy.* Yes, **easy.**

b. (Return to the ball.) Sound it out. Get ready. (Quickly touch **ē, s, y** as the children say:) *ēēēsssyyy.*

c. What word? (Signal.) *Easy.* Yes, **easy.**

d. (Repeat *b* and *c* until firm.)

check

EXERCISE 5

Sound out first

a. (Touch the ball for **check.**) Sound it out. Get ready. (Quickly touch **ch, e,** between **c** and **k** as the children say:) *cheeek.*

b. What word? (Signal.) *Check.* Yes, **check.**

c. (Repeat exercise until firm.)

tall

EXERCISE 6

al word

a. (Point to **al** in **tall.**) What do these letters say? (Signal.) *All.* Yes, **all.**

b. (Touch the ball for **tall.**) Read this word the fast way. Get ready. (Signal.) *Tall.* Yes, **tall.**

tar

EXERCISE 7

ar word

a. (Point to **ar** in **tar.**) What do these letters say? (Signal.) *Are.* Yes, **are.**

b. (Touch the ball for **tar.**) Read this word the fast way. Get ready. (Signal.) *Tar.* Yes, **tar.**

Individual test

(Call on individual children to read a column of words from this lesson. If the column contains only one or two words, direct the child to read additional words from an adjacent column. Praise children who read all words with no errors.)

STORYBOOK

STORY 73
EXERCISE 8

First reading—title and three sentences

a. (Pass out Storybook 1.)

b. Everybody, open your reader to page 191.

c. Everybody, touch the title of the story and get ready to read the words in the title.

d. First word. ✔

• Get ready. (Tap.) *Sandy.*

e. (Tap for each remaining word in the title.)

f. Everybody, say the title. (Signal.) *Sandy and Big Bill.*

Do not touch small letters.

Get ready to read all the words on this page without making a mistake.

EXERCISE 5

Two-part word

a. (Cover **ing.** Point to **gett.**) Everybody, tell me what this part of the word says. Get ready. (Signal.) *Get.* Yes, **get.**

b. (Uncover **ing.** Touch the ball for **getting.**) Now tell me what the whole word says. Get ready. (Signal.) *Getting.* Yes, **getting.**

c. (Repeat exercise until firm.)

EXERCISE 6

Two-part word

a. (Cover **ed.** Point to **grabb.**) Everybody, tell me what this part of the word says. Get ready. (Signal.) *Grab.* Yes, **grab.**

b. (Uncover **ed.** Touch the ball for **grabbed.**) Now tell me what the whole word says. Get ready. (Signal.) *Grabbed.* Yes, **grabbed.**

c. (Repeat exercise until firm.)

EXERCISE 7

Two-part word

a. (Cover **ed.** Point to **slipp.**) Everybody, tell me what this part of the word says. Get ready. (Signal.) *Slip.* Yes, **slip.**

b. (Uncover **ed.** Touch the ball for **slipped.**) Now tell me what the whole word says. Get ready. (Signal.) *Slipped.* Yes, **slipped.**

c. (Repeat exercise until firm.)

getting

grabbed

slipped

(Repeat any troublesome words.)

Individual test

(Call on individual children. Each child reads a different word.)

outside

EXERCISE 8

Two-part word

a. (Cover **side.** Point to **out.**) Everybody, tell me what this part of the word says. Get ready. (Signal.) *Out.* Yes, **out.**

b. (Uncover **side.** Touch the ball for **outside.**) Now tell me what the whole word says. Get ready. (Signal.) *Outside.* Yes, **outside.**

c. (Repeat exercise until firm.)

before

EXERCISE 9

Two-part word

a. (Cover **fore.** Point to **be.**) Everybody, tell me what this part of the word says. Get ready. (Signal.) *Be.* Yes, **be.**

b. (Uncover **fore.** Touch the ball for **before.**) Now tell me what the whole word says. Get ready. (Signal.) *Before.* Yes, **before.**

c. (Repeat exercise until firm.)

g. Everybody, get ready to read this story.

h. First word. ✔

- Get ready. (Tap.) *Sandy.*

i. Next word. ✔

- Get ready. (Tap.) *Ran.*

j. (Repeat *i* for the remaining words in the first three sentences. Have the children reread the first three sentences until firm.)

EXERCISE 9

Remaining sentences

a. I'm going to call on individual children to read a sentence. Everybody, follow along and point to the words. If you hear a mistake, raise your hand.

b. (Call on a child.) Read the next sentence.

┌─ **To Correct** ─────────────────────────┐

word-identification errors (**from,** for example)
1. That word is **from.** What word? *From.*
2. Go back to the beginning of the sentence and read the sentence again.

└───────────────────────────────────────┘

c. (Call on another child.) Read the next sentence.

d. (Repeat *c* for most of the remaining sentences in the story.)

e. (Occasionally have the group read a sentence. When the group is to read, say:) Everybody, read the next sentence. (Tap for each word in the sentence.)

EXERCISE 10

Second reading—sentences and questions

a. You're going to read the story again. This time I'm going to ask questions.

b. Starting with the first word of the title. ✔

- Get ready. (Tap as the children read the title.)

---

sandy and big bill[1]

sandy ran up to the cop.[2] she told him that she had found the missing train car.

one man said, "will you get out of here, little girl?[3] can't you see that we are talking?"

sandy said, "but I found the train car that is missing."

the woman said, "there is no missing train car."

sandy said, "but there is a car missing and I found it." then sandy told them all about the missing car.

after she told what had happened, the cop said, "I think there were one hundred cars in that train. how can we check it?"[4]

one man said, "that's easy. I'll get big bill. he counts the cars on every train that comes in here."[5]

that man left. soon he came back with another man. as he walked back with the other man he shouted, "big bill counted the cars. he says that there are ninety-nine cars."[6]

sandy looked at big bill, and big bill looked at sandy. big bill was the man who had stopped her outside the shed.[7]

more to come

---

c. (Call on a child.) Read the first sentence.

d. (Call on another child.) Read the next sentence.

e. (Repeat *d* for most of the remaining sentences in the story.)

f. (Occasionally have the group read a sentence.)

g. (After each underlined sentence has been read, present each comprehension question specified below to the entire group.)

[1] This story will be about Sandy. Who else will it be about? (Signal.) *Big Bill.*

- I don't know if you'll like Big Bill.

[2] Why did she do that? (The children respond.)

[3] Why is he speaking like that to Sandy? (The children respond.)

[4] Who is talking? (Signal.) *The cop.*

- What does he want to check? (Signal.) *That there were one hundred cars on the train.*

- Tell me a way you could check that. (The children respond.)

- Yes, you could count them.

[5] Who counts the cars? (Signal.) *Big Bill.*

[6] How many cars did Big Bill say there are? (Signal.) *Ninety-nine.*

- And how many do we know there are? (Signal.) *One hundred.*

- So why did Big Bill say that? (The children respond.) I think he is telling a lie.

[7] Had Sandy and Big Bill ever seen each other before? (Signal.) *Yes.*

- Where? (Signal.) *Outside the shed.*

- Tell me something about what happened when they talked before. (The children respond.)

READING VOCABULARY

Get ready to read all the words on this page without making a mistake.

EXERCISE 1

Sound out first

a. (Touch the ball for **stuck.**) Sound it out. Get ready. (Quickly touch **s, t, u,** and between **c** and **k,** as the children say:) *ssstuuuk.*

b. What word? (Signal.) *Stuck.* Yes, **stuck.**

c. (Repeat exercise until firm.)

EXERCISE 2

Sound out first

a. (Touch the ball for **must.**) Sound it out. Get ready. (Quickly touch **m, u, s, t** as the children say:) *mmmuuussst.*

b. What word? (Signal.) *Must.* Yes, **must.**

c. (Repeat exercise until firm.)

EXERCISE 3

Sound out first

a. (Touch the ball for **cōlder.**) Sound it out. Get ready. (Quickly touch **c, ō, l, d, er** as the children say:) *cōōōlllderrr.*

b. What word? (Signal.) *Colder.* Yes, **colder.**

c. (Repeat *a* and *b* for **snōw.**)

EXERCISE 4

Long and short vowel words

a. Read these words the fast way. Remember to look at the end of the word.

b. (Touch the ball for **time.** Pause two seconds.) Get ready. (Signal.) *Time.* Yes, **time.**

c. (Repeat *b* for **hat, hate,** and **tim.**)

stuck

must

cōlder

snōw

(Repeat any troublesome words.)

Individual test

(Call on individual children. Each child reads a different word.)

time

hat

hate

tim

WORKSHEET 73

EXERCISE 11
Picture comprehension

a. Look at the picture.

b. (Ask these questions:)
1. Show me which man is Big Bill.
   (The children respond.)
2. Is he a good guy or a bad guy? (Signal.)
   A bad guy.
   • Right, he's the crook.
3. What happened to Sandy's book?
   (Signal.) *She dropped it.*
   • Why do you suppose that happened?
     (The children respond.)
4. Show me which man is the cop.
   (The children respond.)
   • How do you know he's the cop? (Let the
     children comment for ten seconds. Then
     comment briefly.)

SUMMARY OF INDEPENDENT ACTIVITY
EXERCISE 12

Introduction to independent activity

a. (Pass out Worksheet 73 to each child.)

b. (Hold up side 1 of your worksheet.)
Everybody, you're going to do this
worksheet on your own. (Tell the children
when they will work the items.)
• Let's go over the things you're going to do.

Story items

(Point to the story-items exercise.) Everybody,
remember to write your answers in the blanks.

Following instructions

a. (Touch the sentence in the box.)

b. Everybody, first you're going to read the
sentence in the box. Then you're going to
read the instructions below the box and do
what the instructions tell you to do.

Story-picture items

(Point to the story-picture items on side 2.)
Remember to follow these instructions and
look at the picture when you work these
items.

Reading comprehension

(Point to the story.) You're going to read this
story and then do the items. Remember to
write the answers in the blanks.

END OF LESSON 73

soon sam's kite passed up all the other kites. it went up so far it looked like a little spot.[4]

some of the boys and girls asked sam, "where did you get that kite?"

sam said, "you can get a kit for this kite at the toy store. but I will have to tell you how to fit the parts so that they make a tent kite."[5]

more and more boys and girls asked sam about his kite. at last sam said, "I will make a paper that tells how to make a tent kite from the kit."

and he did.[6] when he got home, he sat down with his mom. his mom helped him with the paper. when they were done, his mom said, "this paper reads very well. you did a good job."

sam said, "that's good. now let's make a lot of these papers so we can give one to everybody who wants one."

the next day sam gave each boy and girl a paper. he told them to read the paper and do what it said.

now there are many tent kites flying over the park. and no one says, "hō, hō." the tent kites fly better than any other kite.[7]

the end

---

[4] Why did it look so small?
(The children respond.)

[5] Who is speaking? (Signal.) *Sam.*

- Why will Sam have to show them how to make the kite? (The children respond.)
- Right, the paper telling how to do it is missing from the kit.

[6] What did he do? (The children respond.)

- Yes, he made a paper that tells you how to make a tent kite.

[7] Why don't people say "ho, ho" anymore? (The children respond.)

EXERCISE 15

Picture comprehension

a. Look at the picture.

b. (Ask these questions:)
   1. What's on those papers Sam is passing out? (The children respond.)
   - Yes, instructions telling how to make a tent kite like his.
   2. What do you think those children will do after they read the paper?
      (The children respond.)
   - Yes, they will make kites.
   3. What kind of kites do you see flying? (Signal.) *Tent kites.*
   4. How do you think they learned to make them? (The children respond.)
   5. Have you ever made a kite?
      (The children respond.)

WORKSHEET 78

SUMMARY OF INDEPENDENT ACTIVITY
EXERCISE 16

Introduction to independent activity

a. (Pass out Worksheet 78 to each child.)

b. (Hold up side 1 of your worksheet.) Everybody, you're going to do this worksheet on your own. (Tell the children when they will work the items.)

- Let's go over the things you're going to do.

Story items

(Point to the story-items exercise.) Everybody, remember to write your answers in the blanks.

Following instructions

a. (Touch the sentence in the box.)

b. Everybody, first you're going to read the sentence in the box. Then you're going to read the instructions below the box and do what the instructions tell you to do.

Story-picture items

(Point to the story-picture items on side 2.) Remember to follow these instructions and look at the picture when you work these items.

Reading comprehension

(Point to the story.) You're going to read this story and then do the items. Remember to write the answers in the blanks.

END OF LESSON 78

READING VOCABULARY

Get ready to read all the words on this page without making a mistake.

sh

EXERCISE 1

sh words

a. (Point to **sh.**) When these letters are together, they usually say **shshsh.**

b. What do these letters usually say? (Signal.) *shshsh.* Yes, **shshsh.**

• (Repeat until firm.)

c. (Point to the words.) These are words you already know. See if you can read them when they look this way.

d. (Point to **sh** in **shop.**) What do these letters say? (Signal.) *shshsh.*

e. (Touch the ball for **shop.**) Read the fast way. Get ready. (Signal.) *Shop.* Yes, **shop.**

f. (Repeat *d* and *e* for **should** and **she's.**)

g. (Repeat the series of words until firm.)

shop

should

she's

their

tracks

EXERCISE 2

Listen, sound out

a. (Point to **their.**) I'll tell you this word. (Pause.) **Their.** What word? (Signal.) *Their.* Yes, **their.**

b. (Touch the ball for **their.**) Sound it out. Get ready. (Quickly touch **th, e, i, r** as the children say:) *thththeeeiiirrr.*

c. What word? (Signal.) *Their.* Yes, **their.**

d. (Repeat *b* and *c* until firm.)

EXERCISE 3

Sound out first

a. (Touch the ball for **tracks.**) Sound it out. Get ready. (Quickly touch **t, r, a,** between **c** and **k, s** as the children say:) *trrraaaksss.*

b. What word? (Signal.) *Tracks.* Yes, **tracks.**

c. (Repeat exercise until firm.)

(Repeat any troublesome words.)

Individual test

(Call on individual children. Each child reads a different word.)

STORYBOOK

STORY 78
EXERCISE 12

First reading—title and three sentences

a. (Pass out Storybook 1.)
b. Everybody, open your reader to page 207.
c. Everybody, touch the title of the story and get ready to read the words in the title.
d. First word. ✔
• Get ready. (Tap.) *Can.*
e. (Tap for each remaining word in the title.)
f. Everybody, say the title. (Signal.)
  Can Sam's kite really fly?
g. Everybody, get ready to read this story.
h. First word. ✔
• Get ready. (Tap.) *When.*
i. Next word. ✔
• Get ready. (Tap.) *Sam.*
j. (Repeat *i* for the remaining words in the first three sentences. Have the children reread the first three sentences until firm.)

EXERCISE 13

Remaining sentences

a. I'm going to call on individual children to read a sentence. Everybody, follow along and point to the words. If you hear a mistake, raise your hand.
b. (Call on a child.) Read the next sentence.

To Correct

word-identification errors (**from,** for example)
1. That word is **from.** What word? *From.*
2. Go back to the beginning of the sentence and read the sentence again.

c. (Call on an another child.) Read the next sentence.
d. (Repeat *c* for most of the remaining sentences in the story.)
e. (Occasionally have the group read a sentence. When the group is to read, say:) Everybody, read the next sentence. (Tap for each word in the sentence.)

can sam's kite rēally flÿ?[1]
when sam made his kite, his mom said that it looked funny. so did the boys and girls in the park. they looked at the kite and said, "hō, hō, that thing looks like a tent. it wōn't flÿ."[2]
sam said, "we will see."
sam's kite began to go up.
up, up it went. it was going up very fast. sam's mom said, "well, would you look at that kite go up."
the boys and girls said, "wow, that kite can rēally flÿ."[3]

EXERCISE 14

Second reading—sentences and questions

a. You're going to read the story again. This time I'm going to ask questions.
b. Starting with the first word of the title. ✔
• Get ready. (Tap as the children read the title.)
c. (Call on a child.) Read the first sentence.

To Correct

word-identification errors (**from,** for example)
1. That word is **from.** What word? *From.*
2. Go back to the beginning of the sentence and read the sentence again.

d. (Call on another child.) Read the next sentence.
e. (Repeat *d* for most of the remaining sentences in the story.)
f. (Occasionally have the group read a sentence.)
g. (After each underlined sentence has been read, present each comprehension question specified below to the entire group.)
[1] What are we going to find out in this story? (Signal.) *If Sam's kite can really fly.*
[2] Did they think Sam's kite would fly? (Signal.) *No.*
[3] Could the kite really fly? (Signal.) *Yes.*
• And what's the title of this story? (Signal.) *Can Sam's kite really fly?*
• And what's the answer? (Signal.) *Yes.*

Do not touch small letters.

Get ready to read all the words on this page without making a mistake.

EXERCISE 4

Sound out first

a. (Touch the ball for **lȳing.**) Sound it out. Get ready. (Quickly touch **l, ȳ, ing** as the children say:) *Illȳȳȳiiing.*

b. What word? (Signal.) *Lying.* Yes, **lying.**

c. (Repeat exercise until firm.)

EXERCISE 5

Sound out first

a. (Touch the ball for **lōading.**) Sound it out. Get ready. (Quickly touch **l, ō, d, ing** as the children say:) *Illōōōdiiing.*

b. What word? (Signal.) *Loading.* Yes, **loading.**

c. (Repeat exercise until firm.)

EXERCISE 6

ou word

a. (Point to **ou** in **about.**) What do these letters say? (Signal.) *ou.* Yes, **ou.**

b. (Touch the ball for **about.**) Read this word the fast way. Get ready. (Signal.) *About.* Yes, **about.**

EXERCISE 7

al word

a. (Point to **al** in **alwāys.**) What do these letters say? (Signal.) *All.* Yes, **all.**

b. (Touch the ball for **alwāys.**) Read this word the fast way. Get ready. (Signal.) *Always.* Yes, **always.**

EXERCISE 8

Two-part word

a. (Cover **thing.** Point to **any.**) Everybody, tell me what this part of the word says. Get ready. (Signal.) *Any.* Yes, **any.**

b. (Uncover **thing.** Touch the ball for **anything.**) Now tell me what the whole word says. Get ready. (Signal.) *Anything.* Yes, **anything.**

c. (Repeat exercise until firm.)

EXERCISE 9

Two-part word

a. (Cover **fore.** Point to **be.**) Everybody, tell me what this part of the word says. Get ready. (Signal.) *Be.* Yes, **be.**

b. (Uncover **fore.** Touch the ball for **before.**) Now tell me what the whole word says. Get ready. (Signal.) *Before.* Yes, **before.**

c. (Repeat exercise until firm.)

about

alwāys

anything

before

(Repeat any troublesome words.)

Individual test

(Call on individual children. Each child reads a different word.)

Get ready to read all the words on this page without making a mistake.

EXERCISE 7

Listen, sound out

a. (Point to **done.**) I'll tell you this word. (Pause.) **Done**. What word? (Signal.) *Done.* Yes, **done.**

b. (Touch the ball for **done.**) Sound it out. Get ready. (Quickly touch **d, o, n, e** as the children say:) *dooonnneee.*

To Correct

(If the children do not say the sounds you point to:)

1. (Say:) You've got to say the sounds I point to.
2. (Repeat *b* until firm.)

c. What word? (Signal.) *Done.* Yes, **done.**

d. (Repeat *b* and *c* until firm.)

EXERCISE 8

ing words

a. (Point to **ing.**) When these letters are together, they usually say **ing.**

b. What do these letters usually say? (Signal.) *ing.* Yes, **ing.**

• (Repeat until firm.)

c. (Point to the words.) These are words you already know. See if you can read them when they look this way.

d. (Point to **ing** in **thing.**) What do these letters say? (Signal.) *ing.*

e. (Touch the ball for **thing.**) Read the fast way. Get ready. (Signal.) *Thing.* Yes, **thing.**

f. (Repeat *d* and *e* for **flȳing.**)

g. (Repeat both words until firm.)

done

ing

thing

flȳing

Individual test

(Call on individual children to read a column of words from this lesson. If the column contains only one or two words, direct the child to read additional words from an adjacent column. Praise children who read all words with no errors.)

park

EXERCISE 9

ar word

a. (Point to **ar** in **park.**) What do these letters say? (Signal.) *Are.* Yes, **are.**

b. (Touch the ball for **park.**) Read this word the fast way. Get ready. (Signal.) *Park.* Yes, **park.**

parts

EXERCISE 10

Read the fast way

a. Read this word the fast way.

b. (Touch the ball for **parts.** Pause two seconds.) Get ready. (Signal.) *Parts.* Yes, **parts.**

everybody

EXERCISE 11

Two-part word

a. (Cover **body.** Point to **every.**) Everybody, tell me what this part of the word says. Get ready. (Signal.) *Every.* Yes, **every.**

b. (Uncover **body.** Touch the ball for **everybody.**) Now tell me what the whole word says. Get ready. (Signal.) *Everybody.* Yes, **everybody.**

c. (Repeat exercise until firm.)

Do not touch small letters.

Get ready to read all the words on this page without making a mistake.

EXERCISE 10

Read the fast way

a. Read these words the fast way.

b. (Touch the ball for **store.** Pause two seconds.) Get ready. (Signal.) *Store.* Yes, **store.**

c. (Repeat b for remaining words.)

store

mēan

saw

mēal

inside

what's

touch

take

crooks

mark

nēar

her

here

then

that's

white

Individual test

(Call on individual children to read a column of words from this lesson. If the column contains only one or two words, direct the child to read additional words from an adjacent column.)

Do not touch small letters.

Get ready to read all the words on this page without making a mistake.

EXERCISE 6

Read the fast way

a. Read these words the fast way.
b. (Touch the ball for **store.** Pause two seconds.) Get ready. (Signal.) *Store.* Yes, **store.**
c. (Repeat *b* for remaining words.)

store

gave

wōn't

passed

pāper

rēally

looked

whȳ

who

how

helped

ōver

sorry

these

(Repeat any troublesome words.)

Individual test

(Call on individual children. Each child reads a different word.)

STORYBOOK

STORY 74

EXERCISE 11

First reading—title and three sentences

a. (Pass out Storybook 1.)

b. Everybody, open your reader to page 194.

c. Everybody, touch the title of the story and get ready to read the words in the title.

d. First word. ✔

- Get ready. (Tap.) *Back.*

e. (Tap for each remaining word in the title.)

f. Everybody, say the title. (Signal.) *Back to the shed.*

g. Everybody, get ready to read this story.

h. First word. ✔

- Get ready. (Tap.) *Sandy.*

i. Next word. ✔

- Get ready. (Tap.) *Saw.*

j. (Repeat *i* for the remaining words in the first three sentences. Have the children reread the first three sentences until firm.)

EXERCISE 12

Remaining sentences

a. I'm going to call on individual children to read a sentence. Everybody, follow along and point to the words. If you hear a mistake, raise your hand.

b. (Call on a child.) Read the next sentence.

To Correct

word-identification errors (**from,** for example)
1. That word is **from.** What word? *From.*
2. Go back to the beginning of the sentence and read the sentence again.

c. (Call on another child.) Read the next sentence.

d. (Repeat *c* for most of the remaining sentences in the story.)

e. (Occasionally have the group read a sentence. When the group is to read, say:) Everybody, read the next sentence. (Tap for each word in the sentence.)

back to the shed[1]

sandy saw that big bill was the big man who had stopped her outside the shed. she shouted, "that's one of the men who was stealing the tv sets.[2] that's him." she told the cop that big bill had stopped her outside the shed.

big bill looked very mean. he said, "what's that girl talking about? I think she's nuts."[3]

sandy said, "no, I'm not nuts. that is one of the men."

EXERCISE 13

Second reading—sentences and questions

a. You're going to read the story again. This time I'm going to ask questions.

b. Starting with the first word of the title. ✔

- Get ready. (Tap as the children read the title.)

c. (Call on a child.) Read the first sentence.

To Correct

word-identification errors (**from,** for example)
1. That word is **from.** What word? *From.*
2. Go back to the beginning of the sentence and read the sentence again.

d. (Call on another child.) Read the next sentence.

e. (Repeat *d* for most of the remaining sentences in the story.)

f. (Occasionally have the group read a sentence.)

g. (After each underlined sentence has been read, present each comprehension question specified below to the entire group.)

[1] Where are they going to go? (Signal.) *Back to the shed.*

- How do you know? (Signal.) *Because the title of the story says back to the shed.*

[2] Let me hear you say it like Sandy did. (Signal.) *That's one of the men who was stealing the TV sets.*

- Who is she talking about? (Signal.) *Big Bill.*

[3] Who is Big Bill talking about? (Signal.) *Sandy.*

- Why did he say that? (The children respond.)

READING VOCABULARY

Get ready to read all the words on this page without making a mistake.

EXERCISE 1

Long and short vowel words

a. Read these words the fast way. Remember to look at the end of the word.

b. (Touch the ball for **kite.** Pause two seconds.) Get ready. (Signal.) *Kite.* Yes, **kite.**

c. (Repeat *b* for **hop, hope,** and **kit.**)

kite

hop

hope

kit

EXERCISE 2

Sound out first

a. (Touch the ball for **last.**) Sound it out. Get ready. (Quickly touch **l, a, s, t** as the children say:) *lllaaassst.*

b. What word? (Signal.) *Last.* Yes, **last.**

c. (Repeat exercise until firm.)

EXERCISE 3

Sound out first

a. (Touch the ball for **every.**) Sound it out. Get ready. (Quickly touch **e, v, er, y** as the children say:) *eeevvverrryyy.*

b. What word? (Signal.) *Every.* Yes, **every.**

c. (Repeat exercise until firm.)

EXERCISE 4

Sound out first

a. (Touch the ball for **tent.**) Sound it out. Get ready. (Quickly touch **t, e, n, t** as the children say:) *teeennnt.*

b. What word? (Signal.) *Tent.* Yes, **tent.**

c. (Repeat exercise until firm.)

EXERCISE 5

Sound out first

a. (Touch the ball for **than.**) Sound it out. Get ready. (Quickly touch **th, a, n** as the children say:) *thththaaannn.*

b. What word? (Signal.) *Than.* Yes, **than.**

c. (Repeat exercise until firm.)

last

every

tent

than

(Repeat any troublesome words.)

Individual test

(Call on individual children. Each child reads a different word.)

big bill said, "I dŏn't knŏw what she is talkiñg about. I never saw her before.[4] and I dŏn't knŏw anythiñg about a shed with a red trāin car in it."

"yes, you do," sandy said.

the cop said, "well, whȳ dŏn't we all take a walk down the tracks and fĬnd out who is lȳiñg?"[5]

so they all walked down the tracks to the shed. when they came nēar the shed, sandy could see a big white truck at one end of the shed. she said, "that must be their truck. the crooks must be inside the shed, lōadiñg the truck."[6]

big bill gave sandy a mēan look.[7]

more to come

[4] Was that true? (Signal.) *No.*
- What do you say when somebody tells things that are not true? (The children respond.) Right, they are lying.

[5] What does the cop want to do? (The children respond.)

[6] Why do they need a truck? (The children respond.)

[7] Show me what a mean look looks like. (The children respond.)
- What a mean look!

EXERCISE 14
Picture comprehension

a. What do you think you'll see in the picture? (The children respond.)
b. Turn the page and look at the picture.
c. (Ask these questions:)
1. Where are the people walking to in this picture? (Signal.) *The shed.*
2. What's that man in the shed doing? (The children respond.)
3. What is Sandy saying? (The children respond.)
4. Who is Sandy talking to? (The children respond.)
5. What could the cop be thinking? (Let the children comment for ten seconds. Then comment briefly.)
6. Do you think they'll catch all the crooks? (The children respond.)
- Next time we'll find out how the story ends.

SUMMARY OF INDEPENDENT ACTIVITY
EXERCISE 15
Introduction to independent activity

a. (Pass out Worksheet 74 to each child.)
b. (Hold up side 1 of your worksheet.) Everybody, you're going to do this worksheet on your own. (Tell the children when they will work the items.)
- Let's go over the things you're going to do.

Story items

(Point to the story-items exercise.) Everybody, remember to write your answers in the blanks.

Following instructions

a. (Touch the sentence in the box.)
b. Everybody, first you're going to read the sentence in the box. Then you're going to read the instructions below the box and do what the instructions tell you to do.

Story-picture items

(Point to the story-picture items on side 2.) Remember to follow these instructions and look at the picture when you work these items.

Reading comprehension

(Point to the story.) You're going to read this story and then do the items. Remember to write the answers in the blanks.

END OF LESSON 74

sam's mom said, "I'm sorry for making fun of your kite, but it looks very funny."

sam said, "I dōn't care how funny it looks. I think it will flȳ."[5]

his mom said, "no, I dōn't think it will. it does not look like a kite that will flȳ."[6]

"we will see," sam said.

so sam and his mom went to the park.[7] there were lots of boys and girls in the park. some of them were flȳing kites. and some of the kites were wāy up in the skȳ.

sam said, "I think mȳ kite will pass up all those kites."

sam's mom said, "I dōn't think your kite will go thrēē fēēt from the ground."

do you think sam's kite will flȳ?[8]

more next time[9]

---

[5] Did Sam think his funny-looking kite would fly. (Signal.) *Yes.*

[6] Did his mom think the kite would fly? (Signal.) *No.*

[7] Why did they go there? (The children respond.)
- A park is a good place to fly kites.

[8] What do you think? (The children respond.)

[9] Next time we'll read the end of the story and see if the kite flies.

EXERCISE 13

Picture comprehension

a. Look at the picture.
b. (Ask these questions:)
   1. Show me Sam and his mom. (The children respond.)
   2. Does Sam's kite look funny to you? (The children respond.)
   3. How many children are sitting on the ground? (Signal.) *One.*
   4. Show me the little girl who is flying her kite. (The children respond.)
   5. How many kites do you see in the sky? (Signal.) *Two.*

SUMMARY OF INDEPENDENT ACTIVITY
EXERCISE 14

Introduction to independent activity

a. (Pass out Worksheet 77 to each child.)
b. (Hold up side 1 of your worksheet.) Everybody, you're going to do this worksheet on your own. (Tell the children when they will work the items.)
- Let's go over the things you're going to do.

Story items

(Point to the story-items exercise.) Everybody, remember to write your answers in the blanks.

Following instructions

a. (Touch the sentence in the box.)
b. Everybody, first you're going to read the sentence in the box. Then you're going to read the instructions below the box and do what the instructions tell you to do.

Story-picture items

(Point to the story-picture items on side 2.) Remember to follow these instructions and look at the picture when you work these items.

Reading comprehension

(Point to the story.) You're going to read this story and then do the items. Remember to write the answers in the blanks.

END OF LESSON 77

READING VOCABULARY

Do not touch small letters.

Get ready to read all the words on this page without making a mistake.

EXERCISE 1

Sound out first

a. (Touch the ball for **didn't**.) Sound it out. Get ready. (Quickly touch **d, i, d, n, t** as the children say:) *diiidnnnt.*

b. What word? (Signal.) *Didn't.* Yes, **didn't**.

c. (Repeat exercise until firm.)

EXERCISE 2

Sound out first

a. (Touch the ball for **next**.) Sound it out. Get ready. (Quickly touch **n, e, x, t** as the children say:) *nnneeext.*

b. What word? (Signal.) *Next.* Yes, **next**.

c. (Repeat exercise until firm.)

EXERCISE 3

Sound out first

a. (Touch the ball for **I'll**.) Sound it out. Get ready. (Quickly touch **I**, between the I's as the children say:) *I'll.*

b. What word? (Signal.) *I'll.* Yes, **I'll.**

c. (Repeat exercise until firm.)

didn't

next

I'll

(Repeat any troublesome words.)

Individual test

(Call on individual children. Each child reads a different word.)

EXERCISE 4

Read the fast way

a. Read these words the fast way.

b. (Touch the ball for **shouted**. Pause two seconds.) Get ready. (Signal.) *Shouted.* Yes, **shouted.**

c. (Repeat *b* for **showed** and **should**.)

shouted

shōwed

should

STORYBOOK

STORY 77

EXERCISE 10

First reading—title and three sentences

a. (Pass out Storybook 1.)

b. Everybody, open your reader to page 204.

c. Everybody, touch the title of the story and get ready to read the words in the title.

d. First word. ✔

- Get ready. (Tap.) *Sam.*

e. (Tap for each remaining word in the title.)

f. Everybody, say the title. (Signal.) *Sam makes a funny kite.*

g. Everybody, get ready to read this story.

h. First word. ✔

- Get ready. (Tap.) *Sam.*

i. Next word. ✔

- Get ready. (Tap.) *Liked.*

j. (Repeat *i* for the remaining words in the first three sentences. Have the children reread the first three sentences until firm.)

EXERCISE 11

Remaining sentences

a. I'm going to call on individual children to read a sentence. Everybody, follow along and point to the words. If you hear a mistake, raise your hand.

b. (Call on a child.) Read the next sentence.

To Correct

word-identification errors (**from**, for example)
1. That word is **from**. What word? *From.*
2. Go back to the beginning of the sentence and read the sentence again.

c. (Call on another child.) Read the next sentence.

d. (Repeat *c* for most of the remaining sentences in the story.)

e. (Occasionally have the group read a sentence.)
(When the group is to read, say:)
Everybody, read the next sentence. (Tap for each word in the sentence.)

---

sam makes a funny kite[1]

sam liked to make things. he had made a toy car from a kit. he did a good job. now sam had a kite kit. but there was no pāper in the kit to tell how to make a kite from the parts.

sam was not very happy.[2] he looked at ēach of the parts. then he began to trȳ to make a kite from the parts in the kit. he worked and worked.

when his mom saw the kite, she said, "hō, hō. that is a funny-looking kite."[3]

it was funny-looking. it looked like a small tent made out of pāper and wood.[4] the top of the kite was very sharp.

EXERCISE 12

Second reading—sentences and questions

a. You're going to read the story again. This time I'm going to ask questions.

b. Starting with the first word of the title. ✔

- Get ready. (Tap as the children read the title.)

c. (Call on a child.) Read the first sentence.

To Correct

word-identification errors (**from**, for example)
1. That word is **from**. What word? *From.*
2. Go back to the beginning of the sentence and read the sentence again.

d. (Call on another child.) Read the next sentence.

e. (Repeat *d* for most of the remaining sentences in the story.)

f. (Occasionally have the group read a sentence.)

g. (After each underlined sentence has been read, present each comprehension question specified below to the entire group.)

[1] What's Sam going to do in this story? (Signal.) *Make a funny kite.*

[2] Why was Sam unhappy? (The children respond.)

- Right, there was no paper telling him how to make a kite.

[3] Everybody, tell me what his mom said. (Signal.) *Ho, ho. That is a funny-looking kite.*

[4] What did the kite look like? (Signal.) *A small tent.*

- And what was it made out of? (Signal.) *Paper and wood.*

Do not touch small letters.

Get ready to read all the words on this page without making a mistake.

EXERCISE 5

Read the fast way

a. Read these words the fast way.

b. (Touch the ball for **crooks.** Pause two seconds.) Get ready. (Signal.) *Crooks.* Yes, **crooks.**

c. (Repeat *b* for remaining words.)

gave

from

like

better

you'll

finding

leaving

waited

paper

rest

about

what's

I've

their

crooks

gift

work

saw

(Repeat any troublesome words.)

Individual test

(Call on individual children. Each child reads a different word.)

Do not touch small letters.

Get ready to read all the words on this page without making a mistake.

EXERCISE 9

Read the fast way

a. Read these words the fast way.
b. (Touch the ball for **does.** Pause two seconds.) Get ready. (Signal.) *Does.* Yes, **does.**
c. (Repeat *b* for **makes, making, fine, wood, sorry, work, worked, what, that, wōn't, I'm,** and **those.**)

*d*oes

makes

making

fine

wood

sorry

work

work*e*d

what

that

wōn't

I'm

those

Individual test

(Call on individual children to read a column of words from this lesson. If the column contains only one or two words, direct the child to read additional words from an adjacent column.)

Get ready to read all the words on this page without making a mistake.

shed

EXERCISE 6

Read the fast way first

a. (Touch the ball for **shed.**) Read this word the fast way. (Pause two seconds.) Get ready. (Signal.) *Shed.* Yes, **shed.**

b. (Return to the ball.) Sound it out. Get ready. (Quickly touch **sh, e, d** as the children say:) *shshsheeed.*

c. What word? (Signal.) *Shed.* Yes, **shed.**

d. (Repeat *b* and *c* until firm.)

EXERCISE 7

Long and short vowel words

a. Read these words the fast way. Remember to look at the end of the word.

b. (Touch the ball for **same.** Pause two seconds.) Get ready. (Signal.) *Same.* Yes, **same.**

c. (Repeat *b* for **kite, fin, kit, sam,** and **fine.**)

same

kite

fin

kit

sam

fine

Individual test

(Call on individual children to read a column of words from this lesson. If the column contains only one or two words, direct the child to read additional words from an adjacent column. Praise children who read all words with no errors.)

STORY 75

EXERCISE 8

First reading—title and three sentences

a. (Pass out Storybook 1.)

b. Everybody, open your reader to page 197.

c. Everybody, touch the title of the story and get ready to read the words in the title.

d. First word. ✔

• Get ready. (Tap.) *Thank.*

e. (Tap for each remaining word in the title.)

f. Everybody, say the title. (Signal.) *Thank you, Sandy.*

Do not touch small letters.

Get ready to read all the words on this page without making a mistake.

mixed

EXERCISE 5

Sound out first

a. (Touch the ball for **mixed.**) Sound it out. Get ready. (Quickly touch **m, i, x, d** as the children say:) *mmmiiixd.*

b. What word? (Signal.) *Mixed.* Yes, **mixed.**

c. (Repeat exercise until firm.)

Job

EXERCISE 6

Sound out first

a. (Touch the ball for **job.**) Sound it out. Get ready. (Quickly touch **j, o, b** as the children say:) *jooob.*

b. What word? (Signal.) *Job.* Yes, **job.**

c. (Repeat exercise until firm.)

sharp

EXERCISE 7

ar word

a. (Touch the ball for **sharp.**) Read this word the fast way. (Pause two seconds.) Get ready. (Signal.) *Sharp.* Yes, **sharp.**

b. (Point to **ar** in **sharp.**) Everybody, what do these letters say? (Signal.) *Are.* Yes, **are.**

c. (Touch the ball for **sharp.**) Sound it out. Get ready. (Quickly touch **sh, ar, p** as the children say:) *shshsharp.*

d. What word? (Signal.) *Sharp.* Yes, **sharp.**

e. (Repeat c and d until firm.)

EXERCISE 8

Long and short vowel words

a. Read these words the fast way. Remember to look at the end of the word.

b. (Touch the ball for **car.** Pause two seconds.) Get ready. (Signal.) *Car.* Yes, **car.**

c. (Repeat b for **note, same, not, care,** and **sam.**)

car

note

same

not

care

sam

(Repeat any troublesome words.)

Individual test

(Call on individual children. Each child reads a different word.)

g. Everybody, get ready to read this story.

h. First word. ✔
- Get ready. (Tap.) *Sandy.*

i. Next word. ✔
- Get ready. (Tap.) *And.*

j. (Repeat *i* for the remaining words in the first three sentences. Have the children reread the first three sentences until firm.)

EXERCISE 9

Remaining sentences

a. I'm going to call on individual children to read a sentence. Everybody, follow along and point to the words. If you hear a mistake, raise your hand.

b. (Call on a child.) Read the next sentence.

To Correct

word-identification errors (**from,** for example)
1. That word is **from.** What word? *From.*
2. Go back to the beginning of the sentence and read the sentence again.

c. (Call on another child.) Read the next sentence.

d. (Repeat *c* for most of the remaining sentences in the story.)

e. (Occasionally have the group read a sentence. When the group is to read, say:) Everybody, read the next sentence. (Tap for each word in the sentence.)

EXERCISE 10

Second reading—sentences and questions

a. You're going to read the story again. This time I'm going to ask questions.

b. Starting with the first word of the title. ✔
- Get ready. (Tap as the children read the title.)

---

thank you, sandy[1]

sandy and the others were near the shed. the cop said, "the rest of you wait here. I'll go inside that shed and see what's going on."[2]

so they waited as the cop went into the shed. as soon as the cop was in the shed, big bill said, "I've got work to do. I'm leaving."[3]

"you better stay here," one of the men said. big bill didn't answer. bill just gave sandy a mean look.

sandy looked at the shed and waited. then she saw some men start to come from the shed. they all had their hands up.[4] the cop was walking behind them. the cop shouted, "that girl found the tv sets. I think big bill is one of the crooks."

one of the men said to sandy, "thank you for finding the missing car." the woman also thanked sandy. so did the cop.[5]

then one of the men said, "this rail road would like to give you a gift for finding the crooks."[6] so the man gave her a very fine gift. what do you think that gift was?[7]

it was a tv set.[8]

this is the end.

---

c. (Call on a child.) Read the first sentence.

d. (Call on another child.) Read the next sentence.

e. (Repeat *d* for most of the remaining sentences in the story.)

f. (Occasionally have the group read a sentence.)

g. (After each underlined sentence has been read, present each comprehension question specified below to the entire group.)

[1] What does this title tell you about what is going to happen? (The children respond.)

[2] Who is talking? (Signal.) *The cop.*
- Why is he going in the shed all by himself? (The children respond.)

[3] Who is speaking? (Signal.) *Big Bill.*
- Why did he say he was leaving? (Signal.) *He had work to do.*
- Why do you think he's really leaving? (The children respond.)

[4] Why did they have their hands up? (The children respond.)

[5] What did the cop say to Sandy? (The children respond.)

[6] What is a gift? (The children respond.)
- Yes, a present. Some people give gifts at Christmas and for birthdays. Why do they want to give her a gift? (The children respond.)

[7] What do you think it was? (The children respond.)
- Let's read and find out.

[8] What was the gift? (Signal.) *A TV set.*
- You were right.

READING VOCABULARY

Do not touch small letters.

Get ready to read all the words on this page without making a mistake.

EXERCISE 1

ing words

a. (Point to **ing**.) When these letters are together, they usually say **ing**.

b. What do these letters usually say? (Signal.) *ing.* Yes, **ing**.

• (Repeat until firm.)

c. (Point to the words.) These are words you already know. See if you can read them when they look this way.

d. (Point to **ing** in **looking**.) What do these letters say? (Signal.) *ing.*

e. (Touch the ball for **looking**.) Read the fast way. Get ready. (Signal.) *Looking.* Yes, **looking**.

f. (Repeat *d* and *e* for **flȳing**.)

g. (Repeat both words until firm.)

ing

looking

flȳing

(Repeat any troublesome words.)

Individual test

(Call on individual children. Each child reads a different word.)

tent

EXERCISE 2

Sound out first

a. (Touch the ball for **tent**.) Sound it out. Get ready. (Quickly touch **t, e, n, t** as the children say:) *teeennnt.*

b. What word? (Signal.) *Tent.* Yes, **tent**.

c. (Repeat exercise until firm.)

ēach

EXERCISE 3

Sound out first

a. (Touch the ball for **each**.) Sound it out. Get ready. (Quickly touch **ē, ch** as the children say:) *ēēēch.*

b. What word? (Signal.) *Each.* Yes, **each**.

c. (Repeat exercise until firm.)

very

EXERCISE 4

Sound out first

a. (Touch the ball for **very**.) Sound it out. Get ready. (Quickly touch **v, e, r, y** as the children say:) *vvveeerrryyy.*

b. What word? (Signal.) *Very.* Yes, **very**.

c. (Repeat exercise until firm.)

EXERCISE 11

Picture comprehension

a. Look at the picture.

b. (Ask these questions:)

1. How many crooks do you see? (Signal.) *Two.*
2. How many cops do you see? (Signal.) *One.*
3. What is the gift Sandy is getting? (Signal.) *A TV set.*
   - She is lucky. Her own TV set.
4. What is happening to Big Bill in this picture? **(The children respond.)**
5. What do you think will happen to him after they leave the railroad yard? **(Let the children comment for ten seconds. Then comment briefly.)**

SUMMARY OF INDEPENDENT ACTIVITY
EXERCISE 12

Summary of independent activities

a. (Pass out Worksheet 75 to each child.)

b. Everybody, now you'll do your worksheet. Remember to do all parts of the worksheet and to read all the parts carefully.

INDIVIDUAL CHECKOUT
EXERCISE 13

2-minute individual fluency checkout: rate/accuracy

a. As you are doing your worksheet, I'll call on children one at a time to read the **first page of the story.** Remember, you get two stars if you read the first page of the story in less than two minutes and make no more than three errors.

b. (Call on each child. Tell the child:) Start with the title and read the first page of the story very carefully. Go. (Time the child. Tell the child any words the child misses. Stop the child as soon as the child makes the fourth error or exceeds the time limit.)

c. (If the child meets the rate-accuracy criterion, record two stars on your chart for lesson 75. Congratulate the child. Give children who do not earn two stars a chance to read the first page of the story again before the next lesson is presented.) 109 words/**2 min** = 55 wpm **[3 errors]**

END OF LESSON 75

sam looked inside the kit. then he said, "what paper? there is no paper in this kit."[7]

sam's mom said, "that is too bad. how will you make the kite if there is no paper in the kit?"

sam said, "I will go back to the store and get a paper that tells how to make a kite from these parts."

when sam got to the store, the man in the store said, "I don't have other papers that tell how to make kites."

sam asked, "how can I make a kite if I don't have the paper?"[8]

the man said, "you will have to do the best you can."[9]

sam was not happy. he went home and looked at all the parts in the kite kit.

more to come[10]

[7] Was there a paper in the kit? (Signal.) *No.*
- I wonder how he'll make the kite without that paper. (The children respond.)
- Let's read and find out.
[8] Everybody, say that question. (Signal.) *How can I make a kite if I don't have the paper?*
[9] Everybody, say the man's answer. (Signal.) *You will have to do the best you can.*
[10] We'll read more next time.

EXERCISE 10
Picture comprehension

a. Look at the picture.
b. (Ask these questions:)
1. (Point to the toy car.) Who made that car? (Signal.) *Sam.*
2. Why did Sam make that car? (Signal.) *He likes to make things.*
3. (Point to the kite parts.) What is that stuff on the floor? (The children respond.) Yes, those are the kite parts.
4. Can you see a paper telling Sam how to make the kite? (Signal.) *No.*
- Why not? (The children respond.)
- Right, the paper is missing.
- I hope he can put all those parts together.

WORSHEET 76

SUMMARY OF INDEPENDENT ACTIVITY
EXERCISE 11

Introduction to independent activity

a. (Pass out Worksheet 76 to each child.)
b. (Hold up side 1 of your worksheet.) Everybody, you're going to do this worksheet on your own. (Tell the children when they will work the items.)
- Let's go over the things you're going to do.

Story items

(Point to the story-items exercise.) Everybody, remember to write your answers in the blanks.

Following instructions

a. (Touch the sentence in the box.)
b. Everybody, first you're going to read the sentence in the box. Then you're going to read the instructions below the box and do what the instructions tell you to do.

Story-picture items

(Point to the story-picture items on side 2.) Remember to follow these instructions and look at the picture when you work these items.

Reading comprehension

(Point to the story.) You're going to read this story and then do the items. Remember to write the answers in the blanks.

END OF LESSON 76

READING VOCABULARY

Do not touch small letters.

Get ready to read all the words on this page without making a mistake.

EXERCISE 1

Sound out first

a. (Touch the ball for **best.**) Sound it out. Get ready. (Quickly touch **b, e, s, t** as the children say:) *beeessst.*

b. What word? (Signal.) *Best.* Yes, **best.**

c. (Repeat exercise until firm.)

best

EXERCISE 2

ing words

a. (Point to **ing.**) When these letters are together, they usually say **ing.**

b. What do these letters usually say? (Signal.) *ing.* Yes, **ing.**

* (Repeat until firm.)

c. (Point to the words.) These are words you already know. See if you can read them when they look this way.

d. (Point to **ing** in **something.**) What do these letters say? (Signal.) *ing.*

e. (Touch the ball for **something.**) Read the fast way. Get ready. (Signal.) *Something.* Yes, **something.**

f. (Repeat *d* and *e* for **looking** and **rēading.**)

g. (Repeat the series of words until firm.)

ing

something

looking

rēa**ding**

parts

EXERCISE 3

ar word

a. (Touch the ball for **parts.**) Read this word the fast way. (Pause two seconds.) Get ready. (Signal.) *Parts.* Yes, **parts.**

b. (Point to **ar** in **parts.**) Everybody, what do these letters say? (Signal.) *Are.* Yes, **are.**

c. (Touch the ball for **parts.**) Sound it out. Get ready. (Quickly touch **p, ar, t, s** as the children say:) *partsss.*

d. What word? (Signal.) *Parts.* Yes, **parts.**

e. (Repeat *c* and *d* until firm.)

kites

EXERCISE 4

Practice final-e rule

a. Read this word the fast way. Remember to look at the end of the word.

b. (Touch the ball for **kites.** Pause two seconds.) Get ready. (Signal.) *Kites.* Yes, **kites.**

c. (Touch the ball for **kites.**) Sound it out. Get ready. (Quickly touch **k, i, t, s** as the children say:) *kīīītsss.*

d. What word? (Signal.) *Kites.* Yes, **kites.**

e. (Repeat *b* through *d* until firm.)

(Repeat any troublesome words.)

Individual test

(Call on individual children. Each child reads a different word.)

g. Everybody, get ready to read this story.

h. First word. ✔
- Get ready. (Tap.) *Sam.*

i. Next word. ✔
- Get ready. (Tap.) *Liked.*

j. (Repeat *i* for the remaining words in the first three sentences. Have the children reread the first three sentences until firm.)

EXERCISE 8

Remaining sentences

a. I'm going to call on individual children to read a sentence. Everybody, follow along and point to the words. If you hear a mistake, raise your hand.

b. (Call on a child.) Read the next sentence.

To Correct
word-identification errors (**from,** for example)
1. That word is **from.** What word? *From.*
2. Go back to the beginning of the sentence and read the sentence again.

c. (Call on another child.) Read the next sentence.

d. (Repeat *c* for most of the remaining sentences in the story.)

e. (Occasionally have the group read a sentence. When the group is to read, say:) Everybody, read the next sentence. (Tap for each word in the sentence.)

EXERCISE 9

Second reading—sentences and questions

a. You're going to read the story again. This time I'm going to ask questions.

b. Starting with the first word of the title. ✔
- Get ready. (Tap as the children read the title.)

---

sam gets a kite kit[1]

sam liked to make things. he liked to make toy cars. so he went to the store and got a toy car kit.[2] his mom said, "that kit has the parts of a car. you have to rēad and fInd out how to fit the parts so that they make a car."

sam said, "I will do that."

so sam began to rēad the pāper that came with the car kit.[3] then he began to fit the parts to make a car. soon he had a toy car.

his mom said, "that is a fine car. you are good at rēading and at making things."[4]

sam did not like to make the same thing again. he said, "I will not make other cars. I will make something else."

so he went to the store and got a kite kit.[5] when he got home, he shōwed his mom the kite kit. his mom said, "that kit has a lot of parts in it. you will have to rēad the pāper that comes with the kit to fInd out how to make the kite."[6]

---

c. (Call on a child.) Read the first sentence.

To Correct
word-identification errors (**from,** for example)
1. That word is **from.** What word? *From.*
2. Go back to the beginning of the sentence and read the sentence again.

d. (Call on another child.) Read the next sentence.

e. (Repeat *d* for most of the remaining sentences in the story.)

f. (Occasionally have the group read a sentence.)

g. (After each underlined sentence has been read, present each comprehension question specified below to the entire group.)

[1] What will Sam get? (Signal.) *A kite kit.*
- What is a kite kit? (The children respond.)
- Yes, in a kite kit you get all the parts to build a kite.

[2] What kind of kit did he get? (Signal.) *A toy car kit.*
- What is he going to make? (Signal.) *A toy car.*

[3] Why does he have to read the paper? (The children respond.)
- Right, the paper tells him how to make the car.

[4] Everybody, say that. (Signal.) *You are good at reading and at making things.*

[5] What did he get this time? (Signal.) *A kite kit.*

[6] Why does he have to read the paper? (The children respond.)
- Right, the paper tells him how to make the kite.

Do not touch small letters.

Get ready to read all the words on this page without making a mistake.

EXERCISE 5

Read the fast way

a. Read these words the fast way.

b. (Touch the ball for **store**. Pause two seconds.) Get ready. (Signal.) *Store.* Yes, **store.**

c. (Repeat *b* for remaining words.)

store

make

makes

making

home

pāper

what

when

then

who

how

from

began

other

else

next

(Repeat any troublesome words.)

Individual test

(Call on individual children. Each child reads a different word.)

Get ready to read all the words on this page without making a mistake.

EXERCISE 6

Long and short vowel words

a. Read these words the fast way. Remember to look at the end of the word.

b. (Touch the ball for **rode.** Pause two seconds.) Get ready. (Signal.) *Rode.* Yes, **rode.**

c. (Repeat *b* for **kite, sam, not, same, rod, note,** and **kit.**)

not

same

rode

kite

sam

rod

note

kit

Individual test

(Call on individual children to read a column of words from this lesson. If the column contains only one or two words, direct the child to read additional words from an adjacent column.)

STORY 76

EXERCISE 7

First reading—title and three sentences

a. (Pass out Storybook 1.)

b. Everybody, open your reader to page 200.

c. Everybody, touch the title of the story and get ready to read the words in the title.

d. First word. ✔

• Get ready. (Tap.) *Sam.*

e. (Tap for each remaining word in the title.)

f. Everybody, say the title. (Signal.) *Sam gets a kite kit.*

Grade 1 Reading Curriculum Map

Reading Mastery Signature Edition, Grade 1

		Lesson 1	Lesson 2	Lesson 3	Lesson 4	Lesson 5
Spelling		Writing sounds: 1 / Writing words: 2–5	Writing sounds: 1 / Writing words: 2, 3	Writing sounds: 1 / Writing words: 2, 3	Writing sounds: 1 / Writing words: 2–5	Writing sounds: 1 / Writing words: 2, 3
		Phonograms review: 1–5 / Segmentation review: 2–5	Phonograms review: 1–3 / Segmentation review: 2, 3	Phonograms review: 1–3 / Segmentation review: 2, 3	Phonograms review: 1–5 / Segmentation review: 2–5	Phonograms review: 1–3 / Segmentation review: 2, 3
Comprehension		Note details: 14, 16	Determine character emotions: 18 / Note details: 16, 18	Note details: 6, 10	Determine character emotions: 6 / Note details: 6, 10	Note details: 17, 18
		Note details: 12, 13 / Visualize: 13 / Determine character emotions: 13 / Drawing inferences:13 / Make deductions: 12 / Predictions: 13	Note details: 14, 15 / Visualize: 15 / Make judgments: 14 / Predictions: 15 / Cause/effect:14 / Drawing inferences: 15			Note details: 15, 16 / Predictions:15 / Make judgments: 15, 16 / Drawing inferences: 15, 16 / Cause/effect: 15 / Determine character emotions: 16
				Following directions: 3	Following directions: 3	Following directions: 12
Fluency						Individual Checkout (I.C.): 19
		Repeated reading: 12 √	Repeated reading: 14 √			Repeated reading: 15 √
		Reading words: 2, 3, 5, 6, 7, 8, 9 / √: 2, 3, 5, 6, 7, 8, 9	Reading words: 2, 3, 4, 5, 6, 8, 9, 10, 11	Repeated reading: 5 √	Repeated reading: 5 √	√: 2–10
Phonics and Word Recognition	**Regular**	Reading words review: 14, 16	Reading words review: 16, 18		Reading words review: 6, 8	Reading words review: 17, 18
		Reading words: 10 / Connected text: 11, 12 / √: 11, 12	Reading words: 12 / Connected text: 13, 14 / √: 13, 14			Reading words: 13 Connected text:14, 15 / √: 14, 15
		Blending sounds into words: 2 (lift), 3 (clap), 5 (far), 9 (road, sitting, went, every, this, that, the, then) / Reading words: 5 (far), 6 (are), 7 (bar), 8 (car), 9 (road, sitting, went, every, this, that, the, then) √	Blending sounds into words: 2 (paint), 3 (mail), 4 (kissed, when), 5 (where), 6 (there), 8, 9 (farm), 10 (charm), 11 (cart) √: 2, 3, 4, 5, 6, 8, 9, 10, 11 / Reading words: 3, 4, 5, 6	Reading words: 2, 4 (them, her, here, didn't, don't, for, she, ate, barn, why) 5 (he, she, ate, barn, why) / √: 2, 4, 5	Reading words: 2, 4 (he, were, at, they, these, those, even, very, did, yard) / √: 2, 4	Blending sounds into words: 2, 3, 4, 6 (stop), 7, 9, 10 / Reading words: 2, 3, 4 (live), 5 (girls, going), 6, 7, 8 (arm), 9, 10, 11
	Irregular			of: 4 √	do: 4 √	walk, talk, walking: 4 / talking: 5 / √: 4, 5
Letter Sound Correspondence		Review: 15, 16	Review: 17, 18	Review: 7, 11	Review: 7, 11	Review: 18
		Introduction: 4 (ar) / Review: 1 (ă, ŭ, th, ĕ, wh, d, ō, h, ī); 5, 7, 8 (ar) / √: 1, 4, 5, 7, 8	Review: 1 (ŭ, th, ĕ, wh, ō, h, ī, sh, er, ī); 7, 8, 9, 10, 11 (ar) / √: 1, 7, 8, 9, 10	Review:1 (ĕ, ī, wh, ū, sh, th, ă, ō, m, ch) / √: 1	Review: 1 (ō, ī, wh, ch, sh, ĭ, ă, er, ĕ, g, l, s) √: 1	Review: 1 (ŭ, ĕ, ch, ī, ă, ō, m, sh, b, f, r) / √: 1
Print Awareness						
Phonemic Awareness		Segmentation review: 16	Segmentation: 18	Segmentation: 18	Segmentation: 6	Segmentation: 6

Reading Mastery Signature Edition, Grade 1

Key: (for Teachers)   √ = informal assessment   Numbers = exercise numbers   Bold face type = first appearance

		Lesson 6	Lesson 7	Lesson 8	Lesson 9	Lesson 10
Phonemic Awareness						
Print Awareness						
Letter Sound Correspondence		Review: 1 (ĭ, ĭ, r, l, ē, ĕ, s, ŏ, h, ŭ, x, t) √: 1	Review: 1 (ĕ, ē, b, h, d, ā, ŏ, l, ĭ, t, ŭ, c), 5 (ar), 6 (ar), 7 (ar) √: 1, 5, 6, 7	Review: 1 (ŏ, ā, ē, ĭ, ō, ŭ, l, m, r, s, t, w) √: 1	Review: 1 (ĕ, ĭ, ŏ, ŭ, t, m, n, w, s, ā, ĭ, ō, th) √: 1	Review: 1 (ĕ, ē, b, d, ŏ, ō, n, m, ŭ, w, s, r), 8 (ar) √: 1, 8
		Review: 19, 20	Review: 18, 19, 20	Review: 7, 8, 9	Review: 7, 8, 9	Review: 17
Phonics and Word Recognition	*Irregular*	3– **away** √				Blending sounds into words: 5 (**other**), 6 (**book**), 7 (**another**) √: 5, 6, 7 Reading words: : 5 (**other**), 6 (**book**), 7 (**another**) √: 5, 6, 7
	Regular	Blending sounds into words: 2, 3 (**can**), 6 (**yarn**), 7 (**start**), 8, 9 (**lived**) √: 2, 6, 7, 8, 9 Reading words: 2, 3 (**can**), 4 (**dig, dog, big, dug, cop, hole**), 5, 6 (**yarn**), 7 (**start**), 8, 9 (**lived**), 10 √: 2 – 9	Blending sounds into words: 2, 3 (**came**), 4 (**made**), 5 (**art**), 6 (**tart**), 7, 9 (**never**) √: 2, 3, 4, 5, 6, 7 Reading words: : 2, 3 (**came**), 4 (**made**), 5 (**art**), 6 (**tart**), 7, 8 (**starting, yes, liked**), 9 (**never**), 10 √: 2–9	Reading words: 2, 4 √: 2, 4	Reading words: 2, 4 √: 2, 4	Blending sounds into words: 2 (**like**), 3 (**with, bath, help, helped, happy, then, when, where, played**) , 9 (**shark**) √: 2, 3, 9 Reading words: 2 (**like**), 3 (**with, bath, help, helped, happy, then, when, where, played**) , 4 (**swim**), 5 (**other**), 6 (**book**), 7 (**another**), 8 (**ark**), 9 (**shark**), 10 (**arf, bark, barked**) √: 2–10 Onset rime: 4 (**swim**) √
		Reading words: 12 Connected text: 13, 14 √: 13, 14	Reading words: 12 Connected text: 13, 14 √: 13, 14			Reading words: 11 Connected text: 12, 13 √: 12, 13
		Reading words review: 16, 18, 20	Reading words review: 16, 18, 20	Reading words review: 5, 7, 9	Reading words review: 5, 7, 9	Reading words review: 15, 16
Fluency		Reading words: 2–10 √: 2–9	Reading words: 2–10 √: 2–9	Reading words:4 √	Reading words: 4 √	Reading words: 2–10 √: 2–10
		Repeated reading: 14 √	Repeated reading: 14 √			Repeated reading: 13 √
						Individual Checkout (I.C.): 18
Comprehension		Following directions: 11	Following directions: 11	Following directions: 3	Following directions: 3	
		Making judgments: 14, 15 Noting details: 14, 15 Making deductions: 14 Determining character emotions: 14 Making connections: 15	Noting details: 14, 15 Drawing inferences: 14 Making connections: 15			Noting details: 13, 14 Making predictions: 13 Drawing conclusions: 13, 14 Determining character emotions: 14 Making connections: 14
		Noting details: 16, 18	Noting details: 16, 18	Noting details: 7 Determining character emotions: 7	Noting details: 7 Determining character emotions: 7	Noting details: 15, 16, 17
Spelling		Phonograms review: 1–3 Segmentation review: 2, 3	Phonograms review: 1, 2 Segmentation review: 2	Phonograms review: 1, 2 Segmentation review: 2	Phonograms review: 1–3 Segmentation review: 2, 3	Phonograms review: 1–3 Segmentation review: 2, 3
		Writing sounds: 1 Writing words: 2, 3	Writing sounds: 1 Writing words: 2	Writing sounds: 1 Writing words: 2	Writing sounds: 1 Writing words: 2, 3	Writing sounds: 1 Writing words: 2, 3

Reading Mastery Signature Edition, Grade 1

Key: (for Teachers) √ = informal assessment   Numbers = exercise numbers   Bold face type = first appearance

		Lesson 11	Lesson 12	Lesson 13	Lesson 14	Lesson 15
Phonemic Awareness						
Print Awareness						
Letter Sound Correspondence		Review: 1 (er, ĕ, ā, ē, th, wh, ch, sh, short-y, g, h, p), 4, 5, 6 (ar) √: 1, 4, 5, 6	Review: 1 (ō, ē, ŏ, ĕ, h, z, g, p, short-y, w), 4, 6 (ar) √: 1, 4, 6	Review: 1 (ĭ, ŏ, ĭ, ō, th, wh, c, v, g, m, r, n)	Review: 1 (f, h, z, k, short-y, long-y, r, p, ĭ, ă, ĭ, ā) √: 1	Review: 1 (short-y, long-y, ă, ō, ă, ŏ, v, p, d, f, m, k) √: 1
		Review: 19, 20, 22	Review: 17, 18, 23, 24	Review: 9, 10	Review: 18, 19	Review: 16
Phonics and Word Recognition	Irregular	Blending sounds into words: 11, 12 **(took)** √: 11, 12 Reading words: 13 **(looked, cooked)** √: 13	Blending sounds into words: 10 **(books)** Reading words: 11 **(looks)** √: 10, 11		Blending sounds into words: 4 **(boy)**, 9 **(touch)** √	
	Regular	Blending sounds into words: 2, 3, 6, 7, 9 **(after, yelled, swimming)** √: 2, 3, 6, 7, 9 Reading words: 2, 3, 5, 6, 7, 8, 9 **(after, yelled, swimming)**, 10 **(funny)** √: 2, 3, 5, 6, 7, 8, 9, 10 Onset rime: 8 **(swam)** √	Blending sounds into words: 2 **(swims)**, 3 **(plays)**, 4, 6, 7 **(better)**, 8, 10 **(horse)** √: 2, 3, 4, 6, 7, 8, 10 Reading words: 2 **(swims)**, 3 **(plays)**, 4, 5, 6, 7 **(better)**, 8, 9, 10 **(horse)**, 11 √: 2–11	Reading words: 4 √: 4	Blending sounds into words: 2 **(ride)**, 3 **(fast)**, 4 **(cow, stopped)** 5 **(try)**, 6 **(fly)** √: 2–6 Reading words: 2 **(ride)**, 3 **(fast)**, 4 **(cow, stopped)** 5 **(try)**, 6 **(fly)**, 7, 8, 9, 10 √: 2–9 Onset rime: 8 **(creek)** √	Blending sounds into words: 2, 3, 4 **(rode, let's faster, next)**, 6, 7, 8 **(stream)**, 9 **(splash)** √: 2, 3, 4, 6, 7, 8, 9 Reading words: 2, 3, 4 **(rode, let's faster, next)**, 5, 6, 7, 8 **(stream)**, 9 **(splash)**, 10 √: 2–10
		Reading words: 14 Connected text: 15, 16 √: 15, 16	Reading words: 12 Connected text: 13, 14 √: 13, 14		Reading words: 12 Connected text: 13, 14 √: 13, 14	Reading words: 12 Connected text: 13, 14 √: 13, 14
		Reading words review: 18, 19, 21, 22	Reading words review: 16, 17, 19, 20	Reading words review: 5		
Fluency		Reading words: 2, 3, 5, 6, 7, 8, 9, 10, 11, 12, 13 √: 2, 3, 5, 6, 7, 8, 9, 10, 11, 12, 13	Reading words: 2–11 √: 2–11	Reading words: 4 √: 4	Reading words: 2–10 √: 2–9	Reading words: 2–10 √: 2–9
		Repeated reading: 16√	Repeated reading: 14 √		Repeated reading: 14 √	Repeated reading: 14 √
		Sentence copying: 25	Sentence copying: 17	Sentence copying: 10	Sentence copying: 18	Sentence copying: 16
						IC: 17
Comprehension				Following directions: 3	Following directions: 11	Following directions: 11
		Noting details: 16, 17 Determining character emotions: 16 Making connections: 17	Noting details: 14, 15 Making predictions: 14 Drawing conclusions: 15 Making connections: 15		Noting details: 14, 15 Making connections: 14, 15 Making predictions: 14, 15 Determining character emotions: 15	Noting details: 14, 15 Making predictions: 14, 15 Making connections: 15
		Noting details: 22, 24, 27	Noting details: 16, 19, 20, 22, 25	Noting details: 5, 7, 8 Determining character emotions: 8	Noting details: 17, 20, 21	Noting details: 16
Spelling		Phonograms review: 1–4 Segmentation review: 3, 4	Phonograms review: 1–5 Segmentation review: 2, 3, 5	Phonograms review: 1–4 Segmentation review: 3, 4	Phonograms review: 1–4 Segmentation review: 3, 4	Phonograms review: 1–5 Segmentation review: 3, 4
						Writing sounds: 1, 2 Writing words: 3, 4, 5
		Writing sounds: 1, 2 Writing words: 3, 4	Writing sounds: 1, 4 Writing words: 2, 3, 5	Writing sounds: 1, 2 Writing words: 3, 4	Writing sounds: 1, 2 Writing words: 3, 4	

3   Objective Chart

Reading Mastery Signature Edition, Grade 1

Key: (for Teachers)   √= informal assessment   Numbers = exercise numbers   Bold face type = first appearance

		Lesson 16	Lesson 17	Lesson 18	Lesson 19	Lesson 20
Phonemic Awareness						
Print Awareness		Sentence copying: 17	Sentence copying: 18	Sentence copying: 9	Sentence copying: 18	Sentence copying: 16
Letter Sound Correspondence		Review: 1 (ŏ, ŭ, ō, b, y, f, t, h, n, y, s, v), 8 (ar) √: 1, 8	Review: 1 (b, ĕ, h, t, k y, m, z, n, y) √: 1	Review: 1 (th, wh, ch, ĭ, ī, d, x, k, r, z, s,ŭ, w) √: 1	Review: 1 (ŏ, x, ch, qu, ing, z, er, w, sh, c, n, y, s), 6 (ar)	Review: 1 (qu, x, ing, er, sh, c, h, z, j, ĕ, ē, ĭ)
		Review: 17, 18	Review: 18, 19	Review: 9, 10	Review: 18, 20	Review: 16
Phonics and Word Recognition	**Irregular**	Blending sounds into words: 4 (come, some), 6 (what)	Blending sounds into words: 5 (water), 9 (circle) √: 5, 9		Reading words: 7 (girl) √	Blending sounds into words: 5 (good) √: 5 Reading words: 2 (mother, brother)
	Regular	Blending sounds into words: 2, 3, 4 (best, same, over),7 (bank), 8 √:2, 3, 4, 7, 8 Reading words: : 2, 3, 4 (best, same, over), 5, 7 (bank), 8, 9	Blending sounds into words: 2, 3 (real), 4 (jumping), 6, 8 √: 2, 3, 4, 6, 8 Reading words: 2, 3 (real), 4 (jumping), 6, 7, 8, 10 √: 2, 3, 4, 6, 7, 8	Reading words: 2, 4 √: 4	Blending sounds into words: 2 (story), 3, 4 (tried, cry, cried), 5, 6 √: 2–6 Reading words: : 2 (story), 3, 4 (tried, cry, cried), 5, 6, 7, 8 √: 2–7	Blending sounds into words: 3 (self), 4 (ask), 5 (reading, really, rabbit), 6, 7 (read), 8 (play) √: 3–8 Reading words: 2, 3 (self), 4 (ask), 5 (reading, really, rabbit), 6, 7 (read), 8 (play), 9 √: 2–8
		Reading words: 11 Connected text: 12, 13 √: 12, 13	Reading words: 12 Connected text: 13, 14 √: 13, 14		Reading words: 10 Connected text:11, 12 √: 11, 12	Reading words: 11 Connected text: 12, 13 √: 12, 13
				Reading words review: 5	Reading words review: 14	Reading words review: 15
Fluency		Reading words: 2–9 √: 2–8	Reading words: 2–10 √: 2–9	Reading words: 4 √: 4	Reading words: 2–8 √: 2–7	Reading words: 2–9 √: 2–8
		Repeated reading: 13	Repeated reading: 14		Repeated reading: 12 √	Repeated reading: 13 √
						IC: 17
Comprehension		Following directions: 10	Following directions: 11	Following directions: 3	Following directions: 9	Following directions: 10
		Noting details: 13, 14 Determining character emotions: 14	Noting details: 14 Making predictions: 14 Cause/effect: 14, 15 Determining character emotions: 15 Making connections: 15		Noting details: 12 Making predictions: 13 Making connections: 13	Noting details: 12, 13 Accessing prior knowledge: 12, 13 Making connections: 14
		Noting details: 16, 19, 20	Noting details: 17, 20, 21	Following directions: 5 Noting details: 7, 8 Determining character emotions: 8	Following directions: 14 Noting details: 16, 17, 19	Following directions: 15 Noting details: 16
						Lesson 20 Curriculum-Based Assessment
Spelling		Phonograms review: 1–3 Segmentation review: 3	Phonograms review: 1–4 Segmentation review: 3, 4	Phonograms review: 1–4 Segmentation review: 3, 4	Phonograms review:1–4 Segmentation review: 3, 4	Phonograms review: 1–4 Segmentation review: 3, 4
		Writing sounds: 1, 2 Writing words: 3, 4	Writing sounds: 1, 2 Writing words: 4, 5	Writing sounds: 1, 2 Writing words: 3–5	Writing sounds: 1, 2 Writing words: 3–5	Writing sounds: 1, 2 Writing words: 3–5

Reading Mastery Signature Edition, Grade 1

Key: (for Teachers) √ = informal assessment Numbers = exercise numbers Bold face type = first appearance

		Lesson 21	Lesson 22	Lesson 23	Lesson 24	Lesson 25
Phonemic Awareness						
Print Awareness						
Letter Sound Correspondence		Review: 1 (ŭ, m, n, q, u, ing, er, sh, f, p, r, h, j), 8 (ar) √: 1, 8	Review: 1 (ĭ, r, ō, b, t, c, n, f, w, x, l, p) √: 1	Review: 1 (sh, b, d, ĭ, ă, ē, g, w, j, z, k, l) √: 1	Review: 1 (ĭ, ă, z, wh, n, d, l, h, ŏ, ĭ, m, v), 5 (ar) √: 1, 5	Review: 1 (ă, ĭ, th, n, s, er, ŭ, ō, j, k, t, y), 7 (ar) √: 1, 7
		Review: 20, 22	Review: 19, 21	Review: 21, 23	Review: 17, 19	Review: 20
Phonics and Word Recognition	**Irregular**			Reading words: 2 **(look)** √	Reading words: 6 **(walked)**	Blending sounds into words: 6 **(who)**, 13 **(answered)** √: 6, 13 Reading words: 8 **(doing)** √
	Regular	Blending sounds into words: 2 **(bake)**, 3, 4 **(bakes, cake)**, 5, 6 **(asked)** √: 2–6 Reading words: 2 **(bake)**, 3, 4 **(bakes, cake)**, 5, 6 **(asked)**, 7 **(kind)**, 8 **(hard)**, 9 **(card)**, 10 √: 2–9	Blending sounds into words: 2 **(hates)**, 3, 4, 5 **(baked, eagle, bones)**, 7 **(spot)** 8 **(smelled)** √: 2, 3, 4, 5, 7, 8 Reading words: 2 **(hates)**, 3, 4, 5 **(baked, eagle, bones)**, 6, 7 **(spot)**, 8 **(smelled)**, 9 √: 2–8	Blending sounds into words: 3 **(getting)**, 4 **(fine)**, 5 **(leave)**, 6 **(side)**, 7 **(pay, meal, well)**, 8, 10 **(street)** √: 3, 4, 5, 6, 7, 8, 10 Reading words: 2 **(get)**, 3 **(getting)**, 4 **(fine)**, 5 **(leave)**, 6 **(side)**, 7 **(pay, meal, well)**, 8, 9, 10, 11 **(street)** √: 2–10 Onset rime: 9 **(broom)** √	Blending sounds into words: 2 **(room)**, 3, 4 **(still)** √: 2–4 Reading words: : 2 **(room)**, 3, 4 **(still)**, 5, 6 **(note, my, pad)**, 7 √: 2–6	Blending sounds into words: 2 **(white)**, 3 **(steps)**, 4 **(must)**, 5, 9, 11 **(told)** √: 2, 3, 4, 5, 9, 11 Reading words: 2 **(white)**, 3 **(steps)**, 4 **(must)**, 5, 6, 7, 8, 9, 10, 11 **(told)**, 12, 14 √: 2–12 Onset rime: 12 **(brush)** √
		Reading words: 12 Connected text: 13, 14 √: 13, 14	Reading words: 11 Connected text: 12, 13	Reading words: 13 Connected text: 14, 15 √: 14, 15	Reading words: 9 Connected text: 10, 11 √: 10, 11	Reading words: 16 Connected text: 17, 18 √: 17, 18
Fluency		Reading words: 2–10 √: 2–9	Reading words: 2–9 √: 2–8	Reading words: 2–11 √: 2–10	Reading words: 2–7 √: 2–6	Reading words: 2–14 √: 2–13
		Repeated reading: 14 √	Repeated reading: 13	Repeated reading: 15 √	Repeated reading: 11 √	Repeated reading: 18 √
		Sentence copying: 21	Sentence copying: 19	Sentence copying: 21	Sentence copying: 17	Sentence copying: 20
						IC: 21
Comprehension		Following directions: 11	Following directions: 10	Following directions: 12	Following directions: 8	Following directions: 15
		Noting details: 13, 14, 15 Making predictions: 15 Making connections: 15	Noting details: 12, 13, 14 Cause/effect: 13	Noting details: 14, 15 Drawing conclusions: 15 Making connections: 15	Noting details: 10, 11, 12 Cause/effect: 11 Drawing conclusions: 11 Making connections: 12	Noting details: 17, 18 Making predictions: 18, 19 Determining character emotions: 19 Making connections: 19
		Noting details: 17, 19, 21 Determining character emotions: 19 Following directions: 18	Noting details: 16, 18, 20 Following directions: 17	Noting details: 18, 20, 22 Following directions: 19	Noting details: 14, 16, 18 Following directions: 15	Noting details: 20 Following directions: 20
Spelling		Phonograms review: 1–3 Segmentation review: 2, 3	Phonograms review: 1, 2 Segmentation review: 2	Phonograms review: 1, 2, 3 Segmentation review: 3	Phonograms review: 1–5 Segmentation review: 3–5	Phonograms review: 1–5 Segmentation review: 3–5
				Writing sounds: 1, 2 Writing words: 3, 4 Writing sentences: 5		Writing sounds: 1, 2 Writing words: 3–6 Writing sentences: 7
		Writing sounds: 1 Writing words: 2–4 Writing sentences: 5	Writing sounds: 1 Writing words: 2, 3 Writing sentences: 4		Writing sounds: 1, 2 Writing words: 3–6 Writing sentences: 7	

Reading Mastery Signature Edition, Grade 1

Key: (for Teachers) √ = informal assessment   Numbers = exercise numbers   Bold face type = first appearance

	Lesson 26	Lesson 27	Lesson 28	Lesson 29	Lesson 30
Phonemic Awareness		Onset rime: 10			
Print Awareness	Sentence copying: 19	Sentence copying: 23	Sentence copying: 19	Sentence copying: 21	Sentence copying: 20
Letter Sound Correspondence	Review: 1 (ĕ, ŏ, ch, f, j, th,wh, m, s, ing) √	Review: 1 (ĭ, ā, th, wh, ch, qu, l, p, r, x, sh, h), 13 (ar) √: 1, 13	Review: 1 (v, ă, er, w, sh, k, b, n, g, ŏ, ē, j), 6 (ar), 7 (ar) √: 1, 6, 7	Review: 1 (ŭ, ĭ, ĕ, th, ing, h, sh, f, p, j, ŏ), 10 (ar) √: 1, 10	Review: 1 (j, ōăĭ, th, wh, n, t, qu, b, d, h), 7 (ar), 11 (al), 12 (al) √: 1, 7, 11
	Review: 19	Review: 23	Review: 19	Review: 21	Review: 20
Phonics and Word Recognition — Irregular	Blending sounds into words: 7 (**from**) √	Blending sounds into words: 7 (**bird**), 8 (**money**), 12 (**because**) √: 7, 8, 12	Blending sounds into words: 4 (**brothers, love**), 8 (**want**), 9 (**buttons**)	Blending sounds into words: 5 (**buy**)	Reading words: 10 (**wanted, one**)
Phonics and Word Recognition — Regular	Blending sounds into words: 2, 3 (**sore**), 4 (**blow**), 5 (**legs**), 6 (**painted, Don's, old, horn**), 8 (**drop**) √: 2–6, 8 Reading words: 2, 3 (**sore**), 4 (**blow**), 5 (**legs**), 6 (**painted, Don's, old, horn**), 8 (**drop**), 9 (**hold, each, dropped**), 10 √: 2–9	Blending sounds into words: 2, 3, 4, 5 (**held**), 6, 9 (**rob, store, robbers, toot**) √: 2–6, 9 Reading words: 2, 3, 4, 5 (**held**), 6, 9 (**rob, store, robbers, toot**), 11 (**dropping, bags**), 13, 14 √: 2–6, 9, 11, 13	Blending sounds into words: 2, 3, 4 (**cannot, jumps, sky**) √: 2–4 Reading words: 2, 3, 4 (**cannot, jumps, sky**), 5 (**grabbed, six, than**), 6, 7, 10 √: 2–7, 10	Blending sounds into words: 2 (**more**), 3 (**pants**), 4, 6 (**think, pink, bag**), 7 (**off**), 8, 10 (**farmer**), 11 √: 2, 3, 4, 6, 8, 10, 11 Reading words: : 2 (**more**), 3 (**pants**), 4, 6 (**think, pink, bag**), 7 (**off**), 8, 9 (**gold, sold**), 10 (**farmer**), 11, 12 √: 2, 3, 4, 6–11	Blending sounds into words: 2, 3 (**lady**), 4 (**yellow**), 5, 6 (**three**), 8 (**trip**), 9, 13 (**selling**) √: 2–5, 6, 8, 9, 13 Reading words: 2, 3 (**lady**), 4 (**yellow**), 5, 6 (**three**),7, 8 (**trip**), 9, 10 (**cold, kept**), 12 (**ball**), 13 (**selling**), 14 √: 2–10, 12, 13
	Reading words: 12 Connected text: 13, 14 √: 13, 14	Reading words: 16 Connected text: 17, 18 √: 17, 18	Reading words: 12 Connected text: 13, 14 √: 13, 14	Reading words: 14 Connected text: 15, 16 √: 15, 16	Reading words: 16 Connected text: 17, 18 √: 17, 18
Fluency	Reading words: 2–10 √: 2–9	Reading words: 2–14 √: 2–13	Reading words: 2–10 √: 2–9	Reading words: 2–12 √: 2–11	Reading words: 2–10, 12, 13, 14 √: 2–10, 13
	Repeated reading: 14 √	Repeated reading: 18 √	Repeated reading: 14	Repeated reading: 16 √	Repeated reading: 18 √
				IC: 21	
Comprehension	Following directions: 11	Following directions: 15	Following directions: 11	Following directions: 13	Following directions: 15
	Accessing prior knowledge: 13, 14 Noting details: 13, 14, 15 Making deductions: 13 Making connections: 15	Noting details: 17, 18, 19 Cause/effect: 18 Determining character emotions: 19 Making deductions: 19	Noting details: 13, 14, 15 Activating prior knowledge: 15 Making connections: 15	Noting details: 16, 17 Making predictions: 16 Cause/effect: 16 Drawing inferences: 17	Accessing prior knowledge: 17 Making judgments: 17 Noting details: 17, 18 Making predictions: 18
	Noting details: 17, 20 Following directions: 18	Noting details: 21, 24 Following directions: 22	Noting details: 17, 20 Following directions: 18	Noting details: 19, 22 Following directions: 20	Noting details: 20 Following directions: 20
Spelling	Phonograms review: 1–4 Segmentation review: 3, 4	Phonograms review: 1–4 Segmentation review: 3, 4	Phonograms review: 1–3 Segmentation review: 3	Phonograms review: 1–4 Segmentation review: 3, 4	Phonograms review: 1–3 Segmentation review: 3
					Writing sounds: 1, 2 Writing words: 3, 4 Writing sentences: 5
	Writing sounds: 1, 2 Writing words: 3–5 Writing sentences: 6	Writing sounds: 1, 2 Writing words: 3–5 Writing sentences: 6	Writing sounds: 1, 2 Writing words: 3, 4 Writing sentences: 5	Writing sounds: 1, 2 Writing words: 3–5 Writing sentences: 6	

Reading Mastery Signature Edition, Grade 1

Key: (for Teachers)	√ = informal assessment	Numbers = exercise numbers	Bold face type = first appearance	

		Lesson 31	Lesson 32	Lesson 33	Lesson 34	Lesson 35
Phonemic Awareness				Onset rime: 11 **(small)** √: 11		Onset rime: 12 **(sleep)**, 18, 19 √: 12, 18, 19
Print Awareness		Sentence copying: 21	Sentence copying: 9	Sentence copying: 22	Sentence copying: 29	Sentence copying: 26
Letter Sound Correspondence		Review: 1 (s, ĕ, ŏ, ä, ĭ, ŭ, ch, b, c, d, g, m), 7–10 (al) √:1, 7–10	Review: 1 (p, b, d, t, h, k, m, ä, ĭ, ă, ŏ, r) √: 1	Review: 1 (ĕ, ŭ, ĕ, ŏ, th, ch, ing, j, sh, b, d, g), 8–9 (al) √: 1, 8, 9	Review: 1 (h, k, ĭ, ĩ, r, wh, qu, er, ŭ, c, f, n), 2 (ar, al), 14 (ar), 15 (al), 17 (al) √: 1, 2, 14, 15, 17	Review: 1 (ĕ, j, ŏ, g, n, w, l, ĕ, s, z, v, ŏ, short y), 2 (ar, al), 13 (ar), 14 (al), 15 (al), 16 (al)
		Review: 21	Review: 9	Review: 22	Review: 29	Review: 26
Phonics and Word Recognition	Irregular				Blending sounds into words: 12 **(saw)** √	Blending sounds into words: 5 **(oh)** √
	Regular	Blending sounds into words: 2 **(rip)**, 4, 5 **(miles)**, 6 √: 2, 4, 5, 6 Reading words: 2 **(rip)**, 3 **(dim)**, 4, 5 **(miles)**, 6, 8 **(fall)**, 9 **(hall)**, 10 **(ball)**, 11**(all)**, 12 √: 2–6, 8–11	Reading words: 2, 4, 6 √: 2, 4, 6	Blending sounds into words: 2, 3 **(left)**, 4, 6, 7 **(playing)** √: 2, 3, 4, 6, 7 Reading words: : 2, 3 **(left)**, 4, 5 **(fat)**, 6, 7 **(playing)**, 9, 10 **(call)**, 11 **(small)**, 12 √: 2–7, 9–11	Blending sounds into words: 3 **(bent)**, 4 **(bug)**, 5, 6, 7 **(last)**, 8, 9 **(lick)**, 11 **(floor)**, 13 **(spotted)** √: 3–9, 11, 13 Reading words: 3 **(bent)**, 4 **(bug)**, 5, 6, 7 **(last)**, 8, 9 **(lick)**, 10 **(mole, box, I'll)**, 11 **(floor)**, 13 **(spotted)**, 14, 15 **(mall)**, 16, 17 **(salt)**, 18 **(tall, stall)**, 19 √: 3–11, 13–18	Blending sounds into words: 3, 4 **(hope)**, 6 **(dream)**, 8 **(picked)**, 9, 10, 11, 13 **(party)** √: 3, 4, 6, 8, 9, 10, 11, 13 Reading words: 3, 4 **(hope)**, 6 **(dream)**, 7 **(dreaming, goes, meets)**, 8 **(picked)**, 9, 10, 11, 12, 13 **(party)**, 14, 15, 16, 17, 18, 19, 20 √: 3, 4, 6–19
		Reading words: 14 Connected text: 15, 16 √: 15, 16		Reading words: 14 Connected text: 15, 16 √: 15, 16	Reading words: 21 Connected text: 22, 23 √: 22, 23	Reading words: 22 Connected text: 23, 24 √: 23, 24
Fluency		Reading words: 2–6, 8–12 √: 2–6, 8–11	Reading words: 2, 4, 6 √: 2, 4, 6	Reading words: 2–7, 9–12 √: 2–7, 9–11	Reading words: 3–19 √: 3– 18	Reading words: 3–20 √: 3–19
		Repeated reading: 16 √		Repeated reading: 16 √	Repeated reading: 23 √	Repeated reading: 24 √
						IC: 27
Comprehension		Following directions: 13	Following directions: 3, 5	Following directions: 13	Following directions: 20	Following directions: 21
		Noting details: 15, 16, 17 Drawing inferences: 16 Accessing prior knowledge: 17		Noting details: 16, 17 Accessing prior knowledge: 16 Drawing inferences: 17	Noting details: 23, 24 Making predictions: 24 Drawing conclusions: 24 Determining character emotions: 24	Noting details: 24, 25 Cause/effect: 24, 25 Making connections: 24, 25 Determining character emotions: 25
		Noting details: 19, 22 Following directions: 20	Noting details: 8 Following directions: 10	Noting details: 19, 21 Following directions: 20	Noting details: 26, 28 Following directions: 27	Noting details: 26 Following directions: 26
Spelling		Phonograms review: 1–3 Segmentation review: 3	Phonograms review: 1–4 Segmentation review: 3, 4	Phonograms review: 1–5 Segmentation review: 3–5	Phonograms review: 1, 2 Segmentation review: 2	Phonograms review: 1–3 Segmentation review: 2, 3
						Writing sounds: 1 Writing words: 2–4 Writing sentences: 5
		Writing sounds: 1, 2 Writing words: 3, 4 Writing sentences: 5	Writing sounds: 1, 2 Writing words: 3–5 Writing sentences: 6	Writing sounds: 1, 2 Writing words: 3–6 Writing sentences: 7	Writing sounds: 1 Writing words: 2, 3 Writing sentences: 4	

Reading Mastery Signature Edition, Grade 1

Key: (for Teachers)	√ = informal assessment	Numbers = exercise numbers	Bold face type = first appearance

		Lesson 36	Lesson 37	Lesson 38	Lesson 39	Lesson 40
Phonemic Awareness						
Print Awareness						
Letter Sound Correspondence		Review: 1 (ĕ, ĭ, ŭ, ā, ē, ī, ō, ū, th, wh, ch, qu, d, b, c), 2 (al, ar), 12 (ar), 16 (al) √: 1, 2, 12, 16	Review: 1 (ŏ, ō, ē, wh, qu, d, sh, b, r, c, l, f, n, g, j), 15 (ar), 16 (al), 17 (al) √: 1, 15–17	Review: 1 (ä, ĕ, ĭ, ō, ŭ, ā, ĕ, ī, ō), 3 (ar), 13 (al), 14 (al) √: 1, 13, 14	Review: 1 (ä, ē, ī, ō, ä, ĕ, ī, ō, ŭ), 12 (ar) √: 1, 13, 14	Introduction: 1, 2 (vowel letter names) √ Review: 13 (al), 15 (ar) √: 13, 15
		Review: 28	Review: 28	Review: 25	Review: 26	Review: 23
Phonics and Word Recognition	Irregular	Blending sounds into words: 9 **(would)**, 15 **(please)**	Blending sounds into words: 12 **(should)** √ Reading words: 4 **(football)** √	Blending sounds into words: 8 **(your)**, 11 **(could)** √: 8, 11 Reading words: 10 **(touching)** √	Blending sounds into words: 2 **(head)**, 8 **(word)**, 9 **(put)**, 11 **(elephant)**	Blending sounds into words: 11 **(any)**
	Regular	Blending sounds into words: 3 **(can't)**, 4 **(silly)**, 5, 10 **(sing)**, 11, 12, 16 √: 3, 4, 6, 10–12, 16 Reading words: 3 **(can't)**, 4 **(silly)**, 5, 6, **(inside)**, 7, 8, 10 **(sing)**, 11, 12, 13, 14 **(stand)**, 16, 17, 18 √: 3–8, 10–14, 16, 17 Two-part words: 6 **(inside)**, 7, 8 √: 6–8 Onset rime: 14 **(stand)** √	Blending sounds into words: 5, 6, 7, 8, 9 **(much)**, 11 **(bet)**, 13 **(chunks)**, 14, 15 **(part)**, 16, 17 **(taller)** √: 5–9, 11, 13–17 Reading words: 2 **(smiled)**, 3, 5, 6, 7, 8, 9 **(much)**, 10, 11 **(bet)**, 13 **(chunks)**, 14, 15 **(part)**, 16, 17 **(taller)**, 18 √: 2, 3, 5–9, 11, 13–17 Onset rime: 2 **(smiled)** √ Two-part words: 3, 4 **(football)** √: 3, 4	Blending sounds into words: 2, 3, 9 **(week, win)**, 12, 14 √: 2, 3, 9, 12, 14 Reading words: 2, 3, 4, 5, 6 **(always)**, 7 **(also)**, 9 **(week, win)**, 10, 12, 13, 14, 15 √: 2–7, 9, 10, 12–14 Two-part words: 4, 5, 6 **(always)**, 7 **(also)** √: 4–7	Blending sounds into words: 3, 4, 5, 7 **(glasses)**, 10, 12, 15 √: 3, 4, 5, 7, 10, 12, 15 Reading words: 3, 4, 5, 6 **(falls, piles)**, 7 **(glasses)**, 10, 12, 13, 14, 15, 16 √: 3–7, 10, 12–15 Two-part words: 13, 14 √: 13, 14	Blending sounds into words: 3, 4, 5 **(table)**, 6, 8 **(rod)**, 9, 10, 12, 13, 15, 16 √: 3–6, 8–10, 12, 13, 15, 16 Reading words: 3, 4, 5 **(table)**, 6, 7, 8 **(rod)**, 9, 10, 12, 13, 14, 15, 16, 17 √: 3–10, 12–17
		Reading words: 20 Connected text: 21, 22 √: 21, 22	Reading words: 20 Connected text: 21, 22 √: 21, 22	Reading words: 17 Connected text: 18, 19 √: 18, 19	Reading words: 18 Connected text: 19, 20 √: 19, 20	Reading words: 18 Connected text: 19, 20 √: 19, 20
						Reading words review: 22
Fluency		Reading words: 3–18 √: 3–17	Reading words: 2–18 √: 2–17	Reading words: 2–15 √: 2–14	Reading words: 3–16 √: 3–15	Reading words: 3–17 √: 3–17
		Repeated reading: 22 √	Repeated reading: 22 √	Repeated reading: 19	Repeated reading: 20 √	Repeated reading: 20 √
		Sentence copying: 28	Sentence copying: 28	Sentence copying: 25	Sentence copying: 26	Sentence copying: 23
						IC: 24
Comprehension		Following directions: 19	Following directions: 19	Following directions: 16	Following directions: 17	
		Noting details: 22, 23 Drawing conclusions: 22, 23 Making predictions: 22 Accessing prior knowledge: 23	Noting details: 22, 23 Making deductions: 22, 23 Making predictions: 23	Noting details: 19, 20 Drawing inferences: 19 Making predictions: 20 Determining character emotions: 20	Noting details: 20, 21 Making deductions: 20 Making connections: 20, 21 Making predictions: 21 Accessing prior knowledge: 21	Noting details: 20, 21 Making deductions: 20 Making connections: 20, 21 Determining character emotions: 21
		Noting details: 25, 27 Following directions: 26	Noting details: 25, 27 Following directions: 26	Noting details: 22, 24 Following directions: 23	Noting details: 23, 25 Determining character emotions: 23 Following directions: 24	Following directions: 22, 23 Noting details: 23
						Lesson 40 Curriculum-Based Assessment
Spelling		Phonograms review: 1 Segmentation review: 1	Phonograms review: 1 Segmentation review: 1	Phonograms review: 1 Segmentation review: 1	Phonograms review: 1, 2 Segmentation review: 1, 2	Phonograms review: 1–3 Segmentation review: 1–3
		Writing words: 1, 2 Writing sentences: 3	Writing words: 1, 2 Writing sentences: 3	Writing words: 1, 2 Writing sentences: 3	Writing words: 1–3 Writing sentences: 4	Writing words: 1–4 Writing sentences: 5

Reading Mastery Signature Edition, Grade 1

Key: (for Teachers) √ = informal assessment Numbers = exercise numbers Bold face type = first appearance

		Lesson 41	Lesson 42	Lesson 43	Lesson 44	Lesson 45
Phonemic Awareness						
Print Awareness						
Letter Sound Correspondence		Review: 1 (vowel letter names), 12 (al), 13 (al) √: 1, 12, 13	Review: 1 (al, ar), 2 (vowel letter names), 7 (ar), 9 (al) √ 1, 2, 7, 9	Review: 1 (vowel letter names), 8 (ar), 9 (al) √: 1, 8, 9	Review: 1 (ar, al), 2 (vowel letter names), 11 (al), 12 (ar) √: 1, 2, 11, 12	Introduction: 6, 7, 8, 9, 10 (ou) Review: 1 (al, ar), 2 (vowel letter names), 4 (al), 5 (ar) √: 1, 4, 5, 6, 7, 8, 9, 10
		Review: 24	Review: 14	Review: 14	Review: 17	Review: 19
Phonics and Word Recognition	**Irregular**	Blending sounds into words: 5 (loved) Reading words: 14 (wouldn't, couldn't)	Reading words: 6 (shouldn't) √	Reading words: 7 (ready) √		
	Regular	Blending sounds into words: 3, 4, 6, 12, 13 (Walter) √: 3, 4, 6, 12, 13 Reading words: 3, 4, 6, 7 (felt, dinner), 8, 9, 10, 11, 12, 13 √: 3, 4, 6-13 Two-part words: 8, 9 (himself), 10 √: 8-10 Onset rime: 11 (score) √	Blending sounds into words: 3 (not), 4, 8, 9 √: 3, 4, 8, 9 Reading words: 3 (not), 4, 5 (team, cheer, cheered, cheering), 6 (game, scored), 7 (cars), 8, 9	Blending sounds into words: 2 (fin), 3, 4 (Walter's, scores, kick) √: 2, 3, 4 Reading words: 2 (fin), 3, 4 (Walter's, scores, kick), 5, 6, 7 (player, falling), 8, 9, (balls) √: 2, 3, 4, 5, 6, 7, 8, 9 Two-part words: 5, 6 √: 5, 6	Blending sounds into words: 3, 4 (hop), 5, 9 √: 3, 4, 5, 9 Reading words: 3, 4 (hop), 5, 6, 7, 8 (runner), 9, 10, 11, 12 √: 3, 4, 5, 6, 7, 8, 9, 10, 11, 12 Two-part words: 7, 8 (runner) √: 7, 8	Blending sounds into words: 4 (wall), 5, 11, 12 √: 4, 5, 11, 12 Reading words: 3 (just, needed, shot, past, time), 4 (wall), 5, 7 (out), 8 (shout), 9 (loud), 10 (cloud), 11, 12, 13, 14 (almost) √: 3, 4, 5, 7, 8, 9, 10, 11, 12, 13, 14 Two-part words: 13, 14 (almost) √: 13, 14
		Reading words: 15 Connected text: 16. 17 √: 16, 17	Reading words: 10 Connected text: 11, 12 √: 11, 12	Reading words: 10 Connected text: 11, 12 √: 11, 12	Reading words: 13 Connected text: 14, 15 √: 14, 15	Reading words: 15 Connected text: 16, 17 √: 16, 17
Fluency		Reading words: 3-14 √: 3-14	Reading words: 3-9 √	Reading words: 2, 3, 4, 5, 6, 7, 8, 9 √	Reading words: 3, 4, 5, 6, 7, 8, 9, 10, 11, 12√	Reading words: 3, 4, 5, 7, 8, 9, 10, 11, 12, 13, 14 √: 3, 4, 5, 7, 8, 9, 10, 11, 12, 13, 14
		Repeated reading: 17 √	Repeated reading: 12 √	Repeated reading: 12 √	Repeated reading: 15	Repeated reading: 17 √
		Sentence copying: 24	Sentence copying: 14	Sentence copying: 14	Sentence copying: 17	Sentence copying: 19
						Individual Checkout: 20
Comprehension		Noting details: 17 Determining character emotions: 17, 18 Making predictions: 18 Drawing inferences: 18 Making connections: 18	Noting details: 12, 13 Identifying literal cause/effect: 12 Activating prior knowledge: 12 Determining character emotions: 13 Making connections: 13	Making predictions: 12 Noting details: 12 Inferring cause/effect: 12 Identifying literal cause/effect: 12 Inferring story details/events: 13 Interpreting character emotions: 13	Making predictions: 15 Identifying literal cause/effect: 15 Noting details: 15, 16 Inferring story details/events: 16 Making connections: 16	Making predictions: 17 Noting details: 17, 18 Inferring cause/effect: 17 Interpreting a character's emotions: 17, 18 Inferring story details/events: 18
		Recalling details: 21 Following directions: 22 Noting details: 23	Recalling details: 14 Following directions: 14 Noting details: 14	Recalling details: 14 Following directions: 14 Noting details: 14	Recalling details: 17 Following directions: 17 Noting details: 17	Recalling details: 19 Following directions: 19 Noting details: 19
Spelling		Segmentation review: 1	Segmentation review: 1	Segmentation review: 1	Segmentation review: 1, 2	Segmentation review: 1, 2
						Word writing: 1, 2, 3 Sentence writing: 4
		Word writing: 1, 2 Sentence writing: 3	Word writing: 1, 2 Sentence writing: 3	Word writing: 1, 2 Sentence writing: 3	Word writing: 1, 2, 3 Sentence writing: 4	

Key: (for Teachers)	√= informal assessment	Numbers = exercise numbers	Bold face type = first appearance

		Lesson 46	Lesson 47	Lesson 48	Lesson 49	Lesson 50
Phonemic Awareness						
Print Awareness						
Letter Sound Correspondence		Review: 1 (al, ar), 2 (vowel letter names), 9 (al), 10 (ar), 11 (ou), 12 (ou), 13 (ou) √: 1, 2, 9–13	Review: 1 (vowel letter names) √	Review: 1 (ou, al), 2 (vowel letter names), 11–13 (ou) √: 1, 2, 11–13	Review: 1 (ou, ar), 2 (vowel letter names), 9–13 (ou) √: 1, 2, 9–13	Review: 1 (vowel letter names), 13 (ou), 14 (ou)
		Review: 23		Review: 23		
Phonics and Word Recognition	Irregular	Reading words: 8 **(wants)** √		Reading words: 14 **(about)** √		Blending sounds into words: 5 **(afraid)**, 11 **(once)**, 12 **(mountain)** √: 5, 11, 12 Reading words: 15 **(around)** √
	Regular	Blending sounds into words: 3, 4, 5, 7, 10 **(star)** √: 3–5, 7, 10 Reading words: 3, 4, 5, 6, 7, 8 **(pick)**, 9, 10 **(star)**, 12, 13 **(bout)**, 14 √: 3–10, 12–14 Two-part word: 6 √	Reading words: 2, 4, 6 √: 6	Blending sounds into words: 3, 4 **(mad)**, 6 **(children)**, 10 **(moo, petted, how)**, 11 **(our)** √: 3, 4, 6, 10, 11 Reading words: 3, 4 **(mad)**, 5, 6 **(children)**, 7 **(Carmen)**, 8, 9 **(teacher)**, 10 **(moo, petted, how)**, 11 **(our)**, 12 **(mouse)**, 13 **(house)**, 14 √: 3–14 Two-part words: 7 **(Carmen)**, 8 √: 7, 8 Introduction of final–e rule: 5	Blending sounds into words: 3, 4, 6, 7 **(saved, grass)**, 12 **(shouted)**, 13 **(sounds)** √: 3, 4, 6, 7, 12, 13 Reading words: 3, 4, 5, 6, 7 **(saved, grass)**, 8 **(mooing, glad)**, 9, 10, 11, 12 **(shouted)**, 13 **(sounds)** √: 3–13 Final–e rule: 5	Blending sounds into words: 2, 3, 10 **(piled, screamed)**, 13 **(hound)**, 14 **(pound)** √: 2, 3, 10, 13, 14 Reading words: 2, 3, 4, 6, 7, 8, 9, 10 **(piled, screamed)**, 13 **(hound)**, 14 **(pound)**, 15 **(clouds)** √: 2, 3, 4, 6–10, 13–15 Two-part words: 7, 8, 9 √: 7–9 Final–e rule: 4
		Reading words: 15 Connected text: 16, 17 √: 16, 17		Reading words: 15 Connected text: 16, 17 √: 16, 17	Reading words: 14 Connected text: 15, 16 √: 15, 16	Reading words: 16 Connected text: 17, 18 √: 17, 18
Fluency		Reading words: 3–10, 12–14 √: 3–10, 12–14	Reading words: 2, 4, 6 √: 6	Reading words: 3–14 √: 3–14	Reading words: 3–13 √: 3–13	Reading words: 2–15 √: 2–15
		Repeated reading: 17 √		Repeated reading: 17	Repeated reading: 16 √	Repeated reading: 18 √
		Sentence copying: 23		Sentence copying: 23		
						IC: 21
Comprehension			Following directions: 3, 5			
		Making predictions: 17 Noting details: 17, 18 Accessing prior knowledge: 17 Inferring story details/events: 17 Interpreting character emotions: 17, 18 Making connections: 18		Noting details: 17, 18 Identifying literal cause/effect: 17 Making predictions: 17, 18 Inferring story details/events: 18 Recalling details: 18 Accessing prior knowledge: 18 Determining character emotions: 18	Making predictions: 15 Recalling details: 15, 17 Identifying literal cause/effect: 16 Noting details: 16, 17 Interpreting character emotions: 16 Inferring story details/events: 17	Making predictions: 18 Noting details: 18, 19 Inferring cause/effect: 18, 19 Interpreting character emotions: 18 Making connections: 19
		Recalling details: 20 Following directions: 21 Noting details: 22	Noting details: 7 Inferring story details/events: 8 Following directions: 9, 11	Recalling details: 20 Following directions: 21 Noting details: 22	Recalling details: 19 Following directions: 20, 22 Noting details: 21	Recalling details: 20 Following directions: 20 Interpreting character emotions: 20
Spelling		Phonograms review: 1 Segmentation review: 1	Phonograms review: 1 Segmentation review: 1	Phonograms review: 1 Segmentation review: 1	Phonograms review: 1 Segmentation review: 1	Phonograms review: 1, 2 Segmentation review: 2
						Writing sounds: 1 Writing words: 2, 3 Writing sentences: 4
		Writing words: 1, 2 Writing sentences: 3	Writing words: 1, 2 Writing sentences: 3	Writing words: 1, 2 Writing sentences: 3	Writing words: 1, 2 Writing sentences: 3	

Reading Mastery Signature Edition, Grade 1

	Lesson 51	Lesson 52	Lesson 53	Lesson 54	Lesson 55
Spelling	Writing sounds: 1 Writing words: 2-4 Writing sentences: 5	Writing sounds: 1 Writing words: 2-4 Writing sentences: 5	Writing sounds: 1 Writing words: 2-4 Writing sentences: 5	Writing sounds: 1 Writing words: 2-4 Writing sentences: 5	Writing words: 1, 2 Writing sentences: 3
	Phonograms review: 1-3 Segmentation review: 2, 3	Phonograms review: 1-3 Segmentation review: 2, 3	Phonograms review: 1-3 Segmentation review: 2, 3	Phonograms review: 1-3 Segmentation review: 2, 3	Phonograms review: 1 Segmentation review: 1
Comprehension	Noting details: 17 Identifying literal cause/effect: 17 Making predictions: 18 Drawing inferences: 18 Recalling details: 20 Following directions: 21, 23 Noting details: 22	Recalling details: 16 Identifying literal cause/effect: 17, 18 Making predictions: 18 Recalling details: 20 Following directions: 21, 23 Noting details: 22	Recalling details: 12 Interpreting character emotions: 14 Recalling details: 16 Following directions: 17, 19 Noting details: 18	Recalling details: 13 Noting details: 14 Reality/Fantasy: 14 Making predictions: 14, 15 Inferring cause/effect: 15 Recalling details: 17 Following directions: 18, 20 Noting details: 19	Recalling details: 13 Noting details: 14, 15 Identifying literal cause/effect: 14, 15 Making connections: 14 Sequencing: 14 Interpreting character motives: 14 Making judgments: 14 Recalling details: 16 Following directions: 16 Noting details: 16
Fluency	Reading words: 2-14 √: 2-14 Repeated reading: 17	Reading words: 3-14 √: 3-14 Repeated reading: 17	Reading words: 1-10 √: 1-10 Repeated reading: 13	Reading words: 3-11 √: 3-11 Repeated reading: 14 √	Reading words: 1-11 √: 1-11 Repeated reading: 14 √ IC: 17

Phonics and Word Recognition

	Lesson 51	Lesson 52	Lesson 53	Lesson 54	Lesson 55
Regular	Blending sounds into words: 2 (rate), 3 (rate) Reading words: 2 (rat), 3 (rate), 4, 7 (steep), 8, 8, 11 2, 3, 4, 5, 7, 8, 10, 11 10 (herself), 11, 12, 13, 14 Final-e rule: 4 (rat, rate) √: 2, 3, 4, 7, 8, 10-14 Two-part word: 10 (herself) √ Reading words: 15 Connected text: 16, 17 √: 16, 17	Blending sounds into words: 3 (rest), 4 (open), 5 (hounds) Reading words: 3 (rest), 4 (open), 5 (before), 6, 7, 8 (slammed), 9, 10, 11 (hanging, only), 12, 13 (ouch), 14 (hounds) 3, 4, 5, 7, 8, 10, 14 Final-e rule: 6 √: 3-14 Reading words: 15 Connected text: 16, 17 √: 16, 17	Blending sounds into words: 6, 7, 8 (door), 9 Reading words: 1, 3, 4 (behind), 5 (slowly, opened), 6, 7, 8 (door), 9 (thousand), 10 (found) 10 (found) Final-e rule: 1 √: 1, 3-10 Reading words: 11 Connected text: 12, 13 √: 12, 13	Blending sounds into words: 10 (elf), 11 (cross) Reading words: 1, 3 (careful), 4 (bigger), 5, 6, 7, 8, 10, 11 3 (careful), 4 (bigger) 10 (found), 11 (cross) Two-part word: 3 (careful), 4 (bigger) √: 3-11 Final-e rule: 5 √: 3, 4 Reading words: 12 Connected text: 13, 14 √: 13, 14	Blending sounds into words: 1 (reached), 2 (tired), 3 (woke), 4 (lie) Reading words: 1 (reached), 2 (tired), 3 (woke), 4 (lie), 5 (cane), 6 (site), 7 (sit), 8, 9, 10, 11 √: 1-4 Final-e rule: 5 (cane) Two-part word: 10 (setting) √: 1-11 Reading words: 12 Connected text: 13, 14 √: 13, 14
Irregular	Blending sounds into words: 5 (magic), 6 (eyes), 9 (father) √: 5, 6, 9	Blending sounds into words: 10 (coming)	Two-part word: 2 (anyone) √ Reading words: 5 (touched) √	Blending sounds into words: 2 (full) Reading words: 9 (many)	Blending sounds into words: 9 (been)

	Lesson 51	Lesson 52	Lesson 53	Lesson 54	Lesson 55
Letter Sound Correspondence	Review: 1 (vowel letter names), 11 (ou), 12 (al), 12-14 (ou) 13 (ar) √: 1, 12, 13	Review: 1 (vowel letter names), 2 (al, ou), 12-14 √: 1, 2, 12-14 (ou)	Review: 9, 10 (ou) √: 9, 10	Review: 1 (ar, ou) √	
Print Awareness					
Phonemic Awareness					

Key: (for Teachers) √ = informal assessment Numbers = exercise numbers Bold face type = first appearance

Reading Mastery Signature Edition, Grade 1

		Lesson 56	Lesson 57	Lesson 58	Lesson 59	Lesson 60
Phonemic Awareness						
Print Awareness						
Letter Sound Correspondence		Review: 17 (ou) √	Review: 2 (al, ou, ar), 7 (ou) √: 2, 7		Review: 2 (al), 3 (ou), 4 (ar) √: 2–4	Review: 1 (ar), 2, (al), 3 (ou) √: 1–3
Phonics and Word Recognition	**Irregular**	Blending sounds into words: 12 (dirty), 13 (does) √: 12, 13 Two-part words: 15 (into), 16 (something) √: 15, 16		Blending sounds into words: 6 (work) √		
	Regular	Blending sounds into words: 1, 2, 3, 4 (rich), 5, 10, 11 (clean),17 (round) √: 1–5, 10, 11, 17 Reading words: 1, 2, 3, 4 (rich), 5, 6, 7, 8 (cam), 9 (hide, hid), 10, 11 (clean), 14 (rubbed), 17 (round) √: 1–11, 14, 17 Final–e rule: 6 √	Blending sounds into words: 7, 8 (stayed), 9, 10 √: 7–10 Reading words: 1 (holding), 3, 4 (pan), 5 (pane), 6, 7, 8 (stayed), 9, 10, 11, 12 (lake), 13 √: 1, 3–13 Final–e rule review: 3, 9, 10, 11, 12 (lake), 13 √: 3, 9–13	Blending sounds into words: 7 Reading words: 1 (keep), 2, 3, 4, 5, 7, 8 (take), 9, 10 √: 1–5, 7–10 Final–e rule review: 2, 5, 8 (take) Two-part word: 9, 10 √: 9, 10	Blending sounds into words: 1, 3, 4, 10 (fix), 12 √: 1, 3, 4, 10, 12 Reading words: 1, 2, 3, 4, 5 (pine, pin), 6, 7, 8, 9 (smile), 10 (fix), 11, 12 √: 1–12 Final–e rule review: 5 (pine, pin), 8, 9 (smile), 12 √: 8, 9, 12	Blending sounds into words: 1 (park), 10, 12 (kite), 13 (kit), 14 (steal) √: 1, 10, 12–14 Reading words: 1 (park), 2, 3, 4, 5, 6, 7, 8 (robber), 9 (running), 10, 11, 12 (kite), 13 (kit), 14 (steal), 15 √: 1–15 Final–e rule review: 4, 7, 10, 12 (kite) √: 4, 7, 10, 12 Two-part words: 8 (robber), 9 (running) √: 8, 9
		Reading words: 18 Connected text: 19, 20 √: 19, 20	Reading words: 14 Connected text: 15, 16 √: 15, 16	Reading words: 11 Connected text: 12, 13 √: 12, 13	Reading words: 13 Connected text: 14, 15 √: 14, 15	Reading words: 16 Connected text: 17, 18 √: 17, 18
Fluency		Reading words: 1–17 √: 1–17	Reading words: 1, 3–13 √: 1, 3–13	Reading words: 1–10 √: 1–10	Reading words: 1–12 √: 1–12	Reading words: 1–15 √: 1–15
		Repeated reading: 20 √	Repeated reading: 16 √	Repeated reading: 13 √	Repeated reading: 15 √	Repeated reading: 18 √ IC: 21
Comprehension		Identifying literal cause/effect: 20 Noting details: 20, 21 Inferring cause and effect: 20, 21 Inferring story details/events: 20 Determining character emotions: 21 Making connections: 21	Recalling details: 15, 16 Inferring story details/events: 16, 17 Noting details: 16, 17 Inferring cause/effect: 16 Interpreting character actions: 16, 17 Making predictions: 16, 17 Determining/interpreting character emotions: 17	Recalling details: 12, 13 Noting details: 13, 14 Inferring cause/effect: 13, 14 Interpreting character motives: 13 Determining character emotions: 14 Making connections: 14	Noting details: 15, 16 Interpreting character actions: 15 Activating prior knowledge: 15 Interpreting character actions: 16	Noting details: 18, 19 Interpreting character motives/ actions: 18, 19 Inferring story details/events: 18 Inferring cause/effect: 18 Making predictions: 18
		Recalling details: 23 Following directions: 24, 26 Noting details: 25	Recalling details: 19 Following directions: 20, 22 Noting details: 21 Inferring cause/effect: 21	Recalling details: 16 Following directions: 17, 19 Noting details: 18 Drawing inferences: 18	Recalling details: 18 Following directions: 19, 20 Noting details: 20 Inferring cause/effect: 20	Recalling details: 20 Following directions: 20 Noting details: 20 Lesson 60 Curriculum-Based Assessment
Spelling		Phonograms review: 1, 2 Segmentation review: 2	Phonograms review: 1, 2, 3 Segmentation review: 2, 3	Phonograms review: 1, 2 Segmentation review: 2	Phonograms review: 1, 2 Segmentation review: 2	Phonograms review: 1, 2, 3 Segmentation review: 2, 3
		Writing sounds: 1 Writing words: 2, 3 Writing sentences: 4	Writing sounds: 1 Writing words: 2, 3, 4 Writing sentences: 5	Writing sounds: 1 Writing words: 2, 3 Writing sentences: 4	Writing sounds: 1 Writing words: 2, 3 Writing sentences: 4	Writing sounds: 1 Writing words: 2, 3, 4 Writing sentences: 5

	Lesson 61	Lesson 62	Lesson 63	Lesson 64	Lesson 65
Spelling	Writing sounds: 1 Writing words: 2, 3, 4 Writing sentences: 5	Writing sounds: 1 Writing words: 2, 3, 4 Writing sentences: 5	Writing sounds: 1 Writing words: 2, 3, 4, 5 Writing sentences: 6	Writing words: 1, 2, 3 Writing sentences: 4	Writing words: 1, 2 Writing sentences: 3
	Phonogram review: 1, 2, 3 Segmentation review: 2, 3	Phonogram review: 1, 2, 3 Segmentation review: 2, 3	Phonogram review: 1, 2, 3, 4 Segmentation review: 2, 3, 4	Phonogram review: 1, 2 Segmentation review: 1, 2	Phonogram review: 1 Segmentation review: 1
Comprehension	Predicting narrative outcomes: 18, 19 Answering literal questions about a text: 18 Interpreting a character's feelings: 19 Inferring causes and effects: 18 Noting details: 18, 19 Drawing inferences: 19 Interpreting a character's feelings: 21 Recalling details: 23 Noting details: 20 Following written directions: 20 Answering literal questions about a text: 24	Predicting narrative outcomes: 18, 19 Answering literal questions about a text: 17 Following directions: 18 Inferring causes and effects: 18 Noting details: 17, 18 Recalling details: 21 Noting details: 19 Following written directions: 22 Answering literal questions about a text: 23	Predicting narrative outcomes: 17, 18 Answering literal questions about a text: 18, 19 Interpreting a character's motives: 17 Inferring causes and effects: 18 Inferring story details and events: 18, 19 Recalling details: 21 Noting details: 23 Following written directions: 22 Answering literal questions about a text: 24	Predicting narrative outcomes: 17, 18 Answering literal questions about a text: 17, 18 Interpreting a character's feelings: 17, 18 Inferring story details and events: 17 Inferring causes and effects: 18 Noting details: 18 Drawing inferences: 17 Recalling details: 20 Noting details: 22 Following written directions: 21 Answering literal questions about a text: 23	Predicting narrative outcomes: 19 Answering literal questions about a text: 19, 20 Interpreting a character's feelings: 20 Inferring causes and effects: 20 Inferring story details and events: 19, 20 Noting details: 20 Recalling details: 21 Following written directions: 21 Answering literal questions about a text: 21
Fluency	Reading words: 1–15 √: 1–15 Repeated reading: 18 √	Reading words: 2–14 √: 2–14 Repeated reading: 17 √	Reading words: 2–15 √: 2–15 Repeated reading: 18 √	Reading words: 2–14 √: 2–14 Repeated reading: 17 √	Reading words: 2–16 √: 2–16 Repeated reading: 19 √ IC: 65
Phonics and Word Recognition — Regular	Blending sounds into words: 2, 3 (**bending**), 4, 9 √: 2–4, 9–11 Reading words: 1, 2, 3 (**bending**), 4, 5, 6 (**bit**), 7 (**sharp**), 10, 11 Final -e rule review: 5, 11, 12, 13 (**save**), 14, 15 (**hugged**) √: 5, 11–13 Two-part words: 14 √ Reading words: 16 Connected text: 17, 18 √: 17, 18	Blending sounds into words: 2, 3 (**string**), 9 (**starts**) √: 2–4, 9 Reading words: 2, 3, 4 (**string**), 5 (**fate**), 6, 7, 8 (**wind**), 9 (**starts**), 10, 11, 12, 13 (**kites**), 14 Final -e rule review: 12 √ (**paper, we'll**) √: 2–13 Two-part words: 13 (**kites**) √ Reading words: 15 Connected text: 16, 17 √: 16, 17	Blending sounds into words: 8, 9, 10, 11 (**lifted**) √: 8–11 Reading words: 2, 3 (**five**), 4, 5 (**no, go, shake**), 8, 9, 10, 11 (**lifted**), 12 (**landed**), 13, 14 Final -e rule review: 3 (**five**), 4 √: 3, 4 Two-part words: 12 (**landed**), 13, 14 √: 12–14 Reading words: 16 Connected text: 17, 18 √: 17, 18	Blending sounds into words: 3, 5 (**happened**), 6 (**proud**), 7 (**darker**), 9 (**thunder**) √: 3, 5, 6, 7, 9 Reading words: 2 (**Tim**), 3, 5 (**happened**), 6 (**proud**), 7 (**darker**), 9 (**thunder**), 13, 14 (**blowing, maker, making, shaking**), 15, 16 √: 2–5, 8–16 Final -e rule review: 13 (**thunder**), 13, 14 (**makes**) Two-part words: 12 (**makes**) √ Reading words: 15 Connected text: 16, 17 √: 16, 17	Blending sounds into words: 9 (**sadder**), 12 (**trapped**), 13, 14 (**float**), 15 √: 9, 12–15 Reading words: 3 (**Sam**), 3 (**fire**), 4 (**while**), 5 (**makes**), 9 (**forest**), 15, 16 Final -e rule review: 3 (**fire**), 4 (**while**) √: 2–5, 8–16 Two-part words: 8 (**forest**) √: 8 Reading words: 17 Connected text: 18, 19 √: 18, 19
Phonics and Word Recognition — Irregular		Reading words: 14 (**wood, you'll**) √	Blending sounds into words: 6 (**know**), 7 (**again**) √: 6, 7	Blending sounds into words: 4 (**pretty**), 11 (**two**) √: 4, 11	Two-part words: 6 (**someone**), 7 (**today**) √: 6, 7
Letter Sound Correspondence	Review: 9 (**ar**), 10 (**al**) √: 9–10	Review: 1 (al, ou, ar), 9 (ar), 10 (ou), 11 (al) √: 9–11	Review: 1 (ar, ou, al), 8 (ou), 9 (ar) √: 1, 8, 9	Review: 1 (ar, ou, al), 6 (ou), 7 (ar), 10 (al) √: 1, 6, 7, 10	Review: 1 (ou, al, ar), 11 (al), 15 (ar), 16 (ou) √: 1, 11, 15, 16
Print Awareness					
Phonemic Awareness					

Key: (for Teachers)   √ = informal assessment   Numbers = exercise numbers   Bold face type = first appearance

Reading Mastery Signature Edition, Grade 1

Key: (for Teachers) √ = informal assessment   Numbers = exercise numbers   Bold face type = first appearance

		Lesson 66	Lesson 67	Lesson 68	Lesson 69	Lesson 70
Phonemic Awareness						
Print Awareness						
Letter Sound Correspondence		Review: 1 (ar. al. ou), 3 (al), 4 (ou), 5 (ar) √: 1, 3, 4, 5	Review: 11 (th) √: 11	Review: 3 (ou), 9 (th) √: 3, 9	Review: 7 (ar), 8 (ou) √: 7, 8	
Phonics and Word Recognition	Irregular	Blending sounds into words: 6 (**first**), 7 (**water**), 13 (**woman**) √: 6, 7, 13 Reading words: 9 (**shook**), 17 (**tv**) √: 9, 17	Blending sounds into words: 1 (**school**) √: 1 Two-part words: 12 (**anything**) √: 12	Blending sounds into words: 8 (**front**) √: 8		
	Regular	Blending sounds into words: 8 (**floated**) √: 8 Reading words: 2 (**hat, hate**), 3, 4, 5, 8 (**floated**), 9 (**plane, soaked**), 10, 11 (**fires**), 12 (**became**), 14 (**scare**), 15 (**wade**), 16 (**wading, or**) √: 2–5, 8, 10–12, 14–16 Final –e rule review: 15 (**wade**) √: 15 Two-part words: 10, 11 (**fires**), 12 (**became**) √: 10–12 Onset rime: 14 (**scare**) √: 14	Blending sounds into words: 4 (**bear**), 5 (**train**), 6 (**hundred**), 7 (**beans, meat, fifty, hunting**) √: 4–7 Reading words: 2 (**gave**), 3, 4 (**bear**), 5 (**train**), 6 (**hundred**), 7 (**beans, meat, fifty, hunting**), 8 (**pile**), 9, 10, 11 √: 2–11 Final –e rule review: 2 (**gave**) √: 2 Two-part words: 9, 10 √: 9, 10	Blending sounds into words: 3 (**counted**) √: 3 Reading words: 1 (**everything**), 2, 3 (**counted**), 4 (**counter**), 5, 6 (**home, nine, standing, tracks**), 7 (**missing, sandy**), 9 √: 1–7, 9 Two-part words: 1 (**everything**), 2, 4 (**counter**) √: 1, 2, 4	Blending sounds into words: 7 (**parked**), 11 √: 7, 11 Reading words: 1 (**Sid**), 2, 3, 4, 5, 6 (**ninety**), 7 (**parked**), 8, 9, 10, 11, 12 √: 1–12 Final –e rule review: 5 √: 5 Two-part words: 2, 3, 4 √: 2, 3, 4	Blending sounds into words: 8 (**rail**) √: 8 Reading words: 1, 2, 3, 4 (**followed, shed, sets**), 5, 6, 7, 8 (**rail**) √: 1–8 Two-part words: 5, 6 √: 5, 6 Onset rime: 7 √: 7
		Reading words: 18 Connected text: 19, 20 √: 19, 20	Reading words: 13 Connected text: 14, 15 √: 14, 15	Reading words: 10 Connected text: 11, 12 √: 11, 12	Reading words: 13 Connected text: 14, 15 √: 14, 15	Reading words: 9 Connected text: 10, 11 √: 10, 11
Fluency		Reading words: 2–17 √: 2–17	Reading words: 1–12 √: 1–12	Reading words: 1–9 √: 1–9	Reading words: 1–12 √: 1–12	Reading words: 1–8 √: 1–8
		Repeated reading: 20 √	Repeated reading: 15 √	Repeated reading: 12 √	Repeated reading: 15 √	Repeated reading: 11 √
						IC: 70
Comprehension		Answering literal questions about a text: 20, 21 Predicting narrative outcomes: 20 Inferring story details and events: 20 Interpreting a character's feelings: 21 Inferring causes and effects: 20, 21 Interpreting a character's motives: 20 Recalling details: 20 Noting details: 20	Answering literal questions about a text: 15 Predicting narrative outcomes: 15, 16 Inferring story details and events: 15 Interpreting a character's feelings: 15 Interpreting a character's motives: 15 Recalling details: 16 Noting details: 16	Answering literal questions about a text: 12,13 Following directions: 13 Predicting narrative outcomes: 13 Inferring story details and events: 13 Activating prior knowledge: 12 Recalling details: 13 Drawing inferences: 12	Answering literal questions about a text: 14, 15 Inferring story details and events: 15, 16 Recalling details: 14, 15, 16 Noting details: 16	Answering literal questions about a text: 11 Following directions: 11 Predicting narrative outcomes: 11, 12 Inferring story details and events: 11 Interpreting a character's feelings: 11 Inferring causes and effects: 12 Noting details: 12
		Recalling details: 23 Following written directions: 24 Noting details: 26 Answering literal questions about a text: 25	Recalling details: 18 Following written directions: 19 Noting details: 20 Answering literal questions about a text: 20, 21	Recalling details: 15 Following written directions: 16 Noting details: 17 Answering literal questions about a text: 18	Recalling details: 18 Following written directions: 19 Noting details: 20 Answering literal questions about a text: 21	Recalling details: 13 Following written directions: 13 Noting details: 13 Answering literal questions about a text: 13
Spelling		Phonogram review: 1, 2 Segmentation review: 2	Phonogram review: 1, 2, 3 Segmentation review: 2, 3	Phonogram review: 1, 2, 3 Segmentation review: 2, 3	Phonogram review: 1, 2, 3 Segmentation review: 2, 3	Phonogram review: 1, 2, 3 Segmentation review: 2, 3
						Writing sounds: 1 Writing words: 2, 3, 4 Writing sentences: 5
		Writing sounds: 1 Writing words: 2, 3 Writing sentences: 4	Writing sounds: 1 Writing words: 2, 3, 4 Writing sentences: 5	Writing sounds: 1 Writing words: 2, 3, 4 Writing sentences: 5	Writing sounds: 1 Writing words: 2, 3, 4 Writing sentences: 5	

Reading Mastery Signature Edition, Grade 1

Category		Lesson 71	Lesson 72	Lesson 73	Lesson 74	Lesson 75
Spelling		Writing sounds: 1 / Writing words: 2, 3 / Writing sentences: 4	Writing sounds: 1 / Writing words: 2, 3 / Writing sentences: 4	Writing sounds: 1 / Writing words: 2, 3 / Writing sentences: 4	Writing words: 1, 2 / Writing sentences: 3	Writing words: 1, 2 / Writing sentences: 3
		Phonogram review: 1, 2 / Segmentation review: 2	Phonogram review: 1, 2 / Segmentation review: 2	Phonogram review: 1, 2 / Segmentation review: 2	Phonogram review: 1 / Segmentation review: 1	Phonogram review: 1 / Segmentation review: 1
Comprehension		Answering literal questions about a text: 11 / Inferring story details and events: 11, 12 / Interpreting a character's feelings: 12 / Inferring causes and effects: 12 / Interpreting a character's motives: 11 / Noting details: 12 / Activating prior knowledge: 11 / Recalling details: 14 / Following written directions: 15 / Answering literal questions about a text: 17	Answering literal questions about a text: 12 / Inferring story details and events: 12, 13 / Predicting narrative outcomes: 12, 13 / Noting details: 12 / Recalling details: 13 / Noting details: 17 / Recalling details: 15 / Following written directions: 16 / Answering literal questions about a text: 18	Answering literal questions about a text: 10 / Inferring story details and events: 11 / Recalling details: 10 / Interpreting a character's motives: 10 / Noting details: 17 / Recalling details: 12 / Following written directions: 12 / Answering literal questions about a text: 12	Answering literal questions about a text: 13 / Following directions: 13 / Predicting narrative outcomes: 13 / Inferring story details and events: 14 / Interpreting a character's thoughts/feelings: 14 / Interpreting a character's motives: 13 / Recalling details: 13 / Noting details: 14 / Recalling details: 16 / Following written directions: 16 / Answering literal questions about a text: 16	Answering literal questions about a text: 10 / Predicting narrative outcomes: 10, 11 / Interpreting a character's motives: 10 / Noting details: 11 / Activating prior knowledge: 10 / Drawing inferences: 10 / Recalling details: 12 / Following written directions: 12 / Answering literal questions about a text: 12
Fluency		Reading words: 1–8 √: 1–8 / Repeated reading: 11 √	Reading words: 1–9 √: 1–9 / Repeated reading: 12 √	Reading words: 1–7 √: 1–7 / Repeated reading: 10 √	Reading words: 1–10 √: 1–10 / Repeated reading: 13 √	Reading words: 1–7 √: 1–7 / Repeated reading: 10 √ / IC: 75
Phonics and Word Recognition	Regular	Blending sounds into words: 5 (truck), 6 (waited), 7 √: 5, 6, 7 / Reading words: 1, 2, 3, 4, 5 (truck), 6 (waited), 7 √: 1–8 / Two-part words: 2, 3, 4 √: 2, 3, 4 / 7, 8 (seem, load) √: 1–9 / Reading words: 9 √: 10, 11 / Connected text: 10, 11 √: 10, 11	Blending sounds into words: 2, 3 (sorry), 4 (lied), 5 (scared) √: 2–5 / Reading words: 1, 2, 3 (sorry), 4 (lied), 5, 6, 7 √: 1–9 / Two-part words: 6, 7 (scared) √: 6, 7 / Reading words: 10 √: 11, 12 / Connected text: 11, 12 √: 11, 12	Blending sounds into words: 4 (easy), 5 (check) √: 4, 5 / Reading words: 1 (dish, wishing), 2, 3 (that's), 4, 5 (easy), 6, 7 (tar) √: 1–7 / Reading words: 8 √: 9, 10 / Connected text: 9, 10 √: 9, 10	Blending sounds into words: 3, 4 (lying), 5 (loading) √: 3–5 / Reading words: 1 (shop, she's), 3, 4 (lying), 5 / 6, 7, 8, 9, 10 (mean, mark, near) √: 1, 3–10 / Two-part words: 8, 9 √: 8, 9 / Reading words: 11 √: 12, 13 / Connected text: 12, 13 √: 12, 13	Blending sounds into words: 1, 2, 3, 6 √: 1–3, 6 / Reading words: 1, 2, 3, 4 (showed), 5 (gift, finding, leaving, I've), 6, 7 √: 1–7 / Reading words: 8 / Connected text: 9, 10
	Irregular	Reading words: 8 (crooks) √: 8		Reading words: 3 (says) √: 3	Blending sounds into words: 2 (their) √: 2 / Reading words: 10 (what's) √: 10	
Letter Sound Correspondence			Review: 1 (sh) √: 1	Review: 1 (sh), 6 (al), 7 (ar) √: 1, 6, 7	Review: 1 (sh), 6 (ou), 7 (al) √: 1, 6, 7	
Print Awareness						
Phonemic Awareness						

Key: (for Teachers)   √= informal assessment   Numbers = exercise numbers   Bold face type = first appearance

		Lesson 76	Lesson 77	Lesson 78	Lesson 79	Lesson 80
Phonemic Awareness						
Print Awareness						
Letter Sound Correspondence		Review: 2 (ing), 3 (ar) √: 2, 3	Review: 1 (ing), 7 (ar) √: 1, 7	Review: 8 (ing), 9 (ar) √: 8–9		Review: 6 (al), 7 (ar), 8 (ou), 9 (ou) √: 6–9
Phonics and Word Recognition	**Irregular**		Reading words: 9 (**worked**) √: 9	Blending sounds into words: 7 (**done**) √: 7		Blending sounds into words: 4 (**ice**), 11 (**close**) √: 4, 11 Reading words: 12 (**closed**) √: 12
	Regular	Blending sounds into words: 1, 3 (**parts**) √: 1, 3 Reading words: 1, 2, 3 (**parts**), 4, 5 (**else**), 6 √: 1–6 Final –e rule review: 4 √: 4	Blending sounds into words: 2 (**tent**), 3, 4, 5 (**mixed**), 6 (**job**), 7 √: 2–7 Reading words: 1, 2 (**tent**), 3, 4, 5 (**mixed**) 6 (**job**), 7, 8 (**care**), 9 √: 1–9	Blending sounds into words: 2, 3, 4, 5 √: 2–5 Reading words: 1, 2, 3, 4, 5, 6 (**passed**), 8 (**thing**), 9, 10, 11 √: 1–6, 8–11 Two-part word: 11 (**everybody**) √: 11	Blending sounds into words: 1 (**stuck**), 2, 3 (**colder, snow**) √: 1–3 Reading words: 1 (**stuck**), 2, 3 (**colder, snow**), 4, 5, 6, 7 (**slipped**), 8, 9, 10 (**ears, window, show, deep**) √: 1–10 Two-part words: 5, 6, 7 (**slipped**), 8, 9 √: 5–9	Blending sounds into words: 1 (**drink**), 2 (**sly**), 5 (**cream**), 6, 7, 8 (**mouth**) √: 1, 2, 5–8 Reading words: 1 (**drink**), 2 (**sly**), 3 (**con, cone**), 5 (**cream**), 6, 7, 8 (**mouth**), 9, 10, 12 (**giving, conned, cool**) √: 1–3, 5–10, 12
		Reading words: 7 Connected text: 8, 9 √: 8, 9	Reading words: 10 Connected text: 11, 12 √: 11, 12	Reading words: 12 Connected text: 13, 14 √: 13, 14	Reading words: 11 Connected text: 12, 13 √: 12, 13	Reading words: 13 Connected text: 14, 15 √: 14, 15
Fluency		Reading words: 1–6	Reading words: 1–9	Reading words: 1–11 √: 1–11	Reading words: 1–10 √: 1–10	Reading words: 1–12 √: 1–12
		Repeated reading: 9 √: 9	Repeated reading: 12 √	Repeated reading: 14 √	Repeated reading: 13 √	Repeated reading: 15 √
						IC: 80
Comprehension		Answering literal questions about text: 9 Predicting narrative outcomes: 9 Inferring story details and events: 9, 10 Inferring causes and effects: 9 Interpreting a character's motives: 10 Activating prior knowledge: 9 Following directions: 9 Noting details: 10	Answering literal questions about text: 12 Predicting narrative outcomes: 12 Inferring story details and events: 12 Interpreting a character's feelings: 12 Following directions: 13 Noting details: 13	Answering literal questions about text: 14 Predicting narrative outcomes: 15 Inferring story details and events: 14, 15 Recalling details: 14 Noting details: 15	Answering literal questions about text: 13 Inferring story details and events: 13 Interpreting a character's feelings: 13 Inferring causes and effects: 13 Activating prior knowledge: 14 Following directions: 13 Noting details: 14 Recalling details: 14	Answering literal questions about text: 15 Predicting narrative outcomes: 15 Interpreting a character's feelings: 16 Inferring causes and effects: 15 Interpreting a character's motives: 15 Following directions: 15 Noting details: 16
		Recalling details: 12 Following written directions: 13 Noting details: 14 Answering literal questions about text: 15	Recalling details: 15 Following written directions: 16 Noting details: 17 Answering literal questions about text: 18	Recalling details:17 Following written directions: 18 Noting details: 19 Answering literal questions about text: 20	Recalling details: 16 Following written directions: 17 Noting details: 18 Answering literal questions about text: 19	Recalling details: 17 Following written directions: 17 Noting details: 17 Answering literal questions about text: 17
						Lesson 80 Curriculum-Based Assessment
Spelling		Phonogram review: 1 Segmentation review: 1	Phonogram review: 1, 2 Segmentation review: 2	Phonogram review: 1, 2, 3 Segmentation review: 2, 3	Phonogram review: 1, 2, 3 Segmentation review: 2, 3	Phonogram review: 1, 2, 3 Segmentation review: 2, 3
		Writing words: 1, 2 Writing sentences: 3	Writing sounds: 1 Writing words: 2, 3 Writing sentences: 4	Writing sounds: 1 Writing words: 2, 3, 4 Writing sentences: 5	Writing sounds: 1 Writing words: 2, 3, 4 Writing sentences: 5	Writing sounds: 1 Writing words: 2, 3 Writing sentences: 4

Category		Lesson 81	Lesson 82	Lesson 83	Lesson 84	Lesson 85
Spelling		Writing sounds: 1 Writing words: 2, 3 Writing sentences: 4	Writing sounds: 1 Writing words: 2, 3 Writing sentences: 4	Writing sounds: 2 Writing word families: 2 Writing sentences: 4	Writing sounds: 1 Writing words: 3 Writing sentences: 4	Writing words: 3 Writing sentences: 4
		Phonogram review: 1, 2, 3 Segmentation review: 2, 3	Phonogram review: 1, 2 Segmentation review: 2	Phonogram review: 1, 2 Segmentation review: 2 Word families: 2	Phonogram review: 1, 2 Segmentation review: 2	Grapheme recognition: 1 √ Phoneme–grapheme correspondence: 2 √
Comprehension		Following directions: 9 Answering literal questions about a text: 11 Activating prior knowledge: 11, 12 Identifying literal cause and effect: 11 Recalling details and events: 11 Predicting narrative outcomes: 11, 12 Interpreting a character's motives: 11, 12 Noting details: 12 Recalling details: 13 Following written directions: 13 Answering literal questions about a text: 13 Noting details: 13	Following directions: 9 Answering literal questions about a text: 11, 12 Recalling details and events: 11 Predicting narrative outcomes: 12 Recalling details: 13 Following written directions: 13 Answering literal questions about a text: 13 Noting details: 13	Following directions: 10 Answering literal questions about a text: 12 Identifying literal cause and effect: 12 Recalling details and events: 12, 13 Predicting narrative outcomes: 13 Following directions: 13 Recalling details: 14 Following written directions: 14 Answering literal questions about a text: 14 Noting details: 14	Following directions: 9 Answering literal questions about a text: 10, 11 Identifying literal cause and effect: 10, 11 Recalling details and events: 10, 11 Predicting narrative outcomes: 10 Activating prior knowledge: 11 Recalling details: 12 Following written directions: 12 Answering literal questions about a text: 12 Noting details: 12 Interpreting a character's feelings: 12	Following directions: 10 Answering literal questions about a text: 11, 12 Recalling details and events: 11, 12 Predicting narrative outcomes: 11 Drawing inferences: 11 Activating prior knowledge: 12 Recalling details: 13 Following written directions: 13 Answering literal questions about a text: 13 Noting details: 13 Interpreting a character's feelings: 13
Fluency		Reading words: 2–7 √ Repeated reading: 11 √	Reading words: 2–7 √ Repeated reading: 11 √	Reading words: 4–8 √ Repeated reading: 12 √	Reading words: 3–7 √	Reading words: 5–8 √ IC: 85
Phonics and Word Recognition	Regular	Blending sounds into words: 6 (got) √: 6 Reading words: 2, 3, 4, 5 (super, plan, trick), 6 (got, fox), 7 (mop) √: 2–7 Underlined parts of words: 4 √: 4 Reading words: 8 Connected text: 10, 11 √: 10, 11	Blending sounds into words: 4 (gas) √: 4 Reading words: 2 (shoot) 3 (stairs, say), 4 (gas, saying) 5 (mopped, moppen) 6 (day) 7 (mop) √: 2–7 Underlined parts of words: 2, 5 (mopped, moppen) √: 2, 5 Reading words: 8 Connected text: 10, 11 √: 10, 11	Reading words: 4 (dark) 5 (tap) 6 (mopping, handed, tapped) 7 (broke, holes, dimes), 8 (times) √: 4–8 Underlined parts of words: 4 (dark), 6 (mopping, tapped) √: 4, 6 Reading words: 9 Connected text: 11, 12 √: 11, 12	Reading words: 3, 4 (tape, mess) 5 (hitting), 6 (smiles, hopped) 7 (pow) √: 3–7 Underlined parts of words: 3, 6 (smiles, hopped) √: 3, 6 Reading words: 8 Connected text: 10 √: 10	Reading words: 5 (crash, walls) 6 (heave, having), 7 (dive), 8 (crashed) √: 5–8 Underlined parts of words: 5 (crash, walls), 8 (crashed) √: 5, 8 Reading words: 9 Connected text: 11 √: 11
	Irregular	Reading words: 5 (buying, woods, somebody) √: 5	Reading words: 3 (continued), 5 (talked) √: 3, 5 Underlined parts of words: 5 (talked) √: 5	Reading words: 8 (answer) √: 8		
Letter Sound Correspondence		Introduction: 4 (ea) √: 4 Review: 4 (th, ar, ou)	Review: 2 (ea, oo, er, wh, ou) √: 2	Introduction: 4 (ee) √: 4 Review: 4 (wh, ar, al, th, ea)	Review: 3 (th, wh, al, ou, ar) √: 3	Review: 5 (sh, ou, wh, ar, al) √: 5
Print Awareness		Grapheme recognition: 6 (g)		Introduction to letter names: 1 (a – z) √: 2	Review letter names: 1 (a–z) √: 2	Review letter names: 1 (a–z), 3 (a–z) √: 2, 4
Phonemic Awareness						

Key: (for Teachers) √ = informal assessment   Numbers = exercise numbers   Bold face type = first appearance

		Lesson 86	Lesson 87	Lesson 88	Lesson 89	Lesson 90
Phonemic Awareness						
Print Awareness		Review letter names: 1 (a-z) √: 2	Introduction to capital letters: 1 (P, C, Y, F, W, K, I, Z, O, J, S, M, N, T, V, X, U)	Review capital letters: 1 (O, I, Z, V, P, J, N, T, C, U, M, F, Y, K, X, S, W)	Introduction to capital letters: 2 (A, R, D, E, Q) Review capital letters: 1 (T, K, N, J, Z, W, U, S, Y, C, P, I, F, X, O, V, M)	Review capital letters: 1 (R, E, A, D, Q)
Letter Sound Correspondence			Review: 4 (ea, al, ar, ch, oo) √: 4	Review: 4 (al, ea, th, wh, ou) √: 4	Review: 7 (ar, ing, er, ou, ee, wh) √: 7	Review: 6 (sh, ou, th) √: 6
Phonics and Word Recognition	Irregular	Reading words: 4 (said, nothing) √: 4 Spell by letter name: 4 (said, nothing) √: 4		Reading words: 3A (you), 5 (anybody) √: 3A, 5 Spell by letter name: 3B (you) √: 3B Underlined parts of words: 5 (anybody) √: 5		Reading words: 2 (words) √: 2
	Regular	Reading words: 3, 4, 5 (throw, men), 6 √: 3, 4, 5, 6 Spell by letter name: 3, 4 √: 3, 4 Underlined parts of words: 6 (throw, men) √: 6	Reading words: 2, 3 (long), 4 (cheek, tear), 5 (longer, nobody) √: 2, 3, 4, 5, 5 Spell by letter name: 2, 3 (long) √: 2, 3 Underlined parts of words: 4 (cheek, tear), 5 (longer, nobody) √: 4, 5	Reading words: 2 (fixed, carry, baby), 3A (moping), 3B (moping), 4, 5 (thanked) √: 2, 3, 4, 5 Spell by letter name: 2 (fixed, carry), 3B (moping) √: 2, 3B Underlined parts of words: 4, 5 (thanked) √: 4, 5	Reading words: 3 (nailed, most), 4A/B (diner), 5, 6 (moped), 7 (need) √: 3, 4, 5, 6, 7 Spell by letter name: 3 (nailed), 4B (taped, diner) √: 3, 4 Underlined parts of words: 6 (moped), 7 (need) √: 6, 7	Reading words: 2 (plants, boss, key), 3A/B (pinned, pined, send, sent), 4, 5 (plant, seed), 6 (sticks, packed) √: 2, 3, 4, 5, 6 Spell by letter names: 2 (plants, boss, key), 3B (pinned, pined, send, sent) √: 2, 3B Underlined parts of words: 6 (sticks, packed) √: 6
		Reading words: 7 Connected text: 9 √: 9	Reading words: 6 Connected text: 8 √: 8	Reading words: 6 Connected text: 8 √: 8	Reading words: 8 Connected text: 10 √: 10	Reading words: 7 Connected text: 9 √: 9
Fluency		Reading words: 3, 4, 5, 6 √: 3, 4, 5, 6	Reading words: 2, 3, 4, 5, 5 √: 2, 3, 4, 5, 5	Reading words: 2, 3, 4, 5 √: 2, 3, 4, 5	Reading words: 3, 4, 5, 6, 7 √: 3, 4, 5, 6, 7	Reading words: 2, 3, 4, 5, 6 √: 2, 3, 4, 5, 6
						Individual Checkout: 90
Comprehension		Following directions: 8	Following directions: 7	Following directions: 7	Following directions: 9	Following directions: 8
		Answering literal questions about a text: 9, 10 Identifying literal cause and effect: 9 Recalling details and events: 9 Predicting narrative outcomes: 9 Interpreting a character's feelings: 9 Following directions: 9 Drawing inferences: 9, 10	Answering literal questions about a text: 8 Identifying literal cause and effect: 8 Recalling details and events: 8 Predicting narrative outcomes: 8, 9 Interpreting a character's feelings: 8, 9 Drawing inferences: 8, 9	Answering literal questions about a text: 8 Identifying literal cause and effect: 8 Recalling details and events: 9 Predicting narrative outcomes: 8 Drawing inferences: 9	Answering literal questions about a text: 10 Identifying literal cause and effect: 10 Recalling details and events: 11 Predicting narrative outcomes: 10, 11 Drawing inferences: 10	Answering literal questions about a text: 9, 10 Identifying literal cause and effect: 9 Recalling details and events: 10 Predicting narrative outcomes: 9 Interpreting a character's feelings: 9 Following directions: 9 Drawing inferences: 9 Activating prior knowledge: 9
		Recalling details: 11 Following written directions: 11 Answering literal questions about a text: 11 Noting details: 11 Interpreting a character's feelings: 11	Recalling details: 10 Following written directions: 10 Answering literal questions about a text: 10 Noting details: 10 Interpreting a character's feelings: 10	Recalling details: 10 Following written directions: 10 Answering literal questions about a text: 10 Noting details: 10 Interpreting a character's feelings: 10	Recalling details: 12 Following written directions: 12 Answering literal questions about a text: 12 Noting details: 12 Interpreting a character's feelings: 12	Recalling details: 11 Following written directions: 11 Answering literal questions about a text: 11 Noting details: 11
Spelling		Grapheme recognition: 1 √ Phoneme-grapheme correspondence: 2 √ Phonogram review: 3 Segmentation review: 3	Grapheme recognition: 1 √ Phoneme-grapheme correspondence: 2 √	Grapheme recognition: 1 √ Phoneme-grapheme correspondence: 2 √	Grapheme recognition: 1 √ Phoneme-grapheme correspondence: 2 √	Grapheme recognition: 1 √ Phoneme-grapheme correspondence: 2 √
						Writing words: 3 Writing sentences: 4
		Writing words: 3 Writing sentences: 4	Writing words: 3 Writing sentences: 4	Writing words: 3 Writing sentences: 4	Writing words: 3 Writing sentences: 4	

Reading Mastery Signature Edition, Grade 1

Key: (for Teachers) √ = informal assessment   Numbers = exercise numbers   Bold face type = first appearance

		Lesson 91	Lesson 92	Lesson 93	Lesson 94	Lesson 95
Phonemic Awareness						
Print Awareness		Review capital letters: 1 (E, D, R, Q, A) Introduction to capital letters: 2 (B, L, H, G)	Review capital letters: 1 (H, L, G, B)	Review capital letters: 1 (D, B, H, L, R, Q, G, A, E)	Review capital letters: 1 (Q, G, R, E, B, L, A, H, D)	
Letter Sound Correspondence		Review: 7 (ou, al, er, wh, ing, ea) √: 7	Review: 6 (ou, ing, th, ar, wh, ou) √: 6	Review: 5 (ing, er, th, wh, ou) √: 5	Review: 3 (ea, ar, ou, ch, oo) √: 3	Review: 2 (al, ea, ou, ar, th, oo), 3 (al) √: 2, 3
Phonics and Word Recognition	Irregular		Reading words: 3 (**right**) √: 3 Spell by letter name: 3 (**right**) √: 3			Reading words: 1 (**early**), 2 (**schools**) √: 1, 2 Spell by letter name: 1 (**early**) √: 1 Underlined parts of words: 2 (**schools**) √: 2
	Regular	Reading words: 3 (**Now**), 4 (**oak, jail, jailer**), 5 (**cane**), 6 (**notes, canned, caned, seems**), 7 √: 3, 4, 5, 6, 7 Spell by letter name: 3 (**Now**), 4 (**oak, jail, jailer**) √: 3, 4 Underlined parts of words: 6 (**notes, canned, caned, seems**), 7 √: 6, 7	Reading words: 2 (**As, Have**), 3 (**slope**), 4A/B (**slop**), 5 (**noted, planted, dumped**), 6 (**swing, tossed**) √: 2, 3, 4, 5, 6 Spell by letter name: 2 (**As, Have**), 3 √: 2, 3 Underlined parts of words: 5 (**noted, planted, dumped**), 6 (**swing, tossed**) √: 5, 6	Reading words: 2 (**Let**), 3 (**swung**), 4 (**yelling**), 5 (**planting**) √: 2, 3, 4, 5 Spell by letter name: 2 (**Let**), 3 (**swung**) √: 2, 3 Underlined parts of words: 4 (**yelling**), 5 (**planting**) √: 4, 5	Reading words: 2 (**If, And**), 3 (**cheese, fool, leaves**), 4 (**hoped, canner**), 5 (**fixes, spent**), 6A (**tapping**), 6B (**teaches**) √: 2, 3, 4, 5, 6A, 6B Spell by letter name: 2 (**If, And**), 6B (**tapping, teaches**) √: 2, 6B Underlined parts of words: 3 (**cheese, fool, leaves**), 4 (**hoped, canner**) √: 3, 4	Reading words: 1 (**Ann, Dan, lucky**), 2 (**smart**), 3 4 (**spell**) √: 1, 2, 3, 4 Spell by letter name: 1 (**Ann, Dan, lucky**), 4 (**spell**) √: 1, 4 Underlined parts of words: 2 (**smart**), 3 √: 2, 3
		Reading words: 8 Connected text: 10 √: 10	Reading words: 7 Connected text: 9 √: 9	Reading words: 6 Connected text: 8 √: 8	Reading words: 7 Connected text: 9 √: 9	Connected text: 5 √: 5
Fluency		Reading words: 3, 4, 5, 6, 7 √: 3, 4, 5, 6, 7	Reading words: 2, 3, 4, 5, 6 √: 2, 3, 4, 5, 6	Reading words: 2, 3, 4, 5 √: 2, 3, 4, 5	Reading words: 2, 3, 4, 5, 6A, 6B √: 2, 3, 4, 5, 6A, 6B	Reading words: 1, 2, 3, 4 √: 1, 2, 3, 4
						Individual Checkout: 95
Comprehension		Following directions: 9	Following directions: 8	Following directions: 7	Following directions: 8	
		Answering literal questions about a text: 10, 11 Identifying literal cause and effect: 10 Recalling details and events: 10 Predicting narrative outcomes: 10, 11 Following directions: 11 Drawing inferences: 10	Answering literal questions about a text: 9, 10 Identifying literal cause and effect: 10 Recalling details and events: 9, 10 Predicting narrative outcomes: 9 Interpreting a character's feelings: 9 Following directions: 10 Activating prior knowledge: 9	Answering literal questions about a text: 8, 9 Identifying literal cause and effect: 8 Recalling details and events: 8 Predicting narrative outcomes: 8, 9 Interpreting a character's feelings: 9 Drawing inferences: 8	Answering literal questions about a text: 9 Identifying literal cause and effect: 9 Recalling details and events: 9 Interpreting a character's feelings: 10 Following directions: 10 Drawing inferences: 9, 10	Answering literal questions about a text: 5, 6 Recalling details and events: 5, 6 Predicting narrative outcomes: 5 Following directions: 6 Drawing inferences: 5, 6
		Recalling details: 12 Following written directions: 12 Answering literal questions about a text: 12 Noting details: 12	Recalling details: 11 Following written directions: 11 Answering literal questions about a text: 11 Noting details: 11	Recalling details: 10 Following written directions: 10 Answering literal questions about a text: 10 Noting details: 10 Interpreting a character's feelings: 10	Recalling details: 11 Following written directions: 11 Answering literal questions about a text: 11 Noting details: 11 Interpreting a character's feelings: 11	Recalling details: 8 Following written directions: 8 Answering literal questions about a text: 8 Using rules to classify objects: 7
Spelling		Phoneme-grapheme correspondence: 1 √ Phonemic segmentation: 2 √: 2 Spelling words: 3 √	Phoneme-grapheme correspondence: 1 Phonemic segmentation: 2 √: 2 Spelling words: 3 √	Phoneme-grapheme correspondence: 1 Phonemic segmentation: 2 √: 2 Spelling words: 3 √	Answering literal questions about a text: 5, 6 Recalling details and events: 5, 6 Predicting narrative outcomes: 5 Following directions: 6 Drawing inferences: 5, 6	Spelling words: 2, 3 √: 2
						Word copying: 1 Phoneme-grapheme correspondence: 1 Writing words: 3
		Writing sentences: 4	Word copying: 1 Phoneme-grapheme correspondence: 1 Writing sentences: 4	Word copying: 1 Phoneme-grapheme correspondence: 1 Writing sentences: 4	Phoneme-grapheme correspondence: 1 Writing sentences: 4	

Reading Mastery Signature Edition, Grade 1

Key: (for Teachers)   √ = informal assessment   Numbers = exercise numbers   Bold face type = first appearance

		Lesson 96	Lesson 97	Lesson 98	Lesson 99	Lesson 100
Phonemic Awareness						
Print Awareness						
Letter Sound Correspondence			Review: 2 (ing, sh, ch, ar) √: 2	Review: 2 (sh, al, th, ea, oo), 3 (ing) √: 2, 3	Review: 2 (ea, wh, th, al, er) √: 2	
Phonics and Word Recognition	Irregular			Reading words: 1 (question), 3 (You're) √: 1, 3 Spell by letter name: 1 (question) √: 1 Underlined parts of words: 3 (you're) √: 3	Reading words: 1 (grew) √: 1 Spell by letter name: 1 (grew) √: 1	Reading words: 1 (None, friend, swan), 3 (become) √: 1, 3 Spell by letter name: 1 (None, friend, swan) √: 1
	Regular	Reading words: 1 (Helper), 2 (hopping, wagged, boys), 3 (begin, tone, tame), 4 (tiger, seat) √: 1, 2, 3, 4 Spell by letter name: 1 (Helper), 4 (tiger, seat) √: 1, 4 Underlined parts of words: 2 (hopping, wagged, boys) √: 2	Reading words: 1 (wait), 2 (stones, cash), 3, 4 (hoping) √: 1, 2, 3, 4 Spell by letter name: 1 (wait), 4 (hoping) √: 1, 4 Underlined parts of words: 2 (stones, cash)	Reading words: 1, 2, 3, 4, 5 √: 1, 2, 3, 4, 5 Spell by letter name: 5 √: 5 Underlined parts of words: 2, 3 √: 2, 3	Reading words: 1 (hatched), 2 (leap, which), 3, 4 (wig) √: 1, 2, 3, 4 Spell by letter name: 1 (hatched), 4 (wig) √: 1, 4 Underlined parts of words: 2 (leap, which), 3 √: 2, 3	Reading words: 1 (Title, Ugly, grown), 2 (names, duckling), 3 (hello, egg), 4 √: 1, 2, 3, 4 Spell by letter name: 1 (Title, Ugly, grown), 4 (pals) √: 1, 4 Underlined parts of words: 2 (names, duckling) √: 2
		Connected text: 5 √: 5	Connected text: 5	Connected text: 6 √: 6	Connected text: 5 √: 5	Connected text: 5 √: 5
Fluency		Reading words: 1, 2, 3, 4 √: 1, 2, 3, 4	Reading words: 1, 2, 3, 4 √: 1, 2, 3, 4	Reading words: 1, 2, 3, 4, 5 √: 1, 2, 3, 4, 5	Reading words: 1, 2, 3, 4 √: 1, 2, 3, 4	Reading words: 1, 2, 3, 4 √: 1, 2, 3, 4
						Individual Checkout: 100
Comprehension		Answering literal questions about a text: 5, 6 Identifying literal cause and effect: 5 Interpreting a character's feelings: 5, 6 Drawing inferences: 5	Answering literal questions about a text: 5, 6 Recalling details and events: 5 Predicting narrative outcomes: 5, 6 Following directions: 6 Drawing inferences: 5, 6 Activating prior knowledge: 5	Answering literal questions about a text: 6, 7 Recalling details and events: 6 Predicting narrative outcomes: 6	Answering literal questions about a text: 5, 6 Identifying literal cause and effect: 5 Predicting narrative outcomes: 5, 6 Interpreting a character's feelings: 5, 6 Drawing inferences: 5, 6 Activating prior knowledge: 5	Answering literal questions about a text: 5, 6 Identifying literal cause and effect: 5 Recalling details and events: 5 Predicting narrative outcomes: 5, 6 Interpreting a character's feelings: 5 Following directions: 6 Drawing inferences: 5, 6 Activating prior knowledge: 5
		Recalling details: 8 Following written directions: 8 Answering literal questions about a text: 8 Interpreting a character's feelings: 8 Using rules to classify objects: 7	Recalling details: 8 Following written directions: 8 Answering literal questions about a text: 8 Noting details: 8 Using rules to classify objects: 7	Recalling details: 9 Following written directions: 9 Answering literal questions about a text: 9 Using rules to classify objects: 8	Recalling details: 8 Following written directions: 8 Answering literal questions about a text: 8 Using rules to classify objects: 7	Recalling details: 7 Following written directions: 7 Answering literal questions about a text: 7 Using rules to classify objects: 7
						Lesson 100 Curriculum-Based Assessment
Spelling		Phonemic segmentation: 1 √: 1 Spelling words: 2, 3 √: 3	Spelling words: 2, 3	Phonemic segmentation: 1 √: 1 Spelling words: 2, 3	Identifying spelled words: 1 Spelling words: 2, 3	Identifying spelled words: 1 Spelling words: 2, 3
		Writing words: 3	Word copying: 1 Phoneme-grapheme correspondence: 1 Sentence copying: 2 Writing words: 3	Writing words: 3	Sentence copying: 2 Phoneme-grapheme correspondence: 2 Writing words: 3	Sentence copying: 2 Phoneme-grapheme correspondence: 2 Writing words: 3

	Lesson 101	Lesson 102	Lesson 103	Lesson 104	Lesson 105
Spelling	Sentence copying: 2 Phoneme–grapheme correspondence: 2 Writing words: 3 Identifying spelled words: 1 Spelling words: 2, 3	Writing sentences: 2 Writing words: 3 Patterns: 1 √ Spelling words: 1, 3	Writing words: 3 Patterns: 1 √ Spelling words: 1, 2, 3	Writing words: 3 Identifying spelled words: 1 Spelling words: 1	Phoneme–grapheme correspondence: 1 Word copying: 1 Writing words: 3 Spelling words: 2, 3
Comprehension	Using rules to classify objects: 8 Answering literal questions about a text: 8 Following written directions: 8 Recalling details: 7, 8 Drawing inferences: 5, 6 Interpreting a character's feelings: 5, 6 Predicting narrative outcomes: 5 Recalling details and events: 5 Identifying literal cause and effect: 5 Answering literal questions about a text: 5, 6	Using rules to classify objects: 8 Answering literal questions about a text: 8 Following written directions: 7, 8 Recalling details: 7, 8 Activating prior knowledge: 6 Drawing inferences: 5, 6 Interpreting a character's motives: 6 Interpreting a character's feelings: 5 Predicting narrative outcomes: 5 Recalling details and events: 5 Answering literal questions about a text: 5, 6	Using rules to classify objects: 7 Answering literal questions about a text: 8 Following written directions: 7 Recalling details: 8 Drawing inferences: 6 Following directions: 5, 6 Predicting narrative outcomes: 5, 6 Recalling details and events: 5 Identifying literal cause and effect: 5 Answering literal questions about a text: 5, 6	Using rules to classify objects: 8 Answering literal questions about a text: 8 Following written directions: 8 Recalling details: 8 Drawing inferences: 7 Interpreting a character's motives: 6 Predicting narrative outcomes: 6 Recalling details and events: 6 Answering literal questions about a text: 6, 7	Using rules to classify objects: 7 Answering literal questions about a text: 7 Following written directions: 7 Recalling details: 8 Activating prior knowledge: 5 Drawing inferences: 5, 6 Interpreting a character's feelings: 5 Predicting narrative outcomes: 5 Recalling details and events: 5 Identifying literal cause and effect: 5 Answering literal questions about a text: 5, 6
Fluency	Reading words: 1–4 √: 1–4	Reading words: 1–4 √: 1–4	Reading words: 1–4 √: 1–4	Reading words: 1–5 √: 1–5	IC: 105 Reading words: 1–4 √: 1–4
Phonics and Word Recognition — Regular	Reading words: 1 (nest, lunch, bowl, kitten), 2 (reach), 3 (eat, needs, wet), 4 √: 1–4 Spell by letter name: 1 (nest, lunch, bowl, kitten), 4 √: 1–4 Underlined parts of words: 2 (reach) √: 2 Connected text: 5 √: 5	Reading words: 1 (milk, king, sheep), 2 (bald, bean), 3 (homes), 4 (arms, kittens) √: 1, 3 Spell by letter name: 1 (milk, king, sheep), 3 (homes), 4 (arms, kittens) √: 2, 4 Underlined parts of words: 2 (bald, bean), 4 (arms, kittens) Connected text: 5 √: 5	Reading words: 1 (Boo), 2 (horses, tricks), 3 √: 1–4 Spell by letter name: 1 (Boo), 4 (games) √: 1–4 Underlined parts of words: 2 (horses, tricks) √: 2 Connected text: 5 √: 5	Reading words: 1 (cast, castle, monster, green, frog), 2 (biggest, planning), 3, 4, 5 √: 1–5 Spell by letter name: 1 (cast, castle, monster, shopping), 5 (shopping) √: 1, 5 Underlined parts of words: 3 √: 3 Connected text: 6 √: 6	Reading words: 1 (tickle, toad, howling), 2 (bead), 3 (stays), 4 (robed, robbed) √: 1–4 Spell by letter name: 1 (tickle, toad, howling), 4 (robed, robbed) √: 1–4 Underlined parts of words: 3 (stays) √: 3 Connected text: 5 √: 5
Phonics and Word Recognition — Irregular	Reading words: 1 (new) √: 1 Spell by letter name: 1 (new) √: 1	Reading words: 1 (people, ghost, laugh) √: 1 Spell by letter name: 1 (people, ghost, laugh) √: 1	Reading words: 2 (sometimes), 4 (night) √: 2 Underlined parts of words: 2 (sometimes) √: 2 Spell by letter name: 4 (night) √: 4	Reading words: 1 (turned, watched), 2 (laughing) √: 1, 2 Spell by letter name: 1 (turned, watched) √: 1	Reading words: 1 (animal, turn) √: 1 Spell by letter name: 1 (animal) √: 1, 2
Letter Sound Correspondence	Review: 2 (ar, ou, wh, ch, ing, ea) √: 2	Review: 2 (al, ar, ou, ea, wh), 4 (ea) √: 2, 4	Review: 2 (ea) √: 2	Review: 3 (wh, th, ea, ou, ing) √: 3	Review: 3 (al, ing) √: 3
Print Awareness					
Phonemic Awareness					

Reading Mastery Signature Edition, Grade 1

Key: (for Teachers)	√= informal assessment	Numbers = exercise numbers	Bold face type = first appearance

		Lesson 106	Lesson 107	Lesson 108	Lesson 109	Lesson 110
Phonemic Awareness						
Print Awareness						
Letter Sound Correspondence			Review: 2 (al, ou, ea, ing) √: 2	Review: 2 (sh, ou, ing, ar, ea) √: 2	Review: 2 (ing) √: 2	Review: 2 (ar, al, ee, ea, ou) √: 2
Phonics and Word Recognition	Irregular	Reading words: 2 (**laughed**) √: 2 Underlined parts of words: 2 (**laughed**) √: 2	Reading words: 1 (**knock**) √: 1 Spell by letter name: 1 (**knock**) √: 1	Reading words: 1 (**along, flew**), 3 (**knocked**) √: 1, 3 Spell by letter name: 1 (**along, flew**) √: 1 Underlined parts of words: 3 (**knocked**) √: 3	Reading words: 1 (**anyhow**), 3 (**doesn't**) √: 1, 3 Spell by letter name: 1 (**anyhow**) √: 1	Reading words: 1 (**might**) √: 1 Spell by letter name: 1 (**might**) √: 1
	Regular	Reading words: 1 (**dress, bode, leaf**), 2 (**dresses, myself**), 3 (**fear**), 4 √: 1–4 Spell by letter name: 1 (**dress, bode**), 4 √: 1, 4 Underlined parts of words: 2 (**dresses, myself**) √: 2	Reading words: 1, 2 (lead, eating, themselves), 3 (**meaner**), 4 (**caped, capped**) √: 1–4 Spell by letter name: 4 (**caped, capped**) √: 4 Underlined parts of words: 2 (lead, eating, themselves) √: 2	Reading words: 1 (**plate**), 2 (**flash, telling, dart, he'll**), 3 (**rammed, spells, floating, heaved**), 4 (**bites**) √: 1–4 Spell by letter name: 1 (**plate**), 4 (**bites**) √: 1–4 Underlined parts of words: 2 (**flash, telling, dart, he'll**), 3 (**rammed, spells, floating, heaved**) √: 2, 3	Reading words: 1 (**bin, flower, scream**), 2, 3, 4 (**cope, hopper**) √: 1–4 Spell by letter name: 1 (**bin, flower**), 4 (**cope, hopper**) √: 1, 4 Underlined parts of words: 2 √: 2	Reading words: 1 (**snake, shy, smiling**), 2 (**feel**), 3 (**we, casts**), 4 (**panes, pans, sip**) √: 1–4 Spell by letter name: 1 (**snake, shy, smiling**), 4 (**panes, pans, sip**) √: 1, 4 Underlined parts of words: 2 (**feel**) √: 2
		Connected text: 5 √: 5	Connected text: 5 √: 5	Connected text: 5 √: 5	Connected text: 5 √: 5	Connected text: 5 √: 5
Fluency		Reading words: 1–4 √: 1–4	Reading words: 1–4 √: 1–4	Reading words: 1–4 √: 1–4	Reading words: 1–4 √: 1–4	Reading words: 1–4 √: 1–4 IC: 110
Comprehension		Answering literal questions about a text: 5, 6 Identifying literal cause and effect: 5 Predicting narrative outcomes: 5 Interpreting a character's feelings: 6 Interpreting a character's motives: 5 Drawing inferences: 5	Answering literal questions about a text: 5, 6 Recalling details and events: 5 Predicting narrative outcomes: 5, 6 Interpreting a character's motives: 5 Drawing inferences: 5, 6	Answering literal questions about a text: 5, 6 Recalling details and events: 5 Predicting narrative outcomes: 5 Interpreting a character's motives: 5 Drawing inferences: 5, 6	Answering literal questions about a text: 5, 6 Identifying literal cause and effect: 6 Recalling details and events: 5, 6 Predicting narrative outcomes: 6 Interpreting a character's feelings: 6 Drawing inferences: 5, 6	Answering literal questions about a text: 5, 6 Recalling details and events: 5 Predicting narrative outcomes: 5, 6 Drawing inferences: 5, 6
		Recalling details: 7 Following written directions: 7 Answering literal questions about a text: 7 Using rules to classify objects: 7	Recalling details: 7 Following written directions: 7 Answering literal questions about a text: 7 Using rules to classify objects: 7	Recalling details: 7 Following written directions: 7 Answering literal questions about a text: 7 Using rules to classify objects: 7	Recalling details: 7 Following written directions: 7 Answering literal questions about a text: 7 Using rules to classify objects: 7	Recalling details: 7 Following written directions: 7 Answering literal questions about a text: 7 Using rules to classify objects: 7
Spelling		Phonemic segmentation: 1 √: 1 Spelling words: 2, 3	Identifying spelled words: 1 Patterns: 2 √ Spelling words: 2, 3	Identifying spelled words: 1 Patterns: 2 √ Spelling words: 2, 3	Spelling words: 2, 3	Phonemic segmentation: 1 √: 1 Patterns: 2 √ Spelling words: 2, 3
						Writing words: 3
		Writing words: 3	Writing words: 3	Writing words: 3	Word copying: 1 Phoneme–grapheme correspondence: 1 Writing words: 3	

Category		Lesson 111	Lesson 112	Lesson 113	Lesson 114	Lesson 115
Spelling		Writing words: 3 Identifying spelled words: 1 Spelling words: 2, 3 ✓ 2, 3	Word copying: 1 Phoneme-grapheme correspondence: 1 Writing sentences: 3 Spelling words: 2 ✓ 2 Patterns: 2 ✓	Writing sentences: 3 Phonemic segmentation: 1 ✓ 1 Spelling words: 2	Sentence copying: 1 Spelling words: 1, 2, 3 Patterns: 2	Writing sentences: 3 Spelling words: 1 ✓ Phonemic segmentation: 2 ✓ 2
Comprehension		Using rules to classify objects: 7 Answering literal questions about a text: 7 Following written directions: 7 Recalling details: 7 Activating prior knowledge: 5 Drawing inferences: 5, 6 Interpreting a character's motives: 5 Predicting narrative outcomes: Identifying literal cause and effect: Recalling details and events: 5 Answering literal questions about a text: 5, 6	Using rules to classify objects: 7 Answering literal questions about a text: 7 Following written directions: 7 Recalling details: 7 Activating prior knowledge: 5 Drawing inferences: Following directions: 6 Interpreting a character's feelings: 6 Interpreting a character's motives: 5 Recalling details and events: 5 Identifying literal cause and effect: Answering literal questions about a text: 5, 6	Using rules to classify objects: 7 Answering literal questions about a text: 7 Following written directions: 7 Recalling details: 7 Activating prior knowledge: 6 Drawing inferences: Following directions: 6 Interpreting a character's feelings: 6 Interpreting a character's motives: 5 Recalling details and events: 5 Answering literal questions about a text: 5, 6	Using rules to classify objects: 7 Answering literal questions about a text: 7 Following written directions: 7 Recalling details: 7 Drawing inferences: 5 Interpreting a character's feelings: 6 Interpreting a character's motives: 5 Predicting narrative outcomes: 5 Recalling details and events: 5 Identifying literal cause and effect: 5 Answering literal questions about a text: 5, 6	Using rules to classify objects: 7 Answering literal questions about a text: 7 Following written directions: 7 Recalling details: 7 Activating prior knowledge: 5 Drawing inferences: 5, 6 Predicting narrative outcomes: 5 Recalling details and events: 5 Answering literal questions about a text: 5, 6
Fluency		Reading words: 1–4 ✓: 1–4	Reading words: 1–4 ✓: 1–4	Reading words: 1–4 ✓: 1–4	Reading words: 1–4 ✓: 1–4	IC: 115 Reading words: 1–4 ✓: 1–4
Phonics and Word Recognition	Regular	Connected text: 5 ✓: 5 Underlined parts of words: 2 (year, peek, wishes) ✓: 2 Spell by letter name: 1 (bumpy, master, rolled, shore, storm), 4 (maybe) ✓: 1, 4 Reading words: 1 (bumpy, master, rolled, shore, storm), 2 (year, peek, wishes), 3, 4 (maybe)	Connected text: 5 ✓: 5 Underlined parts of words: 2 ✓: 2 Spell by letter name: 1 (puff, Ott, alligator, apple, bottles), 4 (smoke) ✓: 1, 4 Reading words: 1 (puff, Ott, alligator, apple, bottles), 2, 3 (rubs), 4 (smoke)	Connected text: 5 ✓: 5 Underlined parts of words: 2 (dimmer) ✓: 2 Spell by letter name: 1 (Test, suddenly, beach), 4 (takes, dimmed) ✓: 1, 4 Reading words: 1 (Test, suddenly, beach), 2 (dimmer), 3, 4 (takes, dimmed)	Connected text: 5 ✓: 5 Underlined parts of words: 2 (lies), 3 (beat, ...) ✓: 2, 3 Spell by letter name: 1 (bust, bunch, junk, melt), 4 (Bide, coned, flies) ✓: 1, 4 Reading words: 1 (bust, bunch, junk, melt), 2 (lies), 3 (beat, smash), 4 (Bide, coned, flies)	Connected text: 5 ✓: 5 Underlined parts of words: 2 (spanking, smash) ✓: 2 Spell by letter name: 1 (remember, forgot, Rome, middle, banking), 4 (waved, able) ✓: 1, 4 Reading words: 1 (remember, forgot, Rome, middle, banking), 2 (spanking, sounded, thousands), 3 (folded), 4 (waved, able)
	Irregular	Underlined parts of words: 2 (appear) ✓: 2 Spell by letter name: 1 (genie) ✓: 1 Reading words: 1 (genie), 2 (appear)	Spell by letter name: 1 (strange, disappear) ✓: 1 Reading words: 1 (strange, disappear)	Underlined parts of words: 2 (genies) ✓: 2 Reading words: 2 (genies)	Spell by letter name: 1 (Carla) ✓: 1, 2 Reading words: 1 (Carla), 2 (alone, icebox) Underlined parts of words: 2 (alone, icebox) ✓: 2	Spell by letter name: 1 (city), 4 (appears) ✓: 1, 4 Reading words: 1 (city), 4 (appears)
Letter Sound Correspondence		Review: 2 (er, ou, ee, sh) ✓: 2	Review: 2 (ee, sh, er, wh, ou) ✓: 2		Review: 2 (ing), 3 (ea, sh, oo, l) ✓: 2, 3	Review: 2 (ing, ea, oo, ou, ch) ✓: 2
Print Awareness						
Phonemic Awareness						

Key: (for Teachers) ✓ = informal assessment   **Numbers** = exercise numbers   **Bold face type** = first appearance

Key: (for Teachers)   √= informal assessment   Numbers = exercise numbers   Bold face type = first appearance

		Lesson 116	Lesson 117	Lesson 118	Lesson 119	Lesson 120
Phonemic Awareness						
Print Awareness						
Letter Sound Correspondence		Review: 2 (er) √: 2	Review: 2 (wh, ea, ou, sh, ing) √: 2	Review: 2 (ing, ea) √: 2	Review: 2 (ar, er, ch, ing, th, ea) √: 2	
Phonics and Word Recognition	Irregular	Reading words: 1 (face) √: 1 Spell by letter name: 1 (face) √: 1	Reading words: 3 (appeared), 4 √: 3, 4 Underlined parts of words: 3 (appeared) √: 3	Reading words: 1 (through, across), 3 (disappears), 4 (believe) √: 1, 3, 4 Spell by letter name: 1 (through, across), 4 (believes) √: 1, 4	Reading words: 1 (believed) √: 1 Spell by letter name: 1 (believed) √: 1	Reading words: 1 (few, wonderful) √: 1 Spell by letter name: 1 (few, wonderful) √: 1
	Regular	Reading words: 1 (air, blushed, spin, poorest), 2 (being, hatter), 3 (hater, poof), 4 √: 1–4 Spell by letter name: 1 (air, blushed, spin, poorest), 4 √: 1, 4 Underlined parts of words: 2 (being, hatter) √: 2	Reading words: 1 (filled, we're, haven't), 2 (streaming, wished), 3, 4 √: 1–4 Spell by letter name: 1 (filled), 4 √: 1–4 Underlined parts of words: 2 (streaming, wished), 3 √: 2, 3	Reading words: 1 (fact, wise), 2 (closer, resting), 3, 4 (splat, formed, flow, copper) √: 1–4 Spell by letter name: 1 (fact, wise), 4 (splat, formed, flow) √: 1, 4 Underlined parts of words: 2 (closer, resting) √: 2	Reading words: 1 (broken, cans, canes), 2, 3 (spank, stick, glass), 4 (windows), 5 √: 1–5 Spell by letter name: 1 (broken, cans, canes) √: 1 Underlined parts of words: 2, 4 (windows) √: 2, 4	Reading words: 1 (blanks, flip), 2 (flipped, parting), 3 (yet), 4 (shade, planned, planed) √: 1–4 Spell by letter name: 1 (blanks), 4 (shade, planned, planed) √: 1, 4 Underlined parts of words: 2 (flipped, parting) √: 2
		Connected text: 5 √: 5	Connected text: 5 √: 5	Connected text: 5 √: 5	Connected text: 6 √: 6	Connected text: 5 √: 5
Fluency		Reading words:1–4 √: 1–4	Reading words: 1–4 √: 1–4	Reading words: 1–4 √: 1–4	Reading words: 1–5 √: 1–5	Reading words: 1–4 √: 1–4
						IC: 120
Comprehension		Answering literal questions about a text: 5, 6 Identifying literal cause and effect: 5 Recalling details and events: 5 Predicting narrative outcomes: 5 Interpreting a character's feelings: 5, 6 Drawing inferences: 6 Following directions: 6	Answering literal questions about a text: 5, 6 Identifying literal cause and effect: 5 Recalling details and events: 5 Predicting narrative outcomes: 6 Interpreting a character's motives: 6 Drawing inferences: 6 Activating prior knowledge: 5	Answering literal questions about a text: 5, 6 Identifying literal cause and effect: 5 Recalling details and events: 5, 6 Predicting narrative outcomes: 6 Interpreting a character's feelings: 6 Interpreting a character's motives: 5 Drawing inferences: 5	Answering literal questions about a text: 6, 7 Identifying literal cause and effect: 6 Recalling details and events: 7 Predicting narrative outcomes: 6, 7 Interpreting a character's motives: 6, 7 Drawing inferences: 6, 7	Answering literal questions about a text: 5, 6 Recalling details and events: 5 Predicting narrative outcomes: 5 Interpreting a character's feelings: 6 Interpreting a character's motives: 5 Drawing inferences: 5
		Recalling details: 7 Following written directions: 7 Answering literal questions about a text: 7 Using rules to classify objects: 7	Recalling details: 7 Following written directions: 7 Answering literal questions about a text: 7 Using rules to classify objects: 7	Recalling details: 7 Following written directions: 7 Answering literal questions about a text: 7 Using rules to classify objects: 7	Recalling details: 8 Following written directions: 8 Answering literal questions about a text: 8 Using rules to classify objects: 8	Recalling details: 7 Following written directions: 7 Answering literal questions about a text: 7 Using rules to classify objects: 7
						Lesson 120 Curriculum-Based Assessment
Spelling		Spelling words: 1 Identifying spelled words: 2 √: 2	Spelling words: 1, 2, 3	Spelling words: 1, 2, 3	Spelling words: 1 Identifying spelled words: 2 √: 2	Spelling words: 1 Phonemic segmentation: 2 √: 2
		Sentence copying: 1 Phoneme–grapheme correspondence: 1 Writing sentences: 3	Sentence copying: 1 Phoneme–grapheme correspondence: 1 Writing words: 3	Sentence copying: 1 Phoneme–grapheme correspondence: 1 Writing words: 3	Sentence copying: 1 Phoneme–grapheme correspondence: 1 Writing sentences: 3	Sentence copying: 1 Phoneme–grapheme correspondence: 1 Writing sentences: 3

	Lesson 121	Lesson 122	Lesson 123	Lesson 124	Lesson 125
Spelling	Writing sentences: 1 Spelling words: 2, 3	Writing words: 3 Identifying spelled words: 1 √: 1 Spelling words: 2, 3	Writing words: 3 Spelling words: 1, 3 √: 2 Phonemic segmentation: 2 Identifying spelled words: 1 √: 1	Writing words: 3 Spelling words: 2, 3 √: 1 Phonemic segmentation: 1 √: 1	Writing words: 3 Spelling words: 2, 3 Phonemic segmentation: 1 √: 1
Comprehension	Answering literal questions about a text: 7, 8 Recalling details and events: 7, 8 Interpreting a character's feelings: 8 Interpreting a character's motives: 7 Drawing inferences: 7, 8 Recalling details: 10 Following written directions: 9, 11 Using rules to classify objects: 10	Answering literal questions about a text: 6, 7 Recalling details and events: 7 Interpreting a character's motives: 6 Drawing inferences: 6 Recalling details: 9 Following written directions: 8, 9 Using rules to classify objects: 9	Answering literal questions about a text: 6, 7 Identifying literal cause and effect: 6 Predicting narrative outcomes: 6 Interpreting a character's motives: 6 Drawing inferences: 7 Recalling details: 9 Written deductions: 8 Following written directions: 9 Using rules to classify objects: 9	Answering literal questions about a text: 6, 7 Recalling details and events: 6 Predicting narrative outcomes: 6 Interpreting a character's feelings: 7 Interpreting a character's motives: 6 Drawing inferences: 6 Recalling details: 9 Written deductions: 8 Following written directions: 9 Using rules to classify objects: 9	Answering literal questions about a text: 5, 6 Drawing inferences: 5, 6 Interpreting a character's feelings: 5 Interpreting a character's motives: 5 Predicting narrative outcomes: 5 Recalling details and events: 5 Written deductions: 7 Following written directions: 8 Recalling details: 8 Using rules to classify objects: 8
Fluency	Reading words: 1–6 √: 1–6	Reading words: 1–5 √: 1–5	Reading words: 1–5 √: 1–5	Reading words: 1–5 √: 1–5	Reading words: 1–4 √: 1–4 IC: 125
Phonics and Word Recognition — Regular	Reading words: 1 (**person, human, impossible, stare**), 2, 3 (**richest, flipping**) 5, 6 (**planner, planer**) √: 1–3, 5–6 Spell by letter name: 1 (**person, human, impossible, stare**), 6 (**planner, planer**) √: 1, 6 Underlined parts of words: 3 (**richest, flipping**) √: 3 Connected text: 7 √: 7	Reading words: 1 (**true, simple, spitting**), 2, 3 (**flowed**), 4, 5 (**dare**) √: 1–5 Spell by letter name: 1 (**true, simple, spitting**), 5 (**dare**) √: 1, 5 Underlined parts of words: 3 (**flowed**) √: 3 Connected text: 6 √: 6	Reading words: 1 (**instant, hug, hungry**), 2, 3 (**he's we've, she'd**) 5 (**planing**) √: 1–5 Spell by letter name: 1 (**instant, hug, hungry**), 5 (**planing**) √: 1, 5 Underlined parts of words: 3 (**he's, we've, she'd**) √: 3 Connected text: 6 √: 6	Reading words: 1 (**vow, class, fingers, snapped**), 2 (**smartest, smarter**), 3, 4, 5 (**taking**) √: 1–5 Spell by letter name: 1 (**vow, class, fingers, snapped**), 5 (**taking**) √: 1, 5 Underlined parts of words: 2 (**smartest, smarter**), 4 √: 2, 4 Connected text: 6 √: 6	Reading words: 1 (**short, spend**), 2 (**ring**) 3 (**patted, vows, masters**), 4 (**biting, wiped, life**) √: 1–4 Spell by letter name: 1 (**short, spend**), 4 (**biting, wiped, life**) √: 1, 4 Underlined parts of words: 2 (**ring**) 3 (**patted, vows, masters**) √: 2, 3 Connected text: 5 √: 5
Phonics and Word Recognition — Irregular	Reading words: 1 (**stood**), 4 (**Marta Flores**) √: 1, 4 Spell by letter name: 1 (**stood**) √: 1	Reading words: 1 (**agreed**), 2 (**fight**) √: 1, 2 Spell by letter name: 1 (**agreed**) √: 1		Reading words: 1 (**obey**), 5 (**knows**) √: 1, 5 Spell by letter name: 1 (**obey**), 5 (**knows**) √: 1, 5	Reading words: 1 (**place**), 3 (**yourself**) √: 1, 3 Spell by letter name: 1 (**place**) √: 1 Underlined parts of words: 3 (**yourself**) √: 3
Letter Sound Correspondence			Review: 3 (**I**) √: 3	Review: 2 (al, sh, ar, er, wh, th, ou), 4 (**I**) √: 2, 4	Review: 2 (ea, ing, th, er, ou) √: 2
Print Awareness					
Phonemic Awareness					

Key: (for Teachers) √= informal assessment   Numbers = exercise numbers   Bold face type = first appearance

Reading Mastery Signature Edition, Grade 1

Key: (for Teachers)   √= informal assessment   Numbers = exercise numbers   Bold face type = first appearance

	Lesson 126	Lesson 127	Lesson 128	Lesson 129	Lesson 130
Phonemic Awareness					
Print Awareness					
Letter Sound Correspondence	Review: 2 (or) √: 2	Review: 4 (ea) √: 4	Review: 2 (er, ea, ou, wh, ing, sh) √: 2	Review: 2 (l) √: 2	
Phonics and Word Recognition — Irregular	Reading words: 1 (**phone, Japan, Alaska, China, move**), 4 (**you've, they've**) √: 1, 4 Spell by letter name: 1 (**phone, Japan, Alaska, China, move**) √: 1 Underlined parts of words: 4 (**you've, they've**) √: 4	Reading words: 1 (**minute**), 2 (**turns**) √: 1, 2 Spell by letter name: 1 (**minute**) √: 1 Underlined parts of words: 2 (**turns**) √: 2	Reading words: 1 (**dollars**), 4 (**phoned**), 5 (**rental**) √: 1, 4, 5 Spell by letter name: 1 (**dollars**), 5 (**rental**) √: 1, 5 Underlined parts of words: 4 (**phoned**) √: 4	Reading words: 1 (**service, dental, trouble**) √: 1 Spell by letter name: 1 (**service, dental, trouble**) √: 1	Reading words: 1 (**honey, moves**), 2 (**already**) √: 1, 2 Spell by letter name: 1 (**honey**) √: 1 Underlined parts of words: 2 (**already**) √: 2
Phonics and Word Recognition — Regular	Reading words: 1 (**trained, hair**), 2 (**belong, hardest**), 3 (**chapped, rush, taken**), 4, 5 (**van, vane**) √: 1–5 Spell by letter name: 1 (**trained, hair**), 5 (**van, vane**) √: 1, 5 Underlined parts of words: 2 (**belong, hardest**), 4 √: 2, 4	Reading words: 1 (**east, clock, rang, too**), 2 (**understand, rushed, spelled**), 3 (**stuff, west, mate**), 4 (**packing, bringing, treat**), 5 (**vaned, hung**) √: 1–5 Spell by letter name: 1 (**east, clock, rang**), 5 (**vaned, hung**) √: 1, 5 Underlined parts of words: 2 (**understand, rushed, spelled**), 4 (**packing, bringing, treat**) √: 2, 4	Reading words: 1 (**until, Trunk, rent, swell**), 2 (**corner, bring**), 3 (**spelling**), 4 (**dragging**), 5 √: 1–5 Spell by letter name: 1 (**until, Trunk**) √: 1 Underlined parts of words: 2 (**corner, bring**), 4 (**dragging**) √: 2, 4	Reading words: 1 (**False, number**), 2 (**rented, where's**), 3 (**teeth**), 4 (**trips**), 5 (**drive**) √: 1–5 Spell by letter name: 1 (**False, number**), 5 (**drive**) √: 1, 5 Underlined parts of words: 2 (**rented, where's**) √: 2	Reading words: 1 (**pocket, loaded**), 2 (**passing**), 3 (**chase**), 4 (**Jan, skates**) √: 1–4 Spell by letter name: 1 (**pocket**), 4 (**Jan, skates**) √: 1, 4 Underlined parts of words: 2 (**passing**) √: 2
Phonics and Word Recognition — Connected text	Connected text: 6 √: 6	Connected text: 6 √: 6	Connected text: 6 √: 6	Connected text: 6 √: 6	Connected text: 5 √: 5
Fluency	Reading words: 1–5 √: 1–5	Reading words: 1–5 √: 1–5	Reading words: 1–5 √: 1–5	Reading words: 1–5 √: 1–5	Reading words: 1–4 √: 1–4 IC: 130
Comprehension	Answering literal questions about a text: 6, 7 Recalling details and events: 6 Interpreting a character's feelings: 7 Drawing inferences: 6, 7	Answering literal questions about a text: 6, 7 Recalling details and events: 6, 7 Predicting narrative outcomes: 6 Interpreting a character's feelings: 7 Interpreting a character's motives: 6 Drawing inferences: 6 Following directions: 6 Activating prior knowledge: 6	Answering literal questions about a text: 6, 7 Recalling details and events: 6, 7 Predicting narrative outcomes: 6 Interpreting a character's motives: 6 Drawing inferences: 6, 7	Answering literal questions about a text: 6, 7 Recalling details and events: 6, 7 Predicting narrative outcomes: 6, 7 Drawing inferences: 7	Answering literal questions about a text: 5, 6 Recalling details and events: 5, 6 Predicting narrative outcomes: 5 Interpreting a character's feelings: 6 Drawing inferences: 5
Comprehension	Written deductions: 8 Recalling details: 8 Following written directions: 8 Answering literal questions about a text: 8 Using rules to classify objects: 8	Written deductions: 8 Recalling details: 8 Following written directions: 8 Answering literal questions about a text: 8 Using rules to classify objects: 8	Written deductions: 8 Recalling details: 8 Following written directions: 8 Answering literal questions about a text: 8 Using rules to classify objects: 8	Written deductions: 8 Recalling details: 8 Following written directions: 8 Answering literal questions about a text: 8 Using rules to classify objects: 8	Written deductions: 7 Recalling details: 7 Following written directions: 7 Answering literal questions about a text: 7 Using rules to classify objects: 7
Spelling	Patterns: 2	Patterns: 2	Identifying spelled words: 1 Spelling words: 1, 2, 3	Phonemic segmentation: 1 √: 1 Spelling words: 2, 3	Spelling words: 2
Spelling					Word copying: 1 Phoneme–grapheme correspondence: 1 Writing sentences: 3
Spelling	Word parts (Affixes): 1 Writing sentences: 3	Word copying: 1 Word parts (Affixes): 1 Writing words: 2 Writing sentences: 3	Writing words: 3	Writing words: 3	

Reading Mastery Signature Edition, Grade 1

Key: (for Teachers) √= informal assessment   Numbers = exercise numbers   Bold face type = first appearance

		Lesson 131	Lesson 132	Lesson 133	Lesson 134	Lesson 135
Phonemic Awareness						
Print Awareness						
Letter Sound Correspondence		Review: 2 (ch, ee, ar, ea, er) √: 2	Review: 2 (ch, ar, ea) √: 2			Review: 2 (ch, wh, ou, th, oo) √: 2
Phonics and Word Recognition	**Irregular**	Reading words: 1 (feathers, turtle) √: 1 Spell by letter name: 1 (feathers, turtle) √: 1	Reading words: 1 (handsome, Caw, nice, mice) √: 1 Spell by letter name: 1 (handsome, Caw, nice) √: 1	Reading words: 1 (world, wear, footprint) √: 1 Spell by letter name: 1 (world, wear, footprint) √: 1		
	Regular	Reading words: 1 (dry, drank), 2 (chicken), 3 (helps, Ellen's), 4 (wide) √: 1–4 Spell by letter name: 1 (dry, drank), 4 (wide) √: 1, 4 Underlined parts of words: 2 (chicken), 3 (helps, Ellen's) √: 2, 3	Reading words: 1 (Crow, branch), 2 (chunk, such, Carl), 3 (lay, black), 4 (slider, wings, singing), 5 (sang) √: 1–5 Spell by letter name: 1 (Crow, branch), 5 (sang) √: 1, 5 Underlined parts of words: 2 (chunk, such, Carl), 4 (slider, wings, singing) √: 2, 4	Reading words: 1 (toe, nail, slid), 2 (pond), 3 (weed, hotter), 4 (cons, cones, shine, shining) √: 1–4 Spell by letter name: 1 (toe), 4 (cons, cones, shine, shining) √: 1, 4	Reading words: 1 (Flame, shell, slide), 2 (tears, cheeks), 3, 4 (coat, cave, gaped, gapped, joke) √: 1–4 Spell by letter name: 1 (Flame, shell), 4 (coat, cave, gaped, gapped, joke) √: 1, 4 Underlined parts of words: 2 (tears, cheeks) √: 2	Reading words: 1 (stool, roots, snap, sneak, strong), 2 (tooth), 3 (sliding) √: 1–3 Spell by letter name: 1 (stool, roots, snap, sneak, strong), 3 (sliding) √: 1, 3 Underlined parts of words: 2 (tooth) √: 2
		Connected text: 5 √: 5	Connected text: 6 √: 6	Connected text: 5 √: 5	Connected text: 5 √: 5	Connected text: 4 √: 4
Fluency		Reading words: 1–4 √: 1–4	Reading words: 1–5 √: 1–5	Reading words: 1–4 √: 1–4	Reading words: 1–4 √: 1–4	Reading words: 1–3 √: 1–3
						IC: 135
Comprehension		Answering literal questions about a text: 5, 6 Identifying literal cause and effect: 5 Recalling details and events: 5, 6 Predicting narrative outcomes: 5 Drawing inferences: 5	Answering literal questions about a text: 6, 7 Identifying literal cause and effect: 6 Recalling details and events: 6 Predicting narrative outcomes: 6 Interpreting a character's feelings: 7 Drawing inferences: 6	Answering literal questions about a text: 5, 6 Recalling details and events: 5 Predicting narrative outcomes: 5 Drawing inferences: 5, 6	Answering literal questions about a text: 5, 6 Recalling details and events: 5 Interpreting a character's feelings: 6 Interpreting a character's motives: 5 Drawing inferences: 5, 6	Answering literal questions about a text: 4, 5 Recalling details and events: 4 Predicting narrative outcomes: 4, 5 Interpreting a character's motives: 5 Drawing inferences: 4 Following directions: 5
		Written deductions: 7 Recalling details: 7 Following written directions: 7 Answering literal questions about a text: 7 Using rules to classify objects: 7	Written deductions: 9 Recalling details: 9 Following directions: 8 Answering literal questions about a text: 9 Using rules to classify objects: 9	Written deductions: 8 Recalling details: 8 Following directions: 7, 8 Answering literal questions about a text: 8 Using rules to classify objects: 8	Written deductions: 8 Recalling details: 8 Following directions: 7, 8 Answering literal questions about a text: 8 Using rules to classify objects: 8	Written deductions: 7 Recalling details: 7 Following directions: 6, 7 Answering literal questions about a text: 7 Using rules to classify objects: 7
Spelling		Spelling words: 1, 2 Word families: 2	Spelling words: 1, 2, 3 Word families: 2	Spelling words: 1, 2, 3	Spelling words: 1, 2, 3	Spelling words: 1 Phonemic segmentation: 2 √: 2
						Sentence copying: 1 Phoneme–grapheme correspondence: 1 Writing sentences: 3
		Sentence copying: 1 Writing sentences: 3	Writing words: 3	Sentence copying: 1 Phoneme–grapheme correspondence: 1 Writing words: 3	Sentence copying: 1 Phoneme–grapheme correspondence: 1	

Reading Mastery Signature Edition, Grade 1

		Lesson 136	Lesson 137	Lesson 138	Lesson 139	Lesson 140
Phonemic Awareness						
Print Awareness						
Letter Sound Correspondence		Review: 2 (l, al) √: 2	Review: 2 (sh, ai, ea, wh, th) √: 2	Review: 2 (er, ou) √: 2	Review: 2 (ea, th, wh, ee) √: 2	Review: 2 (ea, sh, th, wh, ou, ee) √: 2
Phonics and Word Recognition	**Irregular**	Reading words: 1 (**color**), 3 (**light**), 4 (**pulled**) √: 1, 3, 4 Spell by letter name: 1 (**color**), 4 (**pulled**) √: 1, 4	Reading words: 1 (**wolf, wolves, listen, alive**), 4 (**watch**) √: 1, 4 Spell by letter name: 1 (**wolf, wolves, listen, alive**), 4 (**watch**) √: 1, 4	Reading words: 1 (**cookie, race**), 2 (**watching, someday, worker**) √: 1, 2 Spell by letter name: 1 (**cookie, race**) √: 1 Underlined parts of words: 2 (**watching, someday, worker**) √: 2	Reading words: 1 (**Mr., knew**) √: 1 Spell by letter name: 1 (**Mr., knew**) √: 1	Reading words: 4 (**asleep, ahead**) √: 4 Underlined parts of words: 4 (**asleep, ahead**) √: 4
	Regular	Reading words: 1 (**bong, sneaky**), 2, 3 (**stepped**), 4 (**used**) √: 1–4 Spell by letter name: 1 (**bong**), 4 (**used**) √: 1, 4 Underlined parts of words: 2 √: 2	Reading words: 1 (**flock, Croak**), 2, 3, 4 (**biter, bitter**) √: 1–4 Spell by letter name: 1 (**flock, Croak**), 4 (**biter, bitter**) √: 1, 4 Underlined parts of words: 2 √: 2	Reading words: 1 (**lions, sweet**), 2 (**fastest**), 3, 4 (**safe, chasing**) √: 1–4 Spell by letter name: 1 (**lions, sweet**), 4 (**safe, chasing**) √: 1, 4 Underlined parts of words: 2 (**fastest**) √: 2	Reading words: 1 (**pepper, owl**), 2 (**lined**), 3 (**waiting, slowest, dusty**), 4 (**path, mile**) √: 1–4 Spell by letter name: 1 (**pepper**), 4 (**path, mile**) √: 1, 4 Underlined parts of words: 2 (**lined**), 3 (**waiting, slowest, dusty**) √: 2, 3	Reading words: 1 (**Finish, thick**), 2 (**leaned, speed**), 3 (**loudly**), 4 (**crossed, happening**) √: 1–4 Spell by letter name: 1 (**Finish, thick**) √: 1 Underlined parts of words: 2 (**leaned, speed**), 3 (**loudly**), 4 (**crossed, happening**) √: 2–4
		Connected text: 5 √: 5	Connected text: 5 √: 5	Connected text: 5 √: 5	Connected text: 5 √: 5	Connected text: 5 √: 5
Fluency		Reading words: 1–4 √: 1–4	Reading words: 1–4 √: 1–4	Reading words: 1–4 √: 1–4	Reading words: 1–4 √: 1–4	Reading words: 1–4 √: 1–4 IC: 140
Comprehension		Answering literal questions about a text: 5, 6 Recalling details and events: 5, 6 Interpreting a character's feelings: 5 Interpreting a character's motives: 6 Drawing inferences: 5, 6	Answering literal questions about a text: 5, 6 Recalling details and events: 5 Predicting narrative outcomes: 5 Interpreting a character's motives: 5 Drawing inferences: 5, 6	Answering literal questions about a text: 5, 6 Recalling details and events: 5 Predicting narrative outcomes: 5, 6 Interpreting a character's motives: 5 Drawing inferences: 5	Answering literal questions about a text: 5 Identifying literal cause and effect: 5 Predicting narrative outcomes: 5 Interpreting a character's feelings: 5 Interpreting a character's motives: 5 Drawing inferences: 5, 6 Following directions: 6	Answering literal questions about a text: 5, 6 Identifying literal cause and effect: 5 Recalling details and events: 5 Predicting narrative outcomes: 5 Interpreting a character's motives: 5 Drawing inferences: 5, 6
		Written deductions: 8 Recalling details: 8 Following directions: 7, 8 Answering literal questions about a text: 7, 8 Using rules to classify objects: 8	Written deductions: 7 Recalling details: 7 Following written directions: 7 Answering literal questions about a text: 7 Using rules to classify objects: 7	Written deductions: 7 Recalling details: 7 Following written directions: 7 Answering literal questions about a text: 7 Using rules to classify objects: 7	Written deductions: 7 Recalling details: 7 Following written directions: 7 Answering literal questions about a text: 7 Using rules to classify objects: 7	Written deductions: 7 Recalling details: 7 Following written directions: 7 Answering literal questions about a text: 7
						Lesson 140 Curriculum-Based Assessment
Spelling		Spelling words: 1, 2, 3 Identifying spelled words: 2		Phonemic segmentation: 1 √: 1 Spelling words: 3 √	Spelling words: 1	Identifying spelled words: 2 Spelling words: 2
		Sentence copying: 1 Phoneme–grapheme correspondence: 1 Writing words: 3	Sentence writing: 1, 3 Word parts (Affixes): 2	Word copying: 2 Word parts (Affixes): 2	Word copying: 2 Word parts (Affixes): 2 Writing sentences: 3	Word copying: 1 Phoneme–grapheme correspondence: 1 Writing sentences: 3

Reading Mastery Signature Edition, Grade 1

	Lesson 141	Lesson 142	Lesson 143	Lesson 144	Lesson 145
Spelling	Writing sentences: 3 Patterns: 1 Spelling words: 1, 2	Writing sentences: 3 Patterns: 1 Spelling words: 1, 2	Writing words: 3 Phonemic segmentation: 2 √: 2 Spelling words: 1, 3	Writing sentences: 3 Identifying spelled words: 2 Spelling words: 1, 2	Writing words: 3 Patterns: 1 √: 1 Spelling words: 1, 2, 3
Comprehension	Using rules to classify objects: 7 Answering literal questions about a text: 7 Recalling details: 7 Written deductions: 7 Drawing inferences: 5, 6 Predicting narrative outcomes: 5 Answering literal questions about a text: 5, 6	Using rules to classify objects: 8 Answering literal questions about a text: 8 Following written directions: 7, 8 Recalling details: 8 Written deductions: 8 Drawing inferences: 5, 6 Interpreting a character's feelings: 5, 6 Predicting narrative outcomes: 5 Answering literal questions about a text: 5, 6	Using rules to classify objects: 8 Answering literal questions about a text: 8 Recalling details: 8 Written deductions: 8 Drawing inferences: 5, 6 Interpreting a character's feelings: 5, 6 Predicting narrative outcomes: 5 Answering literal questions about a text: 5, 6	Using rules to classify objects: 7 Answering literal questions about a text: 7 Following directions: 7 Recalling details: 7 Written deductions: 7 Drawing inferences: 5, 6 Interpreting a character's motives: 6 Interpreting a character's feelings: 5 narrative outcomes: 5 Answering literal questions about a text: 5, 6	Using rules to classify objects: 8 Answering literal questions about a text: 8 Recalling details: 8 Following written directions: 8 Written deductions: 8 Drawing inferences: 5, 6 Interpreting a character's motives: 5 Interpreting a character's feelings: 5 Predicting narrative outcomes: 5 Identifying literal cause and effect: 5 Answering literal questions about a text: 5, 6
Fluency	Reading words: 1–4 √: 1–4	Reading words: 1–4 √: 1–4	Reading words: 1–4 √: 1–4	Reading words: 1–4 √: 1–4	IC: 145 Reading words: 1–4 √: 1–4
Phonics and Word Recognition — Regular	Connected text: 5 √: 5 Underlined parts of words: 2, 4 √: 2 Spell by letter name: 1 (spider, jungle), 4 (pain, lion) √: 1, 4 Reading words: 1 (spider, jungle, torn, thorn), 2 (hunter, strongest), 3 (eye), 4 (pain, lion)	Connected text: 5 √: 5 Underlined parts of words: 2, 4 √: 2, 4 Spell by letter name: 1 (Casey, salad, insect, chill, chair, bees) √: 1 Reading words: 1 (Casey, salad, insect, chill, chair, bees), 2 (body, kill), 4 (hens)	Connected text: 5 √: 5 Underlined parts of words: 2 (sea, nearly, leaning), 3 (whenever, screaming) √: 2, 3 Spell by letter name: 1 (sinking, raft), 4 √: 1–4 Reading words: 1 (sinking, raft), 2 (sea, nearly, leaning), 3 (whenever, screaming)	Connected text: 5 √: 5 Underlined parts of words: 2 (speak), 3 (sniffed, boomed, crackers, sucked) √: 2, 3 Spell by letter name: 1 (die, band), 4 (shares, saves, waving) √: 1–4 Reading words: 1 (die, band), 2 (speak), 3 (sniffed, boomed, crackers, sucked), 4 (shares, saves, waving)	Connected text: 5 √: 5 Underlined parts of words: 2 (grasshopper, dressed, tramp's, forgot) √: 2 Spell by letter name: 1 (peevish, crown, clothes), 4 (slept, later) √: 1–4 Reading words: 1 (peevish, crown, clothes), 2 (grasshopper, dressed, tramp's, forgot), 3, 4 (slept, later)
Phonics and Word Recognition — Irregular	Underlined parts of words: 2 (animals) √: 2 Spell by letter name: 1 (jerk, bushes, paw), 4 (pull) √: 1, 2, 4 Reading words: 1 (jerk, bushes, paw), 2 (animals), 4 (pull)		Spell by letter name: 1 (fourth, America, gone) √: 1 Reading words: 1 (fourth, America, gone)	Underlined parts of words: 3 (faced) √: 3 (threw) 4 Spell by letter name: 1 (thumb, prince), 4 √: 1, 3, 4 Reading words: 1 (thumb, prince), 3 (faced), 4 (threw)	Spell by letter name: 1 (wizard, shirt, shoe) √: 1 Reading words: 1 (wizard, shirt, shoe)
Letter Sound Correspondence		Review: 2 (ea, al, wh, th, er) √: 2	Review: 2 (al, ea, sh, ch) √: 2	Review: 2 (ea, ou, er, ing, ch) √: 2	
Print Awareness					
Phonemic Awareness					

Key: (for Teachers)   √= informal assessment   **Numbers** = exercise numbers   **Bold face type** = first appearance

Key: (for Teachers) √= informal assessment   Numbers = exercise numbers   Bold face type = first appearance

	Lesson 146	Lesson 147	Lesson 148	Lesson 149	Lesson 150
Phonemic Awareness					
Print Awareness					
Letter Sound Correspondence	Review: 2 (th) √: 2	Review: 2 (ea) √: 2	Review: 2 (ea, al, ch) √: 2	Review: 2 (ea, ou, ar, ch) √: 2	
Phonics and Word Recognition — Irregular	Reading words: 2 **(tonight)**, 3 **(space, dance)**, 4 **(shoes)** √: 2, 3, 4 Spell by letter name: 4 **(shoes)** √: 4 Underlined parts of words: 2 **(tonight)** √: 2		Reading words: 1 **(page, forward)**, 3 **(dancing)** √: 1, 3 Spell by letter name: 1 **(page, forward)**, 3 **(dancing)** √: 1, 3	Reading words: 1 **(banana)** √: 1 Spell by letter name: 1 **(banana)** √: 1	Reading words: 2 **(wooden)** √: 2 Underlined parts of words: 2 **(wooden)** √: 2
Phonics and Word Recognition — Regular	Reading words: 1 **(rule, crump, Jean)**, 2 **(deepest, matter)**, 3, 4 √: 1–4 Spell by letter name: 1 **(rule, crump, Jean)**, 4 √: 1, 4 Underlined parts of words: 2 **(deepest, matter)** √: 2	Reading words: 1 **(brown)**, 2 **(swinging, sixteen, sneaking)**, 3 √: 1–3 Spell by letter name: 1 **(brown)**, 3 √: 1, 3 Underlined parts of words: 2 **(swinging, sixteen, sneaking)** √: 2	Reading words: 1, 2 **(popped)**, 3 √: 1–3 Spell by letter name: 1, 3 √: 1, 3 Underlined parts of words: 2 **(popped)** √: 2	Reading words: 1 **(mammal, tickled, rocky)**, 2 **(remembering)**, 3 **(paths, hasn't, hadn't)** √: 1–3 Spell by letter name: 1 **(mammal)** √: 1 Underlined parts of words: 2 **(remembering)**, 3 **(paths, hasn't, hadn't)** √: 2, 3	Reading words: 1 **(vine, grape, Chop, sleepy)**, 2 **(tallest, longest)**, 3 **(tries)**, 4 **(using)** √: 1–4 Spell by letter name: 1 **(vine, grape, Chop)**, 4 **(using)** √: 1, 4 Underlined parts of words: 2 **(tallest, longest)** √: 2
Phonics and Word Recognition — Connected text	Connected text: 5 √: 5	Connected text: 5 √: 5	Connected text: 5 √: 5	Connected text: 5 √: 5	Connected text: 6 √: 6
Fluency	Reading words: 1–4 √: 1–4	Reading words: 1–3 √: 1–3	Reading words: 1–3 √: 1–3	Reading words: 1–3 √: 1–3	Reading words: 1–4 √: 1–4 IC: 150
Comprehension	Rule introduction: 5 Answering literal questions about a text: 5, 6 Predicting narrative outcomes: 5, 6 Recalling details and events: 5 Interpreting a character's feelings: 5 Drawing inferences: 5 Following directions: 6	Rule introduction: 5 Rule review: 4, 5 Applying rules: 5 Answering literal questions about a text: 5, 6 Recalling details and events: 5 Predicting narrative outcomes: 5 Interpreting a character's feelings: 6 Drawing inferences: 6 Activating prior knowledge:	Rule introduction: 5 Rule review: 4, 5 Applying rules: 5 Answering literal questions about a text: 5, 6 Identifying literal cause and effect: 5 Recalling details and events: 6 Predicting narrative outcomes: 5 Interpreting a character's feelings: 6 Drawing inferences: 5, 6	Rule introduction: 5 Rule review: 4, 5 Applying rules: 5 Answering literal questions about a text: 5, 6 Identifying literal cause and effect: 5 Recalling details and events: 6 Predicting narrative outcomes: Drawing inferences: 5 Following directions: 6	Rule introduction: 6 Rule review: 5 Applying rules: 6, 7 Answering literal questions about a text: 6, 7 Identifying literal cause and effect: 6 Interpreting a character's motives: 7 Drawing inferences: 6
Comprehension (written)	Written deductions: 8 Recalling details: 8 Following written directions: 8 Answering literal questions about a text: 8 Using rules to classify objects: 8 Rule review: 8	Written deductions: 7 Recalling details: 7 Following written directions: 7 Answering literal questions about a text: 7 Using rules to classify objects: 7 Rule review: 7 Applying rules: 7	Written deductions: 7 Recalling details: 8 Following written directions: 8 Answering literal questions about a text: 8 Applying rules: 8	Written deductions: 7, 8 Recalling details: 8 Following written directions: 8 Answering literal questions about a text: 8 Rule review: 8	Written deductions: 8, 10 Recalling details: 10 Following written directions: 10 Answering literal questions about a text: 10 Rule review: 10
Spelling	Patterns: 1 Spelling words: 1 √: 1 Phonemic segmentation: 2 √: 2	Patterns: 1 Spelling words: 1, 3	Patterns: 1 Spelling words: 1, 3	Spelling words: 1	Phonemic segmentation: 1 √: 1 Identifying spelled words: 2 Spelling words: 2, 3 Writing words: 3
Spelling (writing)	Writing sentences: 3	Word parts (Affixes): 2 Writing words: 2	Word copying: 2 Word parts (Affixes): 2 Writing words: 3	Word copying: 2 Word parts (Affixes): 2 Writing sentences: 3	

Key: (for Teachers) √ = informal assessment Numbers = exercise numbers Bold face type = first appearance

		Lesson 151	Lesson 152	Lesson 153	Lesson 154	Lesson 155
Phonemic Awareness						
Print Awareness						
Letter Sound Correspondence		Review: 2 (ou, ea, ch, ing) √: 2	Review: √:		Review: 3 (al, sh, wh, ee, er) √: 3	Review: 2 (l, ing) √: 2
Phonics and Word Recognition	**Irregular**	Reading words: 1 (**third**), 3 (**bananas**) √: 1, 3 Spell by letter name: 1 (**third**) √: 1	Reading words: 1 (**wonder, disappeared**) √: 1 Spell by letter name: 1 (**wonder**) √: 1	Reading words: 1 (**eight**), 4 (**four**) √: 1, 4 Spell by letter name: 1 (**eight**), 4 (**four**) √: 1, 4		Reading words: 1 (**metal, warm, blew**) √: 1 Spell by letter name: 1 (**metal, warm**) √: 1
	Regular	Reading words: 1 (**soft**), 2 (**eaten**), 3 (**rules**), 4 (**filed, striped**) √: 1–4 Spell by letter name: 1 (**soft**) √: 1 Underlined parts of words: 2 (**eaten**), 4 (**filed, striped**) √: 2, 4	Reading words: 1 (**handle**), 2 (**muddy**), 3 (**rid, red**), 4 √: 1–4 Spell by letter name: 1 (**handle**), 4 √: 1, 4 Underlined parts of words: 2 (**muddy**) √: 2	Reading words: 1, 2 (**hated**), 3 (**dear**), 4 (**stripes**) √: 1–4 Spell by letter name: 1, 4 (**stripes**) √: 1, 4 Underlined parts of words: 2 (**hated**) √: 2	Reading words: 1 (**babies**), 2, 3 (**wish, trapper**) √: 1–3 Spell by letter name: 1 (**babies**) √: 1 Underlined parts of words: 2, 3 (**wish, trapper**) √: 2, 3	Reading words: 1 (**monkey, rather, angry**), 2, 3, 4 √: 1–4 Spell by letter name: 1 (**monkey, rather, angry**), 4 √: 1, 4 Underlined parts of words: 2 √: 2
		Connected text: 6 √: 6	Connected text: 6 √: 6	Connected text: 6 √: 6	Connected text: 5 √: 5	Connected text: 6 √: 6
Fluency		Reading words: 1–4 √: 1–4	Reading words: 1–4 √: 1–4	Reading words: 1–4 √: 1–4	Reading words: 1–3 √: 1–3	Reading words: 1–4 √: 1–4
						IC: 155
Comprehension		Rule introduction: 6 Rule review: 5, 6 Answering literal questions about a text: 6, 7 Predicting narrative outcomes: 6 Recalling details and events: 6 Interpreting a character's feelings: 7 Following directions: 7	Rule introduction: 6 Rule review: 5, 6 Answering literal questions about a text: 6, 7 Recalling details and events: 6, 7 Interpreting a character's motives: 7 Drawing inferences: 6 Following directions: 7	Rule introduction: 6 Rule review: 5, 6 Answering literal questions about a text: 6, 7 Predicting narrative outcomes: 6, 7 Recalling details and events: 6 Interpreting a character's feelings: 7 Drawing inferences: 6, 7	Rule introduction: 5 Rule review: 4, 5 Answering literal questions about a text: 5, 6 Predicting narrative outcomes: 5, 6 Recalling details and events: 5 Interpreting a character's feelings: 5, 6 Drawing inferences: 5, 6 Applying rules: 5	Rule introduction: 6 Rule review: 5, 6 Answering literal questions about a text: 6, 7 Predicting narrative outcomes: 6 Recalling details and events: 6, 7 Interpreting a character's feelings: 7 Drawing inferences: 6, 7 Applying rules: 6
		Written deductions: 9 Recalling details: 9 Following written directions: 9 Answering literal questions about a text: 9 Rule review: 9 Interpreting a character's feelings: 9	Written deductions: 9 Recalling details: 9 Following written directions: 9 Answering literal questions about a text: 9 Rule review: 9	Written deductions: 9 Recalling details: 9 Following written directions: 9 Answering literal questions about a text: 9 Rule review: 9 Applying rules: 9	Written deductions: 8 Recalling details: 8 Following written directions: 8 Answering literal questions about a text: 8 Rule review: 8 Applying rules: 8	Written deductions: 8 Recalling details: 8 Following written directions: 8 Answering literal questions about a text: 8 Rule review: 8
Spelling		Phonemic segmentation: 1 √: 1 Spelling words: 2	Identifying spelled words: 1 Spelling words: 1, 2	Spelling words: 2	Phonemic segmentation: 1 √: 1 Spelling words: 2, 3	Identifying spelled words: 1 Spelling words: 1, 2, 3
						Writing words: 3
		Writing sentences: 3	Writing sentences: 3	Word copying: 1 Phoneme–grapheme correspondence: 1 Writing sentences: 3	Writing words: 3	

Key: (for Teachers) √= informal assessment   Numbers = exercise numbers   Bold face type = first appearance

		Lesson 156	Lesson 157	Lesson 158	Lesson 159	Lesson 160
Phonemic Awareness						
Print Awareness						
Letter Sound Correspondence			Review: 4 (wh, al, ea, th, er) √: 4		Review: 2 (ea, ing) √: 2	Review: 2 (ea) √: 2
Phonics and Word Recognition	**Irregular**	Reading words: 1 (**figure, easiest**), 2 (**they'll**), 4 (**anywhere**) √: 1, 2, 4 Spell by letter name: 1 (**figure, easiest**), 4 (**anywhere**) √: 1, 4 Underlined parts of words: 2 (**they'll**) √: 2	Reading words: 1 (**idea**), 2 (**warmer**) √: 1, 2 Spell by letter name: 1 (**idea**) √: 1 Underlined parts of words: 2 (**warmer**) √: 2	Reading words: 1 (**U.S.**) √: 1 Spell by letter name: 1 (**U.S.**) √: 1	Reading words: 3 (**Woof**) √: 3 Spell by letter name: 3 (**Woof**) √: 3	Reading words: 1 (**arrows**) √: 1 Spell by letter name: 1 (**arrows**) √: 1
	Regular	Reading words: 1 (**whale, winter**), 2, 3, 4 √: 1–4 Spell by letter name: 1 (**whale, winter**), 4 √: 1, 4 Underlined parts of words: 2 √: 2	Reading words: 1 (**spring**), 2, 3, 4 (**wheels**) √: 1–4 Spell by letter name: 1 (**spring**), 4 (**wheels**) √: 1, 4 Underlined parts of words: 2 √: 2	Reading words: 1 (**town**), 2 (**Everest, she'll**), 3, 4 (**taper, tapper, loop, stared**) √: 1–4 Spell by letter name: 4 (**taper, tapper, loop, stared**) √: 4 Underlined parts of words: 2 (**Everest, she'll**) √: 2	Reading words: 1 (**Darn, Squeak, breathe, letter**), 2, 3 √: 1–3 Spell by letter name: 1 (**Darn, Squeak, breathe, letter**), 3 √: 1, 3 Underlined parts of words: 2 √: 2	Reading words: 1 (**puppy, Here's**), 2, 3 (**tail**), 4 (**timer**) √: 1–4 Spell by letter name: 1, 4 (**timer**) √: 1, 4 Underlined parts of words: 2 (**licked, licking**) √: 2
		Connected text: 6 √: 6	Connected text: 6 √: 6	Connected text: 6 √: 6	Connected text: 5 √: 5	Connected text: 6 √: 6
Fluency		Reading words: 1–4 √: 1–4	Reading words: 1–4 √: 1–4	Reading words: 1–4 √: 1–4	Reading words: 1–3 √: 1–3	Reading words: 1–4 √: 1–4
						IC: 160
Comprehension		Rule introduction: 6 Rule review: 5, 6 Answering literal questions about a text: 6, 7 Predicting narrative outcomes: 6 Recalling details and events: 6 Drawing inferences: 6, 7	Rule introduction: 6 Rule review: 5, 6 Answering literal questions about a text: 6, 7 Predicting narrative outcomes: 6 Recalling details and events: 6 Drawing inferences: 7	Rule introduction: 6 Rule review: 5, 6 Answering literal questions about a text: 6, 7 Predicting narrative outcomes: 6 Recalling details and events: 6 Interpreting a character's feelings: 7 Drawing inferences: 6, 7	Rule introduction: 5 Rule review: 4, 5 Answering literal questions about a text: 5, 6 Recalling details and events: 5 Interpreting a character's feelings: 6 Drawing inferences: 6	Rule introduction: 6 Rule review: 5, 6 Answering literal questions about a text: 6, 7 Predicting narrative outcomes: 6 Recalling details and events: 6, 7 Interpreting a character's feelings: 7 Interpreting a character's motives: 6 Drawing inferences: 6
		Written deductions: 9 Recalling details: 9 Following written directions: 9 Answering literal questions about a text: 9 Rule review: 9	Written deductions: 9 Recalling details: 9 Following written directions: 9 Answering literal questions about a text: 9 Rule review: 9	Written deductions: 9 Recalling details: 9 Following written directions: 9 Answering literal questions about a text: 9 Rule review: 9	Written deductions: 8 Recalling details: 8 Following written directions: 8 Answering literal questions about a text: 8 Rule review: 8	Written deductions: 9 Recalling details: 9 Following written directions: 9 Answering literal questions about a text: 9 Rule review: 9 Interpreting a character's feelings: 9
						Lesson 160 Curriculum-Based Assessment
Spelling		Spelling words: 2, 3	Phonemic segmentation: 1 √: 1 Spelling words: 2	Identifying spelled words: 1 Spelling words: 1, 2	Spelling words: 2, 3	Spelling words: 1
		Word copying: 1 Phoneme–grapheme correspondence: 1 Writing words: 3	Writing sentences: 3	Writing sentences: 3	Word copying: 1 Phoneme–grapheme correspondence: 1 Writing words: 3	Writing words: 1 Writing sentences: 2